Microsoft Visio 2013

Step by Step

Scott A. Helmers

Published with the authorization of Microsoft Corporation by:
O'Reilly Media, Inc.
1005 Gravenstein Highway North
Sebastopol, California 95472

ISBN: 978-0-7356-6946-8

1 2 3 4 5 6 7 8 9 M 8 7 6 5 4 3

Printed and bound in the United States of America.

Microsoft Press books are available through booksellers and distributors worldwide. If you need support related to this book, email Microsoft Press Book Support at mspinput@microsoft.com. Please tell us what you think of this book at *http://www.microsoft.com/learning/booksurvey*.

Acquisitions and Developmental Editor: Kenyon Brown

Production Editor: Melanie Yarbrough

Editorial Production: Online Training Solutions, Inc. (OTSI)

Technical Reviewer: John Marshall

Indexer: Ron Strauss

Cover Design: Girvin

Cover Composition: Karen Montgomery

Illustrator: Online Training Solutions, Inc. (OTSI)

This book is dedicated to the memory of Judy Lew, 1966-2012. Her skill in guiding the Visio Program Management team toward the release of Visio 2013 was exceeded only by her love of life and her family. Though we only met face to face a few times, and always at Visio-related work events, Judy and I spent far more time talking about our daughters than about work. Esmé and Lila, your mother was a truly special person.

Contents

1   A visual orientation to a visual product   3

2   Creating a new diagram   53

3   Adding sophistication to your drawings   103

4　Creating flowcharts and organization charts　157

5　Adding style, color, and themes　203

6 Entering, linking to, and reporting on data   239

7 Adding and using hyperlinks   291

11   Adding structure to your diagrams   417

12   Creating and validating process diagrams   455

Introduction

Microsoft Visio 2013 is the premier application for creating business and technical diagrams. Far more than a drawing program, Visio is used by millions of people to document the physical world and to convey concepts and data in a visual format.

Microsoft Visio 2013 Step by Step offers a comprehensive look at both the Standard and Professional editions of Visio 2013. By following the exercises in the book, you will learn about important product features by working with them rather than just reading about them. You will also explore the powerful integration between Visio and other members of the Microsoft Office suite of applications, including Microsoft SharePoint 2013 and SharePoint Online.

Who this book is for

Microsoft Visio 2013 Step by Step and other books in the *Step by Step* series are designed for beginning to intermediate level computer users. The examples and exercises in this book apply equally well in small, medium, and large organizations, whether their orientation is commercial, governmental, academic, or non-profit. Many examples teach skills than can be applied for home and personal projects as well. Whether you are already comfortable working in Visio and want to learn about new features, or are new to Visio, this book provides invaluable hands-on experience.

How this book is organized

This book is divided into 13 chapters that explore the rich set of Visio capabilities. In the first two chapters, you learn how to navigate within the Visio user interface, how to find diagram templates to help you get started, and how to create and work with diagrams. Each of the subsequent chapters introduces you to key concepts or diagram types and provides multiple examples. Depending on your experience with Visio, the exercises in each chapter either teach or reinforce important concepts because you are working with real diagrams and real-world examples.

This book has been designed to lead you step by step through the tasks you're most likely to want to perform with Visio 2013. If you start at the beginning and work your way through all of the exercises, you will gain enough proficiency to master the use of Visio. However, if you are only interested in certain topics or features, you can jump in anywhere to acquire exactly the skills you need.

Downloading the practice files

Before you can complete the exercises in this book, you need to download the book's practice files to your computer. The practice files can be downloaded from the following page:

http://aka.ms/Visio2013SbS/files

IMPORTANT Visio 2013 is not available from this page. You should purchase and install that program before using this book.

The following table lists the practice files for this book.

Chapter	File
Chapter 1: A visual orientation to a visual product	None
Chapter 2: Creating a new diagram	Basic ShapesA_start.vsdx
	Basic ShapesB_start.vsdx
	Basic ShapesC_start.vsdx
	Quick Draw_start.vsdx
	Size & Position_start.vsdx
Chapter 3: Adding sophistication to your drawings	Background Exercises_start.vsdx
	Corporate DiagramA_start.vsdx
	Corporate DiagramB_start.vsdx
	International Office.jpg
	Orient Shapes and TextA_start.vsdx
	Orient Shapes and TextB_start.vsdx
	Shape Data_start.vsdx
	Starfish.jpg
	Text ExercisesA_start.vsdx
	Text ExercisesB_start.vsdx

Chapter	File
Chapter 4: Creating flowcharts and organization charts	HR Recruiting Flowchart_start.vsdx
	Org Chart Data_start.xlsx
	Photos folder
Chapter 5: Adding style, color, and themes	Align and Space_Start.vsdx
	HR Recruiting FlowchartA_start.vsdx
	HR Recruiting FlowchartB_start.vsdx
	Network diagram_start.vsdx
Chapter 6: Entering, linking to, and reporting on data	HR Process Data_start.xlsx
	HR Process MapA_start.vsdx
	HR Process MapB_start.vsdx
	HR Process MapC_start.vsdx
	HR Process MapD_start.vsdx
	HR Process MapE_start.vsdx
	HR Process MapF_start.vsdx
Chapter 7: Adding and using hyperlinks	HR Process Map_start.vsdx
	Human Resources Policy Manual.docx
	Sample PDF Document.pdf
	Sample presentation.pptx
	Sample Project file.mpp
	Sample spreadsheet.xlsx
Chapter 8: Printing, reusing, and sharing diagrams	HR Process Map for Chapter08A_start.vsdx
	HR Process Map for Chapter08B_start.vsdx
Chapter 9: Creating network and data center diagrams	Network Diagram (Basic) with data_start.vsdx
	Network Diagram (Basic)_start.vsdx
	Network Diagram (Detailed)_start.vsdx
	Network Diagram (Organized)_start.vsdx
	Network Diagram with RackA_start.vsdx
	Network Diagram with RackB_start.vsdx
Chapter 10: Visualizing your data	Casino Floor.vsdx
	Contoso Network Data.xlsx
	HR Recruiting Flowchart with data graphics_start.vsdx
	HR Recruiting Flowchart_start.vsdx
	Network Diagram_start.vsdx
	Sales Proposal Process TaskMap.pdf
Chapter 11: Adding structure to your diagrams	Containers, Lists and Callouts_start.vsdx
	Data graphics legends_start.vsdx

Chapter	File
Chapter 12: Creating and validating process diagrams	HR Recruiting Flowchart Validation_start.vsdx
	RuleSets -- BPMN 2.0.html
	RuleSets -- Cross-Functional Flowchart.html
	RuleSets -- Flowchart.html
	RuleSets -- SharePoint 2010 Workflow.html
	RuleSets -- SharePoint 2013 Workflow.html
	Theater Ticketing ProcessA_start.vsdx
	Theater Ticketing ProcessB_start.vsdx
	Visio 2007 Flowchart_start.vsd
Chapter 13: Collaborating on and publishing diagrams	Collaboration Brainstorm DiagramA_start.vsdx
	Collaboration Brainstorm DiagramB_start.vsdx
	Theater Ticketing Process Status Data_start.xlsx
	Theater Ticketing ProcessA_start.vsdx
	Theater Ticketing ProcessB_start.vsdx
	Timeline diagram_start.vsdx
Appendix: Looking under the hood	Basic Shapes_start.vsdx
	ShapeSheet_start.vsdx

Your companion ebook

With the ebook edition of this book, you can do the following:

- Search the full text

- Print

- Copy and paste

To download your ebook, please see the instruction page at the back of the book.

Getting support and giving feedback

The following sections provide information about getting help with Office 2013 Professional or the contents of this book and contacting us to provide feedback or report errors.

Errata

We've made every effort to ensure the accuracy of this book and its companion content. Any errors that have been reported since this book was published are listed on our Microsoft Press site at oreilly.com:

http://aka.ms/Visio2013SbS/errata

If you find an error that is not already listed, you can report it to us through the same page.

If you need additional support, email Microsoft Press Book Support at: *mspinput@microsoft.com*.

Please note that product support for Microsoft software is not offered through the previous addresses.

We want to hear from you

At Microsoft Press, your satisfaction is our top priority, and your feedback our most valuable asset. Please tell us what you think of this book at:

http://www.microsoft.com/learning/booksurvey

The survey is short, and we read every one of your comments and ideas. Thanks in advance for your input!

Stay in touch

Let's keep the conversation going! We're on Twitter at: *http://twitter.com/MicrosoftPress/*.

Acknowledgments

As with the 2010 edition of this book, my deepest thanks and love to Marilyn, Sara, and Julie for doing everything that I didn't do while I was in book-writing mode.

Thanks to the Visio team at Microsoft for creating such an incredible product and for being such a welcoming and supportive group. I've had the pleasure of getting to know many team members over the last five years and look forward to continuing to work with them. Special thanks to Jenn Cherwinka and Anurag Sinha for obtaining answers to dozens of obscure questions as well as for moving small mountains to get special product keys and other bits of treasure from deep within Microsoft.

The dozen or so Visio experts in the world who are part of the Microsoft Most Valuable Professional (MVP) program are an amazingly talented group, and it is a pleasure to count many of them as friends. In particular, thanks to: John Marshall for his astute and historically rich technical editing of this book; Chris Roth for maintaining the ever-useful collection of articles, ideas, and forums at the Visio Guy website (*www.visguy.com*); Al Edlund for advice on page scaling; John Goldsmith whose online contributions at *visualsignals.typepad. co.uk/vislog* are cited multiple times in this text; and David Parker for his Rules Tools (*www. visiorules.com*) and for consultation on that subject.

Thanks to two companies who provide complimentary copies of their products to MVPs for use in our work: TechSmith (*www.techsmith.com*) for Snagit, the most amazing screen capture tool imaginable, and VMware (*www.vmware.com*) for VMware Workstation, an essential part of keeping multiple versions and combinations of Windows, Microsoft Office, and Visio organized and accessible at the click of a mouse.

Thanks to the editorial teams at Microsoft Press, O'Reilly, and OTSI for their guidance and support throughout the development of this book. Special thanks to my editor Kenyon Brown for guiding me through the process a second time.

Finally, thanks to Kathy Brennan and Mike Cunningham. Our collective decision to build TaskMap as a Visio add-in started the journey of discovery that led to this book.

Chapter at a glance

Get

Get started with Visio 2013,
page 13

Understand

Understand tool tabs and add-in tabs,
page 32

Manage

Manage the shapes window,
page 39

Zoom

Pan and zoom in Visio,
page 45

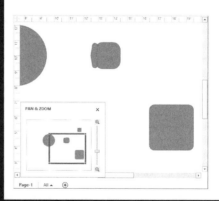

IN THIS CHAPTER, YOU WILL LEARN HOW TO

- Identify the editions and features of Visio 2013.

- Get started with Visio 2013.

- Explore, minimize, and restore the Visio ribbon.

- Understand tool tabs and add-in tabs.

- Understand shapes, masters, stencils, and templates.

- Explore the drawing window and manage the Shapes window.

- Pan and zoom in Visio.

Microsoft Visio is the premier application for creating business diagrams of all types, ranging from flowcharts, network diagrams, and organization charts, to floor plans and brainstorming diagrams. Even though this book contains dozens of examples and sample diagrams, it can only scratch the surface of the hundreds of types of diagrams you can create with Visio.

Microsoft Visio 2013 continues the use of the *fluent user interface* (UI), otherwise known as the *ribbon*, that was introduced with Visio 2010. Regardless of what you might think of the ribbon in other Microsoft Office applications, it feels right at home in Visio, primarily because the goal of a ribbon-style interface is a visual presentation of a related group of functions, and Visio is, first and foremost, a visual product.

In this chapter, you will learn that there are three editions of Visio 2013, and will discover what's new in the 2013 release of the product. You will launch Visio and explore the *Backstage* view and will then explore the tabs on the Visio ribbon. You will compare the permanent tabs on the ribbon with tool tabs sets and add-in tabs. You will learn about stencils, templates, masters, and shapes and how to manage the various windows that comprise the Visio user interface. Finally, you will learn how to pan and zoom the diagram in the drawing window.

Identifying the editions of Visio 2013

Visio 2013 is available in three editions. The first two editions utilize the traditional desktop software purchase and installation model and mirror the two editions that were offered in most prior Visio releases. The third edition is part of the Office 365 suite of subscription-based applications.

- **Visio Standard 2013** Visio Standard is the starter edition of Visio. It provides significant capability for creating business diagrams and includes 26 templates for creating diagrams in six categories.

- **Visio Professional 2013** Visio Professional expands on the Standard edition by offering more than four dozen additional templates for a total of 76 across eight categories. In addition, Visio Pro includes the ability to link diagrams to a wide variety of data sources, and includes a diagram validation capability that is especially well-suited for the expanded set of business process diagrams it supports.

- **Visio Pro for Office 365** This new edition of Visio 2013 provides the identical features and templates as Visio Professional 2013. The key differences in this edition are in packaging and delivery, because it is part of Microsoft Office 365. Office 365 is a cloud-based subscription service. Instead of purchasing Visio Pro for Office 365, you pay a monthly subscription and can install the software on up to five computers running Windows 7 or Windows 8. Each time you install, you automatically receive the latest updates.

Identifying new features of Visio 2013

If you have used any previous version of Visio, you will find a rich set of new features described in the sections that follow. Even if you've never used Visio, it will still be worth reading through the features described here in order to learn more about the capabilities of the software.

If you are upgrading from Visio 2010

Visio 2010 introduced the ribbon user interface and a long list of new features. Visio 2013 continues the momentum with another long list of enhancements and new capabilities.

TIP The data-connected sample diagrams that were included with Visio 2010 and Visio 2007 are no longer included with Visio 2013. In addition, the database reverse engineering add-in is no longer packaged with Visio 2013.

- **Updated, modern shapes** Hundreds of shapes have been completely redesigned for Visio 2013 to make your diagrams look fresh and modern, and to accommodate Visio 2013 themes. The new shapes are included with the stencils used in many familiar templates, enhancing the appearance of Basic Network, Organization Chart, Timeline, Workflow, and SharePoint Workflow diagrams, among others.

- **Professional appearance** Visio 2013 themes have been dramatically enhanced, making it easier than ever to produce eye-catching yet professional-looking diagrams. In addition, themes have been supplemented with pre-designed visual variants that let you add your personal touch. Further, you can apply effects like reflection, glow, and bevel to provide additional emphasis.

- **Integration with the cloud** The Open, Save, and Save As pages in the Visio 2013 Backstage view provide easy access to your SkyDrive account, as well as to Microsoft SharePoint and SharePoint Online sites.

- **Improved integration with SharePoint** Publishing Visio diagrams to SharePoint is easier than ever because SharePoint 2013 can open Visio files directly. Diagrams published to SharePoint can be viewed using almost any web browser.

- **Collaboration (commenting)** Multiple people can read and add comments to a Visio diagram using either Visio or a web browser when diagrams are stored in SharePoint or SharePoint Online.

- **Change shape** With Visio 2013, you can replace one shape with another, and the new shape will retain the connections, text, and data from the original shape.

- **Duplicate page** You can create a duplicate copy of any Visio page with two clicks.

- **Enhanced template and shape search** It's easier in Visio 2013 to locate the right template to begin a new diagram or to find exactly the right shape to enhance your diagram. Search results are sorted and filtered more effectively and duplicate results are eliminated.

- **Organization charts with photos** The Organization Chart wizard has been en-hanced in Visio 2013 to provide bulk import of photographs.

- **Improved Mini Toolbar** The Mini Toolbar that appears when you right-click either the drawing page or a shape has been revamped, further streamlining many actions and reducing mouse movement. The Drawing Tools, Connector Tool, Change Shape, Shape Styles, and alignment features have been added to the Mini Toolbar.

- **Enhanced touch support** Visio 2013 recognizes a greater array of gestures and touch for easier use on tablets and computers with touch screens.

- **New file format** All previous versions of Visio stored drawings in a proprietary file format. Visio 2013 joins other members of the Microsoft Office family in using the Open Packaging Convention, an XML-based format. The new .vsdx file format makes the contents of Visio drawings more accessible to other applications for a variety of purposes, including integration with SharePoint as described previously and following.

The following features are available only in the Professional edition of Visio 2013.

- **Collaboration (coauthoring)** Multiple authors can edit the same Visio 2013 document simultaneously when the document is stored on SkyDrive, SharePoint, or SharePoint Online in Office 365.

- **SharePoint Workflow integration** Visio 2013 supports the Microsoft .NET Framework 4 workflows that are supported in SharePoint 2013. In addition, Microsoft SharePoint Designer 2013 can open and manipulate Visio 2013 files directly. Consequently, you can use Visio's visual workflow design features to create workflows in both Visio and SharePoint Designer, and then execute them with SharePoint Workflow.

- **Updated BPMN and UML templates** The Business Process Model and Notation (BPMN) template now conforms to version 2.0 of that standard, and the Unified Modeling Language (UML) templates conform to UML version 2.4.

SEE ALSO The Visio product team wrote a series of blog posts describing the new features in Visio 2013. Refer to *blogs.office.com/b/visio/archive/2013/03/19/recapping-posts-on-the-new-visio.aspx* for a summary.

If you are upgrading from Visio 2007

Visio 2010 was the most significant upgrade to the capabilities of Visio in years. If you are upgrading from Visio 2007, you will benefit from the following features in addition to ev-erything listed in the previous section.

- **New user interface** Visio 2010 is the first version of the product to incorporate the ribbon user interface (UI) and the Backstage view. In addition, the **Shapes** window presents stencils more logically and can be minimized so it occupies less screen real estate.

- **Enhanced user experience** Live Preview is a tremendous addition to Visio 2010, because it enables you to view potential changes in color, fill pattern, font size, shape type, data graphics, and more, before you commit to the change. Visio 2010 also reduces required mouse movement with features like AutoConnect and QuickShapes (refer to next bullet), and the Mini Toolbar.

- **Diagramming support** Multiple features whose names begin with *Auto* or *Quick* suggest that creating and organizing Visio 2010 diagrams is even easier, and it's true. AutoConnect and QuickShapes add new connectors and shapes; AutoAdd and AutoDelete simplify adding and removing shapes on the page; AutoSize expands and contracts Visio page dimensions. In addition, the **Add page** button creates new pages with a single click, and enhanced copy/paste enables you to control where shapes will be pasted. Finally, the enhanced Dynamic Grid provides excellent visual feedback when placing or moving shapes, dramatically reducing the need to nudge and reposition shapes after they are on the page.

- **Structured diagrams** Visio 2010 introduces a new type of shape called a container that provides more than just a visual grouping for a set of shapes. Shapes in a container know they are contained, and the container knows the members that reside within it. Consequently, when you move, copy, or delete a container, all of the members go with it. However, unlike a group shape, the member shapes are accessible with a single click just as if the container were not there.

  In most containers, you can place member shapes wherever you'd like. However, a list is a special type of container that maintains members in ordered sequence. Each list member knows exactly where it resides within the list.

  The third structured diagram element is a new type of callout. The purpose of a callout is still the same—to add annotations to shapes on the page—but both the callout and the target shape are aware of each other, which dramatically improves shape behavior.

  Not only do containers, lists, and callouts enable users to make more effective diagrams more easily, they also provide significant opportunities to Visio developers for building location-aware shapes and for writing code that takes advantage of diagram structure.

- **Enhanced appearance** Visio 2010 themes and effects add a new professional appearance to your diagrams. The themes gallery, with Live Preview, lets you sample more than two dozen coordinated sets of colors, fonts, patterns, and effects before choosing the one that is just right for your diagram.

- **Improved CAD support** Visio 2010 supports import, conversion, and export of newer file types from Autodesk's AutoCAD software.

- **Save as PDF or XPS** The software to save diagrams in Portable Document Format (PDF) or XML Paper Specification (XPS) format is now bundled with Visio.

The following features are available only in the Professional or Premium editions of Visio 2010.

- **Dynamic web diagrams** Previous versions of Visio have allowed you to save a Visio drawing as a set of webpages but with one key limitation: if the diagram changed, you needed to republish the website. Visio 2010, in conjunction with Visio Services on SharePoint 2010, introduces the ability to create dynamic websites from data-connected diagrams. Now, many changes to the diagram, or to the data behind the diagram, appear automatically for anyone viewing your diagram with a web browser.

- **Business process** Several new features add to your ability to create business process diagrams in Visio 2010: a BPMN template that conforms to the 1.2 version of the BPMN standard; a feature that automatically creates subprocess pages for flowcharts and BPMN diagrams; and a new interchange file type that lets you create SharePoint Workflow diagrams in Visio and export them to SharePoint Designer (you can also import SharePoint Workflow diagrams into Visio to view graphical representations of the workflows).

- **Diagram validation** You can ensure that your diagrams meet a minimum set of predefined conditions before you publish or distribute them using diagram validation rules. Four Visio 2010 templates—Basic Flowchart, Cross Functional Flowchart, Microsoft SharePoint Workflow, and BPMN—include predefined validation rule sets. You can edit the existing rule sets or create your own.

If you are upgrading from Visio 2003

Visio 2007 Professional introduced an important set of data-related enhancements that significantly improved your ability to create data-rich diagrams and to visualize that data creatively and effectively.

- **Themes** Visio 2007 introduces themes—a fast way to add style and a professionally designed look to your diagrams.

- **AutoConnect** You no longer need to return to the stencil every time you want to add a shape to the page. When you click one of the four AutoConnect arrows that appear when you point to an existing shape on the drawing page, Visio adds a connector and a copy of the currently selected *master* shape in the stencil.

- **Save as PDF or XPS** After downloading a free, add-in available from Microsoft, you can save Visio diagrams in either PDF or XPS format.

- **Sample diagrams** Visio 2007 includes five sample diagrams in the new Getting Started category on the startup screen. In the Professional edition, the diagrams are connected to data in Excel workbooks that are also included with Visio.

The following features are available only in the Professional edition of Visio 2007.

- **Data linking** A new linking wizard dramatically simplifies the task of linking shapes on the drawing page to data that resides in Microsoft Excel, Access, SQL Server, SharePoint lists, or almost any ODBC or OLEDB-compatible database. No programming is required to establish connections or to refresh a diagram when the underlying data changes.

- **Data graphics** You can use Visio 2007 data graphics to visualize data by displaying text or a graphic that is based on the data inside the shape.

- **PivotDiagrams** You can build tree-structured data views using the new Pivot-Diagram template.

- **ITIL and Value Stream mapping** New templates enable you to create two important types of diagrams: Information Technology Infrastructure Library (ITIL) process maps and Value Stream maps.

Working with the ribbon

The Office ribbon is a dynamic user interface element; its appearance changes if the width of the window in which it is being viewed changes. As a result, a button might be large or small, it might or might not have a label, or it might even be an entry in a list.

For example, when sufficient horizontal space is available, the buttons on the Home tab are spread out, and the available commands in each group are visible.

If you decrease the horizontal space available to the ribbon, small button labels disappear and groups of buttons might hide under one button that represents the entire group.

Compare the arrangement of buttons in the Font and Paragraph groups in the preceding and following graphics, for example. Also, in the following graphic, notice that the captions for the rightmost buttons in the Arrange group have disappeared, and that the Arrange group has been collapsed to a single button. Collapsed buttons and groups retain all of their functions, as the submenu beneath the Arrange button demonstrates.

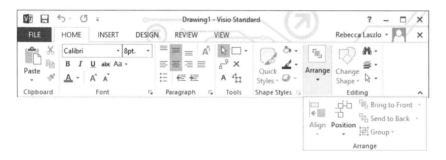

When the ribbon becomes too narrow to display all of the groups, a scroll arrow appears at its right end. Clicking the scroll arrow displays additional groups.

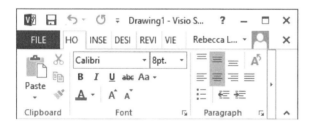

The width of the ribbon depends on three factors:

- **Program window width** Maximizing the program window provides the most space for the ribbon. To maximize the window, click the **Maximize** button, drag the borders of a nonmaximized window, or drag the window to the top of the screen.

- **Screen resolution** Screen resolution is the size of your screen display expressed as pixels wide × pixels high. Your screen resolution options are dependent on the display adapter installed in your computer, and on your monitor. Common screen resolutions range from 800 × 600 to 2560 × 1600. The greater the number of pixels wide (the first number), the greater the number of buttons that can be shown on the ribbon.

To change your screen resolution:

a. Display the **Screen Resolution** control panel item in one of the following ways:

  - Right-click the Windows desktop, and then click **Screen Resolution**.

  - Type **screen resolution** in Windows 8 Search, and then click **Adjust screen resolution** in the **Settings** results.

  - Open the **Display** control panel item, and then click **Adjust resolution**.

b. On the **Screen Resolution** page, click the **Resolution** arrow, click or drag to select the screen resolution you want, and then click **Apply** or **OK**.

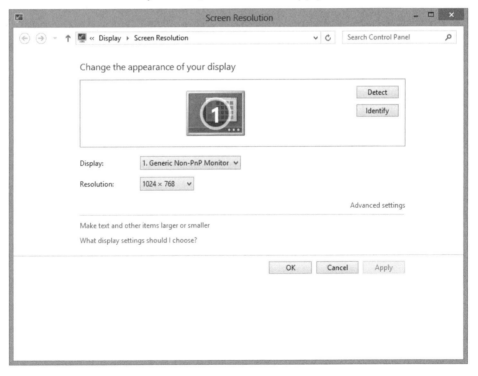

- **The magnification of your screen display** If you change the screen magnification setting in Windows, text and user interface elements are larger and therefore more legible, but fewer elements fit on the screen. You can set the magnification from 100 to 500 percent.

You can change the screen magnification from the Display page of the Appearance and Personalization control panel item. You can display the Display page directly from Control Panel or by using one of the following methods:

- Right-click the Windows desktop, click **Personalize**, and then in the lower-left corner of the **Personalization** window, click **Display**.

- Type **display** in Windows 8 Search, and then click **Display** in the **Settings** results.

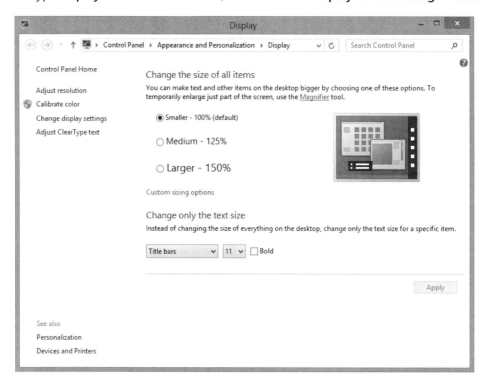

To change the screen magnification to 125 or 150 percent, click that option on the Display page. To select another magnification, click the Custom sizing options link and then, in the Custom sizing options dialog box, click the magnification you want in the drop-down list or drag the ruler to change the magnification even more.

After you click OK in the Custom sizing options dialog box, the custom magnification is shown on the Display page along with any warnings about possible problems with selecting that magnification. Click Apply on the Display page to apply the selected magnification.

Adapting exercise steps

The Visio ribbon consists of multiple tabs, each of which contains a set of related functions. The function buttons on any one tab are organized into named groups. Consequently, the instructions in the book that guide you to a specific function or button will include three parts. For example:

On the **Home** *tab, in the* **Tools** *group, click the* **Pointer Tool** *button.*

The screen shots shown in this book were captured at a screen resolution of 1024 × 768, at 100% magnification. If your settings are different, the ribbon on your screen might not look the same as the one shown in this book, but you can easily adapt the steps to locate the command.

For example, if a button appears differently on your screen than it does in this book, start by clicking the specified tab, and then locate the specified group. If a group has been collapsed into a group list or under a group button, click the list or button to display the group's commands. If you can't immediately identify the button you want, point to likely candidates to display their names in ScreenTips.

Instructions in this book are based on traditional keyboard and mouse input methods. If you're using Visio on a touch-enabled device, you might be taking action by tapping with your finger or with a stylus. If so, substitute a tapping action any time you're instructed to click a user interface element. Also note that when you're instructed to type information in Visio, you can do so by typing on a keyboard, tapping in the entry field under discussion to display and use the onscreen keyboard, or even speaking aloud, depending on your computer setup and your personal preferences.

Getting started with Visio 2013

When you start Visio 2013, it presents a startup page that is new to this version of Visio and is common to both the Standard and Professional editions of Visio 2013.

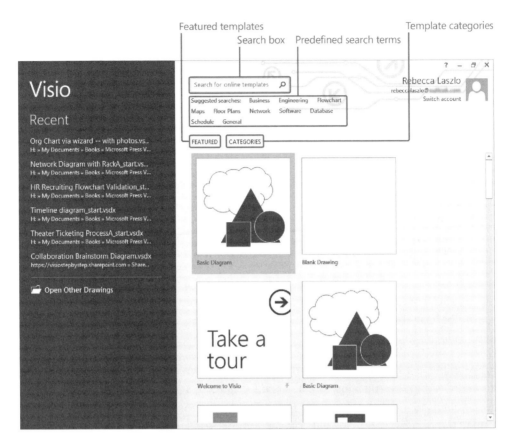

Featured templates   Template categories

Search box   Predefined search terms

Key sections of the start page are described in the following list.

- In the narrower left column is a list of recently opened diagrams. Clicking any diagram name opens it again.

  If you want to open a diagram that is not on the Recent list, click the Open Other Drawings button at the bottom of the list and Visio will take you to the Open page that is described in the next section.

- In the wider right column is a collection of thumbnails representing recently used or recommended templates.

- Above the template thumbnails are four important ways to find Visio templates.

  - You can type any words into the **Search for online templates** box and Visio will present templates that match your keywords.

  - You can click any word in the **Suggested searches** list to initiate an online search for matching templates.

- **Featured** is the default selection for the template thumbnails that appear in the main part of the page (refer to the preceding graphic). The presentation of thumbnails is dynamic; the templates you use most frequently will rise to the top.

- Clicking **Categories** presents a set of template categories that are the same as the categories in previous versions of Visio: Business, Flowchart, General, Maps and Floor Plans, Network, and Schedule. The Professional edition also includes Engineering, and Software and Database categories.

At the end of the template categories list is an additional entry called New from existing. Clicking this thumbnail enables you to select any existing Visio diagram. Visio will then open a copy of the diagram as a new document and will leave the original untouched.

> **IMPORTANT** Clicking a suggested search term will *not* produce the same result as selecting a template category of the same name. For example, clicking the Flowchart search term will yield some of the same templates that you will find in the template category named Flowchart, however, it will also return several—or several hundred—additional templates, both for Visio and for other programs in the Office suite.
>
> If you would like to locate Visio 2013 templates using a method that is most like what you are familiar with from a previous version of Visio, click Categories and then select the desired template category.

SEE ALSO Microsoft has published a series of quick-start guides for the programs in the Office family at *office.microsoft.com/en-us/support/office-2013-quick-start-guides-HA103673669.aspx.*

Exploring the Backstage view

The Backstage view is the central location for managing files and setting the options that control how Visio 2013 operates. You access the Backstage view by clicking the File tab at the top left of the Visio window.

Of the 11 pages in the Backstage view, only four—New, Open, Account, and Options—are available if you do not have a diagram open. The remaining seven appear when you open a diagram.

TIP If you are in the Backstage view and have a diagram open, you can return to the diagram by clicking the left-pointing arrow in the upper-left corner of the Visio window. If you don't have a diagram open, clicking the arrow will return you to the start screen.

The pages in the Backstage view are described in the following sections.

Info

When you have a diagram open and click the File tab, Visio presents the Info page.

The center section of the page includes four command buttons.

- You will learn more about the **Remove Personal Information** button in Chapter 8, "Printing, reusing, and sharing diagrams."

- You can click the **Reduce File Size** button if document size is a major consideration.

- The **Check Compatibility** button checks the current diagram for features that are not compatible with previous versions of Visio.

- You will learn about the SharePoint publishing settings behind the **Set Publish Options and Check Data Connections** button in Chapter 13, "Collaborating on and publishing diagrams."

The right side of the page provides information about the open document, along with a Properties list that you can use to view and set additional document properties. You will use the Properties list in several places in this book, including Chapter 7, "Adding and using hyperlinks," and Chapter 8.

SEE ALSO If you open a file from a previous version of Visio, it will open in compatibility mode, and an additional button, labeled *Convert*, will appear at the top of the Info page. Refer to "The Visio 2013 file formats" in the Appendix for more information about working with files from previous versions of Visio.

New

The New page provides access to both built-in templates and online templates. You access built-in templates by clicking a diagram thumbnail in the lower part of the page. You can either type your own search terms or use the predefined search terms at the top of the page to locate templates from *Office.com*.

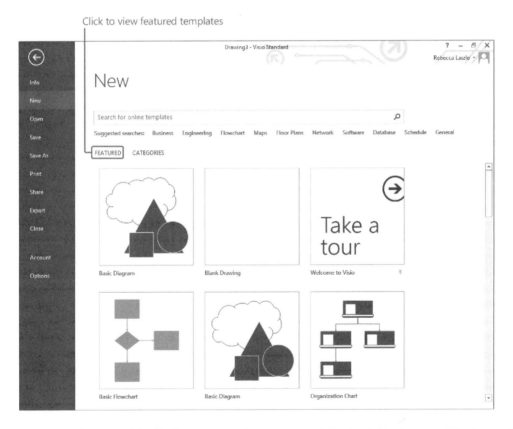

The preceding graphic displays Featured diagrams, while the following graphic shows the template Categories for Visio Standard. Be sure to read about the difference between featured templates and template categories at the beginning of the "Getting started with Visio 2013" section.

Click to view template categories

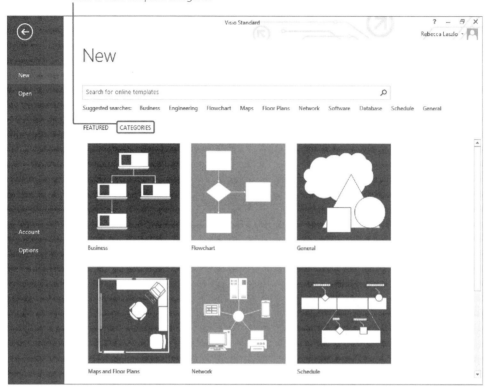

Clicking any template category displays thumbnails for the diagrams in that category.

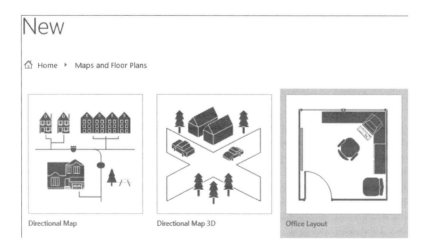

If you click once on a diagram thumbnail, Visio displays information about that template, as shown in the following graphic. If you double-click a diagram thumbnail, Visio launches a new diagram.

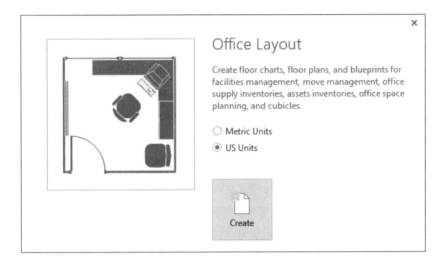

TIP When you create a new diagram, Visio names it Drawing*n*, where *n* is a sequence number that is incremented for each new drawing created within one Visio session. Closing and restarting Visio always resets the sequence number to 1.

Visio templates are provided in two different sets of measurement units.

- **Metric** *Metric* drawings are sized using International Standards Organization (ISO) specified paper sizes; the default size is usually A4. Metric templates also include other ISO drawing and paper sizes. All measurements are in millimeters or other metric measurement units.

- **US Units** Diagrams created with *US Units* use the 8.5-by-11-inch, letter-sized paper that is common in the United States and parts of Canada and Mexico. Templates created for US Units also include additional drawing and paper sizes that are common in those countries. The default measurement units are inches and feet.

Depending on your system configuration, you might be offered a choice between the two, as shown in the preceding graphic.

Open

The Open page provides access to previously stored Visio diagrams.

TIP If you are familiar with the Backstage view in Visio 2010, you will notice that there is no longer a separate Recent page in the Visio 2013 Backstage view; Recent drawings are available on the Open page instead.

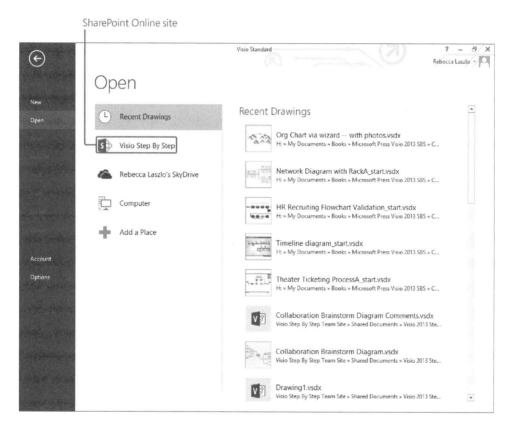

One of the first things you'll notice on the Visio 2013 Open page is that the buttons in the center column make it is just as easy to access diagrams stored on SharePoint or SkyDrive as it is to open documents on your computer. Simply click any of the location buttons in the center column to display a list of recently used folders along with a Browse button for that location. The page that results from clicking the button for the Visio Step By Step SharePoint Online site is shown in the following graphic.

Click Add A Place to pin additional SkyDrive or SharePoint Online locations to the Open page.

When you click the Browse button on the Open page, Visio displays the Windows Open dialog box. The file type filter in the Open dialog is preset to display Visio drawings, templates, and stencils that were created in the new Visio 2013 file format, as well as those created with previous versions of Visio.

SEE ALSO To learn more about the new Visio file formats and about opening and converting files created in previous versions of Visio, refer to "The Visio 2013 file formats" in the Appendix.

Save

Clicking Save for a previously unsaved diagram displays the Save As page shown in the following section. Clicking Save for a previously saved diagram simply saves the changes.

Save As

On the Save As page, you can choose a local or remote location and then either select a recent folder or use the Browse button to navigate to the desired location.

Print

The Print page provides a print preview and printing options. You will learn about print options in Chapter 8.

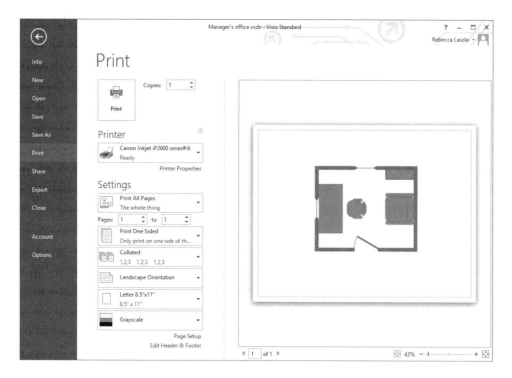

Share

The Share page offers two techniques for sharing your Visio drawing.

You can click Invite People to publicize your diagram via email or social media. The first step is to click the Save To Cloud button to store your diagram to either SkyDrive or SharePoint. After the save operation completes, Visio provides an email form and several buttons you can use to share links to your diagram.

You can click the Email button to share your diagram using any of the options listed on the right side of the following graphic.

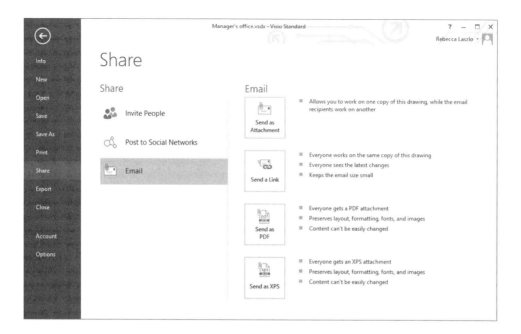

Export

The Export page enables you to create a PDF or XPS document as well as to save in a wide variety of other file formats. You will learn about exporting to other file formats in Chapter 8, "Printing, reusing, and sharing diagrams," and Chapter 12, "Creating and validating process diagrams."

Close

There is no Close page—clicking Close simply closes the active diagram.

Account

The Account page summarizes information about the Microsoft Account (formerly known as Live ID) that you have linked to Visio. Links in the Account column enable you to change your Microsoft Account details and to switch to another Microsoft Account if you have more than one. The same column provides drop-down lists you can use to alter the Office Background and Office Theme used for Visio and all other Office applications.

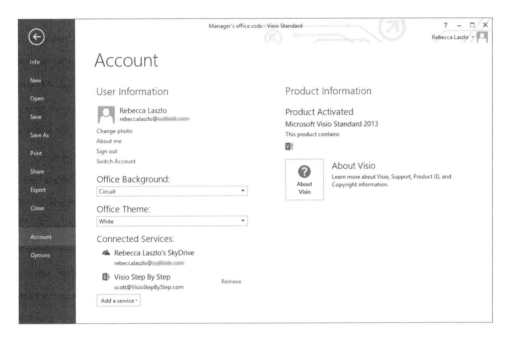

Clicking the About Visio button in the right-hand column displays version information and your product ID. The upper portion of the About Microsoft Visio dialog box is shown in the following graphic.

TIP The About Microsoft Visio dialog box does not indicate whether you are running the Standard or Professional edition of Visio. However, that information is displayed in the title bar of the Visio window as shown in the preceding graphic.

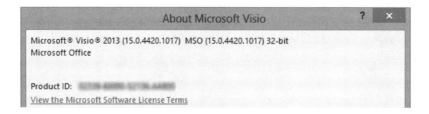

Options

The Options button opens a dialog box that contains dozens of settings you can use to customize the operation of Visio. Many people use Visio 2013 without ever needing to change any of these options, but it's a good idea to examine the option categories for potential future use.

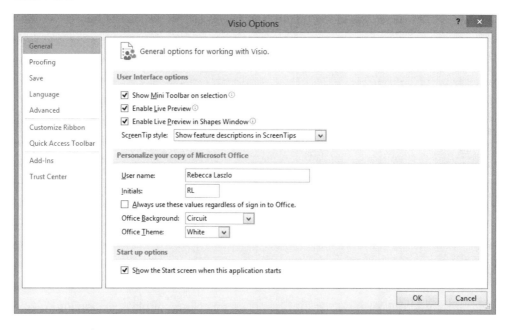

- **General** Type your user name and initials as well as set various global options, including Live Preview and the Visio window color scheme.

- **Proofing** Set autocorrect, spelling, and grammar options.

- **Save** Set the default Visio save format (Visio Document; Visio Macro-Enabled Document; Visio 2003-2010 Document) and the document management check out/check in options.

- **Language** Set editing, display, help, and ScreenTip language parameters.

- **Advanced** Set dozens of options in five categories: Editing, Display, Save/Open, Shape Search, and General.

- **Customize Ribbon** Add/rearrange commands on built-in ribbon tabs; create new tabs and commands.

- **Quick Access Toolbar** Add/remove command buttons on the *Quick Access Toolbar*.

- **Add-ins** View and add/delete Visio add-ins.

- **Trust Center** View and edit macro settings and other trust-related options.

Exploring the Visio ribbon

Earlier in this chapter, the graphics in "Working with the ribbon" demonstrated how the appearance of the ribbon can change depending on the width of the Visio window.

In this exercise, the width of the ribbon will remain constant at 1024 pixels and you will explore each of the Visio tabs.

> **IMPORTANT** Most of the screen shots in this book feature the Professional edition ribbon. Consequently, there might be tabs, buttons, or options in the screen shots that don't apply if you are using the Standard edition. In general, you can ignore any buttons or tabs that do not appear on your computer screen. Where necessary, the text will distinguish those exercises or functions that can only be performed with a specific Visio 2013 edition.

 SET UP **If Visio is already running, click File, and then click New. If Visio is not running, start it. On either the New or startup page, double-click the Basic Diagram thumbnail.**

1   Click the **Home** tab if it is not already selected.

   The Home tab is just what it sounds like: a place where you will spend a consider-able amount of time. The Home tab contains the largest number of buttons by far, because the Visio team at Microsoft tried to fit as many of the most frequently used functions as possible onto this tab. You'll find sets of related buttons organized into groups called Clipboard, Font, Paragraph, Tools, Shape Styles, Arrange, and Editing.

   You will use buttons on this tab in most of the exercises in this book.

TIP Many of the groups on the Visio tabs include a small arrow in the lower-right corner of the group (refer to the Font, Paragraph, and Shape Styles groups above). The arrow button, known as the *dialog box launcher*, opens a dialog box that provides detailed control over multiple functions related to that group. In many cases, the dialog box that opens will look familiar to experienced Visio users, because it is the same one that was used in previous Visio versions.

2   Click the **Insert** tab to access the **Pages**, **Illustrations**, **Diagram Parts**, **Links**, and **Text** groups. Many of the functions available on this tab mirror the items on the Insert menu in Visio 2007 and earlier.

You will use buttons on this tab in multiple chapters including Chapter 3, "Adding sophistication to your drawings," and Chapter 11, "Adding structure to your diagrams."

TIP Ribbon buttons that display a downward-pointing arrow behave in one of two ways. When you point to some buttons, like the Container button on the left in the following graphic, the entire button is illuminated. Clicking this type of button always presents a set of options related to the button title.

When you point to other buttons, like the Text Box button in the following graphic on the right, only half of the button is illuminated. Clicking the half without the arrow performs the default action for the button. Clicking the half with the arrow presents a menu of options.

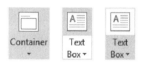

3   Click the **Design** tab to change **Page Setup**, select **Themes** or **Variants**, create or edit page **Backgrounds**, and change page **Layout**.

You will use buttons on this tab in various exercises, including those in Chapter 3, "Adding sophistication to your drawings," and Chapter 5, "Adding style, color, and themes."

4   Click the **Data** tab.

IMPORTANT This tab is available only in the Professional edition.

On the Data tab, you can establish and maintain links to External Data, Display Data using *data graphics*, and Show/Hide both the Shape Data and External Data windows.

You will use buttons on this tab primarily in Chapter 6, "Entering, linking, and reporting on data," and Chapter 10, "Visualizing your data."

5   Click the **Process** tab.

IMPORTANT This tab is available only in the Professional edition.

In the Subprocess group, you can create a new *subprocess* or link to an existing one. In the Diagram Validation group, you can validate a drawing against a set of business rules and manage validation issues. You can also import or export a SharePoint Workflow from this tab.

You will use buttons on this tab in Chapters 12 and 13.

6   Click the **Review** tab for access to functions for **Proofing**, **Language**, **Comments**, and **Reports**.

You will use buttons on this tab in various exercises, including those in Chapters 3 and 6.

7   Click the **View** tab.

As the name suggests, most of the buttons on this tab affect which Visio features are visible on the screen:

- The lone button in the **Views** group sets Visio into full-screen display mode.

    KEYBOARD SHORTCUT Press F5 to enter or exit full-screen view mode.

- The **Show** group controls which drawing aids and task panes are visible.

- Use the **Zoom** buttons to change the magnification level in the drawing window.

- The **Visual Aids** group enables and disables various on-screen drawings aids.

- Use the **Window** buttons to arrange or select among multiple windows when you have more than one drawing open.

- The **Macros** group provides access to the Visio macro programming window and to a list of pre-programmed add-ons that enhance the capabilities of Visio.

You will use buttons on this tab in exercises later in this chapter and throughout the rest of the book.

❌ CLEAN UP **Close the *Drawing1* drawing. It is not necessary to save your changes.**

TIP The buttons and controls on all ribbon tabs display pop-up tooltip text when you point to them. If you are unsure of the function of any button, just point to the button to view the tooltip.

SEE ALSO If you are familiar with versions of Visio prior to Visio 2010 and would like help shifting from toolbars and menus to the ribbon, Microsoft has created an interactive guide to the ribbon for each product in the Office suite. When you click a toolbar or menu item in the guide, it will display the appropriate ribbon button. You can find the Visio guide at *office.microsoft.com/en-us/visio-help/learn-where-menu-and-toolbar-commands-are-in-office-2010-and-related-products-HA101794130.aspx*. Although this guide was created for Visio 2010, the Visio 2013 ribbon is sufficiently similar that you will still find the guide to be helpful.

Where are the keyboard shortcuts?

If you are accustomed to using keyboard shortcuts, you'll be happy to know that they still exist in Visio 2013. Most shortcuts are the same as in previous versions of Visio, although some were changed to make them consistent with other applications in the Office suite.

The keyboard shortcut letters appear when you press the Alt key. The following graphic shows the shortcut letter associated with each tab on the Visio 2013 ribbon. Notice, too, that each button on the Quick Access Toolbar has been assigned a shortcut number based on its position within the Quick Access Toolbar.

Pressing the letter or number for any displayed shortcut key opens the relevant tab and displays the shortcut keys for that tab. For example, pressing the N key when in the view shown in the previous graphic displays the Insert tab and the shortcut letters shown in the following graphic.

TIP Previous versions of Visio used the capital letter *I* as the shortcut key for the Insert menu. Visio 2013 uses the keyboard shortcut *N* to be consistent with other Office applications.

Understanding tool tabs and add-in tabs

All of the ribbon tabs shown in the preceding sections are visible 100 percent of the time as you run Visio. However, there are two types of tabs that only appear when necessary.

A *Tool tab set* only appears in a particular drawing context, usually when a specific type of shape is selected on the drawing page. Tool tab sets usually appear to the right of the View tab and are not activated automatically, that is, you must click the tab to view its contents. A tool tab set includes a colored header and may contain one or more tool tabs under the header. Here are examples of two tool tab sets:

- **Picture Tools** This tool tab set appears whenever you insert or select a graphic on a Visio drawing page. The green Picture Tools header contains a Format tool tab, which includes buttons to crop, rotate, and otherwise modify a picture.

- **Container Tools** This tool tab set appears whenever you insert or select a Visio *container*. The orange Container Tools header contains a Format tool tab, which includes buttons to size and style containers, and to control container membership. You will learn about containers in Chapter 11.

Add-in tabs are associated with software that adds capabilities to Visio. Some add-ins are packaged with Visio by Microsoft; others are sold by third-party software vendors.

Unlike tool tabs, add-in tabs look and behave exactly like permanent Visio tabs with one primary exception: they appear when an add-in application is active and disappear when it is not. Here are two examples:

- **Org Chart** This add-in is included with Visio and is activated whenever you create or edit a drawing that uses either of the Visio organization chart templates. You will learn about organization charts in Chapter 4.

- **TaskMap** This third-party add-in provides easy-to-use process mapping, analysis, and improvement functions that can be used with any edition of Visio.

SEE ALSO For more information about the TaskMap add-in, go to *www.taskmap.com*.

Minimizing and restoring the Visio ribbon

Because the ribbon takes a reasonable amount of space at the top of the Visio window, you may want to minimize it if you need more space for the drawing page. The key to doing so is a very small up arrow located in the lower-right corner of the ribbon.

Clicking this button minimizes the ribbon as shown in the following graphic. To temporarily display a tab when it's minimized, click the tab name.

To restore the ribbon to normal operation after it has been minimized, click the pushpin located in the lower-right corner of the ribbon.

Understanding shapes, masters, stencils, and templates

Before you explore the rest of Visio, it's helpful to understand a number of commonly used terms:

- *Master* An object in a Visio stencil. The vast majority of people who create diagrams with Visio use the masters that ship with Visio or that they download from the Internet. You can create new masters; however, the techniques for doing so are outside the scope of this book.

- *Stencil* A collection of masters.

- *Shape* An object on a Visio drawing page. Often you create shapes by dragging a master from a stencil to the drawing page; however, you can also create shapes in other ways. (You will learn more about shapes in Chapter 2, "Creating a new diagram," and throughout this book.)

  A shape can be very simple: a line, a polygon, an image. A shape can also be a sophisticated object that changes appearance or behavior as data values change, as its position on the page changes, or as properties of another shape change—the possibilities are endless.

- *Template* A Visio document that includes one or more drawing pages with preset dimensions and measurement units. A template may also include one or more stencils; it may include background pages and designs; its pages may contain shapes or text. A template may also include special software that only operates in that template.

- *Workspace* A collection of Visio windows and window settings. At minimum, the workspace consists of the drawing window and the zoom settings for the pages in the drawing; frequently, it also includes a Shapes window containing one or more stencils. The workspace can also include the Shape Data, Size & Position, or Pan & Zoom windows. Unless you have changed the default action, Visio saves the on-screen workspace whenever you save the document. As a result, when you next open the same document, the same collection of windows is restored.

TIP Despite the distinction made in this list between a master and a shape, you will find that many people refer to an object in a stencil as a shape. Indeed, when you think about it, the window that displays stencils is called the *Shapes* window! Consequently, unless the distinction is important in a specific context, the text in this book will refer to *shapes* in a stencil and to *shapes* on the drawing page.

Exploring the drawing window

When you start Visio, two windows normally appear below the ribbon.

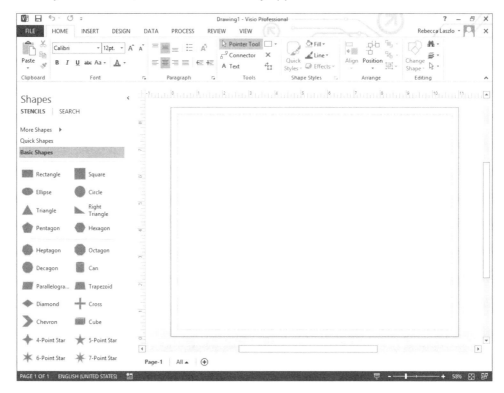

- The *Shapes window* on the left contains one or more stencils, each represented by a header bar containing the name of the stencil. Depending on the number of open stencils in the **Shapes** window, a scroll bar might appear at the right of the headers. You will investigate the **Shapes** window in the next section of this chapter.

  TIP The width of the Shapes window is adjustable, so the one on your system may be wider or narrower than the one that appears in the preceding graphic.

- The larger window on the right is called the *drawing window* because it contains the *drawing page*. The drawing window is bounded on the top and left by rulers that display inches, millimeters, or whatever units you have selected (or your template has selected) for measuring page dimensions.

  TIP All previous versions of Visio displayed the grid on the drawing page by default. However, in Visio 2013, the opposite is true. To make the grid visible, click Grid in the Show group on the View tab.

At the lower left of the drawing window is a set of *page controls*.

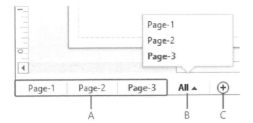

- **A** *Page name tabs* display the name of each page and the active page name is displayed in a different color. Click any tab to change to that page. Right-click any page name tab to access page management functions including the new **Duplicate Page** function.

- **B** Click the **All** button to display a list of all pages in the diagram. The name of the active page is highlighted in the list.

- **C** Click the **Insert Page** button to add a new page.

Below the Shapes and drawing windows is a *status bar* that contains a variety of indicators, buttons, and controls. The buttons and indicators on the left end of the status bar are context sensitive, so they will show different information depending on the state of the drawing.

If nothing is selected on the drawing page, the left end of the status bar looks like the following graphic.

- **A** The **Page Number** button shows which page is active and displays the total number of pages in the current drawing; click this button to open the **Page** dialog box.

- **B** The **Language** area displays the language of the current drawing; the drawing language is normally derived from Windows or Visio language settings.

- **C** Click the **Macros** button to start the macro recorder.

If you have selected a shape on the drawing page, the left end of the status bar looks like the following graphic instead.

- **A** Same as previous A.

- **B** Same as previous B.

- **C** Same as previous C.

- **D** This area contains three buttons. The **Width** and **Height** buttons display the dimensions of the selected shape and the **Angle** button displays its angle of rotation; click any of the three buttons to open the **Size & Position** window.

The right end of the status bar contains a variety of useful buttons and controls.

- **A** Click the **Presentation Mode** button to view the active diagram in full-screen presentation mode.

- **B** Move the **Zoom** slider to zoom in or out.

- **C** The **Zoom Level** button displays the current zoom percentage; click it to open the **Zoom** dialog box.

- **D** Click the **Fit Page To Current Window** button to resize the drawing page so the entire page is visible in the drawing window.

- **E** Click the **Switch Windows** button to switch to another Visio window.

  TIP Most other Office applications require the use of a button on the View tab of the ribbon to switch among multiple open windows. The Visio development team had the foresight to include the Switch Windows button (E) on the status bar where it is much more convenient.

If you right-click anywhere in the status bar, the Customize Status Bar menu appears. You can click any of the options in the Customize Status Bar menu to toggle the display of a button or control.

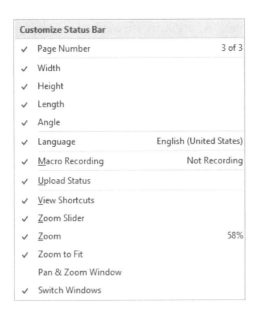

Managing the shapes window

The upper part of the Shapes window contains a list of stencil titles and the lower part displays the shapes from the currently selected stencil.

In this exercise, you will learn various ways to manipulate the Shapes window so it appears in the most useful size and position when you are working on a drawing.

SET UP If Visio is already running, click File, and then click New. If Visio is not running, start it. On either the New or startup page, click Categories, click Maps and Floor Plans, and then double-click the Office Layout thumbnail. Save the new drawing as *Exploring Visio 2013*.

IMPORTANT One of the user interface changes in Visio 2013 is that window boundaries have been designed to fade into the background so they don't interfere visually with the content of the drawing. Consequently, the appearance of some parts of the Shapes window is less obvious than in previous versions of Visio. In particular, the boundary of the Shapes window is not visible. The only way to know where it is located is to move the pointer slowly across it until the pointer changes to a window resize tool.

1   Change the width of the **Shapes** window by dragging the window boundary left or right. The pointer changes to a double-headed arrow as the window border is dragged to a wider or narrower view. (In the following graphic, the pointer is located to the right of the **Search** tab.)

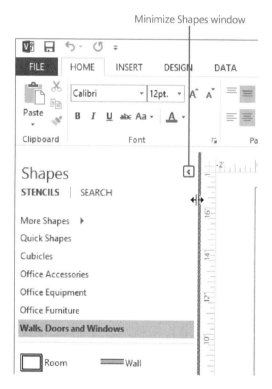

2   Minimize the **Shapes** window by clicking the **Minimize the Shapes window** arrow
    shown in the preceding graphic. Even though the descriptions are now hidden, all of
    the masters in the stencil are still accessible when the **Shapes** window is minimized.
    Consequently, this view is useful when you need more space for the drawing window
    and the icons depicting the masters in the stencil are very recognizable.

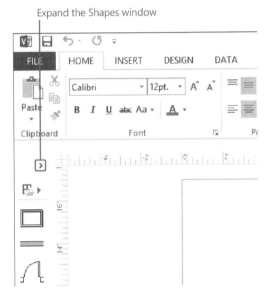

3   Return the **Shapes** window to its former size by clicking the **Expand the Shapes
    window** arrow highlighted in the preceding graphic.

4   To hide the **Shapes** window entirely, on the **View** tab, in the **Show** group, click the
    Task Panes button, and then click **Shapes**.

    TIP The various subwindows that can be opened or closed within the Visio window
    are sometimes referred to as *task panes*.

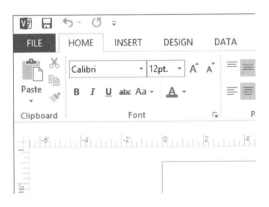

TIP The Shapes window can be reopened by clicking the same button you used to close it.

5   On the **View** tab, in the **Show** group, click **Task Panes**, and then click **Shapes**. If the window does not already show two columns of shapes, adjust the width so it does. The **Walls**, **Doors** and **Windows** title bar is highlighted, indicating that this is the active stencil. However, the Office Layout template includes several additional stencils.

6   In the **Shapes** window, click **Office Furniture**.

TIP When you click the title bar of any stencil, the title bars remain stationary, and the stencil always opens in the same place, below all title bars. This is a significant improvement in behavior over versions of Visio prior to Visio 2010.

You are not restricted to using just the stencils that open in a particular template, as you will discover in the following steps.

IMPORTANT If there is a sufficient number of masters in a stencil to require scroll bars, the scroll bars are only visible if the pointer is inside the stencil portion of the Shapes window. The downside of this visual technique is that you don't necessarily know there are more shapes available (refer to the following graphic on the leftw) unless you move the pointer into the stencil portion of the Shapes window (following graphic on the right).

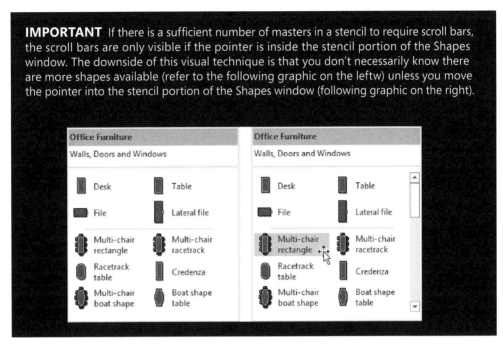

7   In the **Shapes** window, click **More Shapes**, and then point to **General**. (Do not click any stencils in the **General** group yet.) A fly-out menu containing stencil names appears. In the following graphic, the collection of stencils in the **General** group is visible.

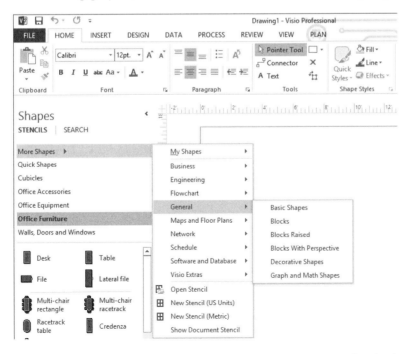

8   With the cascading menus open from step 7, click **Basic Shapes**. Visio opens the **Basic Shapes** stencil. In a behavior change from Visio 2010, a check mark appears to the left of the stencil you selected, but the fly-out menus remain open, allowing you to select additional stencils from the same or another stencil family.

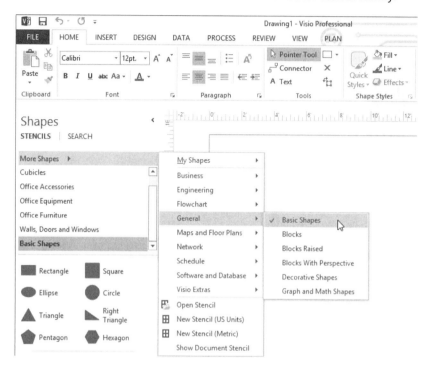

9   Click anywhere in the Visio window to close the cascading menus.

Although it isn't actually necessary in this exercise, it's helpful to know how to close stencils you no longer need, so that's what you will do in the remaining step.

10   Right-click **Basic Shapes**, and then click **Close**.

TIP Although you didn't use it in this exercise, be sure to notice the Search tab at the top of the Shapes window. The enhanced shape search function in Visio 2013 yields more targeted results with fewer duplicate results.

✖ CLEAN UP **Leave the** *Exploring Visio 2013* **drawing open if you are continuing with the next exercise. If not, there is no need to save changes.**

Panning and zooming in Visio

As you work with more detailed Visio diagrams, you will find that you frequently need to *zoom* in and out and *pan*—move left-right and up-down—within the drawing window. Both can be accomplished using a variety of techniques, some of which rely on your mouse, some that use a special Pan & Zoom window, and others that use keyboard shortcuts.

In this exercise, you will learn several techniques to pan and zoom your diagram, beginning with keyboard shortcuts and ending with the Pan & Zoom window.

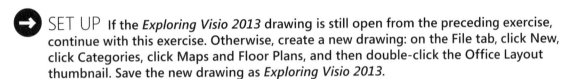 **SET UP** **If the *Exploring Visio 2013* drawing is still open from the preceding exercise, continue with this exercise. Otherwise, create a new drawing: on the File tab, click New, click Categories, click Maps and Floor Plans, and then double-click the Office Layout thumbnail. Save the new drawing as *Exploring Visio 2013*.**

1 Click **Office Furniture** if it is not already the active stencil, and then drag a **Round table** shape onto the drawing page.

2 Drag a **Chair** shape onto a different part of the page.

3 Drag a **Corner table** shape onto yet another part of the page.

4 Drag a **Stool** and a **Square table** onto the page. Space the shapes so they occupy at least half of the drawing page.

Your diagram might look something like the following graphic.

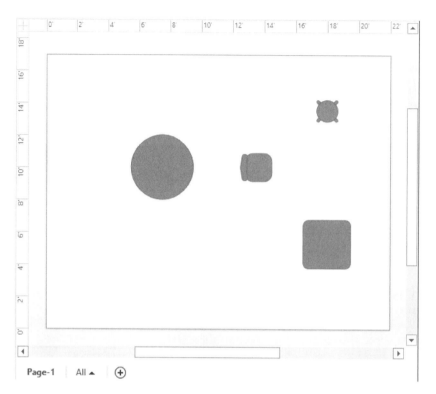

5   Hold down the **Ctrl+Shift** keys (the cursor will change to a magnifying glass with a plus sign), and then drag a rectangle around two of the shapes on the drawing page.

IMPORTANT You must press Ctrl+Shift *before* you click for this zoom technique to work.

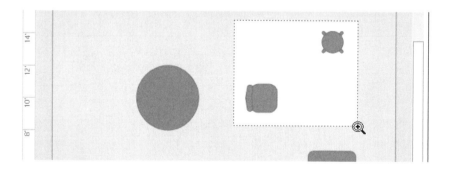

6　Release the mouse button and the keyboard keys. Visio sets the view in the drawing window to just the rectangle you outlined with the mouse.

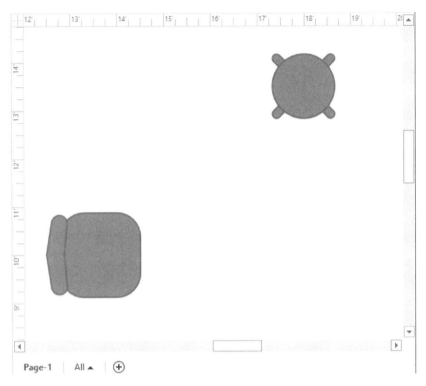

7　Press **Ctrl+Shift+W** to return to a view of the whole drawing page.

TIP Ctrl+Shift+W is an incredibly useful keyboard shortcut to remember because you will frequently zoom in to part of a drawing and then want to return to full page view. To help remember this shortcut, just remember that *W* is the first letter of *whole page*.

IMPORTANT In Visio 2007 and earlier, the keyboard shortcut to view the whole page was Ctrl+W. If you've upgraded from one of those versions of the software, it may take a bit of retraining to get accustomed to using Ctrl+Shift+W instead. To make matters worse, in Visio 2013, Ctrl+W closes the active document. (You will receive a warning if the document has unsaved changes.)

8   Hold down the **Ctrl** key and rotate the mouse wheel. Visio zooms in or out as you rotate the mouse wheel.

> **IMPORTANT** You can only perform this step if your mouse has a wheel.

TIP Sometimes you may want to zoom in on a specific shape. Visio provides an option setting that makes this very easy to do. On the File tab, click Options, and then click Advanced. In the Editing Options section of the Visio Options dialog box, click Center Selection On Zoom. Now when you select a shape and press the Ctrl key while rotating the mouse wheel, Visio automatically zooms in and out on the selected shape.

9   Press **Ctrl+Shift+W** to return to a view of the whole drawing page.

10   On the **View** tab, in the **Show** group, click the **Task Panes** button, and then click **Pan & Zoom**. The **Pan & Zoom** window opens. You can drag it to position it wherever you'd like.

TIP You can also open the Pan & Zoom window by clicking the Pan & Zoom button on the right end of the status bar. (Refer to "Exploring the drawing window" earlier in this chapter for information about the Visio status bar.)

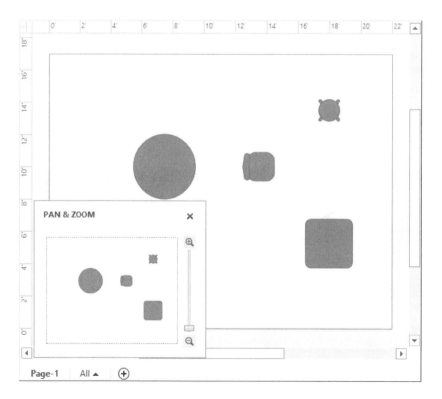

11   Click in the **Pan & Zoom** window, and then drag the cursor to create a rectangle that surrounds any two of the shapes. A blue rectangle appears in the Pan & Zoom window and the drawing window shows only the selected portion of the page.

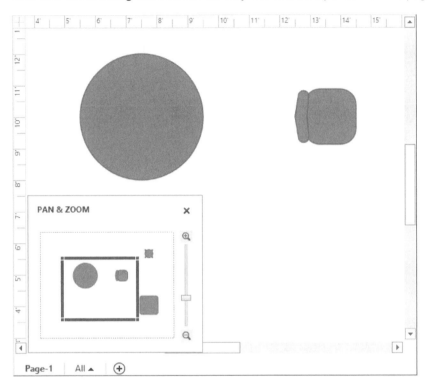

12   In the **Pan & Zoom** window, click in the interior of the blue rectangle, and then drag into another part of the miniature drawing page. The drawing window now shows the newly selected area of the drawing page.

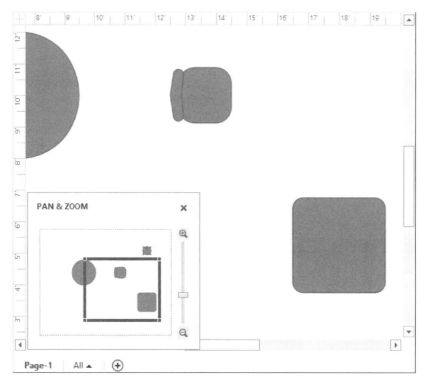

With the Pan & Zoom window open, you can:

- Continue to move the blue rectangle to reposition what appears in the drawing window.

- Drag the edges or the corners of the blue rectangle to resize it and change the zoom level.

- Drag the slider control on the right edge of the **Pan & Zoom** window to change the zoom level.

For many drawings, the Pan & Zoom window isn't necessary and may even be in the way. However, it is extremely helpful when your drawing page is very large, as it may be if you are working on diagrams such as engineering drawings, floor plans, or office layouts.

❌ CLEAN UP **Close the Pan & Zoom window. Save changes and close the drawing.**

TIP If you have a mouse with a wheel button, you can move the drawing page up and down in the drawing window by rotating the mouse wheel. You can reposition the drawing page to the left and right by holding down the Shift key while rotating the mouse wheel.

You can also move the drawing page using the arrow keys on your keyboard. Be sure that no shapes are selected before pressing the arrow keys, however, or you will move the selected shape(s) instead of moving the page.

Key points

- Visio Professional contains templates, stencils, ribbon tabs, and functions that are not included in Visio Standard. A key focus for the additional features in Visio Professional is linking to data sources and then visualizing that data using text callouts and icons. Professional features also enhance diagram collaboration, and enable documenting and managing business processes.

- Visio 2013 is the second version of Visio to employ the Office fluent user interface, commonly known as the ribbon. The Visio ribbon is well-designed and easy to use, in large part because the goal of the ribbon is to present sets of related functions visually, and Visio is a visual product.

- Tool tab sets and add-in tabs provide unique features and are only visible when they are relevant and can be used. Most ribbon tabs are visible all of the time.

- The Backstage view provides file management and option settings for Visio 2013.

- The drawing window and the Shapes window are the primary windows you will use to create and manipulate Visio diagrams.

- Visio provides a variety of keyboard shortcuts, mouse techniques, and specialized subwindows for panning and zooming within a diagram.

Chapter at a glance

Position

Position shapes with rulers and guides,
page 63

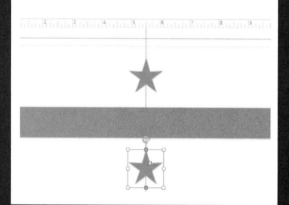

Resize

Resize and reposition shapes,
page 66

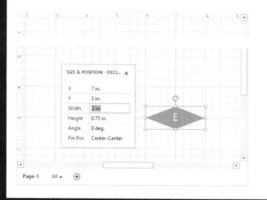

Use

Use AutoAdd and AutoDelete,
page 91

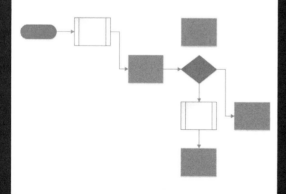

Replace

Replace shapes,
page 95

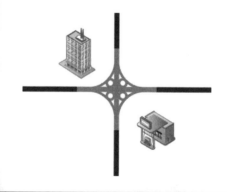

IN THIS CHAPTER, YOU WILL LEARN HOW TO

- Use basic shapes and the Dynamic Grid.

- Select, copy, paste, and duplicate shapes.

- Connect shapes with lines and dynamic connectors.

- Identify one-dimensional shapes and types of glue.

- Position shapes with rulers, guides, AutoConnect, and Quick Shapes.

- Use AutoAdd and AutoDelete.

- Replace shapes in a diagram.

As you discovered in Chapter 1, "A visual orientation to a visual product," Microsoft Visio 2013 includes a variety of templates in either six (Standard edition) or eight (Professional edition) categories. One of the easiest ways to begin a new diagram is to start with one of the templates. Some templates include stencils that contain very simple shapes; others contain stencils with very complex, intelligent shapes.

In Chapter 4, "Creating flowcharts and organization charts" and Chapter 9, "Creating network and data center diagrams," you will learn about templates in the latter category; you may even be surprised how sophisticated some of the shapes in those templates are.

In this chapter, you will use a very basic template to explore some of the key features of Visio 2013 that make it so easy to create new drawings: the Dynamic Grid, AutoConnect, Quick Shapes, AutoAdd, and AutoDelete. In addition, you will learn techniques for copying and pasting, connecting, resizing, and repositioning shapes. Finally, you will discover an exciting new feature that lets you replace a shape in a diagram with an entirely different shape.

Using basic shapes and the Dynamic Grid

Visio 2013 provides an enhanced *Dynamic Grid*. The purpose of the Dynamic Grid is to help you position a shape with greater accuracy as you drop it on the page or when you relocate it, thereby eliminating much of the need to drag and nudge the shape into alignment after you've placed it.

Though the Dynamic Grid was helpful in Visio 2010 and 2007, it's even more useful in Visio 2013 because it reacts more quickly to pointer movement and shape locations, and because it provides a greater variety of visual feedback. In addition, the Dynamic Grid is more valuable for aligning shapes in Visio 2013 because the background page grid is turned off by default.

In this exercise, you will create a drawing from a stencil containing basic Visio shapes. In the process of doing so, you will use several types of Dynamic Grid feedback. You will also create several shapes using Visio's drawing tools.

 SET UP **If Visio is already running, click File, and then click New. If Visio is not running, start it. On either the New or startup page, double-click the Basic Diagram thumbnail. Save the drawing as** *Basic Shapes***.**

1   Drag a **Rectangle** shape onto the drawing page and position it toward the upper-left corner of the page.

2   Drag a **Circle** shape onto the drawing page and position it to the right of the rectangle. Before you release the mouse button to drop the circle, move it up and down on the page. As you move the circle, a green, horizontal Dynamic Grid line appears when the circle is in certain positions relative to the rectangle.

   From left to right in the following graphics, the Dynamic Grid line indicates when the circle is aligned with the top, center, and bottom of the existing rectangle.

2

TROUBLESHOOTING If the Dynamic Grid lines don't appear as you move shapes near others already on the page, it is probably because the feature is turned off for this drawing. To activate the Dynamic Grid, click the Dynamic Grid button in the Visual Aids group on the View tab.

3 Use the Dynamic Grid to align the circle with the middle of the rectangle and drop it so the space between the shapes is approximately 1 inch (2.5 cm).

TIP Use of the Dynamic Grid lines is not restricted to positioning new shapes as you drop them from the stencil. The Dynamic Grid lines also appear when you use the pointer to reposition existing shapes on the page.

4 Click on the circle and drag it closer to the rectangle. The Dynamic Grid centerline appears, and if you've located the circle at a certain distance from the rectangle, a second Dynamic Grid element appears. When the distance between the two shapes matches the default spacing interval for this page, a double-headed arrow appears.

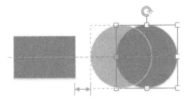

TIP You can change the default inter-shape spacing interval for a page: on the Home tab, in the Arrange group, click Position, and then click Spacing Options. The Spacing Options dialog box that appears enables you to change the horizontal and vertical spacing intervals.

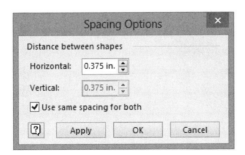

5   Press **Ctrl+Z** to undo the shape movement and position the circle back where you originally dropped it.

6   Drag a **Square** shape onto the page and position it on the right side of the circle but don't release the mouse button yet.

7   Use the Dynamic Grid to align the square with the center of the circle and then move the square left and right until the green double-headed arrow appears.

Notice that the double-headed arrow shown in the following graphic is longer than the double-headed arrow shown in the graphic after step 4 and that there are two of them, not one. In step 4, the double-headed arrow shows that the interval between your shapes matches the drawing's default spacing. In this example, the pair of double-headed arrows indicates that your new shape is the same distance from the circle that the circle is from the rectangle.

TIP To show you that the circle and square are the same height, Visio displays Dynamic Grid lines at the top, middle, and bottom of the pair of shapes.

8   Release the left mouse button to drop the square.

9   Continue to experiment with the Dynamic Grid by dragging an **Octagon** shape below the rectangle on the drawing page. As shown in the following graphic, the Dynamic Grid can provide guidance in two directions at once: the vertical lines indicate alignment with the rectangle; the pair of longer double-headed arrows show horizontal spacing; the short double-headed arrow highlights vertical spacing.

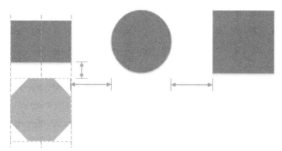

10   Release the left mouse button to drop the shape.

11   Drag a **Triangle** shape to the right of the octagon and below the circle. Once again, notice that the Dynamic Grid operates in two directions simultaneously. The Dynamic Grid also informs you that the triangle and circle are the same width (three vertical lines) but that the triangle and octagon are different heights (one horizontal line).

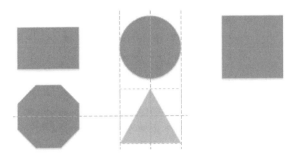

Now that you've added five shapes to the page by using a Visio stencil, it's time to create some shapes of your own using the Visio drawing tools.

12   On the **Home** tab, in the **Tools** group, click the **Rectangle Tool**. Notice that the cursor changes to a plus sign with a rectangle to the lower right.

> **IMPORTANT** The Rectangle Tool is one of six drawing tools that are located on a menu behind a button in the Tools group on the Home tab. The button is located to the right of the Pointer Tool and the image on the button and the accompanying tooltip text show the most recently used of the six tools. Each time you start Visio, however, the button function reverts to the Rectangle Tool.

13   Click anywhere on the drawing page and drag down and to the right to draw a rectangle.

      TIP You can constrain the Rectangle Tool so it only draws squares by holding down the Shift key while dragging the mouse.

14   On the **Home** tab, in the **Tools** group, click the **Ellipse Tool**, and then drag to create an ellipse to the right of your rectangle.

      TIP You can constrain the Ellipse Tool so it draws only circles by holding down the Shift key while dragging the mouse.

TIP To return Visio to normal operating mode after using one of the drawing tools, click the Pointer Tool in the Tools group on the Home tab or use the keyboard shortcut Ctrl+1.

⊗ CLEAN UP **Save your changes to the *Basic Shapes* drawing and close it.**

Although you have used the Dynamic Grid in this exercise while working with simple, geometric shapes, it is also useful with more complex shapes. However, if at any time you prefer to work without the Dynamic Grid, you can turn it off: on the View tab, in the Visual Aids group, click the Dynamic Grid button.

Selecting shapes

You can use several techniques for selecting shapes in Visio. The most obvious is that you can click once on a shape to select it. To select more than one shape using this method, hold down the Shift key or the Ctrl key while clicking additional shapes. You can remove shapes from an existing selection with the same method.

A second common technique is to draw a **bounding box** around one or more shapes. You draw a bounding box by clicking anywhere on the page background and moving the mouse while holding down the mouse button. The bounding box appears as a gray rectangle.

The default behavior in Visio is to select any shapes that are fully surrounded by a bounding box. For example, in the following graphic on the left, the rectangle and octagon will be selected when you release the mouse button. In the graphic on the right, no shapes will be selected.

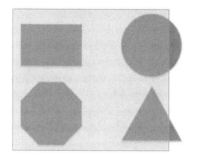 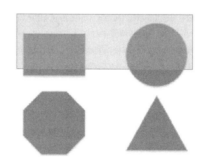

Visio offers an alternative to a bounding box that lets you select shapes with a freeform lasso. To change from **area select** (another name for the bounding box technique) to **lasso select**, on the Home tab, in the Editing group, click the Select button, and then click Lasso Select. To create a lasso selection, click the left mouse button and drag a lasso around the shapes of interest, being certain to end at the same place you began. When you release the mouse button, the enclosed shapes will be selected. The lasso in the following graphic on the left produces the selection on the right.

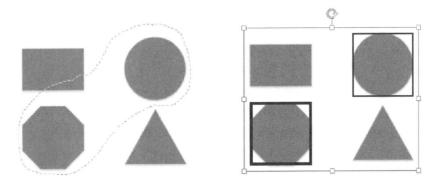

TIP To revert to using bounding boxes, on the Home tab, in the Editing group, click the Select button, and then click Area Select.

You can change selection behavior in Visio so it will select shapes that are partially enclosed by a bounding box or lasso. On the File tab, click Options, and then click Advanced; select the Select Shapes Partially Within Area check box.

Area/lasso selection and click selection are not mutually exclusive. You can select one or more shapes by clicking first, and then add additional shapes by holding down Shift or Ctrl while drawing a bounding box or lasso loop. The reverse works as well: you can start with a bounding box or lasso selection and add additional shapes by using the same keyboard and mouse combination.

KEYBOARD SHORTCUT You can select all shapes on a page by pressing the standard Windows keyboard shortcut Ctrl+A.

Copying, pasting, and duplicating shapes

Pasting copied shapes works more logically in Visio 2013 and Visio 2010 than it did in previous versions of the product. If you copy one or more shapes from Page-1 and then paste them onto Page-2, Visio will paste them into the same position on Page-2 that they occupied on Page-1. Versions prior to Visio 2010 always pasted shapes into the center of the drawing window. Occasionally this was what you wanted, but as often as not, this placement required additional dragging and nudging.

In this exercise, you will use several techniques for copying and duplicating shapes in order to learn the differences in behavior among the techniques.

 SET UP **You need the *Basic ShapesA_start* drawing located in the Chapter02 practice file folder to complete this exercise. Open the drawing in Visio and save it as *Copy & Paste*.**

1   Press **Shift+click** to select the **Octagon** and **Circle** shapes on **Page-1**, and press **Ctrl+C** to copy them.

2   To the right of the **Page-1** name tab (below the drawing page), click the **Insert Page** button.

3   Press **Ctrl+V** to paste the shapes onto **Page-2** (following graphic on the right). Notice that they are placed in the identical position on the page that they occupy on **Page-1** (following graphic on the left).

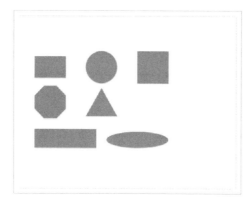   

4   Click the **Page-1** name tab to return to that page.

5   Select and copy the **Triangle** shape on the drawing page.

6   Drag the **Square** shape to the right and drop it beyond the right end of the drawing page. Visio automatically expands the page size to contain the new shape because Auto Size is on by default for this diagram type,

SEE ALSO In Chapter 3, "Adding sophistication to your drawings," you will learn more about the Auto Size function that automatically expands and contracts Visio pages.

7   Scroll the drawing page to the left so that the only visible shape is the square.

8   Press **Ctrl+V** to paste a copy of the triangle onto the drawing page. Visio pastes the shape into the center of the drawing window. If the original triangle had still been visible, Visio would have pasted the new triangle next to the existing one. But because it was not, Visio chose the center of the drawing window.

TIP The paste behavior in this step is different from what happens in Visio 2010. In that version of the software, using Ctrl+V always places the pasted shape next to the original shape (offset a small amount down and to the right), even if you scroll the original shape off the screen. Many people find this frustrating, because if your goal is to paste the copied shape in a distant location, Visio still scrolls back to the original shape.

9   On the **Home** tab, in the **Zoom** group, click **Fit to Window**.

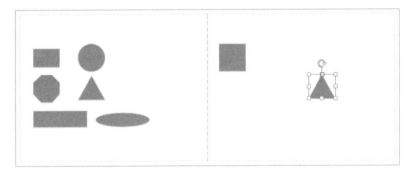

In the next two steps, you will use a technique that enables you to control exactly where pasted shapes will be placed.

10   Select and copy the **Circle** shape.

11   Right-click in the upper-right corner of the page and click **Paste**. Visio pastes the circle at the location where you right-clicked.

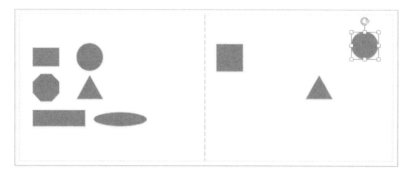

Duplicating shapes is often faster and easier than copying and pasting, especially if you want to reproduce the same shape(s) multiple times. In the final step of this exercise, you will duplicate shapes.

12   Draw a bounding box around the square and triangle shapes on the right side of the page to select them, and then press **Ctrl+D** twice to duplicate the shapes twice.

KEYBOARD SHORTCUT You can also duplicate shapes by holding down the Ctrl key while dragging the shape(s) with the mouse.

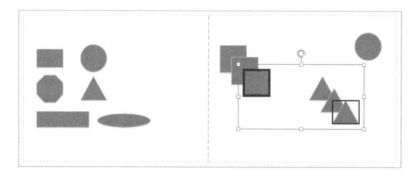

❌ CLEAN UP **Save your changes to the *Copy & Paste* drawing and close it.**

SEE ALSO Visio 2013 includes a new feature to duplicate an entire page. You will use that feature in Chapter 3.

Positioning shapes with rulers and guides

In some of the preceding exercises, you have aligned shapes by using the Dynamic Grid feature of Visio 2013. However, the Dynamic Grid doesn't always do what you need. For example, if there are other shapes between the two you are trying to align, the Dynamic Grid doesn't help. Similarly, you may want to align shapes in ways that the Dynamic Grid doesn't provide.

In this exercise, you will align shapes by using other Visio features.

➡ SET UP **Click the File tab, click New, and then double-click the Basic Diagram thumbnail. Save the drawing as** *Shape Alignment.*

1   Drag a **Rectangle** shape onto the page and position it about one fourth of the way down the page. Drop it so the left end is at the left margin of the page.

2   Use the resize handle on the right end of the rectangle shape to stretch the right edge to the right margin.

TIP As you drag a shape near the edge of the page and it becomes aligned with the page margin, a green Dynamic Grid line appears.

3   From the **Basic Shapes** stencil, drag a **5-Point Star** shape onto the page and drop it above the left half of the rectangle.

In the next step, you will try to align a second star with the one you just placed.

4   Drag a **5-Point Star** shape onto the page below the rectangle and observe that the Dynamic Grid does not help you align the two stars because of the intervening rectangle. Drop the star onto the page.

To align the two stars, you could turn on the grid lines for the page (on the View tab, in the Show group, select Grid) and use them to maneuver the shapes into place. However, using a *guide* will make the task much easier.

5   Position the cursor over the vertical ruler on the left side of the page and observe that the cursor changes to a double-headed arrow. Click the ruler and drag into the middle of the drawing page. The guide appears on the page as a vertical blue line, but be aware that guides do not appear in printed diagrams.

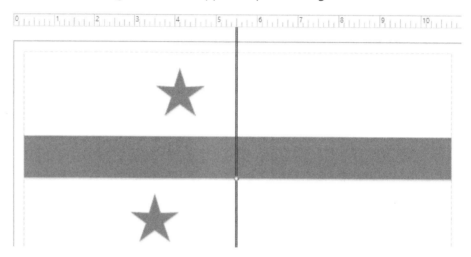

6   Drag the top star toward and over the guide and observe that you can glue the edges and center of the star shape to the guide.

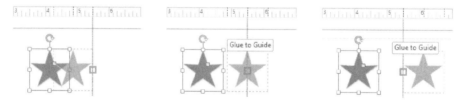

7   Glue the center of the star to the guide.

8   Drag the bottom star and glue its center to the guide.

    TIP Remember that if you hold the Shift key while dragging a shape, you restrict it to moving only horizontally or vertically, but not both.

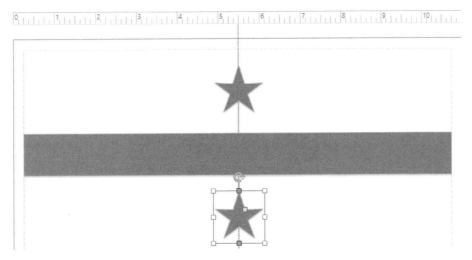

The two stars are now precisely aligned, despite the intervening shape.

Realize that the stars are actually glued to the guide just as lines were glued to shapes in previous exercises. If you move the guide, the stars will move also. However, if you don't need to move the aligned shapes as a unit, you can delete the guide as you would any other shape: just click to select it, and then press the Delete key.

TIP You can create more than one guide by dragging the ruler onto the page again. You can also create horizontal guides by dragging the ruler at the top of the page down.

The rulers provide another means for aligning shapes, as you will discover in the remaining steps.

9   Use the **Zoom** slider at the bottom of the drawing page to set the zoom level to **100%**. Then position the drawing page so the upper-left corner is visible.

10   Drag an **Octagon** shape into the upper-left corner of the page; before releasing the mouse button, observe that there are dashed lines in both the horizontal and vertical rulers (the lines are highlighted in the following graphic).

The lines on the top ruler mark the left, center, and right of the octagon; the lines on the side ruler denote the top, middle, and bottom of the shape. As you move a shape on the drawing page, there are times when it is convenient to place it based on the ruler marks.

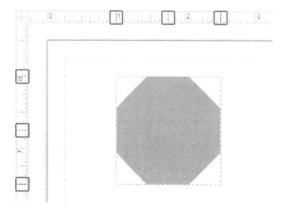

11   Drop the **Octagon** shape onto the page.

⊗ CLEAN UP **Save your changes to the *Shape Alignment* drawing, and then close it.**

Resizing and repositioning shapes

Once you've placed shapes onto the drawing page, you will probably need to move or re-size some of them. Visio provides a variety of techniques for doing so. You can alter shapes using your mouse or keyboard, or a combination of the two. You can also use the Size & Position window.

Not all properties of all shapes can be modified through the user interface, and you may not know which attributes are locked until you attempt to make a change. You may even find that seemingly identical shapes have been designed with very different capabilities and, therefore, behave differently. Sometimes the locked attributes are very simple, like the examples that you will encounter in this exercise. Other times, shape attributes are locked in more complex ways. Regardless of which attributes are locked, the shape designer's goal is typically the same: to ensure that shapes behave in particular ways for particular drawing types.

In this exercise, you will change the characteristics of several shapes by using the mouse, the keyboard, and the Size & Position window. Note that the Visio grid lines have been turned on for this diagram to make the actions in some steps more apparent.

SET UP You need the *Size and Position_start* drawing located in the Chapter02 practice files folder to complete this exercise. Open the drawing in Visio and save it as *Size and Position*.

1   Click once (don't double-click) to select shape **A**.

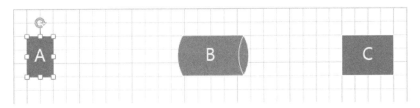

The white squares that appear on a selected shape are referred to as *selection handles*, *resize handles*, or just *handles*, and allow you to alter the shape in the following ways:

- Dragging the square handles in the center of each edge alters the width or height of the shape.

- Dragging the square handles on the corners adjusts the width and height proportionally.

You will use both types of handles in the exercise steps that follow.

2   Drag the middle handle on the right edge of shape **A** to the right to increase the width of shape **A.** When you first begin to drag to the right, notice that green, double-headed arrows appear under shapes **A** and **C**. If fact, if you look at the lower part of the page, you'll notice the same arrows under shapes **D** and **E**. Do not release the shape handle yet.

> **IMPORTANT** The green, double-headed arrows are an important new dynamic feedback feature in Visio 2013. They call attention to the fact that the width of the shape you are modifying matches the width of other shapes on the page. Although this example compares shape widths, the same feedback is provided when shape heights match.

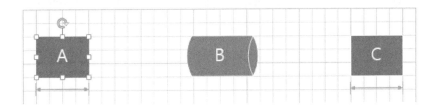

3   Continue to drag the right handle of shape **A** further to the right until the Dynamic Grid feedback informs you that shape **A** is now the same width as shape **B**.

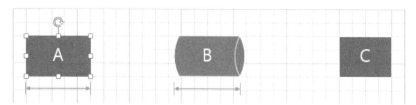

4   Continue to drag the handle until shape **A** is wider than either **B** or **C**, and then release the resize handle.

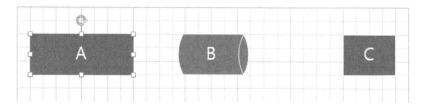

5   Drag the upper-right handle of shape **A** away from the shape to increase the size of the shape proportionally in both dimensions.

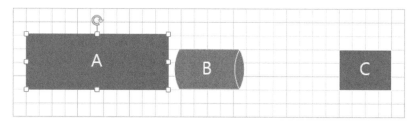

6   Click once (don't double-click) to select shape **B**, and then try to drag either of the height resize handles (top center and bottom center). You will not be able to adjust the height of the shape.

7   With shape **B** still selected, drag the upper-right resize handle toward the upper right. Notice that the shape gets wider but the height doesn't change.

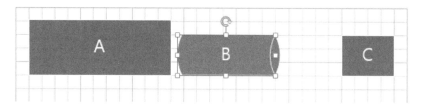

You aren't able to change the height of shape B because the designer of the shape chose to lock that shape property. You are allowed to adjust the width but not the height.

TIP Previous versions of Visio displayed locked handles with a different color than unlocked handles. Visio 2013 does not make any visual distinction.

8   With shape **B** still selected, point to the circular arrow above the shape.

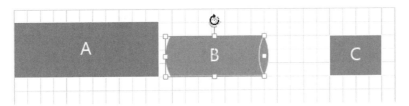

The circular arrow is the **rotation handle**. When you point to it, the cursor changes to a curved arrow and an additional selection handle appears in the center of the shape (it's on top of the letter *B* in the preceding graphic and is connected to the rotation handle by a thin, gray line). The new handle is the Center Of Rotation handle, commonly referred to in Visio as the **pin**.

TIP When you rotate a shape, it rotates around the pin. To envision the purpose of the pin, imagine that shape B is a piece of paper you've stuck on your wall with a pin. If you rotate the piece of paper, it will rotate around the pin.

9   Drag the rotation handle clockwise approximately 90 degrees.

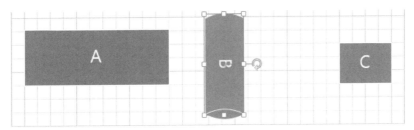

10   Click once to select shape **C** and then try to rotate it.

You are not able to rotate it because that property has been locked for this shape.

11   Select shape **C** and reposition it by dragging it up and down; it behaves quite normally. Then try dragging it side to side and you'll discover that you can't do it, because the horizontal position is locked.

> **TIP** A shape designer might lock a few simple attributes as you've observed in this exercise, or the designer might lock any of dozens of other attributes, in order to make shapes behave as required for a particular type of drawing.

12   Click once to select shape **D**, which is a subprocess shape from the **Basic Flowchart Shapes** stencil. All of the usual handles are available, as shown on the left in the following graphic, but there is a new style of control handle in the lower-left corner of the shape. Drag the yellow control handle to the right and you'll create the variation shown in the right-hand image. As you drag the control handle in either direction, notice that the shape was designed with movement limits for the lines: you can only drag them a certain distance.

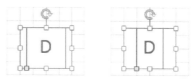

In the subprocess shape, the yellow control handle moves the interior lines. If you drag the control handle far enough back to the left, the interior lines effectively disappear. Even though they aren't visible, the continuing presence of the yellow square suggests that they still exist; if you drag the square back to the right, the lines will reappear.

TIP You will find yellow control handles on a variety of the shapes in Visio stencils. Whenever you select a shape and notice a yellow handle, it's worth experimenting with it to learn how you can use it to alter the shape's appearance. If you make a change that you don't like, simply press Ctrl+Z to undo the modification.

In the remaining steps of this exercise, you will learn to use the Size & Position window as another method for altering shape appearance and location.

13 Click once to select Shape **E**. Then on the **View** tab, in the **Show** group, click the **Task Panes** button, and then click **Size & Position** to open the **Size & Position** window. Position the new window to the left of Shape **E**.

TIP Whenever you have selected one or more shapes, you can also open the Size & Position window by clicking Width, Height, or Angle in the status bar at the bottom of the Visio window.

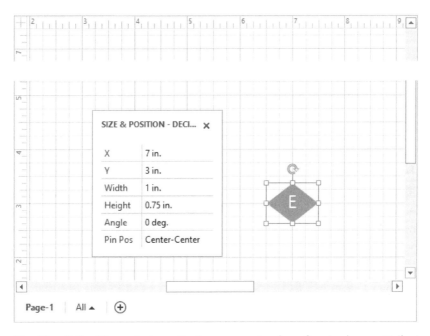

The Size & Position window displays current values for six shape attributes, but it also allows you to change those attributes.

14 Click in the **Width** cell, type **2**, and then press **Enter**. The width of the cell changes to reflect the new value. Notice that you didn't need to type a value for units, because Visio uses the units displayed in the cell as the default. By comparing the width of shape **E** with the ruler shown at the top of the following graphic, you can confirm that the shape is, indeed, 2 inches wide.

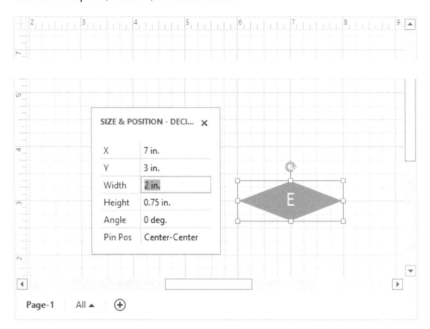

The X and Y cells in the Size & Position window reflect the location of the pin of the shape on the page with respect to the lower-left corner of the page. By comparing the values in the X and Y cells in the preceding graphic with the rulers at the edge of the drawing page, you can verify that the center of shape E is at X=7 inches and Y=3 inches.

15   Click in the **Y** cell, type **4**, and then press **Enter**. By changing the Y value from 3 inches to 4 inches, you have moved the shape higher on the page. You can confirm the new position of the shape on the page by looking at the ruler shown on the left side of the following graphic.

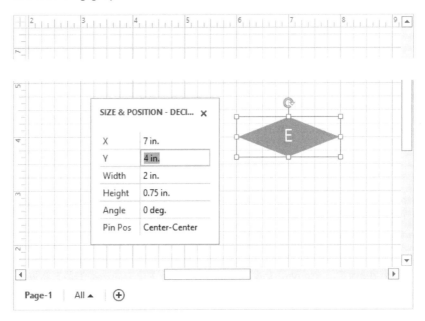

16   Click in the **Pin Pos** cell, click **Center-Left**, and then press **Enter**. Changing this setting moves the pin for the selected shape. The following graphic shows the result of changing the pin to Center-Left. Notice two things:

- The rotation handle is now on the left edge of the shape.

- The shape has shifted to the right on the page. This is because the X and Y coordinates of the shape specify the location of the pin. Because you have moved the pin within the shape, the location of the shape on the page changes.

TIP Using the Pin Pos menu, you can relocate the pin based on a fixed set of pin positions. You can also make freeform changes to the pin location by dragging the Center Of Rotation handle described in step 8.

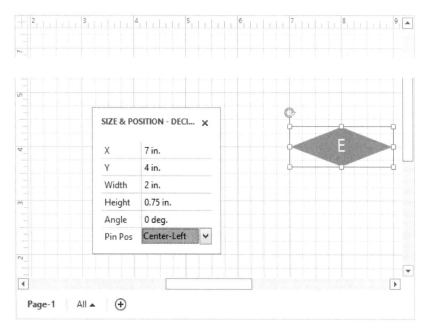

17   Click in the **Angle** cell, type **-90**, and then press **Enter**. Typing -90 degrees is equivalent to dragging the rotation handle clockwise 90 degrees. The following graphic shows that shape **E** rotated around the new pin.

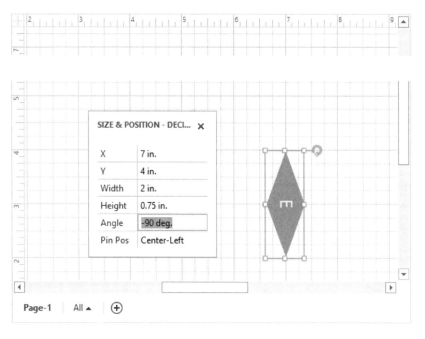

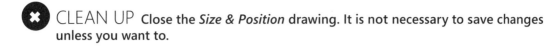 CLEAN UP **Close the *Size & Position* drawing. It is not necessary to save changes unless you want to.**

TIP If you select more than one shape before dragging a resize handle or making changes in the Size & Position window, the changes you make will affect all selected shapes.

In this exercise, you typed numbers into Size & Position window fields to change the physical characteristics of a shape. However, you can also use the Size & Position window in the opposite way—you can move or alter a shape by dragging the control handles and then use the window to observe the new dimensions or position values.

2

Connecting shapes with lines

Visio shapes are either one-dimensional (1-D) or two-dimensional (2-D). ***1-D*** shapes act like lines with endpoints that can be attached to other shapes. ***2-D*** shapes behave like polygons with edges and an interior. However, appearances can be deceiving, because some shapes that appear to be two-dimensional may actually be 1-D shapes in Visio; there's an example in the section titled, "Adding equipment to rack diagrams" in Chapter 9. The reverse can also be true.

In previous exercises, you worked primarily with 2-D shapes. In this exercise, you will connect a variety of 1-D shapes to 2-D shapes.

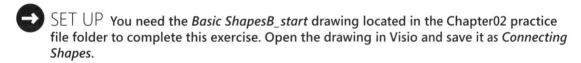 SET UP **You need the *Basic ShapesB_start* drawing located in the Chapter02 practice file folder to complete this exercise. Open the drawing in Visio and save it as *Connecting Shapes*.**

1   On the **Home** tab, in the **Tools** group, click the **Line Tool**. Notice that the cursor changes to a plus sign with a diagonal line to the lower right.

> **IMPORTANT** The Line Tool is one of six tools located behind a button that is immediately to the right of the Pointer Tool. If the Line Tool is not visible, click the arrow next to whichever tool is displayed on the button, and then select the desired tool from the menu.

2   Point near any of the five shapes toward the top of the page. Notice that dark squares appear on the edges and in the center of the shapes.

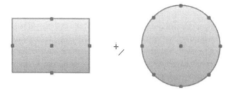

The dark squares are **connection points**. They appear whenever you move near them with a 1-D shape or a tool like the Line Tool.

3   Move the cursor near a connection point and notice that a green square appears. The square indicates that you can click on it to glue one end of the line to the connection point. If you hold the pointer over the square without clicking, tooltip text will appear to confirm that you can glue to the connection point.

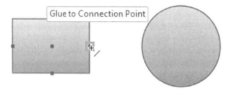

4   Click the connection point on the right end of the rectangle, drag to the connection point on the left edge of the circle, and then release the mouse button.

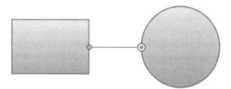

You have drawn a line that is glued to the edges of the two shapes. Notice that the handle on the originating end of the glued line shows a green circle and the handle on the destination end shows a white circle with a green dot.

5   Draw another line above the rectangle but do not glue either end to a shape.

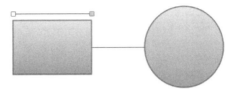

The line shows a white square on the originating end and a solid gray square on the destination end.

TIP The color distinction between the unglued line ends in this step and the glued line ends in the previous step is an important one in Visio. Although it's quite obvious in these two examples whether the line ends are connected, in the next step, you'll find an example in which the color of the line end is very helpful in determining connectedness.

6   Use the **Line Tool** to draw a line from the connection point at the center of the octagon to the long rectangle below it. The long rectangle that you created with the drawing tool in a previous exercise does not contain any connection points. Consequently, you can only drop the end of the line onto the shape and can't glue it. You can confirm which ends are glued by comparing the color and pattern at each end of this line with the handles in the previous two examples.

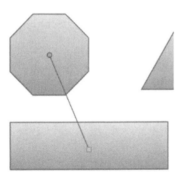

7   On the **Home** tab, in the **Tools** group, click the **Pointer Tool**.

KEYBOARD SHORTCUT Press Ctrl+1 (the number one) to return to the Pointer Tool.

8   Drag the circle up a small distance, and then drag the long rectangle below the octagon down. The following two graphics show the before (left) and after (right).

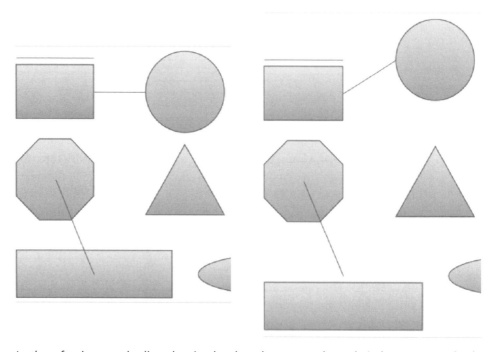

In the *after* image, the line that is glued to the rectangle and circle stays attached at the connection points. However, the line that touched, but wasn't glued to, the rectangle is no longer attached to that shape.

9   On the **Home** tab, in the **Tools** group, click the **Freeform Tool**. Notice that the cursor changes to a plus sign with a squiggly line to the lower right.

10   Click the connection point in the center of the circle and move the cursor randomly, eventually arriving at one of the connection points on the square. Notice that the line develops a bend each time you make a significant change in direction.

There are several important things to note about the line you've drawn:

- If you glued both ends of the line to connection points, the curved line behaves just like the straight line: if you move the shapes, the line will follow. In the case of the freeform line, the line will also retain its unique set of curves. (Try moving the shapes attached to your squiggly line; the results are often quite interesting.)

- There are blue circles at the key points of curvature along the line. These circles are actually handles that you can drag to reshape the line.

- The blue circles are only visible if you select the shape with one of the line tools (Line, Freeform, Arc, or Pencil). If you select it with the Pointer Tool or the Rectangle or Ellipse Tools, only the endpoints are visible, as shown in the following graphic.

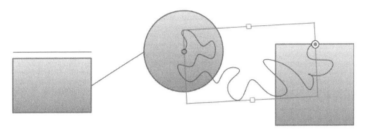

11   In a blank area of the drawing page, draw a freeform line, but be sure to end it at exactly the same point that you started.

Notice the important difference from the line you drew in the previous step: as soon as you finish "closing the loop," Visio applies a fill to your new shape and there are no square handles at the beginning and end of the line. By ending your line at the same place you began, you've actually drawn a 2-D shape, not a 1-D shape.

❌ CLEAN UP **Save your changes to the *Connecting Shapes* drawing but leave it open if you are continuing with the next exercise.**

Though you didn't use them in this exercise, you can experiment with the Arc and Pencil tools to learn about their unique characteristics.

In a previous exercise, you used the Size & Position window with a 2-D shape. If you open the Size & Position window for a 1-D shape, it contains fields that are appropriate to a line. In the following graphic, the coordinates of the beginning and ending points of the line, its length, its angle, and its height are visible. Note that the length is the absolute difference between the beginning and end of the line, and not the linear distance the line traverses.

SIZE & POSITION - D...	Begin X	5.125 in.
	Begin Y	5.375 in.
	End X	6.125 in.
	End Y	7 in.
	Length	1.908 in.
	Angle	58.3925 deg.
	Height	1.625 in.

Connecting shapes with dynamic connectors

In the previous exercise, you learned about four types of 1-D shapes that you can create with the Visio line tools. Although several of those line types can include curves or bends, those features are only present if you place them there. Visio also offers a line called a *dynamic connector*. When you use a dynamic connector, Visio automatically adds and removes bends in the line based on the relative positions of the shapes to which it's glued.

In this exercise, you will perform some of the same steps you completed in the previous exercise, but you'll use dynamic connectors in order to understand the differences in behavior.

 SET UP **You need the *Connecting Shapes* drawing for this exercise. Either continue with the open copy from the previous exercise or open the *Basic ShapesC_start* drawing located in the Chapter02 practice file folder, and then save it as *Connecting Shapes*. Click the Page-2 tab at the bottom of the drawing page to move to Page-2.**

1 On the **Home** tab, in the **Tools** group, click the **Connector** button. Notice that the pointer changes to a black arrow and there is an arrow with two right-angle bends below it.

TIP Just as with the line tools you used in the preceding exercise, you'll find that connection points appear on various shapes as you point near them with the Connector Tool.

2 Drag from the connection point on the right center of the upper rectangle to the connection point on the left edge of the circle, and then release the mouse button, creating **static glue** between the two connection points.

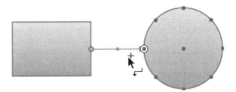

Just as in the preceding exercise, the line you've drawn shows green handles at its endpoints. However, unlike the previous line, a dynamic connector has an arrowhead on its destination end by default. The arrowhead in this graphic is largely obscured by the green handle, but when the dynamic connector is deselected, as in the following graphic, the arrowhead is visible.

3 Draw another dynamic connector above the rectangle but do not glue either end to a shape. Even if you try to draw the connector as a straight line, notice that it appears to have a mind of its own. This will turn out to be one of the most useful characteristics of a dynamic connector, as shown in subsequent steps in this exercise.

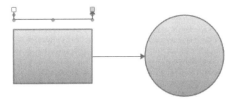

4 Use the Connector Tool to draw a line from the connection point at the center of the octagon to the center of the long rectangle below it.

Something very different happens compared to the preceding exercise where you performed the same step with the line tool. Even though the long rectangle does not contain any connection points, you can still glue a dynamic connector to the shape. Visio provides two visual cues: pop-up text appears above the rectangle, as shown in the following graphic on the left, and the border of the shape is outlined in green. When you release the mouse button, the connector appears as shown in the graphic on the right.

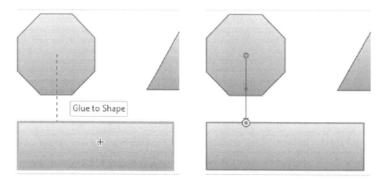

You've just used something Visio calls **dynamic glue** to attach a connector to a shape without any connection points. As you will discover in the next step, you can do the same thing even if a shape has connection points, merely by pointing to a part of the shape where there aren't any.

5   Point to the interior of the octagon until the border of the selection rectangle lights up in red (the following graphic on the left shows the pointer inside the selection rectangle). Drag until the border of the triangle shape turns red and the words *Glue to Shape* appear, as shown on the right. Don't release the mouse button yet.

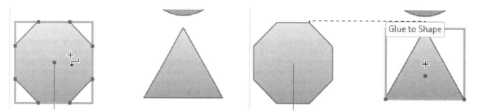

In the graphic on the right, even though the cursor (the plus sign) is above the center of the triangle, the dynamic connector once again seems to have a mind of its own and is connecting to the apex of the triangle.

6   Release the mouse button and observe that the dynamic connector has glued itself to points on the edges of the two shapes.

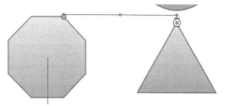

With a few final steps, you will discover the real value of a dynamic connector and learn the difference between static glue and dynamic glue.

7   On the **Home** tab, in the **Tools** group, click the **Pointer Tool**.

     KEYBOARD SHORTCUT Press Ctrl+1 (the number one) to return to the Pointer Tool.

8   Drag the circle up a small distance, drag the long rectangle below the octagon down
     and to the right until it overlaps the ellipse, and then drag the triangle down until it
     also overlaps the ellipse.

     The following graphics show the before (left) and after (right).

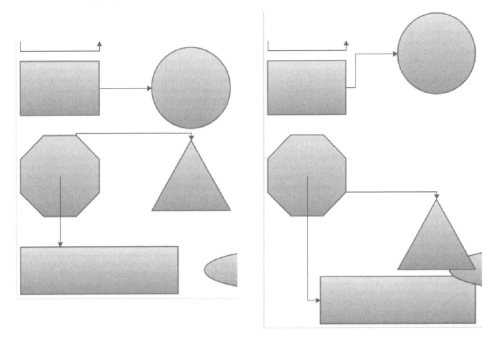

Key observations after moving the three shapes:

- The connector between the upper rectangle and the circle has right-angle bends
  but is still attached at exactly the same two connection points. This is an example
  of static glue: the connector remains attached to a fixed point on both shapes.

- The connector between the octagon and the long rectangle now contains a right-
  angle bend. The tail of the arrow remains glued to the center connection point,
  another example of static glue, but there is also evidence of dynamic glue: the
  head of the arrow is still attached to the long rectangle, but it is connected at a
  different place along the edge of the shape.

- The connector between the octagon and the triangle is glued dynamically at both
  ends. After moving the triangle down, the connector is still glued to both shapes,
  but the points of attachment have changed.

CLEAN UP Save your changes to the *Basic shapes* drawing, and then close it.

By default, dynamic connectors use right-angle bends as you learned in the preceding exercise. You can change the appearance of a dynamic connector by right-clicking it and selecting one of the upper three options shown in the following graphic.

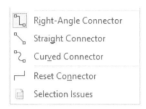

As you move shapes that are linked by dynamic connectors, Visio adjusts the connector segments. In addition, you can manually adjust individual connector segments by dragging the blue control handles that appear at each bend and in the middle of each line segment when you select a connector.

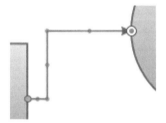

If at any point, a dynamic connector has too many bends or becomes convoluted, you can right-click it and then click Reset Connector. Visio redraws the connector with the minimum number of bends and segments to fit in the required space.

TIP Among the new features on the Visio 2013 *Mini Toolbar* is a single-use *Connector Tool* that is sometimes more convenient than the Connector Tool button in the Tools group on the Home tab. You can add a dynamic connector to your drawing simply by right-clicking either a shape or the drawing page, and then clicking the Connector Tool button shown in the following graphic.

Because you used the Connector Tool in successive steps in the preceding exercise, it made more sense to activate the Connector Tool on the Home tab and then select the Pointer Tool at the end. However, when you are creating your own diagrams and need to draw a single dynamic connector, remember that the Connector Tool is only a right-click away from wherever you are working on the page.

Identifying 1-D shapes and types of glue

In the preceding sections, you learned about several types of 1-D shapes and two forms of glue. This section summarizes the behavior of 1-D shapes and identifies the visual cues Visio uses to differentiate glued and unglued endpoints of 1-D shapes.

- A 1-D shape drawn with any of the line tools (Line, Freeform, Arc, or Pencil) retains its original form when the shapes at the ends are moved.

- A 1-D shape created with the Connector Tool adds or removes bends in the line to accommodate shape movements.

- A line or dynamic connector attached to a connection point forms static glue; the 1-D shape remains attached at that fixed point on the 2-D shape no matter how the 2-D shape is moved.

- A dynamic connector attached to a shape but not to a connection point forms dynamic glue; as the 2-D shape moves, the point at which the dynamic connector attaches to the shape moves.

- A 1-D shape whose endpoints are not glued appears with square control handles that are white on the "from" end and are gray on the "to" end.

- A 1-D shape whose endpoints are glued appears with round control handles; the "from" end is a green circle and the "to" end shows a green dot inside a white circle.

> **IMPORTANT** In previous versions of Visio, the endpoints of 1-D shapes that were attached with static glue looked different than endpoints that were attached with dynamic glue. Visio 2013 no longer provides a visual distinction between the two.

Using AutoConnect and Quick Shapes

AutoConnect was introduced in Visio 2007 and provides a fast means to link shapes using dynamic connectors. *Quick Shapes* were introduced in Visio 2010 and build on AutoConnect to let you create drawings even more quickly.

In this exercise, you will create a new drawing using AutoConnect by itself in the first section, and AutoConnect with Quick Shapes in the second section.

➡ SET UP **Click the File tab, and then click New. Click Categories, click Flowchart, and then double-click the Basic Flowchart thumbnail. Save the new drawing as** *Quick Draw*.

1   Drag a **Start/End** shape into the upper-left corner of the drawing page.

2   Drag **Process** and **Decision** shapes onto the page to create a drawing like the one shown in the following graphic. Be sure you take advantage of the Dynamic Grid you learned about in Chapter 1 to make it easy to align and space the shapes.

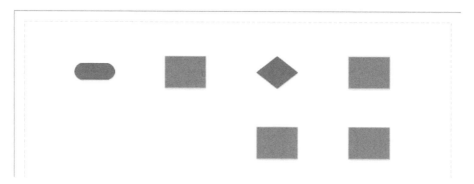

Notice that when you point to any shape on the page, blue AutoConnect arrows appear on the sides that are not yet connected to another shape.

TIP AutoConnect arrows are smarter in Visio 2013 than they were in previous versions of Visio. When you are working on a diagram, if you've used AutoConnect recently, the arrows appear much more quickly when you rest the pointer over a shape. However, if you haven't used them recently, there is a delay before they appear so they don't get in your way.

TROUBLESHOOTING If the AutoConnect arrows don't appear when you point to a shape, it's probably because AutoConnect is turned off for this drawing. To activate AutoConnect, select the AutoConnect check box in the Visual Aids group on the View tab.

3   Point to the **AutoConnect** arrow on the right side of the **start/end** shape. The Live Preview feature of Visio shows a dynamic connector linking the **start/end** to the process shape. A Mini Toolbar containing four shapes also appears; you will learn more about this toolbar later in this exercise.

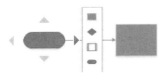

4   Click the **AutoConnect** arrow to connect the shapes.

5   Continue clicking the appropriate **AutoConnect** arrows until the diagram looks like the following graphic.

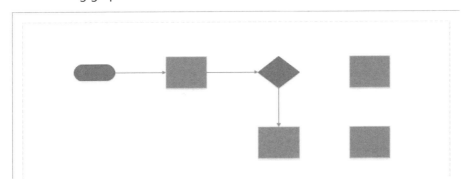

It's clear that AutoConnect makes short work of adding dynamic connectors to existing shapes. Each AutoConnect arrow seeks out a neighboring shape in the direction that the arrow points. You can also use AutoConnect when the desired target shape is not directly in line with the AutoConnect arrow, as you'll discover in the next step.

6   Point to the **Decision** shape until the **AutoConnect** arrows appear, click the **AutoConnect** arrow on the right of the decision shape, and then drag it to the lower of the two rectangles on the right side of the page. As you drag, the screen will look like the following graphic on the left. When you release the mouse button, the shapes are connected, as shown on the right.

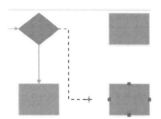 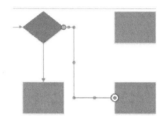

Now that you've used AutoConnect, you will work with a closely related feature to learn another way to create certain types of drawings quickly.

Before moving to the next step, look back at the picture in step 3. In addition to the Live Preview image of a dynamic connector arrow, there are also four small shapes on a Mini Toolbar. These shapes are called Quick Shapes and you will use them to create a drawing that is similar to the one you just built.

7   To the right of the **Page-1** name tab below the drawing page, click the **Insert Page** button. Visio adds a new page called **Page-2**.

8   Drag a **Start/End** shape into the upper-left corner of **Page-2**.

9   Point to the **AutoConnect** arrow on the right side of the **start/end** shape. Live Preview shows two things in addition to the dynamic connector arrow: it displays a preview of the shape that is currently selected in the stencil, along with a Mini Toolbar containing four shapes.

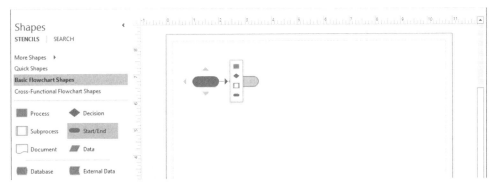

If you want to add another start/end shape to the current drawing, a single click will accomplish that and the new shape will be automatically spaced at the default interval for this page.

However, if you want to add a different shape, Quick Shapes provide an instant solution. Every open stencil in Visio 2013 includes a Quick Shapes section at the top of the stencil window pane, and most stencils include preselected Quick Shapes. If you look closely at the Basic Flowchart Shapes in the Shapes window, you'll notice a fine gray line between the Document/Data shapes and the Database/External Data shapes.

The shapes that appear in the Mini Toolbar are the first four shapes in the Quick Shapes section. If you want different shapes to appear in the Quick Shapes Mini Toolbar, simply drag them to be among the first four shapes in the Quick Shapes section of the stencil.

TIP You can change the order of appearance of shapes in either the Quick Shapes section or the main part of a stencil merely by dragging them to a new location.

10　Point to any of the shapes in the Quick Shapes Mini Toolbar and notice that the Live Preview image changes to reflect that shape.

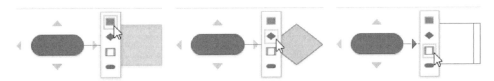

11　Click the **Process** shape in the Mini Toolbar to drop it on the page

12　Point to the process shape and use AutoConnect and the Quick Shapes Mini Toolbar to add a decision shape to its right.

13   Point to the decision shape on the page and drop a process shape below it.

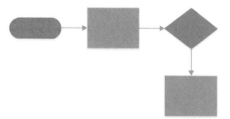

When you click a Quick Shape in the Mini Toolbar, Visio always adds a dynamic connector. Consequently, in order to place two unconnected shapes and finish reproducing the pattern you created on Page-1, it is necessary to place the final two shapes manually.

14   Drag a **Process** shape from the stencil and drop it to the right of the decision shape already on the page. Then drop another **Process** shape below it. Be sure to use the Dynamic Grid to ensure that spacing of the new shapes is consistent with the existing shapes.

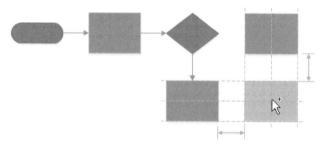

15   Right-click anywhere on the drawing page. On the Mini Toolbar, click the **Connector Tool**, and then use it to link the right end of the decision shape to the left end of the lower-right process shape.

TIP You can also point to the Decision shape and drag a connector from the AutoConnect arrow to the Process shape as you did in step 6.

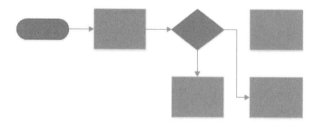

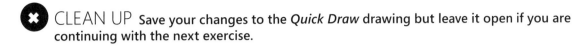 CLEAN UP **Save your changes to the *Quick Draw* drawing but leave it open if you are continuing with the next exercise.**

SEE ALSO The "Visio Blog," written by the Visio product team at Microsoft, contains two posts that were written for Visio 2010 but still apply to Visio 2013 and the exercise in this section:

- *blogs.office.com/b/visio/archive/2009/09/22/autoconnect-in-visio-2010.aspx*

- *blogs.office.com/b/visio/archive/2010/12/08/flowcharts-in-under-a-minute.aspx*

TIP You can turn AutoConnect off for all drawings if you prefer to operate without it. On the File tab, click Options, and then click Advanced. In the Editing Options section, clear the Enable AutoConnect check box.

Using AutoAdd and AutoDelete

Visio 2013 offers enhanced ways to add and delete shapes in a drawing:

- When you add a shape using AutoAdd, Visio rearranges the existing drawing to make the new shape fit. Sometimes the changes it makes are minor; other times they are more significant.

- When you delete a shape that is linked to one other shape with a dynamic connector, AutoDelete automatically removes the now superfluous connector. In addition, if you delete a shape that is between two other shapes, Visio will delete one dynamic connector and reconnect the remaining one to both shapes.

TIP If you don't like the results of an AutoAdd or AutoDelete operation, a single undo command will reset all changes made by the shape addition or deletion.

In this exercise, you will alter a drawing by using AutoAdd and AutoDelete techniques.

SET UP You need the *Quick Draw* drawing for this exercise. Either continue with the open copy from the previous exercise or open the *Quick Draw_start* drawing located in the Chapter02 practice file folder, and then save it as *Quick Draw*.

1　Navigate to **Page-2** if you're not already there.

2　Drag a **Subprocess** shape from the stencil and position it on top of any existing dynamic connector. Both ends of the connector display large green squares that are visible through the semitransparent **Subprocess** shape. Don't release the mouse button yet.

3　Drop the **Subprocess** shape on the connector below the **Decision** shape. Visio pushes the **Process** shape down to make room for the new shape.

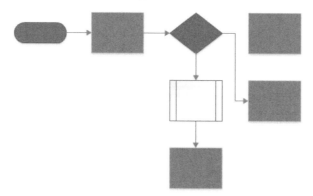

4 Drag a **Subprocess** shape from the stencil and drop it on the connector between the **start/end** shape and the first process box. Visio makes more significant changes in order to accommodate the new shape and avoid the unconnected **Process** shape in the upper right.

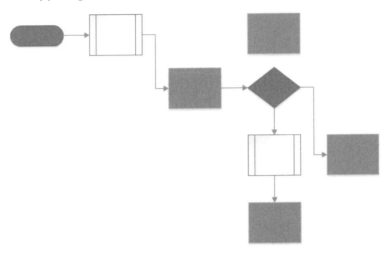

5 Select the **Process** shape at the very bottom of the diagram, and then press the **Delete** key to remove the shape. Visio deletes the selected shape and also removes the dynamic connector that was linked to the **Process** shape.

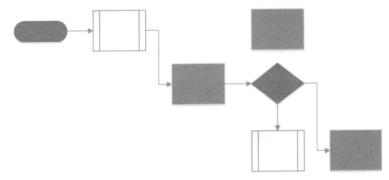

6   Select the **Subprocess** shape between the **Start/End** shape and the first **Process** shape, and then press the **Delete** key. In addition to deleting the **Subprocess** shape, Visio removes one of the two dynamic connectors and reconnects the remaining one between the **Start/End** and the **Process** shapes.

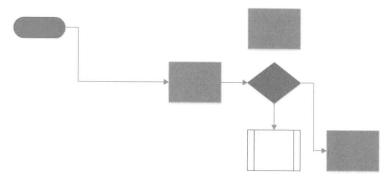

✖ CLEAN UP **Save your changes to the *Quick Draw* drawing, and then close it.**

TIP If you prefer not to have Visio automatically delete connectors when you delete shapes, you can turn this feature off. On the File tab, click Options, and then click Advanced. In the Editing options section, clear the Delete Connectors When Deleting Shapes check box.

The power of undo

As you work on a diagram and make both small-scale and large-scale changes, one of your most powerful allies is the Undo feature in Visio. You can undo nearly any action in Visio. The program defaults to providing 20 undo levels, which means you can undo the most recent 20 actions in your diagram. You shouldn't hesitate to try anything with Visio, because you will be able to undo it if you don't like the result.

If you prefer a larger or smaller number of undo levels, on the File tab, click Options, and then click Advanced, where you will find a setting for Maximum Number Of Undos (the maximum is 99).

Replacing shapes

The exercises up to this point in the chapter have shown you how to add shapes to a page, and then to position, align, resize, and connect them.

In the first part of this exercise, you will create a diagram from a template you haven't used yet. In the second part, you will use an important new Visio feature that enables you to replace any shape with an entirely different shape, and yet retain all of the original shape's key characteristics.

 SET UP **Click the File tab, and then click New. Click Categories, click Maps and Floor Plans, and then double-click the Directional Map (not Directional Map 3D) thumbnail. Save the new drawing as *Change Shapes*.**

1   From the **Road Shapes** stencil, drag a **4-way** shape and use the Dynamic Grid to drop it in the center of the drawing page. Leave the shape selected.

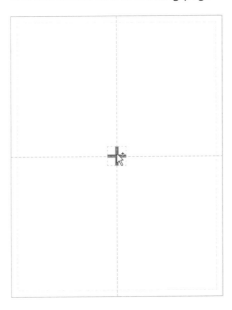

TIP When you drag the first 2-D shape onto an empty drawing page, the Dynamic Grid provides both horizontal and vertical center lines, as shown in the preceding graphic. The center line feedback is not provided if the first shape is a 1-D shape, or if the page contains any other shapes.

2   With the **4-way** shape still selected, on the **Home** tab, in the **Shape Styles** group, click **Line**, and then in the **Standard Colors** section of the color menu, click **Red**. The purpose of the red color is simply to make this shape more visible during the remainder of this exercise.

3   Drag a **Road square** shape onto the page and glue one end to the right end of the **4-way** shape. Then drag and glue a second **Road square** to the left end of the **4-way** shape.

   You'll notice that the road square shapes behave like the dynamic connectors and lines you've used in previous exercises in this chapter: the ends turn green when you attach them to the 4-way shape, indicating that they have been glued.

4   Drag two additional **Road square** shapes onto the page and glue them to the top and bottom of the **4-way** shape.

5   Click the unglued end of the **Road square** shape attached to the top of the **4-way** shape and drag it up and to the right until it is aligned vertically, and then do the same thing with the **Road square** shape attached to the bottom, but drag it down and to the right.

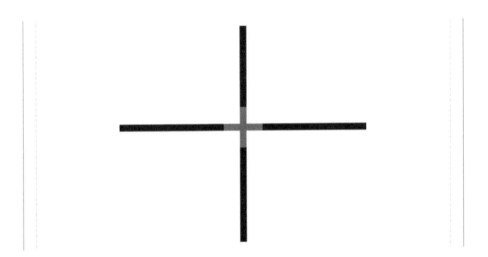

6   In the **Shapes** window, click the **Landmark Shapes** stencil header, and then drag a **Barn** shape into the upper-left quadrant of your roadmap.

7   Drag a **Gas station** shape into the lower-right quadrant of your map.

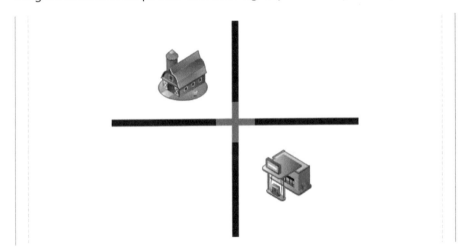

You've now created the basic diagram on which you'll use the Change Shapes feature.

8   Click the **Barn** shape on the drawing page once to select it.

9   On the **Home** tab, in the **Editing** group, click **Change Shape**, and then in the **Change Shape** menu, point to the **Building 1** icon. Notice that Live Preview has replaced the **Barn** shape on the drawing page with the **Building 1** shape.

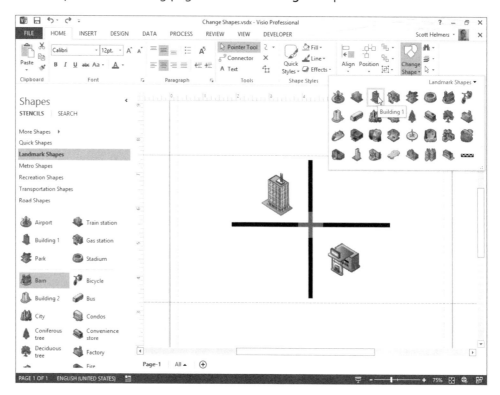

TIP You can also access the Change Shapes button on the right-click Mini Toolbar as shown in the following graphic.

10   Click the **Building 1** icon. Visio has replaced the shape on the page with the one you selected.

11   Right-click the **4-way** shape on the drawing page to select it, and then on the Mini Toolbar click **Change Shape**.

12   In the **Change Shape** menu, click the arrow to the right of **Landmark Shapes** to reveal a list of the other open stencils.

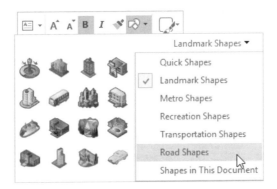

13   Click **Road Shapes.** The **Change Shapes** menu displays icons for the **Road Shapes**.

14 Click **Cloverleaf interchange** as shown in the preceding graphic. Visio replaces the simple four-way intersection with a cloverleaf shape. Notice that the newly inserted shape includes the altered color you applied to the **4-way** shape. In addition, the **Road square** shapes that were glued to the **4-way** shape are now glued to the **Cloverleaf interchange**.

> **IMPORTANT** In general, the shape on the drawing page after a change shape operation retains the formatting, text, and shape data of the original shape. (You will learn about shape data in Chapter 3.

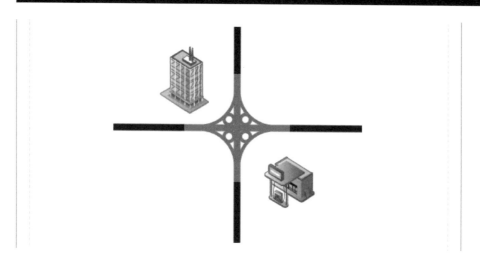

✖ CLEAN UP **Save your changes to the *Change Shapes* drawing, and then close it.**

The ability to replace one shape with another is a long-requested feature in Visio that is finally available in Visio 2013. In this exercise, you replaced one shape at a time, but if you select more than one shape, you can replace all of them at once.

Key points

- The Visio 2013 Dynamic Grid facilitates aligning new and existing shapes on the drawing page and eliminates much of the need to drag and nudge shapes into alignment after you've placed them on the page. You can also use the rulers on the edges of the drawing page, or drag guides onto the page, to assist with shape positioning.

- Visio provides multiple shape selection techniques. Mouse-only techniques allow rectangular selection by bounding box or freeform selection using a lasso. Other techniques use a combination of keystrokes and mouse movements.

- The Visio 2013 paste function is smarter than in previous versions of the product. When you copy shapes from one page to another, the shapes are now pasted into the exact position they occupied on the source page. You can also select a specific paste location or use Paste Special by right-clicking.

- You can connect shapes by using either lines or dynamic connectors. Lines retain their shape characteristics when adjacent shapes are moved. Connectors, on the other hand, dynamically adjust their appearance by adding or removing elbow bends in order to accommodate new shape positions.

- Lines and connectors can be glued either to a specific connection point on a shape or to the shape as a whole. The former is known as static glue; the latter is referred to as dynamic glue. When you reposition shapes that use dynamic glue, the attachment point of a line or connector can change.

- Visio shapes are one of two types: 1-D shapes, which behave like lines; and 2-D shapes, which behave like filled polygons.

- The Visio 2013 AutoConnect and Quick Shapes features can significantly reduce the time it takes to create a drawing consisting of connected shapes.

- With the Visio 2013 AutoAdd function, you can split dynamic connectors merely by dropping a new shape onto them. The reverse is also true: if you delete a shape that is linked by dynamic connectors, AutoDelete removes unneeded connectors.

- Visio 2013 introduces the ability to substitute one shape for another in a diagram. The new shape retains most of the data, formatting, connections, and text of the original shape.

2

Chapter at a glance

Create

Create and format text boxes,
page 105

Comment

Comment on diagrams,
page 117

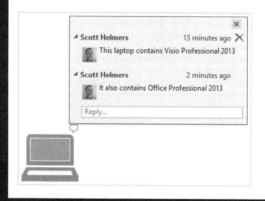

Understand

Understand and use layers,
page 134

Work

Work with background pages and borders,
page 148

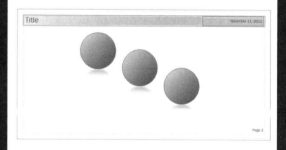

IN THIS CHAPTER, YOU WILL LEARN HOW TO

- Create and format text boxes.

- Orient and group shapes.

- Add, orient, and position shape text.

- Add ScreenTips and comments.

- Use shape data and insert fields.

- Work with pictures, layers, borders, and background pages.

- Manage pages and page setup.

At this point in your Microsoft Visio 2013 journey, you know how to perform many basic tasks: create drawings from templates, add shapes from stencils, create your own shapes, and connect shapes by using lines and dynamic connectors.

In this chapter, you'll move beyond the basics and explore ways to add sophistication to your drawings. In addition to managing pages and page layouts, you will add text to shapes and manipulate shapes and text in new ways. You will also add fields, ScreenTips, and comments to shapes; insert pictures and other objects; learn about layers; and take the first steps in creating data-driven diagrams. (There's more on that last subject in Chapter 6, "Entering, linking to, and reporting on data," and Chapter 10, "Visualizing your data.")

PRACTICE FILES To complete the exercises in this chapter, you need the practice files contained in the Chapter03 practice file folder. For more information, see "Downloading the practice files" in this book's Introduction.

Adding text to shapes

In some Visio diagrams, the shapes are self-explanatory. In many drawings, however, you need to label the shapes.

In this exercise, you'll add text to existing shapes, and you'll change the font size to make the text more readable.

 SET UP **You need the** *Text ExercisesA_start* **drawing located in the Chapter03 practice file folder to complete this exercise. Open the drawing in Visio and save it as** *Text Exercises***. Then follow the steps.**

1   On the left side of the page, click once (don't double-click) on the start/end shape, type **Start**, and then click anywhere on the page background to finish text editing. Notice that Visio zooms the selected shape to the center of the screen when you start typing and returns it to its original shape and location when you finish.

2   Press **Ctrl+A** to select all shapes. Then on the **Home** tab, in the **Font** group, in the **Font Size** list, click **14 pt.** The text in your start/end shape is more legible.

3   Double-click the process shape to the right of the start shape, type **Prepare expense report**, and then click anywhere on the background of the page. When you click outside of the shape, notice that the dimensions of the shape change— it grows taller. The process box is an example of a shape that expands automatically when the amount of text exceeds its size.

4   Click once (don't double-click) on the decision shape, press **F2**, type **Amount > $1000**, and then press **F2** again.

   KEYBOARD SHORTCUT   Press F2 to enter and exit text edit mode.

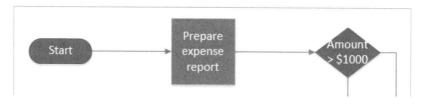

 CLEAN UP **Save your changes to the** *Text Exercises* **drawing but leave it open if you are continuing to the next exercise.**

TIP You added text to shapes in steps 1, 3, and 4 in this exercise. You may have noticed that you were instructed to use a different method each time. For most Visio shapes, the three methods of entering text edit mode—single-click and start typing; double-click; select the shape and press F2—are interchangeable. You will find exceptions to this rule, but most shapes behave as described in this exercise.

Creating and formatting text boxes

3

Although a picture can be worth a thousand words, sometimes you still need a few words.

In this exercise, you'll use the Text Tool on the Home tab to create and format a text box to use as a page title.

 SET UP **You need the *Text Exercises* drawing for this exercise. Either continue with the open copy from the previous exercise or open the *Text ExercisesB_start* drawing located in the Chapter03 practice file folder and save it as *Text Exercises*. Then follow the steps.**

1　On the **Home** tab, in the **Tools** group, click the **Text** button. The cursor changes to a plus sign with a page icon below it.

　　TIP As an alternative, the Visio 2013 Mini Toolbar introduces a single use Text Tool: the pointer reverts to the Pointer Tool as soon as you draw one text box. To open the Mini Toolbar, right-click anywhere on the drawing page.

2　Click in the upper-left corner of the drawing page and drag to create a text box that is approximately 6 inches (150 mm) long. Visio automatically zooms in so you can type in the text box.

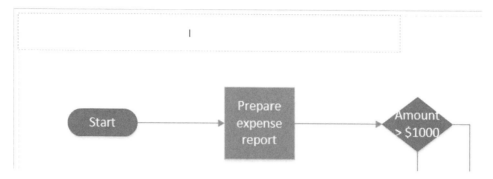

3   Type **Sample Flowchart for Expense Report Processing**.

4   On the **Home** tab, in the **Tools** group, click the **Pointer Tool** button. Visio closes the text box, returns to the previous zoom level, and leaves the text box selected.

TIP If you want to continue working with the Text Tool to create another text box, you can close the current text box by pressing the Esc key or by clicking the drawing page.

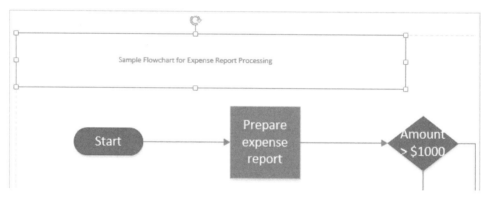

The text in the page title box is a bit small!

5   On the **Home** tab, in the **Font** group, click the **Font Size** arrow. As you point to various font sizes, notice that Visio provides a live preview of the results on the drawing page.

TIP You can also change font sizes by clicking the Grow Font and Shrink Font buttons located immediately to the right of the Font Size drop-down list box.

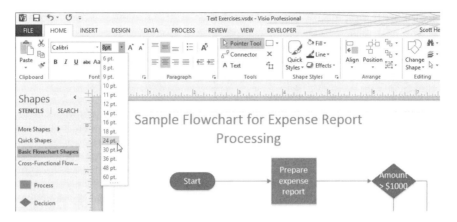

6   Select **24 pt.** as the new font size.

7   Because the text wraps inside the text box at this font size, drag the right resize handle to the right until the text no longer wraps.

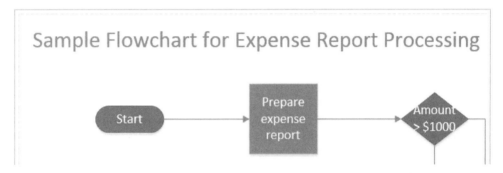

At this point, you can use all of the usual text manipulation tools in the Font and Paragraph groups on the Home tab to apply other fonts, colors, and text styles or to add bullets or numbers and reposition the text within the text box.

❌ CLEAN UP **Save your changes to the *Text Exercises* drawing, and then close it.**

In this exercise, you created a page title text box manually, but Visio offers a number of pre-formatted page title boxes. An example appears in "Working with background pages and borders" later in this chapter.

TIP If you are a long-time Visio user and prefer to use the legacy text formatting dialog boxes, they are still available. Just click the dialog box launcher in either the Font or Paragraph groups on the Home tab.

TIP To apply changes to all of the text in a text box, select the box by using the Pointer Tool before making changes. To change only part of the text, double-click the text box to enter edit mode, and then select the specific text you want to change. (As an alternative to double-clicking the text box, you can select the text box by using the Text Tool, which automatically enters edit mode.)

Orienting shapes on the page

When you drop shapes onto the Visio drawing page, they are usually oriented the way you want them to be. However, there are times when you will want the shapes to appear at a different angle. Visio provides several ways to accomplish this.

In this exercise, you will add several shapes to the Visio drawing page and rotate the shapes to different angles.

TIP The font size for some of the graphics in this exercise has been increased for readability. The font in your shapes may be smaller.

 SET UP **Click the File tab, and then click New. Click Categories, click General, and then double-click the Block Diagram thumbnail. To improve visibility of key diagram elements for this exercise, on the Design tab, in the Themes group, click the More button in the lower-right corner of the Themes gallery, and select No Themes. Save the drawing as** *Orient Shapes and Text*. **Then follow the steps.**

1 On the **View** tab, in the **Zoom** group, click the **Page Width** button, and then position the page so you can view the top edge.

2   Drag a **Box** shape from the **Blocks** stencil and drop it so the center is approximately 8 inches (200 mm) up from the bottom and 3 inches (75 mm) in from the left side of the page.

TIP Use the ruler on the left and top edges of the drawing page to guide shape placement.

IMPORTANT The shapes in the US Units version of the Block Diagram stencil contain the word *text*, whereas the same shapes in the Metric Units version of the stencil do not. Because the examples in this chapter were created using the US version, you will notice the word *text*. If you are using the Metric stencil, add the word *text* to each shape.

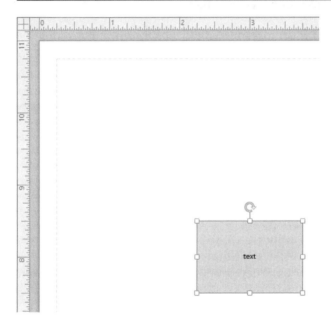

In addition to the regular selection handles surrounding the box, notice the rotation handle at the top center just above the box.

When you point to the rotation handle, the cursor changes from an arrow to a circular arrow. Notice also that a dot appears in the center of the rectangle. This dot shows the geometric center of the shape, that is, the point around which the shape will rotate when you drag the rotation handle. Though you won't do it in this exercise, you can alter the rotation characteristics of the shape by dragging the center of rotation handle to a different location.

TIP If a rotation handle does not appear above a shape, it's because the shape designer has turned off the rotation feature.

3   Grab the rotation handle and rotate the shape 90 degrees to the left (counterclockwise). Both the shape and the text rotate.

TIP If you keep the cursor near the rotation handle as you drag it, the shape rotates in 15-degree increments. However, if you move the cursor away from the rotation handle as you drag it, the shape rotates in 5-degree increments, giving more precise control.

4   Drag the rotation handle counterclockwise another 90 degrees so the box is inverted. Notice that the text is also upside down—more about that in the next exercise.

5   Return the box to its original upright position to continue with this exercise, thereby demonstrating that you can rotate the shape freely through 360 degrees of arc.

6   Drag a **Circle** onto the page so its center is approximately 3 inches (75 mm) to the right of the center of the box, using the **Dynamic Grid** to align it with the box.

7   Right-click the drawing page and select the **Connector Tool** from the **Mini Toolbar**.

TIP The Visio 2013 Mini Toolbar introduces a single use Connector Tool: the pointer reverts to the Pointer Tool as soon as you draw one connector.

8   Draw a connector from the right side of the box to the left side of the circle.

9   With the new connector still selected, type **Demonstration Text** and then press the **Esc** key.

10   Draw a bounding box around all three shapes to select them.

11   On the **Home** tab, in the **Font** group, in the **Font Size** list, click **14 pt.** to make it easier to read the text in the steps that follow.

TIP You can apply the same change to multiple shapes at one time.

12   Draw a bounding box around all three shapes to select them, and then rotate the entire selection 90 degrees clockwise. Notice the difference in behavior between the text in the box or circle and the text on the connector.

TIP You can rotate selections of shapes as easily as you can rotate individual shapes.

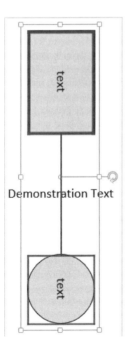

13   Rotate the selection another 90 degrees clockwise so the shapes are inverted.

At this point, it's quite obvious that the text in some shapes seems to behave better—or at least differently—than the text in other shapes when the shapes are rotated. The next exercise will make this even clearer and will show you how to change the text orientation.

✖ CLEAN UP **Press Ctrl+Z twice to undo the last two rotations. Save your changes to the *Orient Shapes and Text* drawing but leave it open if you are continuing with the next exercise.**

Orienting shape text

As you observed in the preceding exercise, shape text does not always rotate as you rotate the containing shape. Whether it does depends on how the underlying shape was designed.

In this exercise, you'll discover additional examples of automatic text rotation, and you'll rotate text manually and reposition text blocks on shapes.

➡ SET UP **You need the *Orient Shapes and Text* drawing for this exercise. Either continue with the open copy from the previous exercise or open the *Orient Shapes and TextA_start* drawing located in the Chapter03 practice file folder and save it as *Orient Shapes and Text*. Then follow the steps.**

1   Drag a **2-D single arrow** shape from the **Blocks** stencil onto the drawing page and position it below the box shape from the preceding exercise.

2   While the arrow is still selected, type **ABC**.

3   In the **Shapes** window, click **Blocks Raised**, drag a **Right arrow** onto the page, and position it to the right of the arrow you placed in the previous step.

4   While the arrow is still selected, type **ABC**.

5   Draw a bounding box around both arrows to select them, and change the font size
     to **14 pt.**

6   Select the arrow on the left and use the rotation handle to turn it 180 degrees, and
     then do the same thing with the right arrow.

Although the two arrow shapes are similar in some respects, their designers made
different choices for how text should be handled. In the left arrow, the text rotates
along with the shape. In the right arrow, the text responds to *gravity*, or more correctly, it responds to a mathematical function that sets the text angle based on the
shape angle so that it appears to be responding to gravity.

TIP For the technically inclined, if you look in the TxtAngle cell in the Text Transform
section of the ShapeSheet for the right arrow, there is a function named GRAVITY().
You will learn the basics of the ShapeSheet in the Appendix.

To get a better sense of how the gravity function works, rotate the right arrow in
several steps from its current position to its original position.

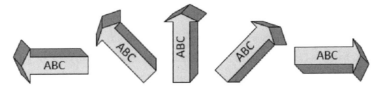

As shown, some shapes are designed so the text will be upright as the shape is rotated, but what do you do with shapes that aren't designed that way? Enter the Text
Block Tool.

7   On the **Home** tab, in the **Tools** group, click the **Text Block** button.

8   Click the left arrow one time and notice that the selection handles appear as usual.

9   Drag the selection handle clockwise. Notice that because you are using the **Text Block Tool** and not the **Pointer Tool**, only the text rotates. Stop when you have rotated the text 180 degrees.

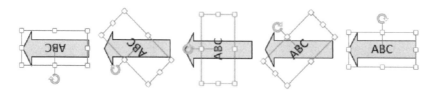

You can use the Text Block Tool to reorient the text in virtually any shape. However, be aware that a shape designer can lock the text in a shape so that the text can neither be altered nor repositioned. If you click with the Text Block Tool on a shape whose text is locked, the rotation handle will not appear, as shown in the following graphic. (If you zoom in on such a shape, you'll notice that the resize handles include a dotted diagonal line.)

❌ CLEAN UP **Save your changes to the *Orient Shapes and Text* drawing but leave it open if you are continuing with the next exercise.**

Positioning shape text

The text on a Visio shape is located in a ***text block***. You can reposition the text within a text block with several buttons located on the Visio ribbon. You can also reposition the entire text block by using the Text Block Tool you learned about in the previous exercise.

In this exercise, you'll reposition text within a text block, and you'll move the text block to a new location.

➡ SET UP **You need the *Orient Shapes and Text* drawing for this exercise. Either continue with the open copy from the previous exercise or open the *Orient Shapes and TextB_ start* drawing located in the Chapter03 practice file folder and save it as *Orient Shapes and Text*. Then follow the steps.**

1   Click once in the rectangle that contains the word *text*.

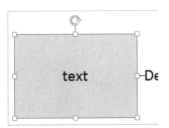

TIP When you select a shape, the illuminated buttons in the Paragraph group show the current text alignment for that shape. For example, after clicking the rectangle, the Paragraph group should look like the following graphic, indicating that the text is centered both vertically and horizontally.

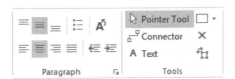

2   On the **Home** tab, in the **Paragraph** group, click any of the buttons to observe the effect. For example, if you click the **Align Top** button and then the **Align Left** button, the shape will look like the following graphic.

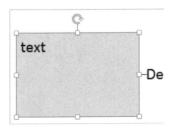

3   On the **Home** tab, in the **Tools** group, click the **Text Block** button, and then click once on the rectangle that contains the word *text*.

4   Click anywhere on the edge of the text block and drag the text block up and to the left. When the **Text Block Tool** is active, the text block moves independently from the underlying shape. If you subsequently use the **Pointer Tool** to move the underlying shape, the text block also moves and remains in the same position relative to the shape.

TIP If the shape designer has locked the text block in a shape, the rotation handle will not appear, and the resize handles will display a dotted diagonal line. You will not be able to move, resize, or rotate the text block.

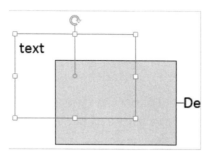

You can also resize the text block whenever the Text Block Tool is active by dragging any of the resize handles. Although moving the text block on this particular shape may not make a lot of sense, there are situations where knowing how to move and rotate text can be very helpful as the remaining steps in this exercise illustrate.

5   Press **Ctrl+1** to activate the **Pointer Tool**.

6   In the **Shapes** window, click **More Shapes**, point to **Network**, and then click **Computers and Monitors - 3D**. After the **Computers And Monitors - 3D** stencil opens, click anywhere on the drawing page to close the fly-out menus.

7   Drag an **LCD monitor** shape onto the page, drop it below the circle shape, and type **Hello**. Notice that this shape was designed so that the text block is located below the shape.

8   On the **Home** tab, in the **Tools** group, click the **Text Block** button.

9   Click the word *Hello* and then reposition and rotate the text block so the word *Hello* appears on the LCD screen at approximately the same angle as the screen itself.

TIP Repositioning and rotating the text in the LCD monitor is an excellent situation in which to use the zoom feature in Visio. Zoom in to enlarge the shape before attempting to relocate and rotate the text. This will enable you to complete this step more easily and more precisely.

❌ CLEAN UP **Save your changes to the *Orient Shapes and Text* drawing, and then close it.**

SEE ALSO For another perspective on text block positioning, go to *www.visguy.com/2007/11/07/text-to-the-bottom-of-the-shape/*.

Adding ScreenTips and comments

In some drawings, you want to provide your reader with additional information that doesn't need to be visible at all times. Visio provides two convenient options with very different characteristics:

- *ScreenTips* display pop-up text when you point to a shape, but they are otherwise invisible. Indeed, there is no way to know that a ScreenTip exists unless you point to a shape containing one and a pop-up appears.

> **IMPORTANT** ScreenTips are part of a shape. Consequently, they move with a shape and are deleted when you delete a shape.

- *Comments* provide a visible indication of their presence, but require you to click the indicator in order to view the text of the comment. Each comment stores and displays the name of the comment author and the date when it was created. New in Visio 2013, one comment shape can contain multiple comments from multiple authors; individual entries are displayed in chronological order. You will learn more about commenting in Chapter 13, "Collaborating on and publishing diagrams."

IMPORTANT If one shape is selected when you add a comment, the comment will be attached to that shape. If more than one shape is selected when you add a comment, the comment will be attached to the *anchor shape* (you will learn more about anchor shapes in Chapter 5, "Adding style, color, and themes"). If no shapes are selected, the comment will be attached to the drawing page.

In general, use ScreenTips to provide useful but noncritical information about a shape. You should make the assumption that the reader may discover a ScreenTip, but also may not. Use comments when it is vital that the reader know that they exist and when it is important to know who created the comment and when.

In this exercise, you'll add a ScreenTip to a shape. You'll also add and edit a comment.

 SET UP **Click the File tab, and then click New. Click Categories, click Network, and then double-click the Basic Network Diagram thumbnail. Save the drawing as *Text and Data on Shapes*. Then follow the steps.**

1   In the **Shapes** window, click **Computers and Monitors**. The **Computers And Monitors** stencil opens.

2   Drag a **PC** shape onto the page.

3   On the **Insert** tab, in the **Text** group, click the **ScreenTip** button to open the **Shape ScreenTip** dialog box.

4   Type **I need a new PC** in the dialog box, and then click **OK**.

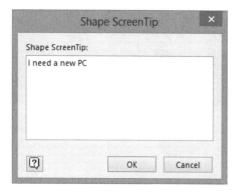

5   Point to the PC and observe the pop-up text that you've created.

6   Drag a **Laptop** shape from the **Computers and Monitors** stencil onto the page.

7   With the laptop shape still selected, on the **Review** tab, in the **Comments** group, click the **New Comment** button.

TIP Comments are part of the review feature set in Visio. Consequently, you will find comment buttons on the Review tab and not on the Insert tab where you found ScreenTips.

Visio drops a comment indicator and an edit box for the comment body onto the page. The indicator is located in the upper-right corner of the shape and looks like a cartoon dialog balloon; the edit box appears above or near it.

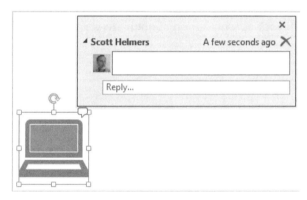

8   Type **This laptop contains Visio Professional 2013.**

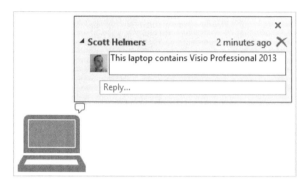

9   Click anywhere on the background of the page to close the comment edit box.

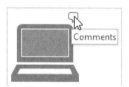

10   Point to the comment balloon but don't click it, which causes Visio to display the word *Comments* but only for as long as you continue to point to the indicator.

11   Click once on the comment indicator to view the Visio display of the comment edit box.

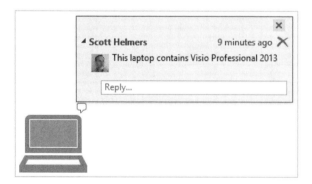

12 Click in the **Reply** area of the edit box and type **It also contains Office Professional 2013**.

> **TIP** If you click on the text of the previous comment, you can edit it instead of typing a reply.

13 Click anywhere outside the comment balloon to close it and then click the balloon again to reopen the comment box.

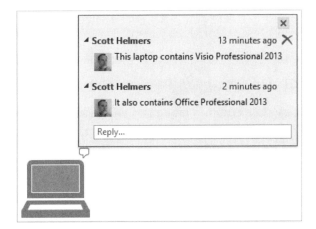

The comment feature in Visio 2013 is much more robust than in previous versions because it supports threaded conversations. Although both comments in the preceding graphic were entered by the same person, in Chapter 13 you'll discover examples of coauthoring that feature comments from multiple people.

TIP If you prefer not to view pictures of the person who made a comment, click the blue triangle to the left of the person's name to collapse the view.

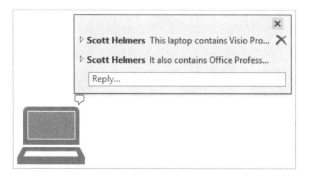

⊗ CLEAN UP **Save your changes to the *Text and Data on Shapes* drawing, and then close it.**

TIP You can turn all comment indicators in your drawing on or off by clicking the lower part of the Comments pane button in the Comments group on the Review tab, and then clicking Reveal Tags.

Using shape data

A significant part of what gives Visio diagrams uniqueness and value is the data that resides inside Visio shapes. Called **shape data** starting with Visio 2007, data fields were known as **custom properties** in previous versions of Visio.

Many of the masters in the built-in Visio stencils already contain shape data fields. In this exercise, you'll work with existing data fields. In Chapter 6, you'll work with data in more detail, including creating new shape data fields.

In this exercise, you'll add and edit values in computer and network shapes.

SET UP **Click the File tab, and then click New. Click Categories, click Network, and then double-click the Basic Network Diagram thumbnail. Save the drawing as** *Shape Data.* **Then follow the steps.**

1   In the **Network and Peripherals** stencil, drag a **Server**, a **Printer**, and a **Fax** shape onto the page, arranging them from top to bottom on the page.

2   Click once on the server shape to select it.

3   On the **View** tab, in the **Show** group, click the **Task Panes** button, and then click **Shape Data**. The **Shape Data** window appears and displays the names and current values, if any, for data fields that are contained within the server shape.

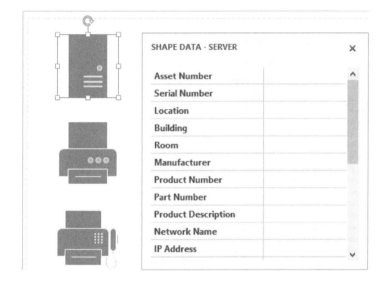

TIP The Shape Data window can appear anywhere on the screen, but you can relocate it by dragging the window header. If you drag it toward any edge of the drawing window, it will attach itself there; if you drag it a bit further, it will dock outside the drawing window. You can also let the Shape Data window float over the drawing window as shown in the graphic.

4   Click in the **Asset Number** field, and type **6789-001**.

5   Click in the **Serial Number** field, and type **13579**.

6   Click in the **Network Name** field, and type **FileServer-A32**.

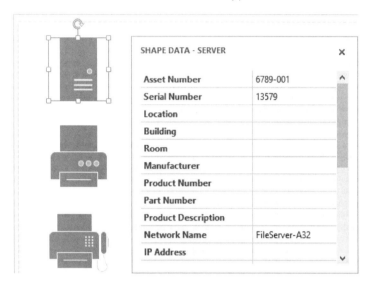

TIP Note the scroll bar on the right side of the Shape Data window. This shape has additional data fields that are not visible in the graphic.

7   Click once on the printer to select it. Notice that the **Shape Data** window now shows the fields that are defined for the printer.

8   Click in the **Asset Number** field, and type **6449-001**.

9   Click in the **Network Name** field, and type **HR-Printer6**.

10   Click once on the fax to select it. Notice that there are fewer fields defined for the fax machine.

11   Click in the **Manufacturer** field, and type **Contoso**.

12   Click in the **Product Number** field, and type **FX351**.

⊗ CLEAN UP **Save your changes to the *Shape Data* drawing but leave it open if you are continuing with the next exercise.**

Inserting fields: the basics

Now that you have entered data into several shapes, wouldn't it be nice if some of it appeared on the drawing?

In this exercise, you'll insert a field onto a shape and link the field to shape data.

 SET UP **You need the** *Shape Data* **drawing for this exercise. Either continue with the open copy from the previous exercise or open the** *Shape Data_start* **drawing located in the Chapter03 practice file folder and save it as** *Shape Data.* **Then follow the steps.**

1 Click once on the server shape to select it.

2 On the **Insert** tab, in the **Text** group, click the **Field** button. The **Field** dialog box opens and displays eight categories of field data that can be inserted into a shape.

3 In the **Category** section of the **Field** dialog box, click **Shape Data**. The **Shape Data** fields for this shape appear in the **Field** name section.

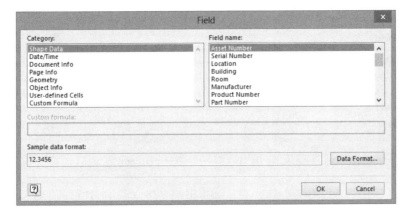

4 Scroll down in the **Field name** section, click **Network Name**, and then click **OK**. The field you inserted appears under the server.

TIP For the server shape and the other shapes on this page, the default text position is centered below the shape. In previous sections in this chapter, you worked with shapes whose text appeared in the middle of a shape or somewhere else. You've also learned how to reposition shape text if you prefer a different location.

5   Click once on the printer to select it, and then repeat steps 2–4 to display the network name for the printer.

6   Click once on the fax to select it, and repeat steps 2 and 3, but this time, click the **Product Number** field to produce a diagram that looks like the following graphic.

⊗ CLEAN UP **Save your changes to the *Shape Data* drawing, and then close it.**

There is a lot more that you can do with fields than simply displaying the contents of one field. You will learn more about fields in the Appendix.

Grouping shapes

Most of the exercises you've done in this book so far have involved using or manipulating individual shapes. Sometimes it's more convenient to work with a set of shapes as a single unit.

In this exercise, you'll create and work with a group shape.

SET UP **Click the File tab, and then click New. Click Categories, click Flowchart, and then double-click the Work Flow Diagram thumbnail. Save the drawing as** *Corporate Diagram*. **Then follow the steps.**

1   In the **Shapes** window, click the **Department** stencil if it is not already selected.

2   Drag a **Headquarters** shape to the drawing page and use the **Dynamic Grid** to position it at the top center of the page. The two **Dynamic Grid** lines provide visual assurance that you are at the top center.

3   On the status bar, click either the **Width** or **Height** button to open the **Size & Position** window.

SEE ALSO For more information about the status bar and the Size & Position window, refer to Chapter 1, "A visual orientation to a visual product."

4   In the **Size & Position** window, double both the **Width** and **Height** to 2 inches for US units or 60 mm. for metric. The increased height of the shape has triggered the *Auto Size* feature and Visio has added a new page above the current page.

5   Press the **Down Arrow** key until the resized shape is at the top margin of the original page.

6   Drag the following shapes onto the page and position them around the headquarters icon: **Customer Service**, **Management**, **Legal Department**, **Human Resources**.

7   Draw a bounding box around all five shapes.

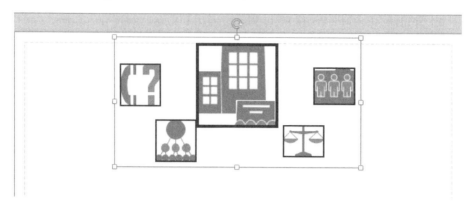

8   On the **Home** tab, in the **Arrange** group, click the **Group Objects** button, and then click **Group**. Notice that the blue selection rectangles around the individual shapes have disappeared, indicating that the group operation was successful.

KEYBOARD SHORTCUT Press Ctrl+G to group selected shapes.

TIP Like the individual shapes that comprise it, a group is also a shape. You can apply borders or fills, add fields and text, and add shape data—in short, you can do anything with a group shape that you can with any other shape.

9   Drag the group to the upper-left corner of the page. All shapes that are part of the group move together.

10 Click anywhere on the page background to deselect the group.

11   Click once on any shape in the group. Notice that the entire group is selected.

12   With the group still selected, click once on the **Legal Department** shape. The selection rectangle around the group changes from a solid line with resize handles to a dashed line to indicate that the group no longer has the focus. The **Legal Department** shape, on the other hand, now displays resize handles and a rotation handle, because it is now the selected shape.

The default behavior for grouped shapes is what you have observed in the preceding two steps: the first click selects the group; the second click selects a shape within the group. It is possible to change this behavior, but you won't do that in this exercise.

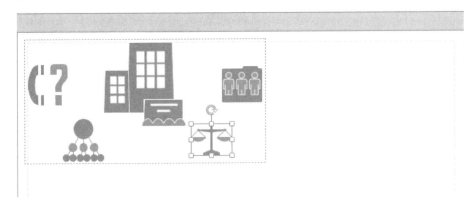

13   Click the dashed line surrounding the group to change the focus back to the group.

14   Drag the lower-right resize handle to enlarge the group. Notice that all shapes within the group resize proportionally.

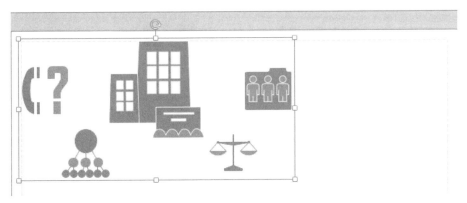

15   Drag a **Bank** shape from the **Department** stencil and drop it somewhere within the boundary of the group.

16   Select and drag the group back to the center of the page. Dropping a shape onto a group does not add it to the group.

TIP By default, shapes dropped on a group are not added to the group. However, if you run Visio in developer mode, you can change the behavior of a group so it will accept dropped shapes. You will learn about developer mode in the Appendix.

17   Right-click any shape in the group, then on the context menu, click **Group,** and then click **Ungroup**. The shapes remain on the page, but Visio removes the group. Any styles, text, or data associated with the group are now gone as well. Once again, each shape now shows its own selection rectangle.

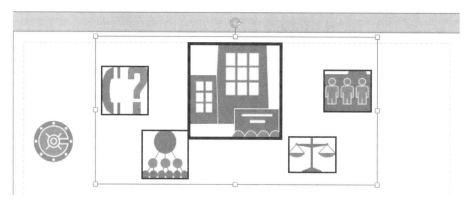

IMPORTANT Ungrouping the shape in this step is perfectly safe. In general though, ungrouping a shape can be very destructive unless you know exactly what you're doing. The reason is that to Visio, a group is just another shape, and it can have its own data and properties. Compounding the problem, the shapes in many groups derive some of their own behavior and data from the group. Consequently, when you ungroup the parent shape, you destroy the shape properties that were derived from the group.

✖ CLEAN UP **Save your changes to the *Corporate Diagram* drawing, but leave it open if you are continuing with the next exercise.**

Inserting pictures

As is true for Microsoft Word, PowerPoint, and many other programs, Visio lets you import pictures of various types into a drawing. You may want to add a picture of a specific object, a piece of clip art or a general background image—either way, you can import almost any type of image or picture into Visio.

In this exercise, you'll import several pictures to add value to and enhance the appearance of your drawing.

➜ SET UP **You need the *Corporate Diagram* drawing for this exercise. Either continue with the open copy from the previous exercise or open the *Corporate DiagramA_start* drawing located in the Chapter03 practice file folder and save it as *Corporate Diagram*. You also need the *International Office* image from the same practice file folder. Then follow the steps.**

1   On the **Insert** tab, in the **Illustrations** group, click the **Picture** button.

    KEYBOARD SHORTCUT Press Alt+N and then press P to insert a picture.

2   Navigate to the **Chapter03 practice file folder**, click **International Office.jpg**, and then click **Open**. (This image originated in the Microsoft Office Clip Art gallery.)

3   Drag the inserted photo to the bottom center of the page.

4   Drag an **International Division** shape from the **Department** stencil and drop it on the right face of the building.

5   On the **Insert** tab, in the **Illustrations** group, click the **Online Pictures** button to open the new Office 2013 **Insert Pictures** dialog box.

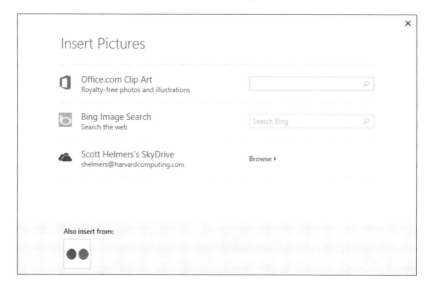

6   In the **Office.com Clip Art** box, type **EU flag** and then press **Enter**. Several flag images appear.

7   Double-click one of the flag images to add it to your drawing.

8   Reduce the size of the flag image, and then position it in the upper-left corner of the building image. Your drawing now includes an iconic representation of various headquarters' functions at the top of the page, and images that represent the international division office at the bottom.

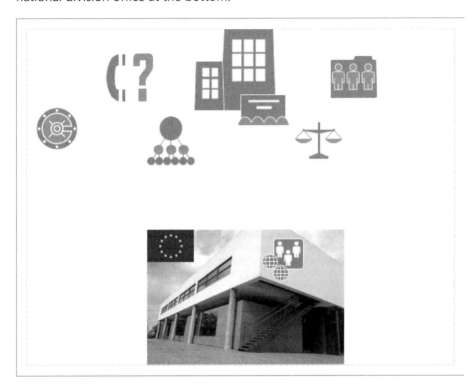

❌ CLEAN UP **Save your changes to the Corporate Diagram drawing, but leave it open if you are continuing with the next exercise.**

Once inserted into your drawing, an image becomes a shape, much like the group did in the preceding exercise. Consequently, you can use any of the various tools in Visio to alter or adjust the shape's properties. You can also add data to the image shape by using a technique you will learn in Chapter 6.

As you completed the steps in this exercise, you may have noticed that when you selected an image, the Picture Tools tool tab set appeared. You can use the buttons on the Format tool tab to alter the properties of an image.

TIP Like most of the other applications in the Microsoft Office suite, you can insert more than just pictures into a Visio drawing. On the Insert tab, click Object, and you will find two dozen or more document and object types (the actual list varies from computer to computer depending which Office products you have installed).

Understanding and using layers

You can organize objects in a Visio drawing into layers and control various properties of all layer members at once. For example, you can control whether layer members will print, be visible on the drawing page, or be selectable. In a town map, for instance, you might put roads on one layer, sewer lines on a second, water pipes on a third, and buildings on a fourth. Organized this way, you can lock certain layers to prevent accidentally moving or selecting that collection of objects while working with shapes on other layers. Similarly, you could print a map showing roads and buildings, but not water pipes.

SEE ALSO You can also use layers to select a subset of the shapes on a page, and you'll learn this technique in "Setting glow, reflection and other effects" in Chapter 5.

Layers offer considerable flexibility in managing the parts of a sophisticated drawing. However, working with layers requires some planning, because things can get complex: a drawing page can have multiple layers; each layer has multiple properties; and any shape can be on zero, one, or multiple layers.

TIP Every layer belongs to exactly one page. When you create a new layer, it is added to the current page. If you copy layer members to a different page, the layer is added to the destination page. (If a layer of the same name already exists on that page, the copied shapes are added to the existing layer.)

The Layer Properties dialog box that you will use in this exercise includes seven check boxes for setting layer properties. The y are described in the following paragraphs; default settings for each property are shown for the Flowchart layer in the graphic following step 7.

- **Visible** Controls whether a layer's shapes are visible on the drawing page.

- **Print** Includes or excludes a layer's members from printing.

  TIP Because the Visible and Print check boxes are separate, you can create a drawing in which members of a layer are visible in the drawing but do not print, and vice versa.

- **Active** Causes all new shapes added to the page to be added to the layer. More than one layer can be active at once, in which case new shapes are added to all active layers.

- **Lock** Prevents you from selecting, moving, or editing any shapes on the layer. In addition, you cannot add shapes to a locked layer.

- **Snap and Glue** Allows and disallows snapping or gluing other shapes to the shapes on this layer.

- **Color** Temporarily overrides the colors of all objects on a layer; clearing this option returns layer members to their original colors. When you select the Color property for a layer, the Layer Color and Transparency settings in the lower right of the dialog box are activated.

In this exercise, you'll create layers and assign shapes to them. You'll also change layer properties, which will show you the effects on the drawing.

 SET UP **You need the *Corporate Diagram* drawing for this exercise. Either continue with the open copy from the previous exercise or open the *Corporate DiagramB_start* drawing located in the Chapter03 practice file folder and save it as *Corporate Diagram*. Then follow the steps.**

1 Click once on the photograph of the building at the bottom of the page to select it.

2 On the **Home** tab, in the **Editing** group, click the **Layers** button, and then click **Assign to Layer** to open the **Layer** dialog box. When the **Layer** dialog box opens, notice that the **Flowchart** layer is already listed because the shapes that are used in the **Work Flow Diagram** template are pre-assigned to that layer.

3   Click the **New** button.

4   In the **New Layer** dialog box, type **Building Photo** and then click **OK**. The **Building Photo** layer is added to the **Layer** dialog box, and the selected shape is added to the new layer.

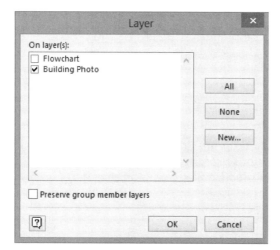

5   Click **OK**.

6   On the **Home** tab, in the **Editing** group, click the **Layers** button, and then click the **Layer Properties** button.

7   In the **Layer Properties** dialog box, select the check box below **Lock** for the **Building Photo** layer.

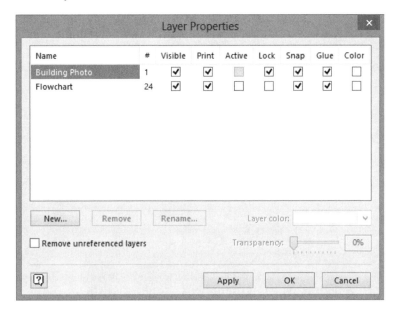

8   Click **OK**. You have now created a new layer, added a shape to it, and locked the layer.

9   Draw a bounding box around the International Division symbol, the EU flag, and the photograph of the building. Notice that you cannot select the building because it is on a locked layer.

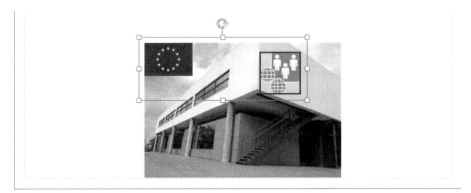

10   On the **Home** tab, in the **Editing** group, click the **Layer Properties** button, and then click **Assign to Layer** to open the **Layer** dialog box. Notice that the **Building Photo** layer does not appear in the list, because you cannot assign shapes to a locked layer.

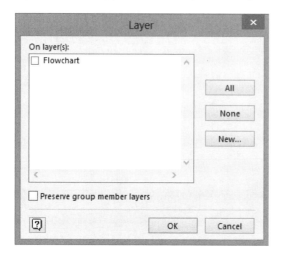

11   Click the **New** button, type **International**, and then click **OK**.

12   Click **OK**. The drawing doesn't look any different at this point, but there is evidence of the new layer in subsequent steps.

13   On the **Home** tab, in the **Editing** group, click the **Layers** button, and then click **Layer Properties**.

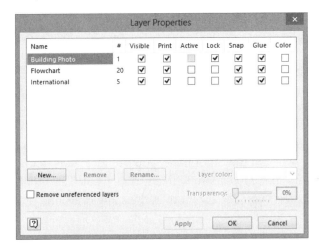

14   In the **Layer Properties** dialog box, clear the check box below **Visible**, for the **International** layer, and then click **Apply**.

TIP The Apply button provides a preview of the intended change without closing the Layer Properties dialog box. If you make a change in the Layer Properties dialog box and want that change to affect your drawing immediately, it is not necessary to click Apply—just click OK.

In the graphic on the right, the two shapes on the International layer are no longer visible. Compare this graphic to the one following step 13.

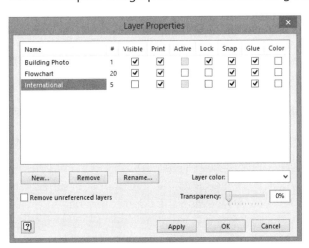

15   Click **OK** to close the **Layer Properties** dialog box.

❌ CLEAN UP **Save your changes to the *Corporate Diagram* drawing, and then close it.**

In this exercise, you saw that flowchart shapes are pre-assigned to a layer. The same thing is true for a number of other Visio templates. In addition, dynamic connectors are always on a layer, so dropping the first one onto any page creates a layer called *Connector*.

TIP Although they both help you organize sets of shapes, groups and layers serve different purposes and have different behaviors. For example, you can select a group and then move it or resize it and the changes affect all of the shapes in the group; you can't perform those actions with the shapes in a layer. On the other hand, you can lock, hide, and otherwise affect shapes in a layer in ways that you cannot with a group. Realize also that groups and layers are not mutually exclusive—you can use both in the same drawing.

Managing pages and page setup

A Visio drawing can contain any number of pages, and each page can have its own dimensions, measurement units, and other characteristics. In addition, the on-screen drawing page can have different dimensions from the physical printer page.

Setting the drawing page size to be different from the physical page lets you do things like:

- Compress a large drawing to fit on a smaller sheet of paper.

- Print a drawing on a very large sheet of paper.

- Print a drawing across multiple sheets of paper.

Indeed, Visio gives you remarkable flexibility in setting page attributes that are useful for virtually any diagram type and any form of printed or electronic output.

Visio drawings also support two types of drawing pages:

- *Foreground pages* contain the active drawing content and are typically the pages that are printed or published in some form.

- *Background pages* contain page elements that can appear on one or more pages but cannot be selected unless you are viewing the background page.

By associating a background page with a foreground page, all text and graphics on the background page appear on the foreground page. One common use for background pages is to add consistent borders or titles to a set of foreground pages. Another is to include the company logo, a legal notice, or any other graphic or text on multiple pages.

In this exercise, you'll add, delete, and reorder pages, as well as change various page settings. You'll also use the new Visio 2013 duplicate page feature. You will work with background pages in the next exercise.

SET UP Click the File tab, and then click New. Click Categories, click General, and then double-click the Basic Diagram thumbnail to create a new drawing. Save the drawing as *Pages and Page Setup*. Then follow the steps.

1   On the **Insert** tab, in the **Pages** group, click the lower part of the **New Page** button, and then click the **Blank Page** button. Visio adds a page called **Page-2**.

2   Notice that you can also add a background page or duplicate the current page from the same drop-down menu.

    TIP Clicking the Blank Page button is equivalent to clicking the Insert Page button that you learned about in Chapter 2, "Creating a new diagram" (it's the button to the right of Page-2 in the following graphic).

    Next you'll change some of the attributes of Page-2 using convenient new features of Visio 2013.

3   On the **Design** tab, in the **Page Setup** group, click the **Orientation** button, and then click **Portrait**. Clicking this button changes the orientation of both the drawing page and the printer page.

4   Drag a **Square** from the **Basic Shapes** stencil onto the top edge of the page so that part of it is on the page and part is on the canvas. Because the Visio 2013 *Auto Size* feature is on by default in this template, as it is in many others, Visio added a page for you. The dashed line is the boundary between *tiles*, each of which represents the portion of the drawing page that will print on a single physical page.

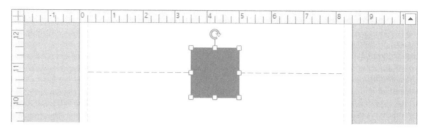

5   Drag the square down so it is below the dashed line. Visio removes the added page because it is no longer needed.

You can turn off the Auto Size feature if you want to use the drawing canvas to store shapes temporarily that you don't want to be on the drawing page.

6   On the **Design** tab, in the **Page Setup** group, click the **Auto Size** button, which removes the illumination from the **Auto Size** button.

TIP The Auto Size option is applied per page. Consequently, changing the setting for the current page does not affect other pages.

7   In the **Shapes** window, click **Arrow Shapes**, and then drag a **Simple Arrow** onto the canvas just above the page. The arrow remains on the canvas and Visio does not expand the drawing page.

TIP Items on the drawing canvas but not on the drawing page do not print.

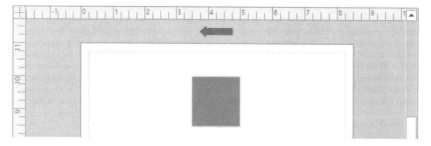

8   Click the **Insert Page** button below the drawing window to add a new page.

IMPORTANT When you added a page in step 1, the new page had landscape orientation; however, this time the new page has portrait orientation. The difference demonstrates an important point: when you add a page, Visio copies all of the characteristics of the *active page*. Consequently, if the pages in your drawing have different attributes, be sure to activate a page with the desired attributes before adding a new page.

You've now used several buttons in the Orientation group on the Design tab that simplify some page-related functions. There are times, however, when you need to make more sophisticated changes to page attributes. The Page Setup dialog box, which will be familiar to users of previous Visio versions, is still available for that purpose.

9   On the **Design** tab, in the **Page Setup** group, click the **Auto Size** button. This action turns **Auto Size** behavior back on for this page.

10   Right-click the page name tab for **Page-3**, and click **Page Setup**. The **Page Setup** dialog box opens to the **Page Properties** tab.

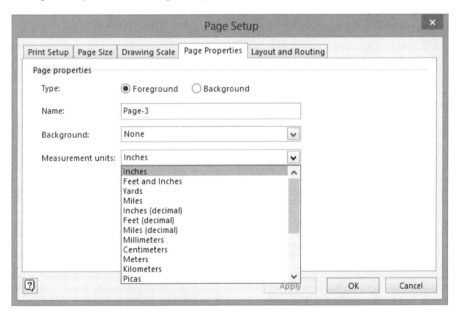

In addition to selecting the page type and changing the page name, you can assign a background page (refer to the next exercise) and select from a large number of measurement units. Be sure to notice the scroll bar in the Measurement units menu—you have a total of 20 choices. If you change the measurement units, the result is visible in the rulers on the top and left of the drawing page.

11 In the **Page Setup** dialog box, click the **Print Setup** tab.

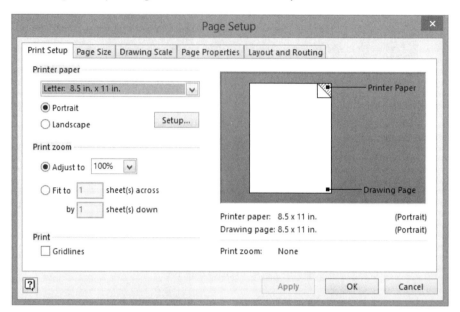

You use the options on the Print Setup tab primarily to affect the size and layout of the physical page, although the zoom settings on this tab also affect the drawing page size.

The Print Setup tab contains three configuration sections on the left and a preview pane on the right. The preview pane changes dynamically to reflect your current print settings and displays them in both visual and text form:

- **Printer paper** Choose the paper size for your desired printer. Most US Units templates default to letter-sized paper as shown in the previous graphic. Metric templates typically default to A4. Regardless of the default, there is a long list of alternate, predefined paper sizes available in the list at the top of this section. You can also select Portrait or Landscape orientation.

    The Setup button opens the printer setup dialog box for the current printer.

- **Print zoom Adjust to 100%** is the default zoom for many templates, but you can select a different zoom level if you want your drawing to print larger or smaller than normal. Choosing a zoom setting greater than 100% causes your drawing to be split across multiple sheets of paper; choosing a setting less than 100% scales your drawing down to fit onto a portion of the printer page.

- **Fit To** Provides an alternate way to scale your drawing for printing.

- **Print** The single setting in this section includes or excludes gridlines from printed output. The default in most templates is to exclude gridlines.

12 In the **Printer paper** section, click **Landscape**. The preview section reflects your choice.

13 In the **Page Setup** dialog box, click the **Page Size** tab.

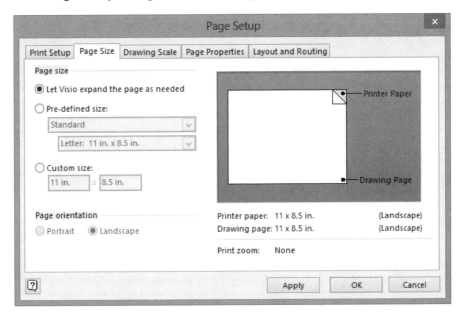

You use the Page Size tab to change attributes of the drawing page; changes you make on this tab do not directly affect the printed page.

The Page Size tab includes two configuration sections plus a preview pane:

- **Page size** The first option in this section enables the dynamic **Auto Size** behavior you used in steps 3 through 5. As an alternative, the second and third options let you set a fixed page size, either from a list of preset sizes or by typing specific dimensions.

- **Page orientation** The options in this section are only active if you choose **Predefined size** or **Custom size** in the **Page size** section. You can use these options to set a different orientation for the physical page than the one that is set for the drawing page.

14   Click **OK**. The dialog box closes and **Page-3** now has landscape orientation.

15   Double-click the page name tab for **Page-2** (not Page-3), type **Portrait with Square**, and then press **Enter**.

As you saw in step 10, you can change the page name on the Page Properties tab in the Page Setup dialog box, but double-clicking the page name tab is usually more convenient.

In addition to changing page names, you can also change the sequence of pages in a drawing.

16   Drag the page name tab for **Page-3** to before **Page-1**.

As you drag the page name tab, the cursor displays a page icon, and a black down arrow points to the junctions between pages.

When you release the mouse button, the page tabs reflect the new page sequence.

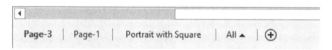

TIP Dragging page name tabs is an easy way to resequence pages when the destination tab location for your page is visible. However, if your diagram has a lot of pages and the destination tab is not visible, there is a simple alternative: right-click any page name tab and select Reorder Pages. In the Reorder Pages dialog box that opens (shown in the following graphic), use the Move Up or Move Down buttons.

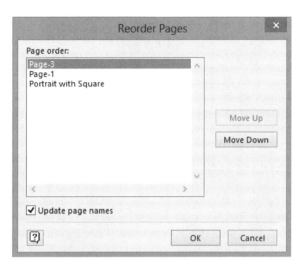

17   Right-click the **Portrait with Square** page name tab and then click **Duplicate**.
      Visio creates a new page that is an exact copy of the source page.

      TIP Duplicating a page and all of its contents is a long-desired feature that is new in
      Visio 2013.

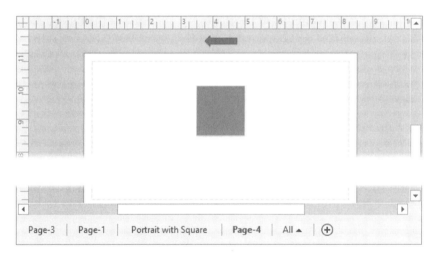

![x] CLEAN UP **Save your changes to the** *Pages and Page Setup* **drawing, and then
close it.**

      KEYBOARD SHORTCUT Visio provides two convenient shortcuts for navigating back and
      forth among the foreground pages in your drawing: Ctrl+Page Up and Ctrl+Page Down.

Working with background pages and borders

You can create background pages manually and assign them to selected foreground pages. You can also take advantage of several Visio features that automatically create and assign background pages.

In this exercise, you'll create background pages manually and assign them to selected foreground pages

TIP In the previous section, you adjusted the sizes and attributes of foreground pages. You can use the same techniques to resize and adjust attributes of background pages.

 SET UP **You need the** *Starfish* **image and the** *Background Exercises_start* **drawing located in the Chapter03 practice files folder to complete this exercise. Open the drawing in Visio and save it as** *Background Exercises*. **Then follow the steps.**

1   The drawing you just opened contains four pages, each of which contains a collection of shapes, and each page has a different theme applied to it. In addition, each page name reflects the contents of the page. The shapes and themes on each page exist so you can quickly tell one page from another as you complete the steps in this exercise. Notice, also, that the drawing for this exercise was created using the metric template.

2   On the **Insert** tab, in the **Pages** group, click the **New Page** arrow (not the button), and then click **Background Page**. The same **Page Setup** dialog box that you saw in the previous exercise opens to the **Page Properties** tab, however, in this case the **Type** is preset to **Background** and the default page name is **Background-1**.

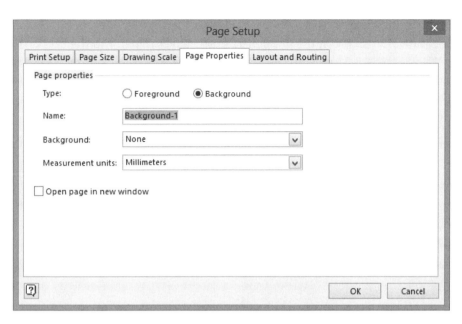

3   Click **OK**. Visio creates the background page.

TIP If the tab for the new page doesn't show the entire name *Background-1*, click any other page name tab, and then click back to the background tab.

TIP Remember that the attributes of the active page determine the attributes of each new page. If your drawing contains pages with different orientations or settings, activate the page that is like, or most like, your desired background page before creating the new page.

4   On the **Insert** tab, in the **Illustrations** group, click the **Picture** button, navigate to the **Starfish.jpg** in the **Chapter03** practice files folder, and then click **Open**. Visio inserts the picture into the center of the drawing window. You will use this picture as a stand-in for a company logo.

5   Drag the starfish picture to the upper-right corner of the page, and then resize it so it is approximately 25 mm (1 inch) wide.

TIP Remember that when you have selected a shape, its current width and height are displayed in the status bar at the bottom of the Visio window. As you drag the corner resize handle, the status bar updates dynamically to show the current size.

TIP You can include "Company Confidential" or other text on the pages in your diagram by adding a text box to the background page.

Now that you've created a background page, you can apply it to one or more fore-ground pages.

6   Right-click on the **Squares** page name tab, and then click **Page Setup**. The **Page Setup** dialog box opens to the **Page Properties** tab.

7   Use the **Background** list, select the name of the background page, **Background-1**, and then click **OK**. The **Squares** page now includes the "logo" and any other objects or text you might have placed on that page. Three important notes:

   ■ Because the starfish is on a background page, you cannot select, change, or relo-cate it on this page. You must go to the background page to make changes.

   ■ Applying background pages is done per page. When you navigate to the **Circles** or **Triangles** pages, they do not show the background.

- If you create a new page from an active page that includes a background page, the new page will also include the background page.

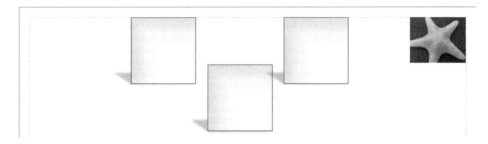

8   Go to the **Circles** page. Notice that the background was not applied to this page.

9   On the **Design** tab, in the **Background** group, click the **Borders & Titles** button to open the **Borders & Titles** gallery. As you point to any thumbnail in the gallery, its name is displayed as pop-up text. Be sure to notice that there is a scroll bar at the right giving you access to additional selections.

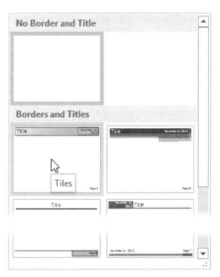

10 Click the **Tiles** thumbnail, which should be toward the upper left. Visio creates a background page containing the title shapes and applies it to the **Circles** page. Most of the title box that appears across the top of the page is reserved for the document title, but the right portion contains today's date. There is also a page number in the lower-right corner.

TIP The page number will be updated dynamically if you add, delete, or reorder pages.

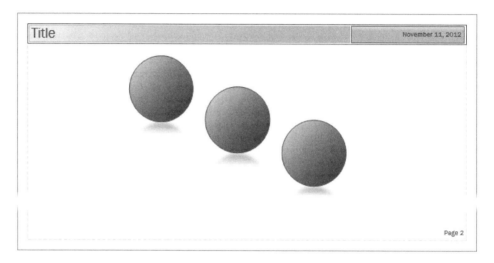

TIP The automatically generated background page is called VBackground-1. Visio includes the letter *V* to distinguish the background page it created from the one you created manually.

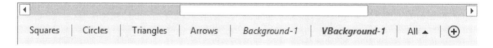

11 Go to **VBackground-1**, click in the **Title** text box, and then type **Tailspin Toys**.

12   Go to **Circles**. The **Circles** foreground page reflects the change you made on the background page.

13   Go to the **Triangles** page.

14   On the **Design** tab, in the **Background** group, click the **Backgrounds** button to view a gallery of available backgrounds. Each thumbnail displays the colors and effects of the theme applied to this page. The name is viewable when you point to any background.

15   Scroll down in the background gallery and click once on the **Verve** background. Visio creates a new background page called **VBackground-2**, and applies it to **Triangles**.

16   Go to the **Arrows** page. Note that it does not include any of the backgrounds you've created for other pages in the drawing.

17   Right-click the **Arrows** page name tab, and then select **Page Setup**.

18   In the **Background** list, select **Background-1**, and then click **OK**.

You have now assigned the same background page to both Triangles and Squares.

❌ CLEAN UP **Save your changes to the *Background Exercises* drawing, and then close it.**

Five final thoughts about background pages:

- Changes you make to a background page appear on all pages using that background page.

- If you have foreground pages with different orientations or sizes, you are likely to need multiple background pages with attributes that match the foreground pages.

- Background pages can have background pages. It is possible, therefore, to build a set of foreground pages that all display shapes from a common background page. (Think of it as the "deep background" page.) Those same foreground pages can also display the contents of other background pages that are unique to an individual page or to a group of pages.

- The page name tabs for background pages always appear to the right of all foreground pages and they cannot be reordered.

- Background page names are italicized.

Key points

- You can add text to almost any Visio shape. In addition, you can create "text only" shapes to add titles, labels, and other information to a drawing.

- Visio provides a set of tools for changing the size, position, and orientation of shapes on a page. There is a complementary set of tools for altering the size, position, and orientation of the text displayed on a shape.

- ScreenTips and comments are two different ways to add text annotations to a drawing. Each behaves differently and is suited for a different purpose.

- Many Visio shapes contain one or more data fields. Shape data can turn a drawing into far more than just a "pretty picture"—the drawing can become the single source for viewing structure, content, form, and function.

- One way to display shape data on a drawing page is to insert a field into a shape and link that field to shape data.

- You can insert photographs, clip art, or other images onto foreground pages; you can also insert them onto background pages so they can appear on multiple foreground pages.

- The Visio 2013 duplicate page function replicates all attributes of a page including its dimensions, contents, and background page, if any.

- Visio provides several ways to organize collections of shapes. You can use groups to tie a set of shapes together so you can move, resize, and work with them as a unit. You can use layers to hide, print, recolor, or lock a set of shapes, while allowing each shape to retain its individuality in ways that aren't true in a group. In Chapter 11, "Adding structure to your diagrams," you'll learn about another option called a *container*.

3

Chapter at a glance

Create
Create flowcharts,
page 161

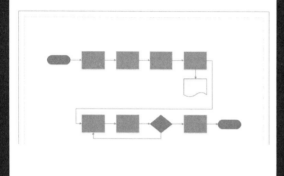

Create
Create swimlane diagrams,
page 166

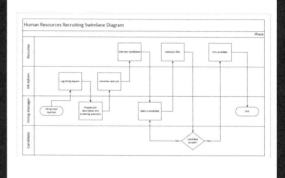

Create
Create org charts by hand,
page 175

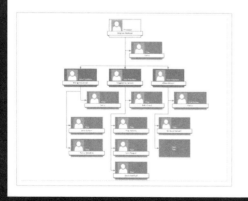

Create
Create org charts with pictures,
page 193

IN THIS CHAPTER, YOU WILL LEARN HOW TO

- Select a flowchart type.

- Create flowcharts and add flowchart labels.

- Understand and create swimlane diagrams.

- Understand and build organization charts.

- Use the Organization Chart Wizard with existing or new data.

- Alter org chart layout and appearance.

- Add photos and change styles in org charts.

In the first three chapters, you learned many of the basic capabilities of Microsoft Visio 2013. In this chapter, you'll apply that knowledge to creating real-world diagrams. There is no better place to start than with the humble *flowchart*, because creating flowcharts is one of the most common tasks for which people use Visio. In fact, according to Microsoft, more than one-third of all Visio diagrams are based on templates from the flowchart category.

Whether the end goal is to diagram the logic of a current or future software module, or to document the way that a work procedure is, or could be, performed, Visio flowcharts are the standard. Also, Visio is frequently used to create an alternative type of flowchart called a *cross-functional flowchart* or a *swimlane diagram*.

Another common application for Visio is to create **organization charts**, often known as **org charts**. You can create org charts manually by dragging the intelligent organization chart shapes from the Visio stencil onto the drawing page, or you can run the Organization Chart Wizard to automate the work of creating your drawing. As you'll discover later in this chapter, the Visio 2013 org chart add-in has been totally redesigned to let you create more attractive, modern, dynamic charts—even ones that include photographs.

In this chapter, you'll learn about different types of flowcharts and will create both conventional flowcharts and swimlane diagrams. You'll also learn how to add text to Visio flowchart shapes. Finally, you'll learn how to build an organization chart by hand as well as by using the wizard, and how to enhance organization charts with pictures.

PRACTICE FILES To complete the exercises in this chapter, you need the practice files contained in the Chapter04 practice file folder. For more information, refer to "Downloading the practice files" in this book's Introduction.

Selecting a flowchart type

Visio provides different flowchart templates, depending on the edition that you use.

Visio Standard

Microsoft Visio Standard 2013 includes four flowchart templates, as shown in the following graphic. You will work with the Basic Flowchart and Cross-Functional Flowchart templates in this chapter. The Work Flow Diagram template is a brand new, theme-capable template for creating workflow diagrams. The corresponding template from previous versions of Visio was retained in Visio 2013 and is now called Work Flow Diagram - 3D.

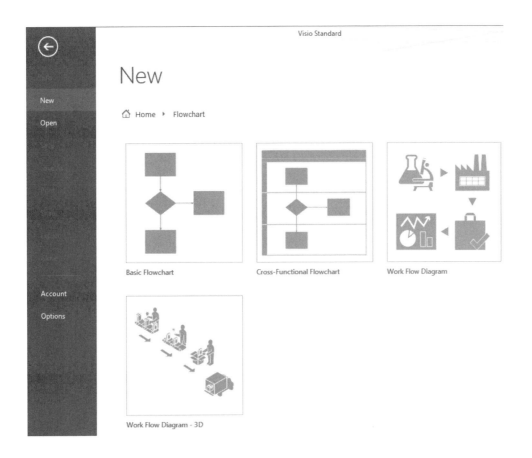

Visio Professional

Visio Professional 2013 includes the same four templates as the Standard edition, but also includes five additional flowchart templates: Business Process Model and Notation (BPMN), IDEF0, Specification and Description Language (SDL) Diagram, and two variations of Microsoft SharePoint Workflow, one for SharePoint 2010 and one for SharePoint 2013.

You'll learn more about the BPMN and SharePoint Workflow templates in Chapter 12, "Creating and validating process diagrams."

SEE ALSO For additional information about IDEF0, go to *en.wikipedia.org/ wiki/IDEF0*. For additional information about SDL, go to *en.wikipedia.org/wiki/ Specification_and_Description_Language*.

Vertical or horizontal?

Should you draw your flowcharts with vertical (portrait) or horizontal (landscape) orientation? Vertical flowcharts, with tasks arranged from top to bottom, are probably more common, but there have always been advocates for the left-to-right, horizontal view.

One interesting note if you have created flowcharts with previous versions of Visio: the Visio 2013 and Visio 2010 Basic Flowchart templates default to horizontal orientation, whereas previous versions presented a vertical view by default. Although this may frustrate people with a long-standing preference for the portrait view, there is some logic to this choice, because computer screens have grown wider over the years.

4

Creating flowcharts

In this exercise, you'll create a new flowchart for a simple human resources recruiting process. The flowchart will have seven process steps and one decision.

 SET UP **Click the File tab, and then click New. Click Categories, click Flowchart, and then double-click the Basic Flowchart thumbnail. Save the new drawing as *HR Recruiting Flowchart*. Then follow the steps.**

1 Drag a **Start/End** shape from the **Basic Flowchart Shapes** stencil onto the drawing page.

2 Point to the start shape you added to the drawing page, click the right-facing blue triangle that appears, and then click the **Process** shape from the **Quick Shapes** menu.

SEE ALSO For a refresher on using Quick Shapes, refer to "Using AutoConnect and quick shapes" in Chapter 2, "Creating a new diagram."

3 Use the same technique to add three more **Process** shapes to the page.

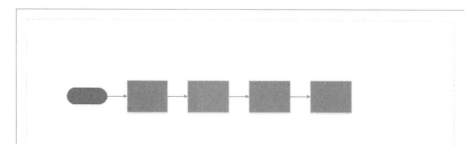

4 Drag a **Process** shape onto the drawing page. Then use the Dynamic Grid to position the new process shape below the leftmost process shape.

SEE ALSO For more information about the Dynamic Grid in Visio, refer to "Using basic shapes and the Dynamic Grid" in Chapter 2.

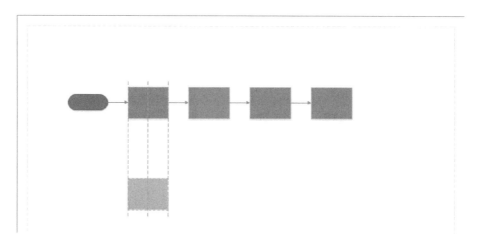

5 From the **Quick Shapes** menu, add the following four shapes:

- Another **Process** shape to the right of the one from step 4.
- A **Decision** diamond to the right of the previous process shape.
- Another **Process** shape to the right of the decision diamond.
- A **Start/End** shape to the right of the final process shape.

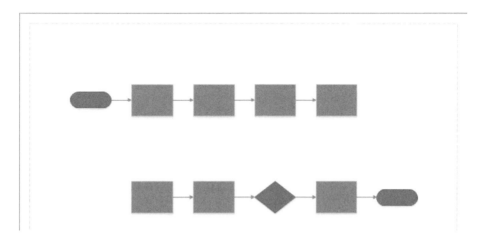

At this point, the flowchart is nearly complete with the exception of two connectors: one that links the end of the first row to the beginning of the second row, and one that links the decision diamond back to a previous step in the flowchart.

6   Right-click anywhere on the drawing page, select the **Connector Tool** from the Mini Toolbar, and then move the cursor near the last shape in the first row.

TIP The Visio 2013 Mini Toolbar introduces a single use Connector Tool: the pointer reverts to the Pointer Tool as soon as you draw one connector.

7   Click the connection point on the right of the top-right process shape, and then drag to the leftmost connection point on the first process shape in the second row.

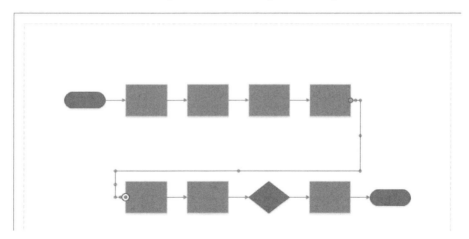

8   Click the blue **AutoConnect** arrow under the decision shape and drag it to the connection point on the bottom of the leftmost process shape in the same row.

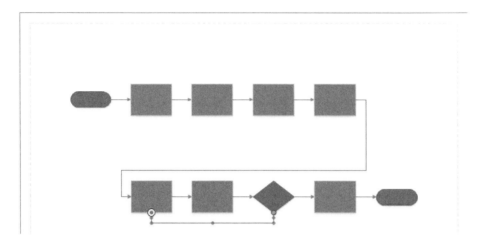

9   Drag a **Document** shape to just below the last process shape in the top row.

> **IMPORTANT** Do not drop the document shape on a connector line or else Visio will break the connector in two and connect your document shape to both lines. This feature is called *AutoAdd* and is described in Chapter 2.

10   Drag a bounding box around all of the shapes in the bottom row. Then hold down the **Shift** key while you drag that row down to make more room. Once again, Visio will reposition the connector line to accommodate the new location of the bottom row.

> **TIP** Holding down the Shift key constrains Visio to moving the selected shapes only vertically or horizontally, whichever is the first direction you move the cursor.

11   Click the blue **AutoConnect** arrow under the upper-right process shape to connect it to the document shape. The layout of your flowchart is now complete.

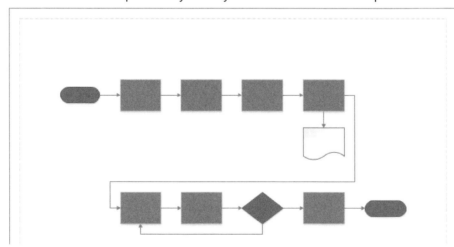

CLEAN UP Save your changes to the *HR Recruiting Flowchart* drawing, but leave it open if you are continuing with the next exercise.

Adding labels to flowcharts

In the preceding exercise, you learned the mechanics of creating a flowchart, but your diagram isn't very useful yet because your shapes have no labels, data, or identifying information.

SEE ALSO For information about adding data to your shapes, refer to Chapter 6, "Entering, linking to, and reporting on data."

In this exercise, you'll add text labels to your flowchart shapes.

SET UP You need the *HR Recruiting Flowchart* drawing for this exercise. Either continue with the open copy from the previous exercise or open the *HR Recruiting Flowchart_ start* drawing located in the Chapter04 practice file folder and save it as *HR Recruiting Flowchart*. Then follow the steps.

1 Click the **Start/End** shape in the upper-left of your diagram, and then type **Hiring need reported**.

2 Click the first **Process** shape in your flowchart, type **Log hiring request**, and then continue from left to right across the top row to add the following labels to the remaining shapes:

- **Prepare job description and screening questions**

- **Advertise open job**

- **Interview candidates**

3 Click and type the following text into the five shapes in the bottom row, from left to right:

- **Select a candidate**

- **Make job offer**

- **Candidate accepts?**

- **Hire candidate**

- **End**

4   Click the connector between the **Candidate accepts?** shape and the **Hire candidate** shape and type **Yes**.

5   Click the connector between the **Candidate accepts?** shape and the **Select a candidate** shape and type **No**.

6   Add a text box to the top of the page, type **Human Resources Recruiting Process** as a title for the flowchart, and then set the font to **24 pt.** and bold. Your finished flowchart should look something like the following graphic.

❌ CLEAN UP **Save your changes and close the *HR Recruiting Flowchart* drawing.**

Understanding swimlane diagrams

Swimlane diagrams are a popular variation on flowcharts, because they correct one significant failing of flowcharts: very few flowcharts show who is responsible for each of the steps or who makes the key decisions.

A swimlane diagram, on the other hand, is specifically organized by role, function, or department. Each process step is placed into a specific lane based on who does the work or who has the responsibility for that process step. For example, a swimlane diagram with a focus on roles might include lanes marked *Accounts Payable Clerk*, *Accounting Supervisor*, and *Chief Financial Officer*. Similarly, a department-focused swimlane drawing might show lanes labeled *Sales*, *Marketing*, *Order Processing*, and *Manufacturing*.

A swimlane diagram is also known as a *cross-functional flowchart* (CFF), because it shows work steps as they cross the functional boundaries in an organization. In this context, individual swimlanes are usually referred to as ***functional bands***.

Regardless of the terminology, swimlane diagrams can be laid out with horizontal or vertical lanes. Using Visio, you can choose the orientation you prefer, as described in the exercise in the following section.

TIP Some Visio templates employ additional software, outside of Visio itself, to perform their functions. The cross-functional flowchart diagram is an example of this type of Visio add-in. And, like many add-ins, cross-functional flowcharts present a custom tab on the ribbon, as shown in the following graphic.

4

Creating swimlane diagrams

In the preceding exercises, you created a flowchart of a human resources recruiting process. However, the flowchart does not indicate who is responsible for each task.

In this exercise, you'll create a swimlane diagram of the same process. In doing so, you'll organize the work steps into role-based lanes to make responsibilities clear.

➡ SET UP **Click the File tab, and then click New. Click Flowchart in the Suggested Searches list. Then follow the steps.**

1   Double-click the **Cross-functional Flowchart** thumbnail. The orientation selection dialog box opens.

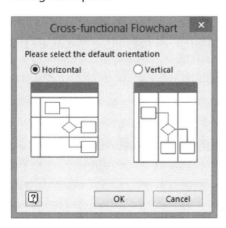

TIP If you have previously selected a default orientation, this dialog box will not appear again. However, you can still change both the orientation of a single diagram and the default for future diagrams. On the Cross-Functional Flowchart tab, in the Arrange group, click the Orientation button and make your selection.

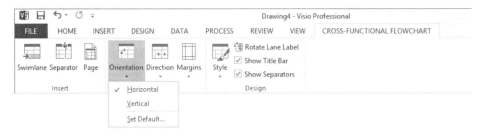

2   Click **OK** to accept the **Horizontal** layout option. The CFF add-in places a title band and two swimlanes onto the drawing page.

3   On the **Cross-Functional Flowchart** tab, in the **Insert** group, click the **Swimlane** button to add another lane to your diagram.

TIP There are three other ways to add swimlanes, each of which is useful at various times:

- Right-click the header of an existing lane, and Visio offers you a choice of adding a new swimlane above or below the one you've selected.

- Drag a **Swimlane** shape from the stencil and drop it on top of an existing lane.

- Point to the boundary between lanes, with the cursor just outside the swimlane structure, and click the blue insertion triangle. (You will learn about this method in the exercise titled, "Finding containers and lists in Visio" in Chapter 11, "Adding structure to your diagrams.")

4   Click the **Title** bar and type **Human Resources Recruiting Swimlane Diagram**.

5   Click the **Function** title bar for the top swimlane and type **Recruiter**.

6   Type **HR Admin** as the title for the second swimlane, and **Candidate** for the third swimlane.

TIP You've probably already figured this out, but swimlane diagrams are so named because they resemble a swimming pool viewed from above.

Human Resources Recruiting Swimlane Diagram

IMPORTANT The remaining screen shots for this exercise were captured using a black and white *theme* to improve legibility in the print edition of this book. Your swimlane diagram will continue to show the default theme colors, as seen in the preceding graphic, unless you have changed themes.

7   Drag a **Swimlane** from the **Cross-Functional Flowchart** stencil but before you drop it onto the page, pause briefly over the boundary between the **HR Admin** and **Candidate** swimlanes. An orange *insertion bar* appears indicating that the lane you drop will be inserted between the two existing lanes.

SEE ALSO Visio 2013 swimlanes are built from a combination of *containers* and *lists*. You will learn more about both in Chapter 11.

Human Resources Recruiting Swimlane Diagram

8   Drop the swimlane onto the page, and while it is still selected, type **Hiring Manager**.

> Human Resources Recruiting Swimlane Diagram
>
> Phase
>
> Recruiter
>
> HR Admin
>
> Hiring Manager
>
> Candidate

9   On the **Home** tab, in the **Tools** group, click the **Connector** button.

> **IMPORTANT** If you select a shape with the Connector Tool and then drag another
> shape onto the page, Visio automatically adds a connector from the first shape to
> the second. In this exercise, you accomplish this by leaving each shape selected after
> dragging it onto the page and typing text into it.
>
> You can stop the automatic addition of connectors by deselecting a shape before
> dragging the next one onto the page. Alternatively, you can select a different shape
> at any time to change which shapes will be connected automatically.

10   Drag a **Start/End** shape from the **Basic Flowchart Shapes** stencil onto the drawing page, and use the Dynamic Grid to position it toward the left end of the **Hiring
Manager** lane.

11   With the **Start/End** shape still selected, type **Hiring need reported**.

TIP It is not necessary to exit text edit mode before continuing to the next step.

12   Drag a **Process** shape into the **HR Admin** lane, dropping it above and to the right of the **Start/End** shape, and then type **Log hiring request**.

TIP To fit the shapes for this exercise onto a single page, ensure that the left edge of each new shape you add to the page overlaps horizontally with the preceding shape as shown in the two graphics that follow.

13   Draw a connector from the top of the **Hiring need reported** shape to the left side of the **Log hiring request** shape.

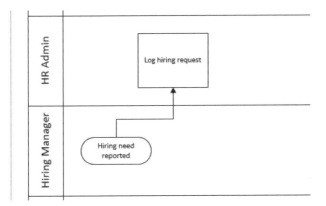

14   Drag a **Process** shape into the **Hiring Manager** lane, and then type **Prepare job description and screening questions**.

15   Use the **Connector Tool** to link the previous process step to your new task.

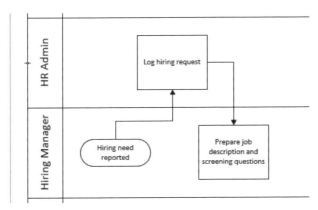

16   Continue adding flowchart shapes to your diagram using the information in rows 4-10 of the following table. (Rows 1-3 represent the shapes you've already added.)

	Shape	Swimlane	Shapetext
1	Start/End	Hiring Manager	Hiring need reported
2	Process	HR Admin	Log hiring request
3	Process	Hiring Manager	Prepare job description and screening questions
4	Process	HR Admin	Advertise open job
5	Process	Recruiter	Interview candidates
6	Process	Hiring Manager	Select a candidate
7	Process	Recruiter	Make job offer
8	Decision	Candidate	Candidate accepts?
9	Process	Recruiter	Hire candidate
10	Start/End	Hiring Manager	End

17 Add a connector from the **Candidate accepts?** shape to the bottom of the **Select a candidate** shape, and then type **No**.

18 Click the connector from the **Candidate accepts?** shape to the **Hire candidate** shape and type **Yes**.

Your swimlane diagram should look something like the following graphic. It's unlikely that your drawing will look exactly like this one, because you probably made different decisions about placing shapes. However, after the general placement and connectivity are correct, you can adjust and tweak your diagram to make it look the way you'd like.

If you think your diagram is too crowded, realize that the cross-functional flowchart template used the default paper size for your region. If you need more space, you can increase the drawing page size as described in Chapter 3, "Adding sophistication to your drawings."

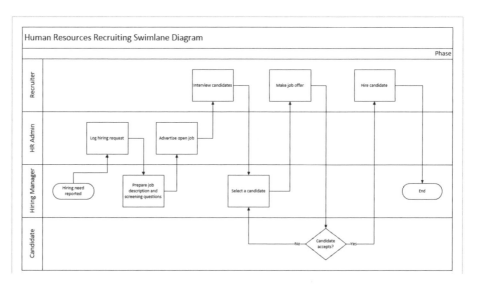

Human Resources Recruiting Swimlane Diagram

Phase

Recruiter: Interview candidates · Make job offer · Hire candidate

HR Admin: Log hiring request · Advertise open job

Hiring Manager: Hiring need reported · Prepare job description and screening questions · Select a candidate · End

Candidate: Candidate accepts? — No — Yes

✕ CLEAN UP **Save the drawing as *HR Recruiting Swimlane*, and then close it.**

One final note about the Visio 2013 take on cross-functional flowcharts: although the end result looks very much as it has in previous versions of Visio, the underlying structure is very different. In fact, structure is the operative word in the previous sentence. In Visio 2013, each swimlane is a *container*, and the overall framework is a *list*. Containers and lists are key components of Visio 2013 structured diagrams and are described in Chapter 11.

Understanding organization charts

An organization chart is typically used to reflect the structure of an organization by showing who reports to whom. The Visio organization chart solution is based on a hierarchical model in which each employee has one boss. Consequently, it doesn't lend itself to organizations that use a matrix or other nonhierarchical structures. However, it is well-suited for most organizations.

The Visio org chart template that has been part of the product since its earliest days has been totally revamped for Visio 2013 and includes exciting new capabilities based on the concept of styles. Each style, accompanied by six brand-new intelligent shapes, provides a totally new look to Visio organization charts. You can switch between styles with one click in order to try out new looks until you find one you like.

You can further customize Visio 2013 charts with a few additional clicks, because the new org chart shapes take advantage of the enhanced themes and embellishments available in Visio 2013. Visio 2013 organization charts also include a long-requested feature: the ability to import photographs, either one shape at a time or in bulk.

The Visio org chart template is assisted by add-in software that is packaged with Visio. The combination of the two simplifies the creation of org charts by handling nearly all of the sizing and spacing chores when you do things like drop an employee shape on top of a manager shape. In addition, the add-in software includes a wizard that you can use to import organization data from Microsoft Excel or other data sources.

The org chart add-in displays an add-in tab on the Visio ribbon whenever an org chart is the active drawing.

SEE ALSO For more information about add-in tabs, refer to "Understanding tool tabs and add-in tabs" in Chapter 1, "A visual orientation to a visual product."

The Visio 2013 Org Chart tab includes many more buttons that in previous Visio versions, making it easier than ever to modify the layout, style, and spacing of your charts. You also have easy access to import and export features, including the ability to import pictures.

At the screen resolution used for the preceding graphic, all 10 new org chart styles aren't visible without clicking the More button highlighted at the lower right of the Styles pane. With a wide-screen monitor, all 10 styles appear, as shown in the following graphic.

In the sections that follow, you'll create a simple org chart manually and a more complex org chart by importing data from an Excel workbook. You'll also import several dozen photographs and learn how to export org chart data to Excel.

Building organization charts by hand

Although you will use the Organization Chart Wizard in subsequent exercises, it's helpful to understand first how easy it is to create org charts by hand.

When you look in the Business template category, you'll find two org chart templates called *Organization Chart* and *Organization Chart Wizard*. The only difference between them is that the latter automatically starts a wizard when you create a new document. If you should ever select the Organization Chart Wizard template by mistake, just cancel the wizard and continue. If you happen to select the template without the wizard and then decide you want to use it, click the Import button in the Organization Data group on the Org Chart tab.

In this exercise, you'll create a new org chart by dragging shapes onto the page and using the org chart template's auto-positioning features. You'll also enter data for each shape in the chart.

 SET UP **Click the File tab and then click New. Click Categories, click Business, and then double-click the Organization Chart thumbnail. Save the new drawing as *Org Chart by Hand*. Then follow the steps.**

1   Drag the **Executive** shape from the **Belt – Organization Chart Shapes** stencil to the top center of the drawing page.

   TIP The title of the Organization Chart Shapes stencil in Visio 2013 is preceded by the name of the currently selected org chart style. When you start a new drawing, it defaults to the Belt style; consequently, Belt – Organization Chart Shapes is displayed in the title bar.

2   With the shape still selected, type **President**, click the word **Name**, and then type **Magnus Hedlund**.

   TIP Just as the title of the Organization Chart Shapes stencil includes the name of the currently selected org chart style, certain master names in the stencil also include the style name. For example, if you are using the Belt style, the masters include Executive Belt, Manager Belt, and others with similar names.

3   Drag a **Manager** shape onto the **Magnus Hedlund** shape. Then type **Vice President**, click the word **Name**, and then type **Magdalena Karwat**. Notice that the org chart software automatically positions the new shape below the *Hedlund* shape.

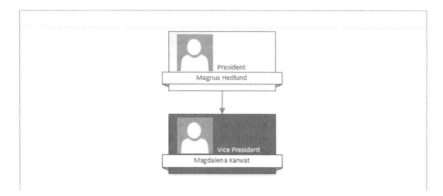

4   Repeat step 3 and notice that the org chart add-in has positioned the second manager shape to the side of the first one. With the new shape still selected, type **Vice President**, click the word **Name**, and then type **Allison Brown**.

5   Drag one more **Manager** shape onto the **Hedlund** shape. Type **Vice President**, click the word **Name**, and then type **Giorgio Veronesi**.

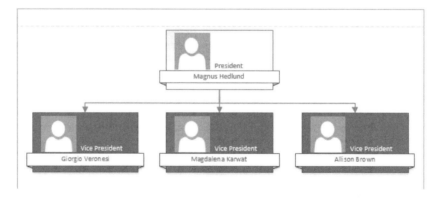

6   Drag a **Position** shape onto the **Giorgio Veronesi** shape, open the **Shape Data** window, and then type **Janet Schorr** into the **Name** field.

SEE ALSO Refer to Chapter 3 for information about opening and using the Shape Data window.

7   Drag a **Position** shape onto the **Giorgio Veronesi** shape, and type **Reina Cabatana** into the **Name** field in the **Shape Data** window.

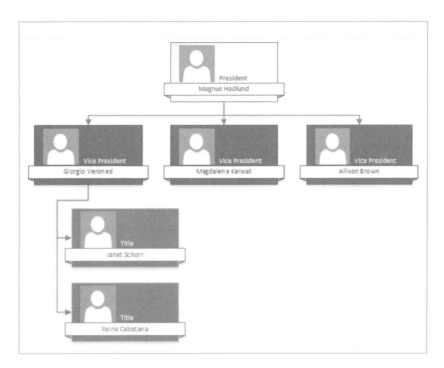

8   Drag the **Three positions** shape onto the **Magdalena Karwat** shape, and use the **Shape Data** window to enter the following names from top to bottom: **Filip Rehorik**, **April Reagan**, and **Scott Rockfeld**.

TIP The Three Positions shape makes it very easy to add three people to the chart at once. Note that there is also a stencil shape called *Multiple Shapes*. When you drop it onto an existing org chart shape, it prompts you to select a shape type and to specify how many of them you'd like to add to the chart.

9   Drag a **Consultant** shape onto the **Allison Brown** shape and enter **Sandeep Kaliyath**.

TIP Notice that the Belt org chart style does not provide any visual differentiation between Consultant and Position shapes. However, the appearance of the Consultant shape is different in other styles as you'll discover later in this exercise.

10   Drag a **Vacancy** shape onto the **Allison Brown** shape and type **Open** as the name. Notice that vacancy shapes do not include a photo placeholder.

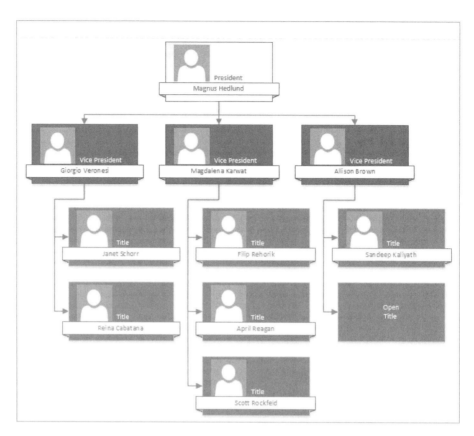

11　Drag an **Assistant** shape onto each of the **Vice President** shapes and type the following names:

	Shape	Shapetext
1	Giorgio Veronesi	Yan Li
2	Magdalena Karwat	Gabe Frost
3	Allison Brown	Erik Rucker

12　Drag an **Assistant** shape onto the **Magnus Hedlund** shape and type **Cassie Hicks** as the name. The org chart add-in has rearranged your drawing to position all of your shapes. Notice that **Assistant** shapes are automatically positioned differently than other subordinate shapes.

At this point, you've built a reasonably sophisticated organization chart by doing little more that dragging shapes and typing text.

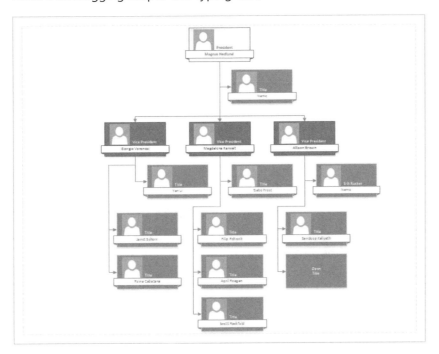

⊗ CLEAN UP **Save your changes to the *Org Chart by Hand* drawing, and then close it.**

TIP Later in this chapter you'll learn how to insert images into the picture placeholders that are included in all of the new org chart styles. However, if you do not plan to include any photos, select all the shapes on the page and then click the Show/Hide button in the Picture group on the Org Chart tab.

As you work with the org chart add-in, you'll find that Visio usually moves existing shapes to accommodate new shapes as you add them to the page. On occasion, however, shapes may overlap. You can resolve the problem by clicking the Re-Layout button in the Layout group on the Org Chart tab. You can also initiate page layout by right-clicking anywhere on the background of an org chart page and then selecting Re-layout from the context menu.

Using the Organization Chart Wizard with existing data

What if you already have your organization data available in electronic form? For example, you might have:

- An Excel workbook that already contains names and reporting information.

- A human resources or Enterprise Resource Planning (ERP) system that can generate an Excel file or a text file.

- Organization data in a Microsoft Exchange Server directory.

- Organization data in a Microsoft Access, dBase, or other database.

In all of those situations, the org chart wizard can help you create your chart.

In this exercise, you'll use data in an Excel workbook to build an organization chart.

SET UP **You need the *Org Chart Data_start* workbook located in the Chapter04 practice file folder to complete this exercise. Then follow the steps.**

1   Start Excel and open the **Org Chart Data_start** workbook so you can look at the data that will be used in this exercise. In particular, notice that there are columns for Name, Title, Reports To, Employee Number, and Extension.

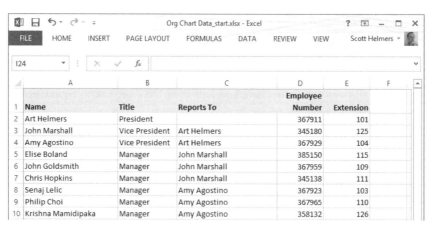

2   Close Excel, and then start Visio.

3   On the **New** page, click **Categories**, click **Business**, and then double-click the **Organization Chart Wizard** thumbnail. The first page of the wizard appears.

TIP If the wizard doesn't appear, simply click the Import button in the Organization Data group on the Org Chart tab.

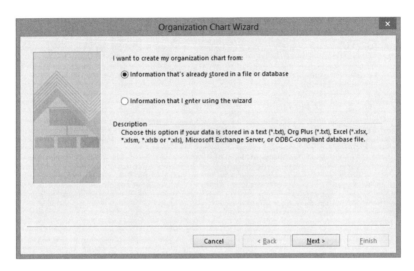

4   Click **Next**. The data source type page appears.

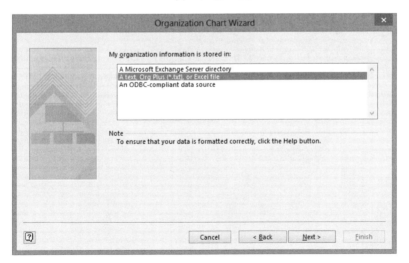

5   Click **A text, Org Plus (*.txt), or Excel file**, and then click **Next**. The file selection page appears.

6   Click the **Browse** button on the file selection page, and then, in the resulting file open dialog box, navigate to the **Org Chart Data_start** workbook that you viewed in step 1. After selecting the correct file, click the **Open** button, which causes the file name you selected to appear in the **Locate the file that contains your organization information** box.

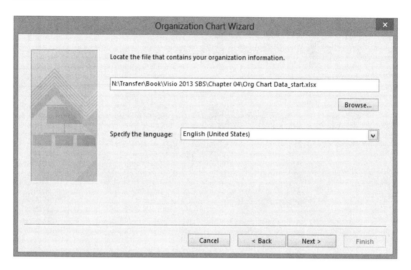

7   Click **Next**. There is a slight pause as Visio opens and reads the data in your spreadsheet.

The Organization Chart Wizard uses the column names, if any, in your spreadsheet to determine which columns hold the name and reporting structure information. It displays the column names that seem to be the best match in the next wizard page.

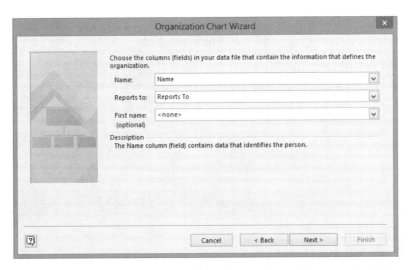

Because the *Org Chart Data* workbook contains columns called *Name* and *Reports To*, the assumptions made by Visio are correct as shown. If the assumptions are not correct, click the arrows to the right of Name and Reports To in order to select the correct columns. Notice you can specify that a separate column contains employees' first names, if that is the case.

8   Click **Next** to display a page where you can indicate which employee data will be displayed on each shape in the chart. The wizard assumes that you want to display the name and title fields, so those fields are preselected on the right side of the page.

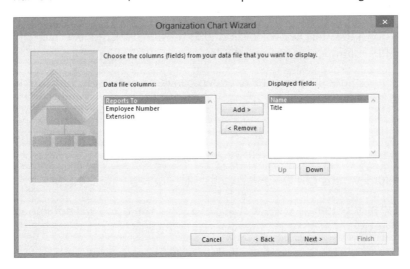

9   In the **Data file columns** section of the page, click **Employee Number**, and then click the **Add** button to move it to the **Displayed fields** section. Finally, click **Next**.

On the wizard page that appears, you determine which spreadsheet data, if any, should be stored in each organization chart shape. This is a separate and unrelated decision from the one on the previous page. You can still display data on the org chart shapes even if you don't store data in the shapes.

TIP The primary reason to store data in org chart shapes is so you can run reports or use the data in other ways without the need to revert to your original data source.

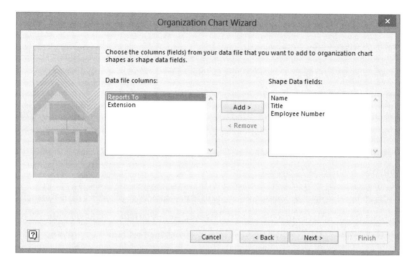

10   Hold down the **Shift** key while clicking **Extension**, which selects everything in the **Data file columns** section, click **Add**, and then click **Next**.

TIP You can use the standard Windows conventions for selecting multiple items in the Data File Columns section:

- Hold down the **Shift** key and click to select everything from the current selection up to and including the item you click.

- Hold down the **Ctrl** key and click to select noncontiguous items.

11   On the picture import page that appears, click **Next**. You will not import pictures in this exercise, but you will in the one that follows.

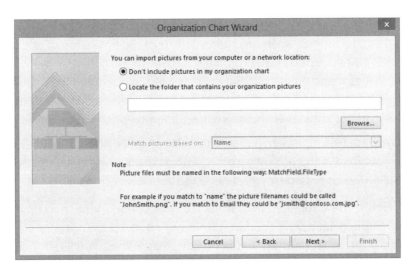

12   On the final wizard page, you can choose among some of the Organization Chart Wizard's powerful layout options.

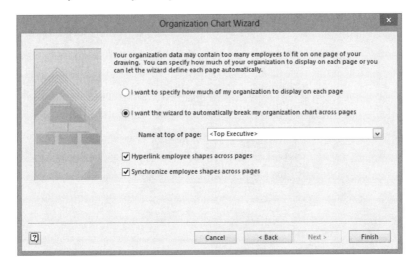

Accepting the default selection of I Want The Wizard To Automatically Break My Organization Chart Across Pages lets the wizard figure out how much to fit on each Visio page. The <Top Executive> option tells Visio to select the person who doesn't report to anyone else as the top shape on the first page of the org chart. If you prefer to select a specific person, such as a department head, you can click the arrow to choose anyone in your list.

Clicking I Want To Specify How Much Of My Organization To Display On Each Page takes you to a wizard page not shown here, and allows you to more directly control how much to fit on each org chart page.

The Hyperlink Employee Shapes Across Pages check box specifies whether the wizard should add hyperlinks when org charts consist of multiple pages. For example, if a manager's direct reports don't fit on the page with the manager, the wizard will leave the Manager shape on the original page and also place it on a subsequent page, along with that manager's direct reports. A check mark in this option tells Visio to add links in both Manager shapes, making page-to-page navigation simpler.

The Synchronize Employee Shapes Across Pages check box also applies to the scenario described in the preceding paragraph. A check mark in this option tells Visio to update the second shape if you change the data in the first one.

13   Click **Finish**. The completed organization chart appears in the Visio drawing window, however, the default style and layout that were applied are not very practical for this particular organization chart. In the exercise that follows, you'll reformat the organization chart using alternate styles and layouts.

> **TIP** Notice that the Belt org chart style uses different shades of color to indicate different position levels in the organizational hierarchy.

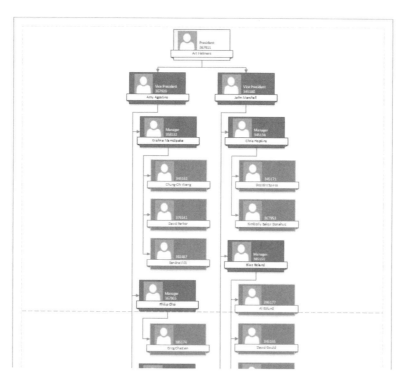

❌ CLEAN UP **Save your drawing as** *Org Chart using Wizard* **and then close it.**

TIP The org chart wizard correctly connects each group of people to its respective boss, but you cannot control where the wizard places people on the page. You can use the buttons in the Arrange group on the Org Chart tab to relocate people and groups after the wizard has created the diagram. However, you can't control how the wizard does the initial placement.

Altering org chart layout and appearance

Whether you create an organization chart manually or automatically using the wizard, you might want to modify the appearance and attributes of the org chart shapes after they're on the page. Previous versions of Visio allowed you to resize org chart rectangles, adjust spacing, and use more than a dozen alternate layouts.

You can still do all of those things with Visio 2013, but you also have the ability to create radically different looking organization charts if you choose. Visio 2013 includes 10 highly varied org chart styles and more than one hundred new theme-compatible shapes. In addition, the Org Chart tab on the Visio ribbon has been redesigned so that many features that were difficult to find in previous versions are now much more accessible.

Layout

You can change the layout of an org chart by using more than a dozen predefined layouts, each of which varies the spacing and connections between shapes. On the Org Chart tab, in the Layout group, click Layout to select from a variety of options.

TIP When the Apply Automatic Layouts to Shape Styles option at the bottom of the layout options list is selected, Visio will re-layout your org chart every time you apply a style. You can retain your current layout when you change styles by clearing the option first.

As an alternative, right-click any shape with subordinates, and then click Arrange Subordinates. Visio opens a dialog box showing all of the built-in layouts.

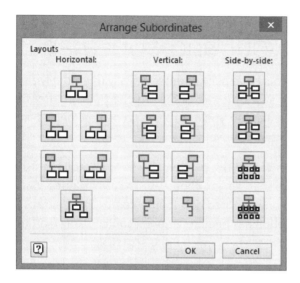

TIP If you don't like the results of any re-layout operation—no matter how radical the changes—you can restore the previous layout with a single undo. Simply type Ctrl+Z or click the Undo button on the *Quick Access Toolbar*.

If you've made manual adjustments to shape position or size, the Re-Layout button, also in the Layout group, will move required shapes to ensure correct positions.

The Best Fit To Page button relocates the entire org chart to better fit on the current page.

Arrange

You rearrange an organization chart by increasing or decreasing the vertical spacing between shapes or groups of shapes using the Spacing buttons in the Arrange group. Also in the Arrange group, the left and right Move arrows change the horizontal spacing.

If you want to hide some sections of your org chart, select an Executive or Manager shape, and then click Show/Hide Subordinates (you can accomplish the same thing by right-clicking a shape and then clicking Show Subordinates or Hide Subordinates). A Manager shape with hidden subordinates displays an icon in the lower–right corner of the shape to indicate their presence.

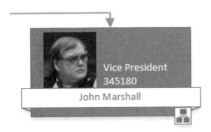

Shapes

The Shapes group contains the Org Chart style gallery that you can use to change the appearance of your chart. From top to bottom, the following graphic shows three of the 10 org chart styles: Belt, Bound, and Stone.

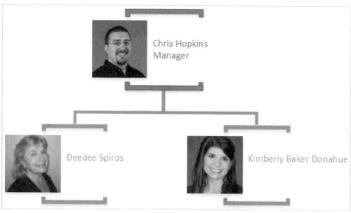

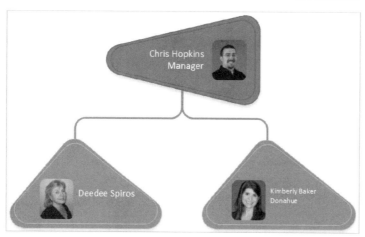

The Shapes group contains buttons that let you adjust the height and width of some or all of the shapes in the org chart; you can select specific shapes to adjust them or click the buttons with no shapes selected to affect all shapes on the page. The final button in the Shapes group lets you convert a shape to a different type of shape, for example, to change a Manager to a Position, or a Vacancy to a Consultant.

Picture

In the following exercise, you'll import photographs during the process of creating a new organization chart. However, that technique is not the only way to manage org chart photos. The Insert button in the Picture group lets you add one or multiple pictures to an existing organization chart. Additional buttons allow you to change, delete, or show/hide an existing picture. All of these functions can also be performed by right-clicking an org chart shape.

4

Themes

Though themes are located on the Design tab and not the Org Chart tab, don't forget that all Visio 2013 org chart shapes were designed to accept theme settings. You can apply any range of colors, effects, and embellishments to create exactly the look you want. The three examples in the following graphic use, from top to bottom, the Bound style and the Whisp theme; the Pip style and the Bubble theme; the Coin style and the Organic theme.

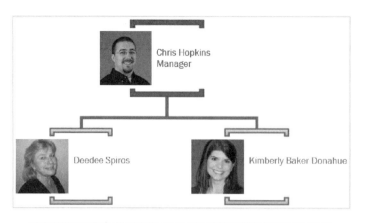

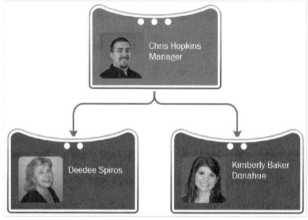

SEE ALSO For more information about Visio themes, refer to "Applying themes to your diagrams" in Chapter 5, "Adding style, color, and themes."

Adding photos and changing styles in org charts

Previous versions of Visio allowed you to insert photographs into organization chart shapes—but only one shape at a time! Visio 2013 allows you to import multiple photographs at once, either into an existing org chart, or as you create one from externally stored data. In the latter case, you can import photos from a folder on your computer or a server. In addition, if you import organization data from Microsoft Exchange Server, you can import the same photos that people use in their Microsoft Outlook profiles.

In this exercise, you'll create an org chart using data from Excel and will import photographs at the same time. You will also use styles to change the appearance and layout of your org chart.

4

 SET UP **You need the *Org Chart Data_start* workbook located in the Chapter04 practice file folder to complete this exercise. You also need the Photos folder contained within the Chapter04 practice file folder. Start Visio if it's not already running. Then follow the steps.**

> **IMPORTANT** Some of the steps in this exercise are based on the specific placement of shapes using the US Units version of the Org Chart template. If you are using the Metric version of the template, you may need to make small adjustments in the exercise steps.

1   Repeat steps 3 through 10 from the preceding exercise.

2   On the **Picture Import** page, click the **Locate the folder that contains your organization pictures** radio button and then use the **Browse** button to navigate to and select the **Photos** folder. After clicking **Open**, the folder name appears in the text box.

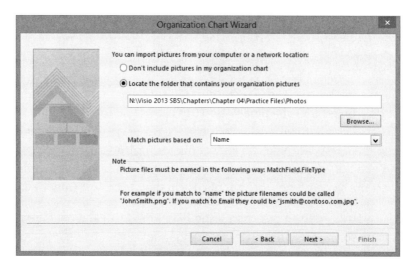

3   Use the arrow to the right of **Match pictures based on** to select **Name**, click **Next**, and then click **Finish** on the final wizard page. The new org chart will look very similar to the one you created in the previous exercise, but this one will contain photographs.

   TIP The image files in the Photos folder are named as described at the bottom of the wizard page in the preceding graphic: each file name includes "FirstnameLastname" and an image file extension ("Firstname Lastname" is also acceptable) and matches a person listed in the Excel data file.

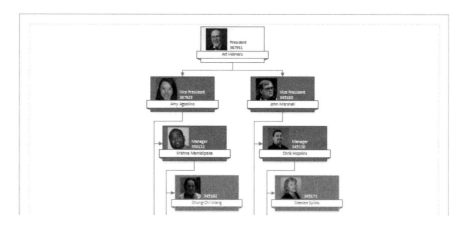

4   On the **Org Chart** tab, in the **Shapes** group, click **Shapetacular** style in the shapes gallery.

       TIP Notice that the Shapetacular org chart style uses both color shades and the geometry of the shape containing the photograph to indicate different position levels in the organizational hierarchy. Each style uses various combinations of shape geometry, fill color, fill gradients, line style, and ornamentation to differentiate position levels.

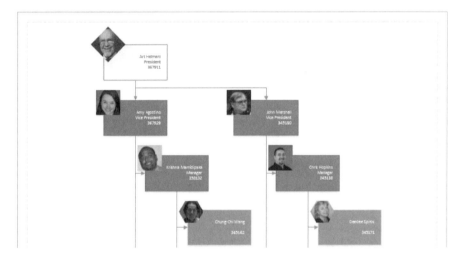

The Shapetacular style highlights the photographs you've imported, but the layout doesn't show very much of the chart.

5   On the **Org Chart** tab, in the **Layout** group, click **Single Top**. Notice that Visio has added new pages automatically to accommodate the new layout.

6   Press **Ctrl+Shift+W** to show the whole page.

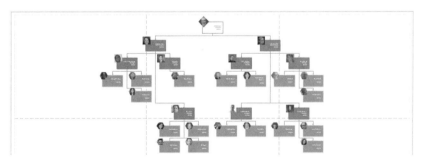

7   Select the **Art Helmers** shape at the top of the page and hold down the **Shift** key while dragging it to the left. (Holding **Shift** while dragging a Visio shape constrains motion to a single direction, either horizontal or vertical.) Position it anywhere near the dashed tile boundary line separating the two upper-leftmost pages. Notice that Visio removes pages that are no longer required.

   TIP Moving an Executive shape also moves all subordinate shapes. The same is true if you relocate a Manager shape.

8   On the **Org Chart** tab, in the **Arrange** group, click **Best Fit to Page**. Visio centers the entire organization chart on the pages.

   TIP You may want to press Ctrl+Shift+W again to center the set of pages in the drawing window.

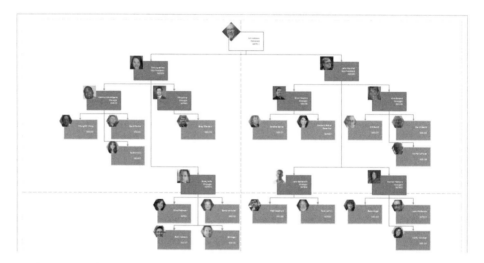

At this point, the organization chart looks reasonably good, but it will require four sheets of paper to print. In the remaining steps of this exercise, you'll use several additional org chart features to position and size the chart to fit the fewest number of sheets. You'll begin with buttons that allow you to reduce either the horizontal or vertical space required for each shape (refer to the following graphic).

9 Ensure that no shapes are selected, and then on the **Org Chart** tab, in the **Shapes** group, click **Decrease the Height** button twice.

10 Select and drag the **Art Helmers** shape upward so the top edge of his photo is at the top margin of the page.

11 On the **Org Chart** tab, in the **Layout** group, click **Re-Layout**. The organization chart now fits comfortably on two printer pages.

12 To finalize your organization chart, drag the **Title/Date** shape from the stencil into the upper-left portion of the drawing page. Double-click the **Company Name** text box and replace *Company Name* with **Trey Research**. The resulting organization chart should look like the following graphic.

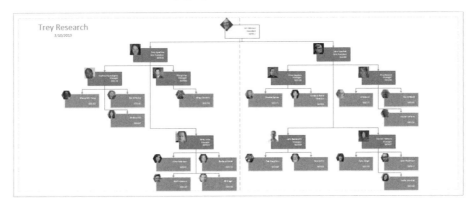

✖ CLEAN UP **Save your drawing as** *Org Chart using Wizard-Photos* **and then close it.**

Depending on the size and position of peoples' heads in the photographs you import into your org chart, you'll find that most are positioned reasonably well within the photo frame provided by the various Visio org chart styles. However, there may be cases where you'll want to reposition the photo. You can do so by selecting the photo, and then on the green Picture Tools Format tab, in the Arrange group, click Crop Tool. A preview of the entire image is displayed and the portions that are outside the photo frame will be grayed out.

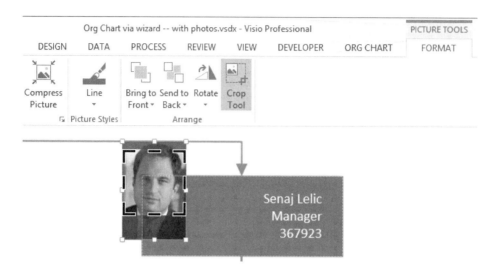

Simply drag the picture to position it the way you want it, and then click outside the picture to complete your changes.

Using the Organization Chart Wizard with new data

If your organization data is not in a format that Visio can read, and you would like to type it into a spreadsheet but don't want to start from scratch, the Organization Chart Wizard can create a preformatted spreadsheet for you.

In this exercise, you'll use the Organization Chart Wizard to create an Excel workbook into which you'll enter your organization data.

 SET UP **Click the File tab, and then click New. Click Categories, click Business, and then double-click the Organization Chart thumbnail. Then follow the steps.**

1   On the first page of the **Organization Chart Wizard**, click **Information that I enter using the wizard**. The description text for this option confirms that you will be creating a new data source.

2   Click **Next**. The **File Type** selection page appears.

3   On the **File Type** selection page, click **Excel**, and then click the **Browse** button. In the resulting dialog box, select a folder in which to save the file, type **Org Chart Data via Wizard** in the **File name** box, and then click the **Save** button. The selected file name appears in the **New file name** box.

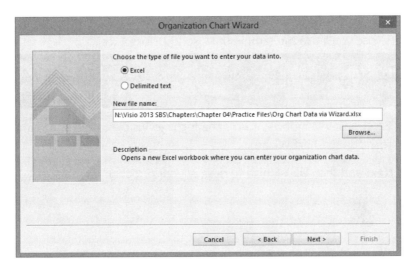

4 Click **Next**. Visio instructs you to type your data over the sample data provided in the Excel workbook it has created.

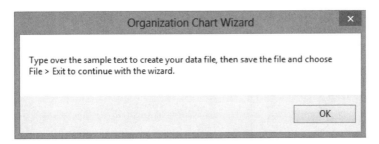

5 Click **OK**. Excel opens to display the formatted workbook. As shown in the following graphic, each column heading includes a comment with instructions for entering data in that column.

6   Ordinarily, you would type your data into the worksheet at this point; however, for this exercise you'll use the sample data, so just close Excel.

> **IMPORTANT** Closing the worksheet isn't sufficient; you must close the Excel application.

After Excel closes, Windows returns the focus to Visio and the photo import page of the Organization Chart Wizard.

7   Click **Next** and then click **Finish** to display your org chart.

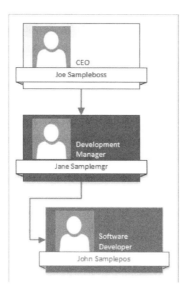

⊗ CLEAN UP **Save the sample file if you want to keep it.**

In the preceding exercise, you created an org chart by typing data into Excel. What if you prefer to start by dragging and dropping shapes, yet you still want to work with an external data source? Consider using an approach that combines things you've learned in this and the preceding sections of this chapter:

- Drag and drop org chart shapes as you did in "Building organization charts by hand."

- Export the data to Excel as you did in the exercise in this section.

- Add and edit the data in your Excel workbook to fill out your organization's details.

- Create a new org chart from the data in Excel as you did in "Using the Organization Chart Wizard with existing data."

- Repeat as needed.

An unconventional use for organization charts

Occasionally, you find a use for a Visio template that its designers might not have envisioned. The author of this book and another Visio expert did exactly that with the Organization Chart Wizard by using it to display the folder structure on a Windows computer. After all, groups of people and folders on a disk drive are both organized hierarchically, so it seemed like a logical thing to do.

SEE ALSO To read an article about viewing the Windows disk drive as an "organization chart," go to *www.experts-exchange.com/viewArticle.jsp?articleID=2802.*

4

Key points

- Creating flowcharts is one of the most common uses for Visio. The built-in templates make it very easy for you to create both conventional flowcharts and swimlane diagrams.

- Swimlane diagrams, also known as cross-functional flowcharts, offer one key advantage over regular flowcharts: each process step resides in a swimlane that identifies which role, department, or function is responsible for that step.

- You can create organization charts manually by dragging shapes from the org chart stencil onto the drawing page.

- The Organization Chart Wizard automates most of the creation of org charts by letting you import data from Excel spreadsheets, text files, and databases. In addition, the wizard can provide you with a preformatted spreadsheet that you can use to enter your organization's data prior to running the wizard.

- Visio 2013 lets you import photographs while building an org chart. You can also import either a single photo or a folder full of photos into an existing chart.

Chapter at a Glance

Align

Align and space shapes,
page 204

Apply

Apply themes, variants and quick styles,
page 212

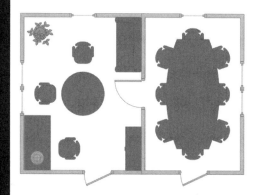

Add

Add theme effects,
page 228

Apply

Apply line styles and colors,
page 231

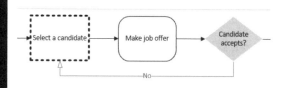

IN THIS CHAPTER, YOU WILL LEARN HOW TO

- Align and space shapes with and without the Auto Align & Space feature.

- Apply themes, variants, and quick styles to your diagrams.

- Customize themes and set theme options.

- Apply fill colors, patterns, line styles, and colors.

- Set glow, reflection, and other effects.

- Use the Format Painter.

In Chapter 4, "Creating flowcharts and organization charts," you created flowcharts, swim-lane diagrams, and organization charts. They were functional and, perhaps, moderately pleasing to the eye, but you might have wanted to make them more attractive.

In this chapter, you'll enhance your diagrams by aligning and spacing shapes. You will also add style and aesthetic appeal by applying themes, variants and Quick Styles. Even if you've used themes in Microsoft Visio 2010 or Visio 2007, you'll find that Visio 2013 themes are much more advanced and capable, although they are just as easy to use. After applying themes, you'll continue your enhancements by adding glows, reflections, and other effects. Finally, you'll apply specific colors and patterns, which you'll also copy using the Format Painter.

PRACTICE FILES To complete the exercises in this chapter, you need the practice files contained in the Chapter05 practice file folder. For more information, see "Downloading the practice files" in this book's Introduction.

Aligning and spacing shapes

Parents and teachers often admonish children by saying, "Neatness counts!" Although children tire of hearing that phrase, neatness is an important factor when you create Visio drawings. It is remarkable how much more effective your diagram can be if the viewer isn't distracted by lines that cross unnecessarily or shapes that are almost, but not quite, aligned.

Chapter 1, "A visual orientation to a visual product," and Chapter 2, "Creating a new diagram," explored many of the ways that Visio helps you create neat drawings—rulers, guides, the dynamic grid—so that you can position, drag, and nudge individual shapes in any way you'd like. However, Visio includes additional tools that make it easy to position and align multiple shapes at once.

What's on top?

When you drop shapes onto a Visio drawing page, their horizontal (X-axis) and vertical (Y-axis) positions are obvious. Less obvious is each shape's position on the Z-axis. You see evidence of the placement on the Z-axis when shapes on a page overlap each other; some shapes appear to be "in front of" or "behind" other shapes.

Even when shapes are not on top of each other, however, Visio keeps track of the **Z-order**, that is, the position of each shape along the Z-axis. The first shape you drop on a page is at the back, and every subsequent shape you add is one step in front of the previous one. If you're in doubt, try the following experiment:

1. Drop three shapes in separate parts of the drawing page so none of the shapes are touching.

2. Drag the second shape you dropped so it partially overlaps the third. Notice that it appears behind the third shape.

3. Drag the first shape so it overlaps part of the second and part of the third. The first shape will maintain its Z-order and appear behind the other two.

You can alter the Z-order of any shape or shapes by using the Bring to Front or Send To Back buttons in the Arrange group on the Home tab. You can also right-click a shape and select Bring To Front or Send To Back from the Mini Toolbar.

TIP The buttons on both the Home tab and the Mini Toolbar move the shape(s) the full distance in one direction. However, they also offer drop-down menus that include Bring Forward and Send Backward buttons to move one step at a time.

In this exercise, you'll work with several valuable Visio tools that align and distribute shapes on the drawing page. After creating a collection of randomly placed shapes, you'll rearrange them into neat rows and columns without dragging a single shape.

SET UP **Click the File tab and then click New. Click Categories, click Flowchart, and then double-click the Basic Flowchart thumbnail. Save the new drawing as** *Align and Space BEFORE.* **Then follow the steps.**

1 Drag four **Process** shapes into a row but deliberately space them very irregularly and don't align them with each other. Repeat with four additional shapes in a second row. Finally, drag the resize handles so some shapes are wider or narrower than others.

   TIP Your diagram doesn't need to look exactly like the one shown here, but this is an example of the type of "messy diagram" you should create.

   Your first task is to rearrange the shapes in the upper row so they are vertically aligned.

2 Draw a bounding box around the shapes in the top row.

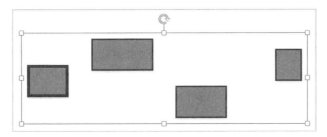

IMPORTANT The leftmost shape in the previous graphic has a bolder selection outline than the others. This is the shape Visio will use as the *anchor shape* for the operations you'll perform in this exercise. Just as its name suggests, the anchor will stay in place— the other shapes will move relative to it.

It's important to notice which shape is the anchor, because the results can be very different with different anchor shapes. For that reason, it's also important to understand how Visio selects the anchor shape so you can change it if you want to:

▪ If you use a bounding box or another technique to select multiple shapes at once, the anchor will be the shape that is farthest to the back. This will usually be the shape that you placed on the page first unless you have changed the Z-order by using the **Send Backward** or **Send Forward** functions.

▪ You can override the Z-order by manually selecting multiple shapes: hold down the **Shift** key and click a series of shapes. The anchor shape will be the first shape you select.

3   On the **Home** tab, in the **Arrange** group, click the **Align** button, and then point to a series of entries on the menu to observe the Live Preview results. For example, point to **Align Left**, **Align Center**, and then **Align Right** to see shapes aligned along their left edges, centers, or right edges.

When you point to either **Auto Align** or **Align Middle**, the preview shows the desired result, so you can click either entry.

TIP If you want to prove to yourself that your choice of anchor shape does make a difference, try this experiment: Undo the alignment action so the shapes in the top row are back where they started; click any shape so it will be the anchor; hold down Shift and click the remaining shapes in the row; align the shapes. The result is that the row has been aligned to your chosen anchor.

4   Repeat step 3 with the second row, using **Align Middle**.

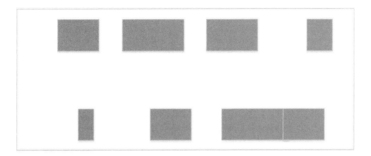

Now that the vertical alignment looks better, you can correct the irregular spacing between shapes.

5   Select all of the shapes in the top row. Then on the **Home** tab, in the **Arrange** group, click the **Position** button. In the **Space Shapes** section of the menu, point to (but don't click) **Auto Space**. Note that Visio leaves the anchor shape in place and arranges the remaining shapes so the distance between the edges of each pair of shapes is identical.

6   Although **Auto Space** can be useful in many situations, in this case, click **Distribute Horizontally**. Though **Auto Space** leaves only the anchor shape in place when it sets equal spacing between pairs of shapes, **Distribute Horizontally** leaves the two outermost shapes in place prior to adjusting the inter-shape spacing.

7   Select the leftmost shape in the top row. Then hold down the **Shift** key and click the leftmost shape in the bottom row.

8   Right-click either of the selected shapes, click the **Align** button, and then click **Align Center**.

TIP The Visio 2013 Mini Toolbar includes a button for Align but not for Position; the Position button exists only in the Arrange group on the Home tab.

9   Hold down **Shift** and click the next shape to the right in each row, and then repeat step 8.

KEYBOARD SHORTCUT In Visio, you can press F4 to repeat the previous operation. For example, after clicking Align Center in step 8, you can complete steps 9 and 10 by selecting a pair of shapes and then pressing F4 to align them.

10 Use the same technique to align the third and fourth pair of shapes in each row.

⊗ CLEAN UP **Save your modified drawing as *Align and Space AFTER* and close it.**

In this exercise, you arranged the shapes on the page by using Align Middle and Distribute Horizontally. You may find it worthwhile to experiment with other align and distribute options so you understand the full range of choices provided by Visio.

Using the Auto Align & Space feature

After completing the preceding exercise, you might be wondering, "Isn't there an easier way to arrange the shapes on a page?" The answer, in many cases, is yes. Visio 2013 includes a powerful Auto Align & Space feature that makes a best effort to position the shapes in your drawing for you.

In this exercise, you'll use the flowchart you created in Chapter 4 to better understand the Visio 2013 auto-arrange features.

➡ SET UP **You need the *HR Recruiting FlowchartA_start* drawing located in the Chapter05 practice file folder to complete this exercise. Open the drawing in Visio. Then follow the steps.**

1   Move various shapes around to make the flowchart less understandable. The graphic below shows one "messy diagram" arrangement.

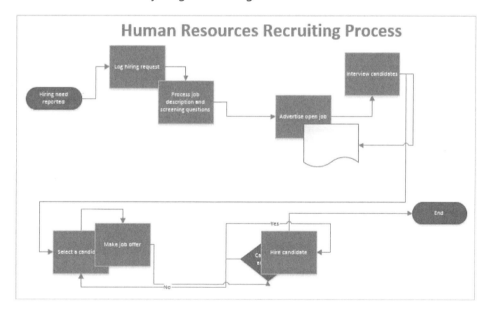

2 On the **Home** tab, in the **Arrange** group, click the **Position** button, and then click **Auto Align & Space**.

TIP If you want Visio to arrange all the shapes on the page, ensure that nothing is selected before you click the Auto Align & Space button. If any shapes are selected when you invoke the Auto Align & Space command, only those shapes will be affected.

The auto-arrange feature made a significant improvement in the diagram, although you may still want to do some fine tuning, for example, aligning the End shape with the second row.

It's important to understand that the results you achieve using Auto Align & Space are closely tied to the location of each shape on the page before you click the button. Sometimes, if you move just one shape a short distance before clicking Auto Align & Space, you will get very different results. Consequently, if your Auto Align & Space results are not satisfactory, press Ctrl+Z to undo the operation, move a shape or two, and try again. Live Preview is also extremely helpful for viewing the results before you commit.

❌ CLEAN UP **Close the Visio drawing; it is not necessary to save it first.**

What other arrangements are possible?

In addition to the spacing and distribution functions you used in the preceding exercises, Visio offers other auto-arrange options.

If you would like to see how these other options work, open the *Align and Space_Start* drawing in the Chapter05 practice file folder. Select all shapes in the top row. On the Home tab, in the Arrange group, click the Position button, and then click More Distribute Options. The Distribute Shapes dialog box that opens may take a moment to understand but does provide multiple options for horizontal and vertical spacing.

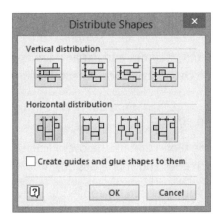

You can change the vertical and horizontal spacing used by any Visio auto-arrange options from the Spacing Options dialog box. To open this dialog box, on the Home tab, in the Arrange group, click Position, and then click Spacing Options.

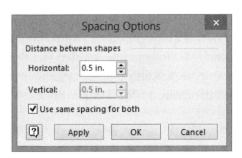

Applying themes, variants, and Quick Styles to your diagrams

Microsoft introduced the idea of themes in Visio 2007 and made them even easier to use in Visio 2010 with the introduction of *Live Preview*.

In Visio 2013, the theme concept has been completely redesigned. Although there are many similarities to themes from Visio 2010, you can use the new themes to create a much broader range of diagram looks. You can assign themes that utilize simple shapes with minimal color and ornamentation, or you can choose themes that incorporate bright, bold, colorful designs, in which shapes are embellished with reflections, glows, and other special effects. And themes are so easy to use that you can try out multiple looks in a matter of seconds.

There are three levels in the Visio 2013 design hierarchy; themes and variants are applied to all shapes on a page or all pages in a diagram, while Quick Styles only affect the currently selected shape(s).

- *Theme* A coordinated set of colors, fonts, and *effects*.

- *Variant* A set of four variations on each theme that maintain the overall character of the theme while providing distinctive color schemes and shape designs.

- *Quick Style* A set of color and style combinations that can be applied to individual shapes while still maintaining the essential nature of the theme and variant you've selected.

Themes, variants and Quick Styles are all supported by Live Preview so you can try a new look before committing to the change.

Hundreds of Visio 2013 shapes have been redesigned to take advantage of the new theming concepts. For example, the generations-old network and computer shapes from previous Visio versions now look modern and fresh and react fully to themes. Org charts shapes, in addition to offering their own new and unique styles, are also theme compatible. Even flowchart shapes and the shapes you create with the *Drawing Tools* display theme colors and effects.

Many of the redesigned shapes consist of multiple subshapes that take on different accent colors within a theme. When you apply themes that are primarily monochromatic, such shapes have a uniform appearance. But when you select themes that employ varied accent colors, you can create skillfully accented diagrams.

In this exercise, you'll create a new type of diagram—an office plan—and then use it to work with themes, variants and Quick Styles.

➡️ SET UP **Start Visio, or if it's already running, click the File tab and then click New. Click Categories, click Maps and Floor Plans, and then double-click the Office Layout thumbnail. Save the new drawing as *Office Plan with themes*. Then follow the steps.**

1   Drag a **Room** shape from the **Walls, Door and Windows** stencil and position it in the upper-left corner of the drawing page. Drag the resize handles so the room is 11 feet wide and 14 feet high (3350 mm by 4300 mm).

      TIP You can set the width, length, or height of most floor plan shapes via their shape data fields, which is often easier than trying to drag a shape to an exact dimension. Simply open the Shape Data window and then type your desired size into one of the appropriate fields. You can type just a number and Visio will apply the default units, or you can type a number followed by an abbreviation, such as ft, in, m, cm, mm to use any units you'd like.

2   Drag a second **Room** shape and position it to the right of the first one so the interior walls are aligned, and then resize the room to be 9 feet wide by 14 feet high (2700 mm by 4300 mm).

3   Drag and position the following shapes in the room on the left:

      ▪ From the **Office Furniture** stencil: **Desk**, three **Desk chairs**, **Lateral file**, **2 seat sofa**

      ▪ From the **Office Accessories** stencil: **Large plant**, **Table lamp** (place on desk)

4 From the **Office Furniture** stencil, drag a **Multi-chair boat** shape into the right-hand room. Feel free to add windows and doors from the **Walls, Door and Windows** stencil if you'd like. Your room arrangement may look something like the following graphic.

5 On the **Design** tab, in the **Themes** group, click the **More** button at the right end of the **Themes** gallery, then point to various theme icons to see the results. The graphics below illustrate four examples of themes with differing characteristics. In the upper left, **Clouds** uses solid fills in some shapes and features gradients in other shapes; **Whisp**, on the right, employs bold, solid fills throughout, but relies on contrasting colors for things like walls. In **Prominence**, on the left in the lower row, the walls and shape borders are more pronounced while the shapes themselves have white fill. **Facet**, in the lower right, features bold, diagonal gradients in selected shapes.

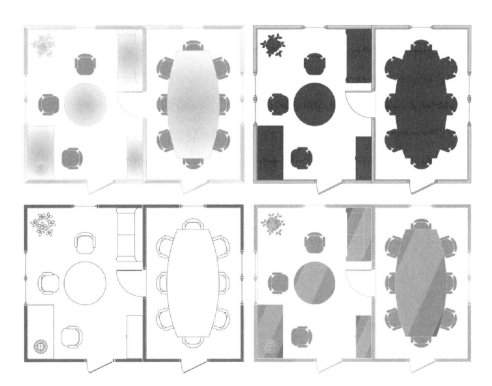

6   On the **Design** tab, in the **Variants** group, click the **More** button at the right end of the **Variants** gallery, then point to various variant icons to see the results. The following graphics feature Variant 3 for the same four themes shown in the preceding graphic. Notice how easy it is to select a variant that changes the character of the office layout by emphasizing certain shape types while reducing the prominence of others.

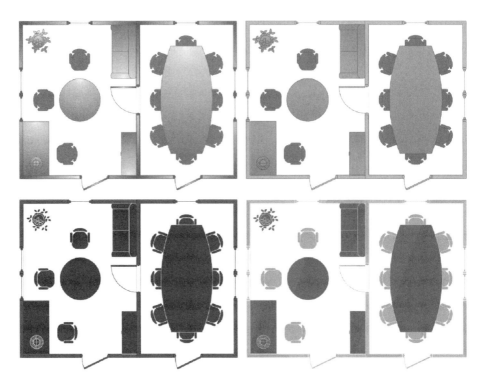

7   Apply the **Clouds** theme to your diagram. Notice that some shapes, such as the desk lamp, are barely visible in this and some other themes.

8   Select the **Desk Lamp** shape.

9   On the **Home** tab, in the **Shape Styles** group, click the **Quick Styles** button. The resulting quick styles gallery has two primary sections that allow you to apply special styling to the selected shape(s) rather than to the entire diagram:

-   Four *Variant Styles*.

-   A six-by-seven matrix of *Theme Styles* that provide theme-appropriate color and style alternatives. The rows of the matrix offer style changes that range from subtle to intense; the columns offer variations numbered from one to seven.

    TIP You can also access Quick Styles by clicking the Styles button on the Mini Toolbar that appears when you right-click a shape. However, one aspect of the gallery's appearance is different when you use this technique. The following graphic on the left shows the gallery when opened from the Home tab; the graphic on the right shows a shorter gallery pane with a scroll bar. It's easy to miss the scroll bar and not realize that all of the same choices are available.

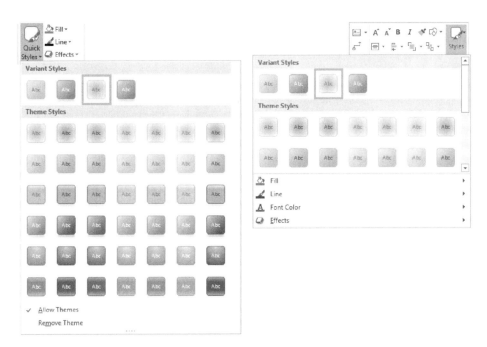

10   In the **Quick Styles** gallery, click **Intense Effect – Aqua, Variant Accent 6** to give the desk lamp a golden color.

     TIP While the columns in the Variants gallery show easily identifiable color differences, realize that each row incorporates different gradients, bevels, and other effects.

11   Apply other themes and variants. Notice that no matter what combination you select, the desk lamp always stands out, because you've assigned a separate style to it. It's important to understand that it does not remain a fixed color—its color changes as you change themes—but it always looks different than the surrounding shapes.

12   Right-click the **Large Plant** shape, click **Styles**, click **Fill** to open the fill colors gallery, and then in the **Standard Colors** section, click **Green**. You have now applied a permanent color to the plant shape; it is not affected when you change themes.

     TIP You will learn more about the fill color gallery in the next exercise.

13   Apply other themes and variants to see that the plant always remains the same color. (The following graphic was created using the **Whisp** theme with **Variant 2**.

     TIP With a shape like the plant, you may also want to set a fixed line color, because some themes apply line colors that you may not want.

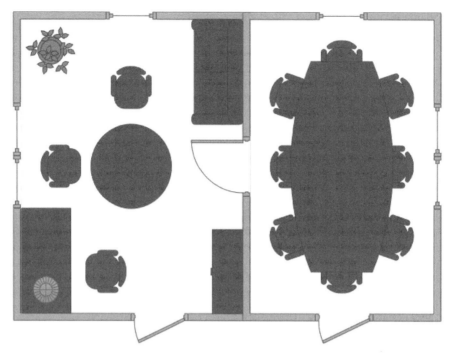

CLEAN UP Save your changes to the *Office Plan with themes* drawing and close it.

Customizing themes

In the preceding exercise, you learned how to use the "out of the box" themes, variants and Quick Styles. In Visio 2013, you can also create your own themes: the theming structure is modular and flexible, allowing you to apply your own choices of colors and effects to create custom themes.

To create a custom theme, on the Design tab, in the Variants group, click the More button in the lower-right corner of the Variants gallery.

More button

- Click **Colors** to choose either a predefined color set or to design your own color scheme by clicking **Create New Theme Colors** at the bottom of the gallery. If you choose to create your own set of colors, Visio presents a dialog box in which you select accent colors as well as colors for text on light and dark fills and an overall shape background color (below, left). Your custom color set will appear under the **Custom** heading in the **Color** gallery (below, right).

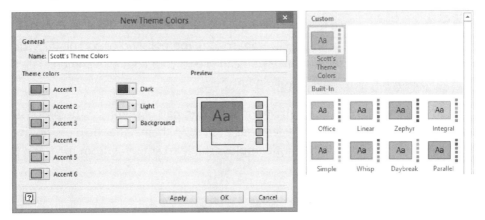

- Click **Effects** to select one of 26 theme effects.
- Click **Connectors** to apply one of 26 styles to a *dynamic connector*.

The Color gallery is on the left in the following graphic; the Effects gallery is in the center; the Connectors gallery is on the right.

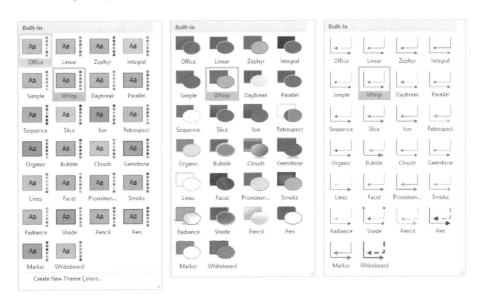

Although it is not shown in the preceding graphic, you can also set the *Embellishment* level.

TIP Creating a custom color set disables Variants, and they will appear grayed out in the Variants gallery.

Hand-drawn themes

Have you ever wanted to show a diagram to an audience in order to get their feedback, but you didn't want the diagram to look too polished or complete? Visio 2013 offers an intriguing set of themes you can use so your audience immediately understands that the drawing is a work in progress.

Compare the network diagrams in the following pair of graphics. The professional, finished-looking image on the left uses the Whisp theme; the "help me finish the network layout" graphic on the right employs the Marker theme from the Hand Drawn section of the themes gallery.

 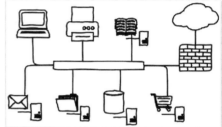

Similarly, the flowchart on the left below appears to be a well-thought out depiction of a company's workflow, while the one on the right begs viewers to help sketch out and refine the process.

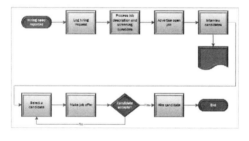 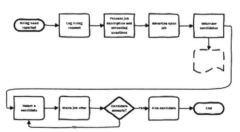

Setting theme options

When you apply a theme, you can apply it to the current page or to all pages in your drawing. The default action when you click the thumbnail for a theme is for Visio to apply it the same way the previous theme was applied. If you're not sure how that was done, right-click the theme thumbnail instead of left-clicking it and you can make an explicit choice from the menu.

You can also choose whether Visio should apply your selected theme to new shapes as they are dropped on the page. You set your preference by selecting or clearing the check box at the bottom of the Themes gallery as shown on the left in the following graphic. If you choose the option to apply a theme to new shapes, Visio also applies your theme settings to the masters in the current stencil; this is shown in the graphic on the right.

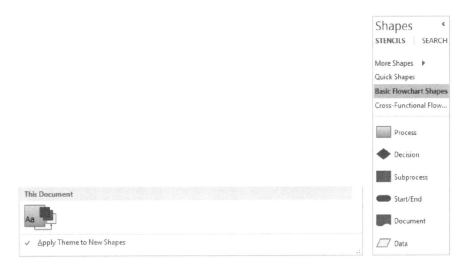

TIP If you want to copy a theme from one Visio drawing to another, merely copy a shape containing the theme from the first drawing and paste it into the second one. You can then delete the shape—the theme will remain behind. Your copied theme will not appear in the Theme gallery but will appear under the Custom heading in the Colors gallery.

You cannot delete the built-in colors, effects, or themes. However, you can delete custom colors sets. To do so, open the theme Colors gallery, right-click the custom color set, and then click Delete.

Applying fill colors and patterns

Visio 2013 themes and effects provide so many options to customize the appearance of your diagrams that you may not need to apply specific fills and patterns as often as in previous versions of the product. However, there may be a time when you need a special color or fill pattern, so the exercise in this section shows you how to apply colors and patterns to shapes. You'll learn about an automatic, data-driven alternative for applying fill colors, called *color by value*, in Chapter 10, "Visualizing your data."

When you need to apply colors and patterns to a small number of shapes, or only need to do it occasionally, two techniques are available: use the Fill button on a shape's right-click menu or click the Fill button on the Home tab. If you used either Fill button in Visio 2010, you should know that their locations have changed slightly.

- When you right-click a shape, click the **Styles** button on the Mini Toolbar to see the **Fill** menu.

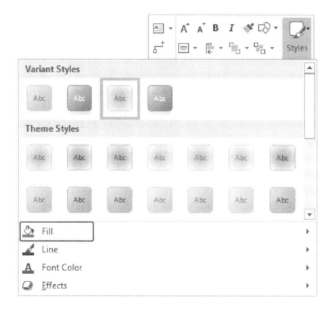

- The **Fill** button on the **Home** tab is located in the **Shape Styles** group.

Visio 2013 introduces a new method for applying styles to shapes that is particularly useful when you want to change the appearance of a series of shapes. The Format Shape window contains everything you need for altering shapes and is accessible by clicking Fill Options at the bottom of the Fill menu, or by right-clicking a shape and then clicking Format Shape. The following graphics show three Format Shape window options that you'll use in this exercise for changing fills: solid, gradient (new in Visio 2013), and pattern. You'll also use the Format Shape window in subsequent exercises to enhance lines and add shape effects.

By the way, the Format Shape window might look familiar—the same window is used for shape formatting in Microsoft PowerPoint and other Microsoft Office 2013 applications.

5

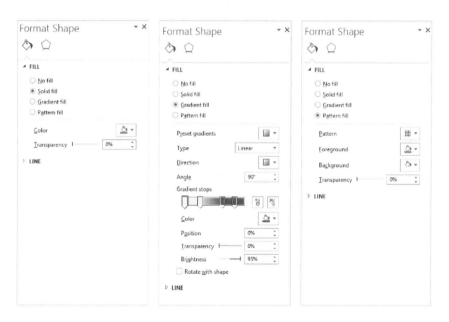

Regardless of the technique you use to open the Fill menu, you can use its color picker to apply a solid fill to selected shapes. The key to taking advantage of the color schemes that are built into themes is to restrict your choices to **theme colors**. To see the distinction between theme colors and other colors, look more closely at the color picker menu shown in the following graphic.

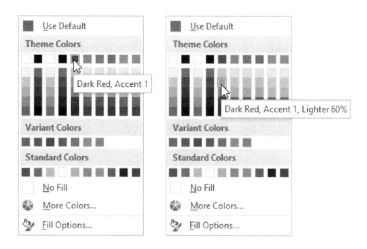

Notice that the color choices are grouped into Theme Colors, Variant Colors, and Standard Colors. If you choose a color from the Theme Colors or Variant Colors section, the fill in your shape will change color as you change themes. However, if you pick a Standard Color or use the More Colors option, you have locked the color of your shape; it will not be affected by themes.

You can use this knowledge to your advantage: set fixed colors in shapes you always want to look the same; set theme colors in shapes you want to look different as you switch themes.

Pointing to any color box in the gallery will display a tooltip with information about that color. For example, the previous left graphic shows a tooltip for Dark Red, *Accent1*, while the graphic on the right shows a shade of the Accent 1 color that is 60% lighter. In general, each column in the Theme Colors section contains a primary color at the top, with lighter or darker shades below.

In this exercise, you'll apply fill colors and patterns to various shapes in a network diagram. You will start by applying a theme color, a variant color, and a standard color so that you can see the result of each as you change themes.

SET UP You need the *Network diagram_start* drawing located in the Chapter05 practice file folder to complete this exercise. Open the diagram in Visio and save it as *Network diagram with colors and patterns*. Then follow the steps.

1   Hold down **Shift** and click the first and third **Server** shapes in the bottom row.

2   Right-click either selected server, on the Mini Toolbar, click **Styles**, and then click **Fill**.

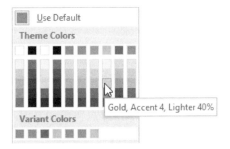

3   In the **Theme Colors** section, click **Gold, Accent 4, Lighter 40%**.

4   Right-click the second **Server** shape in the bottom row, click **Styles**, click **Fill**, and then click **Fill Options** to open the **Format Shape** window. If the **Fill** submenu is not open, click the triangle to the left of the word Fill to open it.

Now that you've opened the Format Shape window, you will use it for the rest of the formatting steps in this exercise.

5   In the **Fill** section, click **Solid fill**, click the **Fill Color** button to open the **Color Picker**, and then in the **Variant Colors** section, click **Blue-Gray, Variant Accent 3**.

6   Select the **Laptop** shape in the upper row; with **Solid Fill** still selected, click the **Fill Color** button and then in the **Standard Colors** section click **Green**.

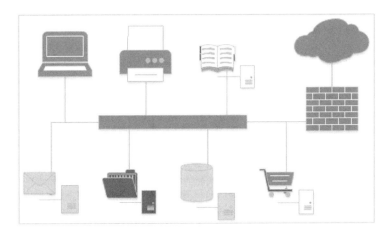

7   On the **Design** tab, in the **Themes** group, click the **More** button at the right end of the **Themes** gallery, then point to various theme icons to view the results. The three shapes in the bottom row that you changed will take on new colors while the laptop computer will retain its green color.

8   Select the **Cloud** shape in the upper-right corner of the diagram, and then in the **Format Shape** window, click **Gradient fill**. Visio applies a multi-stop gradient, a new feature in Visio 2013.

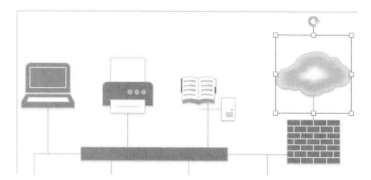

TIP The Format Shape window provides many ways to configure and fine tune gradient settings. You can select preset gradients, add and remove gradient stops, apply various colors, transparency, brightness, direction, and much more.

9   In the **Format Shape** window, in the **Gradient stops** section, click the leftmost gradient stop slider, and then apply a light gray color from the **Theme Colors** section of the **Color Picker**. Repeat with the rightmost gradient stop slider.

10   Also in the **Gradient stops** section, click one of the interior gradient stop sliders, click the **Color** button, and then apply the **Blue** color from the **Standard Colors** palette. Repeat with any other interior gradient stops.

11   Move the **Gradient fill** sliders and adjust any other settings until you have a fill pattern that you like. The pattern in the graphic following step 14 is merely representative; yours will look different.

12   Select the **Printer** shape in the upper row of the diagram, and then in the **Format Shape** window, click **Pattern fill**.

13   Click the **Pattern** button, scroll through the many available patterns, and then click
      pattern **5**.

14   Click the **Foreground** button, and in the **Standard Colors** section, click **Dark Red**.

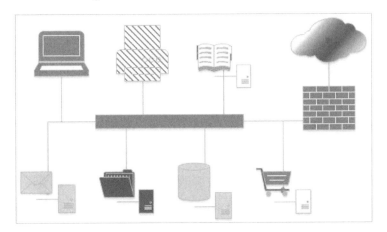

15   On the **Design** tab, open the **Themes** gallery, and in the **Professional** section, click
      the **Ion** thumbnail. Notice which shapes have changed colors with a new theme and
      which have retained a fixed color. Although you aren't likely to use a diagram with
      this crazy of a combination of fills and colors, you should have a good understanding
      of how varied and powerful the shape formatting options in Visio have become.

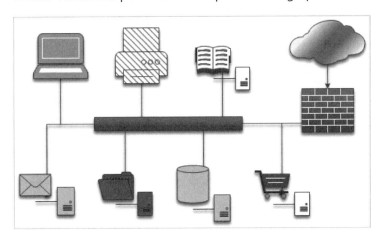

✖ CLEAN UP **Save your changes to the *Network diagram with colors and patterns* drawing and close it.**

Although the preceding exercises have demonstrated multiple ways to select colors from predefined palettes, you still have additional options. If you click More Colors at the bottom of the Fill menu, the Colors dialog box will be displayed with two tabs. The Standard tab lets you click to select from dozens of colors. On the Custom tab, you can use sliders, or you can type specific values, to create colors using the RBG or HSL color schemes.

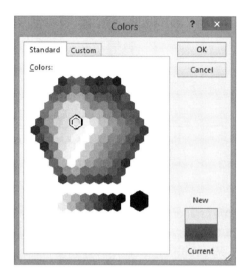
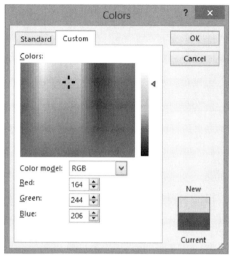

Setting glow, reflection, and other effects

Even after taking advantage of themes, variants, and Quick Styles, and then setting specific colors and fill patterns, there may be occasions when you want something extra. Visio 2013 provides a collection of special effects that can add sophistication or provide extra emphasis to part of your diagram. Some of the effects you will work with in this exercise are used in certain themes, but you can apply them to individual shapes as well.

In this exercise, you'll enhance a flowchart with bevels and reflections, and will call attention to specific shapes using a glow.

 SET UP **You need the *HR Recruiting FlowchartA_start* drawing located in the Chapter05 practice file folder to complete this exercise. Open the diagram in Visio and save it as *HR Recruiting Flowchart with effects*. Then follow the steps.**

1　On the **Design** tab, in the **Themes** group, click the **More** button to open the **Themes** gallery, and then in the **Professional** section, click the **Ion** thumbnail.

2   Press **Ctrl+A** to select all shapes on the page.

3   On the **Home** tab, in the **Shape Styles** group, click **Effects**, point to **Bevel**, and then click the **Hard Edge** thumbnail.

> **TIP** Notice that Live Preview is operating as you point to the Bevels menu in the preceding step, and point to the Glow menu in the following step.

4   Click the **Select a candidate** shape, open the **Effects** menu, point to **Glow**, and then click the **Dark Red, 11 pt glow, Accent color 1** thumbnail.

5

5   On the **Home** tab, in the **Editing** group, click **Select**, and then click **Select by Type**.

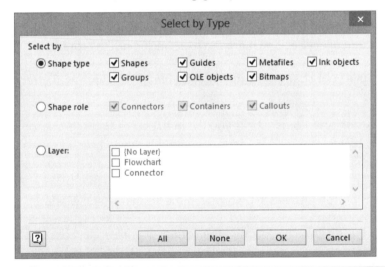

> **IMPORTANT** The goal in the remaining steps in this exercise is to apply a reflection to the flowchart shapes but not to the lines or the text box. You will take advantage of the fact that Visio flowchart shapes are located on a special layer.

> **SEE ALSO** For more information about layers in Visio diagrams, refer to "Understanding layers" in Chapter 3, "Adding sophistication to your drawings."

6   In the **Select by Type** dialog box, click **Layer**, click **Flowchart**, and then click **OK** to select all flowchart shapes on the page.

7   Open the **Effects** menu, point to **Reflection**, and then click **Tight Reflection, 4 pt offset**. You have used Visio effects to turn an ordinary flowchart into one with style and that calls attention to one of the process steps.

You used several effects in the preceding exercise, but you may want to experiment with the additional effects that are available, including 3-D rotation.

✖ CLEAN UP **Save your changes to the *HR Recruiting Flowchart with effects* drawing and close it.**

Applying effects from the Home tab, as you did in the preceding exercise, only gives you access to preset effects. The Format Shape window, which you used in several earlier exercises in this chapter, lets you adjust effect properties with very precise control. The following graphics display several examples. (Notice that the menu entry that is called Bevels on the Home tab Effects button is called 3-D Format in the Format Shape window.)

TIP The Presets button in each section of the Format Shape window displays the same Effects galleries that you used in the preceding exercise. However, there is one important difference: there is no Live Preview in these Presets galleries. If you want to see Live Preview for effects, you need to use the Effects button in the Shape Styles group on the Home tab.

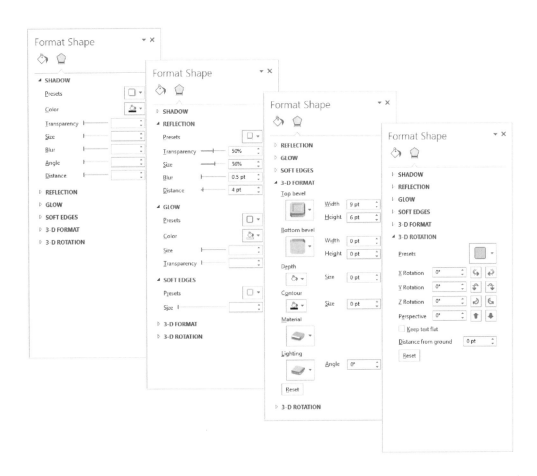

Applying line styles and colors

Now that you have added color, style, and effects to two-dimensional shapes, you can explore line formatting options. Although not quite as exciting visually, line styles can also add value and meaning to your drawings.

In this exercise, you'll alter the types and patterns used for shape borders and connectors. You will also apply line colors.

SET UP You need the *HR Recruiting FlowchartA_start* drawing located in the Chapter05 practice file folder to complete this exercise. Open the diagram in Visio and save it as *HR Recruiting Flowchart with line styles*. Then follow the steps.

1   On the **Design** tab, in the **Themes** group, click the **More** button to open the **Themes** gallery, and then in the **Professional** section, click the **Simple** thumbnail.

2   Right-click the **Select a candidate** shape; on the Mini Toolbar, click **Styles**, click **Line**, point to **Weight**, and then click 2¼ **pt** on the submenu. The selected shape now shows a bold border and the Mini Toolbar remains on the screen.

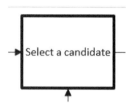

   TIP In this exercise, you'll select line colors and patterns using the Mini Toolbar that is available when you right-click a shape. You can access all of the same functions by clicking the Line button in the Shape Styles group on the Home tab.

3   On the Mini Toolbar, click **Styles**, point to **Dashes** and click the fourth line pattern from the top.

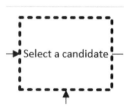

4 Right-click the **Make job offer** shape and then click **Format Shape** to open the
Format Shape window. If the **Line** section isn't already open, click the triangle to
the left of the word Line to open it.

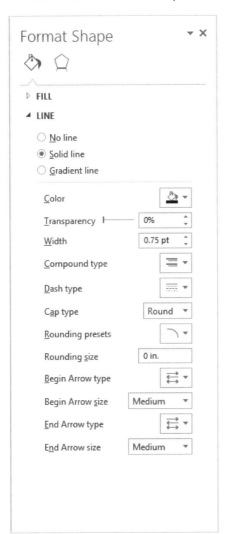

5   In the **Format Shape** window, click **Rounding presets**, and then click the **Small rounding** thumbnail.

6   Click the **Candidate accepts?** Shape; in the **Format Shape** window, and then click **No line**.

7   Because you have turned off the border line, apply a light gray fill color to the **Candidate accepts?** shape to make it more visible.

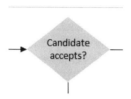

8   Click the line labeled **No;** in the **Format Shape** window, click the **Color** button, and then click **Red, Accent 1** in the **Theme Colors** section. Notice that the line has turned red but the color of the text label has not changed.

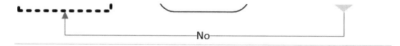

9   Right-click the line labeled **No;** on the Mini Toolbar, click **Styles**, point to **Font Color**, and then click **Red, Accent 1** in the **Theme Colors** section. Both the line and the text are now red. In the remaining steps of this exercise, you'll change the format of the arrowhead.

10   Click the line labeled **No;** in the **Format Shape** window, click the **End Arrow type** button. The current arrow type, number **05**, is highlighted.

11   Scroll down and click arrow style **14**. Be sure to scroll through the amazing selection of arrow end styles both before and after number 14. Your line now has an open-headed arrow, and the bottom row of your flowchart looks like the following graphic.

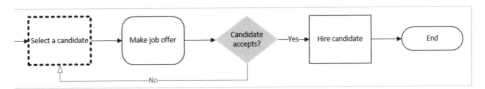

❌ CLEAN UP **Save your changes to the** *HR Recruiting Flowchart with line styles* **drawing but leave it open if you are continuing with the next exercise.**

Using the Format Painter

Like many other applications in the Microsoft Office suite, Visio includes a Format Painter feature, which is an easy way to transfer the formatting from one shape to another. You can copy simple formatting as well as more sophisticated themes, variants and Quick Styles.

In this exercise, you'll copy formatting between shapes.

➡ SET UP **You need the** *HR Recruiting Flowchart with line styles* **drawing for this exercise. Either continue with the open copy from the previous exercise or open the** *HR Recruiting FlowchartB_start* **drawing located in the Chapter05 practice file folder and save it as** *HR Recruiting Flowchart with line styles*. **Then follow the steps.**

1   Right-click the **Candidate accepts?** shape.

2　On the Mini Toolbar, click the **Format Painter** button. The pointer turns black and displays a paintbrush to its right when it is over the page background (in the graphic that follows, this is the image on the left). When you point to a shape, the pointer still displays the paint brush, but the arrow turns white again (the image on the right).

3　Click the **Make job offer** shape so that it takes on the appearance of the selected **Candidate accepts?** shape.

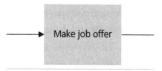

4　Right-click the **Select a candidate** shape, and then double-click the **Format Painter** button. Double-clicking causes the Format Painter to be persistent—you can click several shapes in a row to apply the same style to all of them.

5　Click the **Hire candidate** and **End** shapes once each. Notice that the pointer still shows the **Format Painter** paintbrush, so you can continue to click additional shapes if you want.

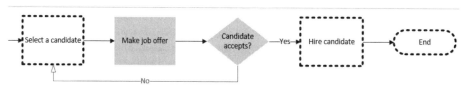

6　Press the **Esc** key to return the pointer to pointer mode.

TIP You can also click either the Format Painter button or the Pointer Tool button to resume normal Visio operation.

❌ CLEAN UP **Save your changes to the *HR Recruiting Flowchart with line styles* drawing and close the drawing.**

Key points

- Visio 2013 includes powerful tools for aligning shapes and setting the spacing between them. Some tools are semi-automated, allowing you to select among various alignment and spacing options. Others are fully automated and attempt to enhance your drawing for you.

- Themes are a powerful way to add visual appeal and professionalism to your diagrams. Each theme is a predesigned collection of colors, patterns, fonts, and styles. Visio 2013 themes range from professional to trendy to hand drawn.

- Variants and Quick Styles let you add your own flair to any theme you select.

- You can apply specific colors to selected shapes, either In addition to, or instead of, using themes. If you want your shapes to retain fixed colors, choose Standard Colors in the color picker; if you want your shapes to adjust to themes settings, use Theme or Variant Colors.

- You can enhance the appearance of shapes by applying any of several dozen predefined fill patterns and line patterns, or you can create your own.

- Visio 2013 offers a range of shape effects that include shadows, reflections, glows, soft edges, 3-D formats (bevels), and 3-D rotation.

5

Chapter at a glance

Edit

Edit shape data,
page 244

Define

Define new shape data fields,
page 256

Link

Link data to shapes,
page 258

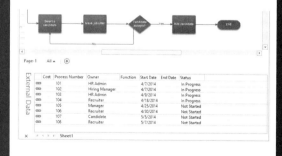

Create

Create a new report,
page 281

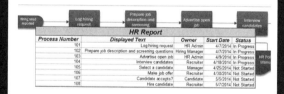

IN THIS CHAPTER, YOU WILL LEARN HOW TO

- Understand, view, and edit shape data.

- View and change shape data attributes.

- Define new shape data fields.

- Link diagrams to external data sources.

- Refresh data in linked diagrams.

- Schedule data refresh.

- Link data to shapes automatically.

- Run a predefined report, create a new report, and modify an existing report.

One of the most significant ways you can add value to your Microsoft Visio drawings is to store relevant data in the shapes on the drawing page. Although this capability has been a part of Visio since the beginning, Visio 2013, like Visio 2010 and Visio 2007, adds a significant level of sophistication to the program's ability to import, store, manipulate, visualize, and report on critical business data.

In this chapter, you will discover ways to make your drawings even more valuable by creating data-driven diagrams. You will learn how to use, create, and edit shape data fields. You will also learn techniques for linking shapes in a Visio drawing to data stored in spreadsheets, databases, and other sources. Finally, you will learn to extract data from a Visio diagram by creating, modifying, and running reports.

PRACTICE FILES To complete the exercises in this chapter, you need the practice files contained in the Chapter06 practice file folder. For more information, see "Downloading the practice files" in this book's Introduction.

Understanding shape data

Many Visio shapes contain data fields, referred to collectively as *shape data*, that you can use to quantify and describe various properties of the shape.

TIP The data fields that are called *shape data* in Visio 2013 were called *Custom Properties* in Visio 2003 and earlier.

Visio 2013 supports eight types of shape data:

- **String** Free-form text

- **Number** Any numeric data; can be restricted to integers or a specific number of decimal places

- **Fixed List** A drop-down list from which users must make a selection; users cannot add additional values to the list

- **Variable List** A drop-down list from which users can make a selection; users can add additional values to the list by typing in the text box

- **Duration** Time value expressed in one of five time units supported by Visio: seconds (es.), minutes (em.), hours (eh.), days (ed.), weeks (ew.); users enter a number followed by one of the time unit abbreviations shown

- **Date** Calendar date; users can either type a date or use a drop-down calendar to select a date

- **Currency** Currency value expressed in currency units based on user's region and language settings in Windows

- **Boolean** True or False

Viewing shape data

To view the shape data for any Visio object, right-click the shape, and click Data, which displays the data submenu. Then click Shape Data on the submenu.

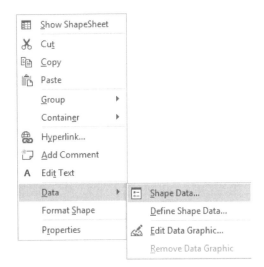

The Shape Data window typically appears somewhere within the main Visio window, usually in whatever position it was located the last time it was opened. The following graphic shows the data associated with a pump/motor 1 shape from the Fluid Power template in the Engineering template that is provided with Visio.

You can position the floating Shape Data window (shown on the left) wherever you would like it. Note that you can also resize the window or dock it in a fixed position by dragging it to any edge of the drawing window (shown in the center).

TIP The pushpin button in the docked window lets you turn AutoHide on or off for the docked window. If you turn AutoHide on, the window "rolls up" into the header when you're not using it (shown on right).

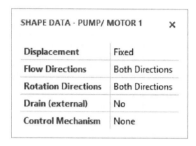
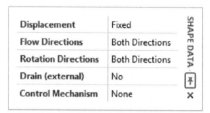

TIP If the Shape Data window is already open when you right-click a shape, clicking Data, and then clicking Shape Data will close it. This may not be what you expect, especially if you didn't notice that the window was already open and can't figure out why it didn't appear.

If you look closely at the following two graphics, you'll notice a subtle difference. It turns out that the Shape Data menu entry is actually a toggle that alternately shows and hides the window. In the graphic on the left, the window is closed so the icon to the left of Shape Data looks normal. However, in the one on the right, the icon is highlighted, indicating that the window is open.

Other ways to view shape data

Because shape data is so vital to Visio diagrams, there are several additional ways to view a shape's data.

When you right-click some shapes, you can click Properties instead of Data. Although the Properties menu entry usually opens the same Shape Data window as the Data submenu technique, in some Visio templates, it opens a Shape Data dialog box instead. Although the dialog box and the window look a bit different, you can edit data in either.

TIP When it is present, the Properties entry is usually at the very bottom of the context menu.

For example, the following Shape Data dialog box for the Fluid Power Pump/Motor 1 was opened by using the Properties menu entry; compare it with the corresponding Shape Data window, shown previously.

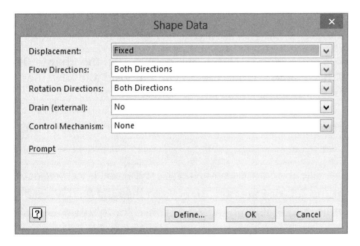

You can also open the Shape Data window from the Visio ribbon. On the Data tab, in the Show/Hide group, select the Shape Data Window check box.

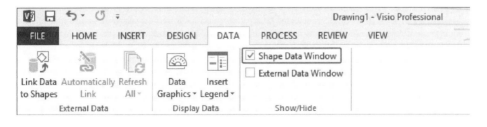

Editing shape data

After you have the Shape Data window open, you can change a shape's data. As you do so, you'll notice that some shape data fields behave differently than others. Visio enforces various rules based on the data type and formatting applied to each shape data field.

SEE ALSO For a list of the shape data types supported by Visio, see "Understanding shape data" earlier in this chapter.

As a simple example, you cannot enter text into a number or currency field. Similarly, Visio prevents you from entering anything other than a number and one of the five valid time unit abbreviations in a duration field.

In this exercise, you will edit some of the data associated with the Human Resources Recruiting Process you worked with in Chapter 4, "Creating flowcharts and organization charts." There are two differences between this map and the one from Chapter 4: the spacing between shapes has been expanded to open up the drawing; and additional shapes have been added to represent a database and several documents.

 SET UP **You need the** *HR Process MapA_start* **drawing located in the Chapter06 practice file folder to complete this exercise. Open the drawing in Visio and save it as** *HR Process Map***. Then open the Shape Data window, and follow the steps.**

1   Click the shape labeled **Log hiring request**. Its data appears in the **Shape Data** window.

2   For an example of data validation based on field type, type **abc** into the **Cost** field. When you press either the **Tab** or **Enter** key to move to the next field, Visio displays an error dialog box, indicating that your entry is not valid for this field, because the **Cost** field expects a currency entry.

Human Resources Recruiting Process

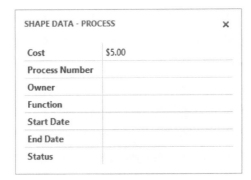

3   Click **OK** to close the error dialog box.

4   Type **5** and then press either the **Tab** or **Enter** key to move to the next field.

SHAPE DATA - PROCESS	
Cost	$5.00
Process Number	
Owner	
Function	
Start Date	
End Date	
Status	

TIP Because the copy of Windows on which these graphics were made uses United States Region and Language settings, the currency amount appears in dollars. Your computer will display currency values based on your regional settings.

5   Type **101** in the **Process Number** field.

6   Press either the **Tab** or **Enter** key to move to the **Owner** field, and then type **John Smith**.

7   Click in the **Start Date** field. Notice that a browse button appears in the right end of the field.

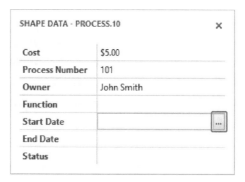

TIP In a Visio date field, you can either type a date or use the calendar field browse button to select a date.

8   Click the calendar field browse button and click a date in the pop-up calendar. The calendar closes and the selected date appears in the **Shape Data** window.

9   Click in the **Status** field. Notice that a down arrow appears in the right end of the field, because this is a Visio list field.

10   Click the arrow to reveal the predefined choices for this list.

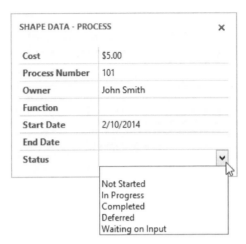

11   Click **In Progress** in the list.

> **TIP** Visio supports two types of list fields: *fixed lists* and *variable lists*. In a fixed
> list field, you must select an entry from the list. In a variable list field, you have the
> option to select one of the list entries, or you can type your own text into the field
> if you prefer. If you type your own text, it gets added to the bottom of the list. The
> Status field in the preceding graphic is an example of a variable list field, so you can
> either select or type an entry in the field.

You can continue to enter or edit data for this process step, or you can select a different shape and edit its data.

✖ CLEAN UP **Save your changes to the *HR Process Map* drawing but leave it open if
you are continuing with the next exercise.**

> **TIP** Though it is not advertised in any obvious way, you can edit data for more than one
> shape at a time. If you select multiple shapes before opening the Shape Data window, the
> changes you make will be applied to *all* selected shapes. This feature can be very powerful
> or very destructive, so it is important to be cautious.

Note that if you do select multiple shapes prior to opening the Shape Data window, the
only visible fields are those fields that all selected shapes have in common, and the values
shown will be those of the *anchor shape* in your selection.

Viewing shape data attributes

When you want to add or edit data fields in a Visio shape, you need to open the Define Shape Data dialog box. To open it, right-click a shape, point to Data, and then click Define Shape Data.

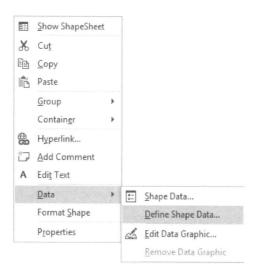

TIP You can also open the Define Shape Data dialog box by right-clicking anywhere in the Shape Data window and then clicking Define Shape Data.

The Define Shape Data dialog box looks like one of the following two samples. The one on the left appears for most Visio users. The one on the right appears if you are running Visio in developer mode, and offers several additional options.

SEE ALSO For information about developer mode, refer to the Appendix.

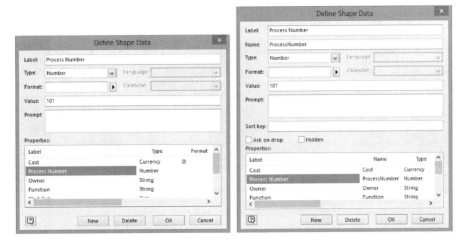

In both variations of the dialog box, notice that each data field has multiple attributes:

- **Label** Field name

- **Type** One of the eight types described in "Understanding shape data" earlier in the chapter

- **Format** Determines how data entered by the user will be presented; different field types have different format options

- **Value** The data value entered when a shape was defined or that was entered by the user

- **Prompt** Tooltip text that appears when the user points to the shape's name in the Shape Data window

In developer mode, the additional attributes that will be displayed are described in the following list. Although some of them are primarily for use by programmers or Visio solution developers, one or two may be of value to power users:

- **Name** An internal name used by Visio developers; can be the same as **Label** except that **Name** cannot contain spaces or most special characters (however, an underscore character is OK).

- **Sort key** Visio uses the alphanumeric value in this field to determine the sequence in which fields will be presented in the **Shape Data** window.

> **IMPORTANT** Visio treats the contents of the Sort key field as text even if you enter a number, which means that it arranges fields based on alphabetic sequence rather than numeric sequence. For example, if field A has a sort key of "1", field B has a sort key of "2", and field C has a sort key value of "10", Visio will place them in the Shape Data window in the sequence A, C, B, because the first character "1" in field C is less than the "2" in field B. To yield a sorted sequence of A, B, C, use sort key values of "01," "02," and "10," respectively.

- **Add on drop** If selected, Visio opens the **Shape Data** dialog box whenever the user drops a shape containing this field onto a page.

- **Hidden** If selected, Visio hides this field; that is, the field does not appear in either the **Shape Data** window or **Shape Data** dialog box. Fields like this are often intended to hide data from all or selected viewers.

TIP The shape data exercises that follow all use the regular Define Shape Data dialog box and not the developer version.

Although it is not advertised in any obvious way, you can create, edit, or delete shape data fields for more than one shape at a time. If you select multiple shapes before opening the Define Shape Data window, the changes you make will be applied to *all* selected shapes. This feature can be very powerful or very destructive, so use it with caution.

Changing shape data attributes

In previous sections of this chapter, you edited shape data and learned about the attributes that comprise each shape data field. In order to appreciate just how flexible and powerful the data features of Visio really are, it's helpful to do two more things: change the attributes of several existing data fields (this exercise), and create new data fields (the following exercise).

In this exercise, you will explore and change the attributes of the data fields in one of the process shapes in the Human Resources Recruiting Process map.

→ SET UP **You need the *HR Process Map* drawing for this exercise. Either continue with the open copy from the previous exercise or open the *HR Process MapB_start* drawing located in the Chapter06 practice file folder and save it as *HR Process Map*. Open the Shape Data window, and then follow the steps.**

1   Click the **Advertise open job** shape to view its shape data. Spend a moment looking at the names of the data fields for this shape.

2   Right-click in the **Shape Data** window, and then click **Define Shape Data** to view the attributes of the first data field, *Cost*. Notice that the **Label** field displays *Cost*, which is the label that appears in the **Shape Data** window. Notice, also, that the **Type** field is set to *Currency*.

3   Click the right-facing arrow next to the **Format** field to view a list of alternate formats in which the currency value can be displayed. (The list that appears depends on the region and language settings for your copy of Windows.) It usually makes sense to leave the format set to **System Setting**, especially if your diagram will be opened in countries that use currencies other than the one you use.

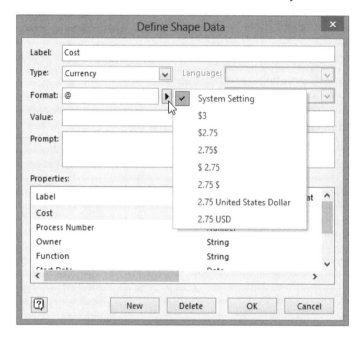

4   Click in the **Value** field and then type **125**. This value will appear as the default value for the **Cost** field the next time you open the **Shape Data** window for this shape. You can still change the value via the **Shape Data** window, but this provides a way for you to specify default values.

5   Type **Enter cost for this process step** into the **Prompt** field. These words will appear as a tooltip for this field later in this exercise.

6 In the **Properties** section of the dialog box, click **Process Number** to view the attributes of this field. Note that this is a *Number*-type field.

7 Click the arrow next to the **Format** field to explore the various formatting options Visio provides for numeric data.

8 Click **Owner** in the **Properties** section of the dialog box. Note that the **Language** field is now enabled, allowing you to specify the preferred language for this text field.

9 Click the arrow next to the **Format** field to explore the various formatting options Visio provides for text data.

10 Click **Start Date** in the **Properties** section of the dialog box. Note that this field has a **Date** type and that the **Language** and **Calendar** attributes are now enabled. These two settings enable you to change properties that affect the presentation of the date.

11 Click the arrow next to the **Format** field to explore the various formatting options Visio provides for date fields.

12 Click **Status** in the **Properties** section of the dialog box. Note that **Status** is a **Variable List**-type field.

The Format field is used quite differently for Variable and Fixed List fields than for the other field types you've explored thus far. For list fields, Format holds a semicolon-separated list of values that will appear in the drop-down list in the Shape Data window.

In the case of the Status field, the Format field holds the following string of characters:

;Not Started;In Progress;Completed;Deferred;Waiting on Input

> **IMPORTANT** The semicolon at the very beginning of the list causes a null (blank) entry to appear at the top of the list. If you do not include a null entry, the user will not be able to leave the field blank after he or she has clicked something in the list. Both options may be appropriate in different situations: in some cases, a blank entry is not acceptable, so you want to force the user to select an entry from the list; in other cases, a blank entry is desirable.

13　Type **;Waiting Manager Approval** at the end of the character string in the **Format** field.

> **IMPORTANT** List entries are delimited by semicolons (";"). Be sure to type the semi-colon before *Waiting Manager Approval* so that the new text becomes a separate entry in the list.

14　Type **In Progress** in the **Value** field.

TIP If you want a value from the list to appear as the default for this field whenever the Shape Data window is opened, type it in the Value field. Be sure that the entry you type exactly matches a list item in the Format field, including upper and lower-case letters.

15　Click **OK** and notice that the **Shape Data** window reflects the changes you made to the fields: there is a default dollar amount in the **Cost** field and the **Status** is preset to *In Progress*.

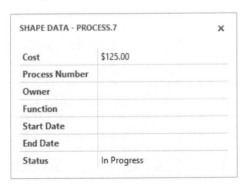

16　Point to the label for the **Cost** field. *Enter cost for this process step* appears as tooltip text because you typed it in the **Prompt** field in step 5 of this procedure.

17   Click in the **Status** field and then click its arrow to display the list. Note that **Waiting Manager Approval** appears at the end of the list.

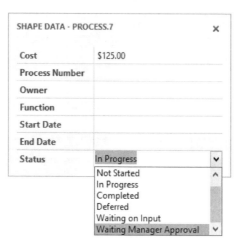

⊗ CLEAN UP **Save your changes to the *HR Process Map* drawing, but leave it open if you are continuing with the next exercise.**

Defining new shape data fields

Now that you have successfully modified data fields for Visio shapes, you are ready to create a new shape data field.

In this exercise, you will add a new field to a shape that already contains other data fields.

➡ SET UP **You need the *HR Process Map* drawing for this exercise. Either continue with the open copy from the previous exercise or open the *HR Process MapC_start* drawing located in the Chapter06 practice file folder and save it as *HR Process Map*. Open the Shape Data window, and then follow the steps.**

1   Click the **Advertise open job** shape, right-click in the **Shape Data** window, and then click **Define Shape Data**.

2   At the bottom of the **Define Shape Data** dialog box, click the **New** button. The focus shifts to the **Label** field, enabling you to type a label for this field.

3   Type **Estimated Duration**.

4   Click the down arrow to the right of **Type**, and then click **Duration**.

5   Click the right arrow next to **Format**.

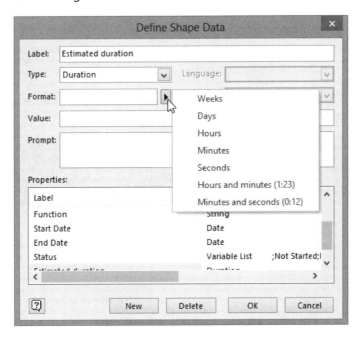

6   Click **Days**.

   TIP You can set the format for a duration field to display the time in any of the standard Visio durations, ranging from seconds to weeks, or you can display the duration in one of the listed time formats.

7   Click **OK** to close the **Define Shape Data** dialog box and return to the **Shape Data** window. Note that the field you created has been added to the bottom of the window.

SHAPE DATA - PROCESS.7	✕
Cost	$125.00
Process Number	
Owner	
Function	
Start Date	
End Date	
Status	In Progress
Estimated Duration	

❌ CLEAN UP **Save your changes to the *HR Process Map* drawing, and then close it.**

TIP In a similar manner that was described at the end of the section titled "Editing shape data" earlier in this chapter, you can add, edit, or delete data fields for more than one shape at a time. To do so, select multiple shapes before opening the Define Shape Data dialog box.

If you select multiple shapes prior to opening the Shape Data window, you will only be able to view the fields that all selected shapes have in common.

IMPORTANT The information in the following section applies only to the Professional edition of Visio 2013. In addition, the data-related features described in this section may not be available while you are using the coauthoring functions of Visio 2013.

Linking diagrams to external data sources

Earlier in this chapter, you learned how to add and edit shape data fields. It's convenient to be able to do so manually, but it's also easy to imagine situations in which you would like to populate your drawings with data from a spreadsheet, database, or other external source.

Prior to Visio 2007, it was possible to link Visio shapes to external data, but it was rather cryptic, somewhat confusing, and the procedures often required programming or at least some technical knowledge.

Microsoft Visio 2007 Professional changed that, and the Professional edition of Visio 2013 includes the same *data linking* facility. In general, there are two steps involved in data linking:

1 Link the diagram to a data source.
2 Link individual shapes to data.

In this exercise, you will perform both steps for the *Human Resources Process Map* drawing using data from the Excel workbook shown in the following figure. Be sure to pay attention to the column headings because you will encounter them during the exercise.

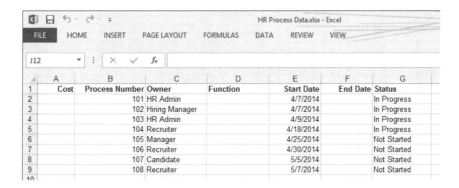

SET UP You need the *HR Process MapD_start* drawing and the *HR Process Data_start* workbook located in the Chapter06 practice file folder to complete this exercise. Open the drawing in Visio and save it as *HR Process Map with data*. Then open the *HR Process Data_start* workbook and save it as *HR Process Data*. Then follow the steps.

1 In Visio, on the **Data** tab, in the **Display Data** group, click the **Data Graphics** button, and then clear the **Apply after Linking Data to Shapes** check box so Visio will not apply any data graphics after you link shapes to data later in this exercise.

SEE ALSO You will learn about data graphics in Chapter 10, "Visualizing your data."

TIP Although you are turning data graphic activation off for this exercise, in many situations, it is valuable to turn it on so you can immediately view the results of your data-linking operation.

2   In Visio, on the **Data** tab, in the **External Data** group, click the **Link Data to Shapes** button. The first page of the **Data Selector** wizard appears.

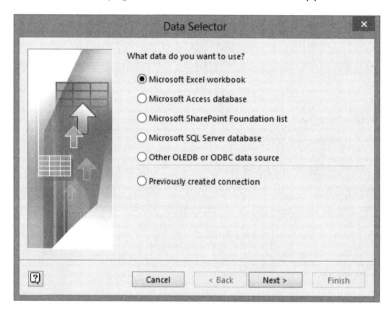

TIP The default data type on the first page of the Data Selector wizard is Microsoft Excel Workbook, which is the one you will use for this exercise. However, notice that you can link to data stored in Microsoft Access, SharePoint, SQL Server, or almost any other database.

3   Click **Next**.

4   On the next **Data Selector** wizard page that appears, click the **Browse** button, and in the resulting file open dialog box, navigate to the **HR Process Data** Excel workbook. After selecting the correct file, click the **Open** button and the file name you selected will appear in the **What Workbook Do You Want To Import?** box.

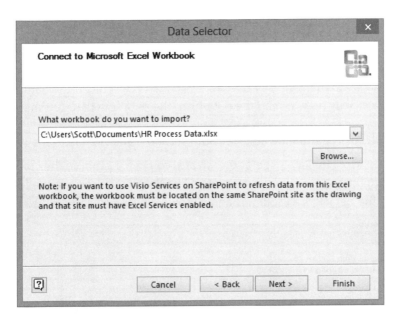

5   Click **Next**.

On this page of the wizard, you can use the What Worksheet Or Range Do You Want To Use? drop-down list box to select the data to which you want to link. The Data Selector wizard usually defaults to the first worksheet in the workbook, which is correct for this exercise.

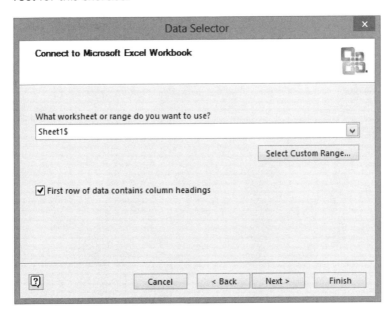

6   Select the **First row of data contains column headings** check box to indicate that the worksheet data includes column headings.

> **TIP** It is very helpful if your Excel workbook contains column headings, and if they match exactly to the names of the shape data fields in Visio. If the names match, Visio will know exactly how to map the data from the data source to the shapes.

7   Click **Next** to accept the defaults for both settings on this page of the wizard.

On the Connect To Data page of the wizard, you can customize the columns and rows from the selected worksheet that will be linked. As shown in the following graphic, the default is all columns and all rows, which works for this exercise.

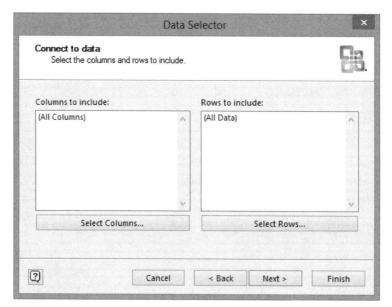

8   Click **Next**.

On this page, Visio recommends a field that appears to uniquely identify each row of data based on its analysis of your data. You can change to a different field if there is a better choice.

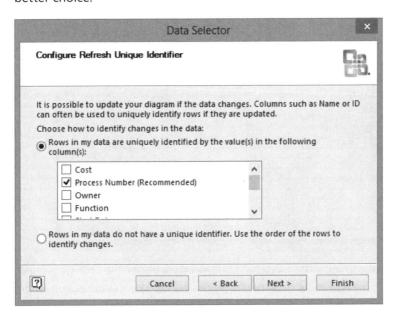

TIP You can select more than one field to constitute the unique ID if a single field is not sufficient.

The guesses Visio makes for the unique ID are generally very good. However, you should always think about the recommendation to determine whether there is a different field or combination of fields that is a better choice.

If your data does not contain a unique value for each row, you can click the option at the bottom of this page of the wizard to signify this, enabling Visio to use the sequence of the rows to identify them. Although this choice will work fine for reasonably stable data sets, be aware that using this option has potentially serious consequences later on if you reorder, add, or delete rows.

9   Click **Next** to display the final page of the wizard.

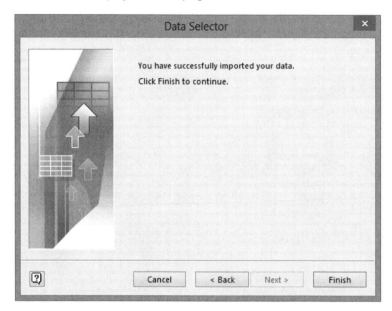

10 Click **Finish** to view the **External Data** window under the **Drawing** pane. The **External Data** window contains one row for each row of data in your spreadsheet.

TIP In this exercise, you will link to only one Excel worksheet. However, it is possible to link a single diagram to more than one data source, whether the sources are all of the same type or consist of a mix of databases, spreadsheets, and SharePoint lists.

TIP You can link a single shape to multiple data sources, for example, some shape data fields can draw their values from a SharePoint list, while other fields in the same shape can replicate data from a SQL database.

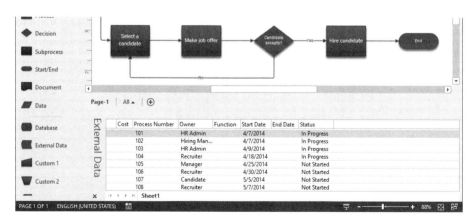

11   Drag data row **101** onto the **Log hiring request** process shape.

As you drag the data row, notice that the pointer appears to be dragging an outline of a shape across the page (graphic on the left). Also, notice that the pointer is accompanied by a plus sign (+). This is the method Visio uses to let you know that you are dragging the data for a specific shape type across the page.

As the mouse pointer moves onto the target shape, the plus sign is replaced by a linking symbol. In addition, the outline shapes take on a thicker, blue border (graphic on the right).

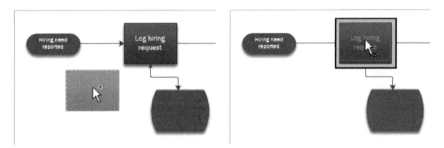

6

TIP If you are dragging a data row onto a shape that is already on the page, as you are in this exercise, it doesn't matter whether the shape under the mouse pointer matches the target shape. Visio will add the data to the existing shape.

In addition to dragging data rows onto existing shapes, you can create new shapes by dragging a data row onto a blank area of the drawing page. To do this, click once on the desired master in the stencil to select it, and then drag a data row onto the page. The shape under the pointer will reflect the master you've selected.

The end result of the drag and drop process doesn't change the appearance of the shape on the page, but you'll notice the addition of a linking symbol at the left end of the top data row, as shown in the following graphic.

TIP If you need to know which row is linked to which shape, right-click on the row, and then click Linked Shapes for the answer. If you need to remove the link between a data row and a shape, just right-click on the row, and then click Unlink.

Cost	Process Number	Owner	Function	Start Date	End Date	Status
🔗	101	HR Admin		4/7/2014		In Progress
	102	Hiring Man...		4/7/2014		In Progress
	103	HR Admin		4/9/2014		In Progress
	104	Recruiter		4/18/2014		In Progress
	105	Manager		4/25/2014		Not Started
	106	Recruiter		4/30/2014		Not Started
	107	Candidate		5/5/2014		Not Started
	108	Recruiter		5/7/2014		Not Started

External Data ✕ | ◄ ◄ ► ►| Sheet1

12 Open the **Shape Data** window for the **Log hiring request** shape to verify that data from the Excel spreadsheet now resides in the Visio shape. It's important to realize that this is a live link from Visio to the data, as you'll discover when you complete the exercise in the next section.

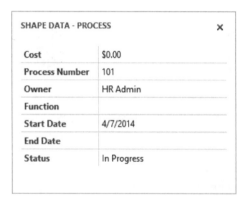

13 Drag the remainder of the data rows onto the shapes on the page. Shapes 102–104 are left-to-right in the top row, and shapes 105–108 are left-to-right across the bottom row. (The **End** shape does not have a data row.) The final result is a fully linked set of data rows.

Cost	Process Number	Owner	Function	Start Date	End Date	Status
🔗	101	HR Admin		4/7/2014		In Progress
🔗	102	Hiring Man...		4/7/2014		In Progress
🔗	103	HR Admin		4/9/2014		In Progress
🔗	104	Recruiter		4/18/2014		In Progress
🔗	105	Manager		4/25/2014		Not Started
🔗	106	Recruiter		4/30/2014		Not Started
🔗	107	Candidate		5/5/2014		Not Started
🔗	108	Recruiter		5/7/2014		Not Started

External Data ✕ | ◄ ◄ ► ►| Sheet1

TIP The name on the tab at the bottom of the External Data window is the name of the worksheet in the linked Excel workbook. If you will be linking a diagram to more than one worksheet or even to worksheets in more than one workbook, it is useful to give each worksheet a unique name.

CLEAN UP Save your changes to the *HR Process Map with data* drawing in Visio and save your changes to the *HR Process Data* workbook in Excel. Leave both files open if you are continuing to the next exercise.

TIP When you populate shapes with data from the External Data window, Visio matches the external data column names with the names of the shape data fields in the target shape. If there are no matching shape data fields, Visio creates new shape data fields to accommodate the external data.

IMPORTANT The information in the following section applies only to the Professional edition of Visio 2013. In addition, the data-related features described in this section may be disabled while you are using the coauthoring functions of Visio 2013.

Refreshing data in linked diagrams

After you have linked data to a Visio drawing, there is a live connection between the files. In fact, you can make changes to the data source and have those changes appear either manually or automatically in the Visio drawing. This is true whether the drawing is linked to a single data source or to multiple sources.

In this exercise, you will change data values in the Excel data source and then view those changes in the Visio shapes.

SET UP You need the *HR Process Map* drawing for this exercise. Either continue with the open copy from the previous exercise or open the *HR Process MapE_start* drawing located in the Chapter06 practice file folder and save it as *HR Process Map with data*. You also need the *HR Process Data_start* workbook located in the Chapter06 practice file folder; open it and save it as *HR Process Data*. Then follow the steps.

1　In the Excel spreadsheet, type **Hiring Manager** in the **Owner** cell for process number **104** (it currently contains **Recruiter**).

2　Type **4/16/2014** in the **Start Date** cell for process step **104** that currently contains **4/18/2014**.

3　Type **In Progress** in the **Status** cell for process step **105** that currently contains **Not Started**.

The following graphic highlights the three changes you've just made.

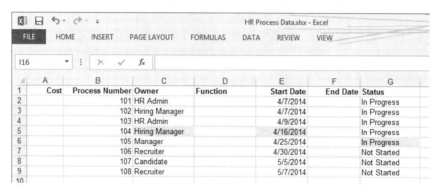

4　Save the changes to the Excel workbook.

TIP It is not necessary to close the spreadsheet or other data source in order to update the Visio drawing.

5　Switch to Visio. Then on the **Data** tab, in the **External Data** group, click the upper half of the **Refresh All** button (do not click the arrow). Visio reads data from all linked data sources and shows the result in the **Refresh Data** dialog box.

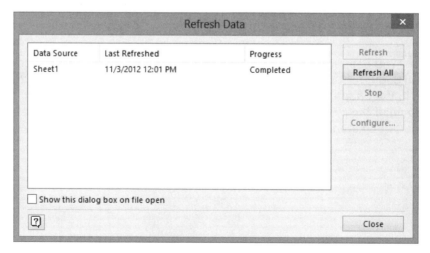

TIP If your diagram is linked to multiple data sources, and you only want to refresh data from some of them, click the lower portion of the Refresh All button and then click Refresh Data. The Refresh Data dialog box will open enabling you to select the specific data source(s) you want to refresh.

6   In the **Refresh Data** dialog box, click **Close**.

7   Open the **Shape Data** window for the shape titled **Interview candidates**. The shape correctly reflects the new data in the Excel workbook; the **External Data** window also displays the new data.

6

⊗ CLEAN UP Save changes to the *HR Process Map with data* drawing and the *HR Process Data* workbook but leave them open if you are continuing with the next exercise.

IMPORTANT The data linking mechanism in Visio is designed for one-way data transfer, that is, for importing data *into* a Visio diagram. The opposite does not work. In other words, you can refresh the data in a drawing after making changes in a linked data source, but you cannot make changes to data in Visio and then push those changes to the linked data source.

Scheduling data refresh

The preceding two exercises showed you how to manually update the data in your diagram by rereading the data sources. It's easy to imagine situations in which you would like to have Visio update the data without manual intervention. Each scenario in the following list would be a good candidate for this feature:

- A network or rack diagram that is used to display a near real–time network and server status

- A call center seating chart that shows which agents are on the phone and which are available

- A process map that shows up-to-date task status

- A factory floor plan that displays production statistics, performance threshold warnings, and safety issues

In this exercise, you will set a schedule so Visio will refresh your drawing automatically.

 SET UP **If they are not already opened, open the** *HR Process Map with data* **Visio drawing and the** *HR Process Data* **Excel workbook that you worked with in the previous exercise. Then follow the steps.**

1   In Visio, right-click anywhere in the **External Data** window, and then click **Configure Refresh** to open the **Configure Refresh** dialog box.

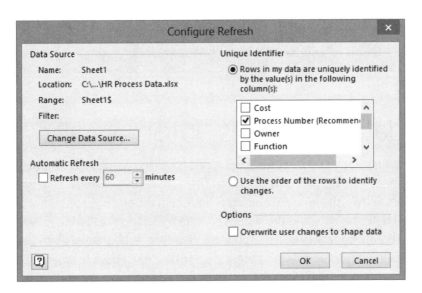

TIP As an alternative to step 1, you can open the Refresh Data dialog box shown in the previous two sections, select one or more data sources, and then click the Configure button.

2   In the **Configure Refresh** dialog box, select the **Refresh every nnn minutes** check box.

3   Type **10** or use the spinner control to set the desired refresh interval, and then click **OK**.

From this point forward, whenever your drawing is open, the data will refresh automatically at the specified time interval. The data will not refresh when the drawing is closed.

✖ CLEAN UP **Save and close the** *HR Process Map with data* **Visio drawing and the** *HR Process Data* **Excel workbook.**

Linking data to shapes automatically

After completing steps 11–13 in the section titled "Linking diagrams to external data" earlier in this chapter, you were probably thinking "There must be a better way to link data to shapes!" Fortunately, there is. Visio includes an automatic linking facility that works very nicely when both the data and the shapes contain matching unique identifiers. The key to the automatic linking facility is in the previous sentence—the shapes on the drawing page and the data in your spreadsheet or other data source must have matching IDs.

In this exercise, you will first prepare your drawing by adding IDs to the shapes, and then you will automatically link the data to the shapes.

 SET UP **You need the *HR Process MapA_start* drawing and the *HR Process Data_start* workbook located in the Chapter06 practice file folder to complete this exercise. Open the drawing in Visio. Then open the *HR Process Data_start* workbook and save it as *HR Process Data*. Then follow the steps.**

1   Click the **Log hiring request** process shape and then type **101** into the **Process Number** field.

2   Click the **Prepare job description and screening questions** process shape and then type **102** into the **Process Number** field.

3   Continue assigning sequential numbers to the process and decision shapes in the flowchart, numbering from left to right in the top row and then the bottom row.

4   Save the drawing as **HR Process Map with IDs**.

Now that you've prepared the drawing, it is easy to link data to shapes automatically.

5   Follow steps 2–10 in the section "Linking diagrams to external data sources" earlier in this chapter. This will connect your drawing to the spreadsheet and open the **External Data** window.

6   On the **Data** tab, in the **External Data** group, click the **Automatically Link** button.

> **IMPORTANT** If you did not select any shapes before performing this step, the wizard page shown in the following graphic will appear exactly as shown. If you did select one or more shapes before performing this step, the Selected Shapes option will be selected. For this exercise, ensure that All Shapes On This Page is selected.

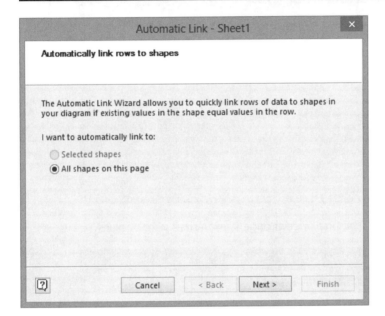

7   Click **Next**.

On this page of the wizard, you tell Visio how to match data with shapes by indicating the column name in the data and the field name in the shapes that are equivalent.

8   Under the **Data Column** heading, click **Process Number** in the list.

9 Under the **Shape Field** heading, click **Process Number** in the list.

TIP If you need to specify multiple conditions for matching data to shapes, click the And button and enter additional conditions.

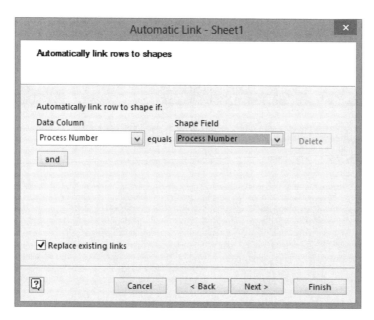

10 Click **Next**. The final wizard page summarizes your choices.

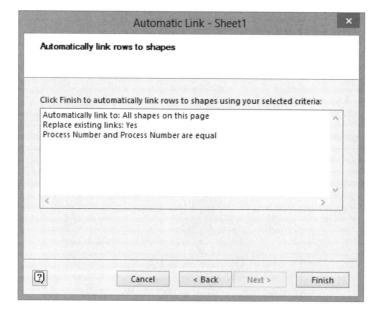

11 Click **Finish**. The appearance of the link symbol at the left end of each data row in the **External Data** window indicates that each row has been successfully linked to a shape on the drawing page.

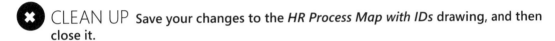

	Cost	Process Number	Owner	Function	Start Date	End Date	Status	
∞		101	HR Admin		4/7/2014		In Progress	
∞		102	Hiring Man...		4/7/2014		In Progress	
∞		103	HR Admin		4/9/2014		In Progress	
∞		104	Recruiter		4/18/2014		In Progress	
∞		105	Manager		4/25/2014		Not Started	
∞		106	Recruiter		4/30/2014		Not Started	
∞		107	Candidate		5/5/2014		Not Started	
∞		108	Recruiter		5/7/2014		Not Started	

⊗ CLEAN UP **Save your changes to the *HR Process Map with IDs* drawing, and then close it.**

Running a predefined report

6

Now that you know how to use, modify, and create data fields, as well as how to link data from external sources to your Visio shapes, the next logical step is to explore ways to use all of that data.

Visio 2013 provides a reporting facility that lets you extract data in a variety of ways in order to summarize and present it. Many of the built-in Visio templates include predefined reports. You can also design your own reports by stepping through the provided report definition wizard.

In this exercise, you will run one of the built-in reports.

➡ SET UP **You need the *HR Process MapE_start* drawing located in the Chapter06 practice file folder to complete this exercise. Open the drawing in Visio and save it as *HR Process Map Reports*. Close the External Data window if it is open. Then follow the steps.**

1 On the **Review** tab, in the **Reports** group, click the **Shape Reports** button to open the **Reports** dialog box.

2   In the **Reports** dialog box, click once on **Flowchart** in the list of reports.

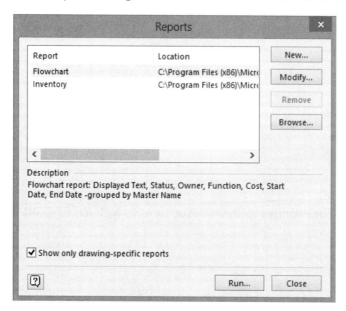

At the top of the Reports dialog box, there are two predefined reports: Flowchart and Inventory. The Flowchart report is part of the flowchart template in Visio and will appear whenever you create a diagram using that template. The Inventory report is a generic Visio report that counts shapes and is present every time you open the Reports dialog box.

Because you selected the Flowchart report, notice that there is a description of the report in the center of the dialog box.

3   Click **Run** to open the **Run Report** dialog box.

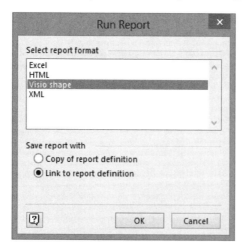

The Run Report dialog box offers four different report output options:

- **Excel** Drops the formatted report data into Excel. The report data can then be edited.

- **HTML** Drops the report into Windows Internet Explorer. This report format is read only.

- **Visio shape** Creates a new Visio shape that contains the report data. (For the technically inclined, this shape is actually an embedded Excel object, so after creating it, you can double-click the report shape and edit the data as though you were using Excel.

- **XML** Creates an XML file containing the formatted report. The report data can be imported into an XML-aware application, or it can be edited.

4   Click **Excel**, and then click **OK** to open the **Flowchart** report.

TIP This report includes subtotals for each entry in the Master Name column.

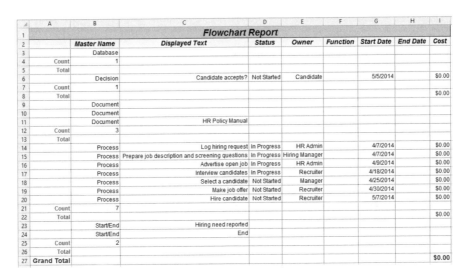

	Master Name	Displayed Text	Status	Owner	Function	Start Date	End Date	Cost
		Flowchart Report						
	Database							
Count	1							
Total								
	Decision	Candidate accepts?	Not Started	Candidate		5/5/2014		$0.00
Count	1							
Total								$0.00
	Document							
	Document							
	Document	HR Policy Manual						
Count	3							
Total								
	Process	Log hiring request	In Progress	HR Admin		4/7/2014		$0.00
	Process	Prepare job description and screening questions	In Progress	Hiring Manager		4/7/2014		$0.00
	Process	Advertise open job	In Progress	HR Admin		4/9/2014		$0.00
	Process	Interview candidates	In Progress	Recruiter		4/18/2014		$0.00
	Process	Select a candidate	Not Started	Manager		4/25/2014		$0.00
	Process	Make job offer	Not Started	Recruiter		4/30/2014		$0.00
	Process	Hire candidate	Not Started	Recruiter		5/7/2014		$0.00
Count	7							
Total								$0.00
	Start/End	Hiring need reported						
	Start/End	End						
Count	2							
Total								
Grand Total								$0.00

5   On the **Review** tab, in the **Reports** group, click the **Shape Reports** button. Then click **Flowchart** and the **Run** button in the **Reports** dialog box to run the **Flowchart** report again.

6   In the **Run Report** dialog box, click **HTML**, and then click **OK**. Internet Explorer opens and displays the report.

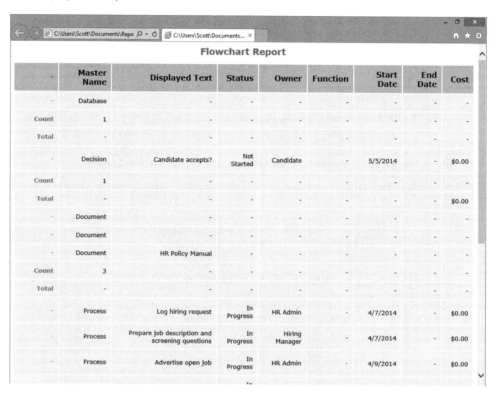

7   Run the **Flowchart** report again, but this time, click **Visio shape** in the **Run Report** dialog box and then click **OK**. As shown in the following graphic, the new shape object can be quite large, so in many cases, you'll want to cut and paste it onto a separate page.

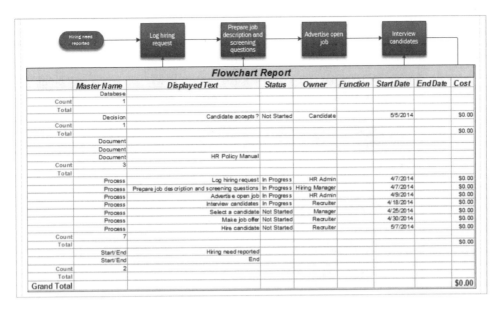

Flowchart Report

	Master Name	Displayed Text	Status	Owner	Function	Start Date	End Date	Cost
	Database							
Count	1							
Total								
	Decision	Candidate accepts?	Not Started	Candidate		5/5/2014		$0.00
Count	1							
Total								$0.00
	Document							
	Document							
	Document	HR Policy Manual						
Count	3							
Total								
	Process	Log hiring request	In Progress	HR Admin		4/7/2014		$0.00
	Process	Prepare job description and screening questions	In Progress	Hiring Manager		4/7/2014		$0.00
	Process	Advertise open job	In Progress	HR Admin		4/9/2014		$0.00
	Process	Interview candidates	In Progress	Recruiter		4/18/2014		$0.00
	Process	Select a candidate	Not Started	Manager		4/25/2014		$0.00
	Process	Make job offer	Not Started	Recruiter		4/30/2014		$0.00
	Process	Hire candidate	Not Started	Recruiter		5/7/2014		$0.00
Count	7							
Total								$0.00
	Start/End	Hiring need reported						
	Start/End	End						
Count	2							
Total								
Grand Total								$0.00

8   On the **Review** tab, in the **Reports** group, click **Shape Reports**.

9   In the **Reports** dialog box, click **Inventory**. Notice the description of this report—it essentially just counts all occurrences of every shape on the page.

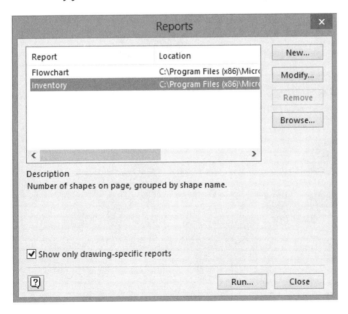

TIP The Show Only Drawing-Specific Reports option at the bottom of the dialog box is selected by default. Generally, this is a good thing, because it prevents Visio from showing you a list of extraneous reports. However, if you're looking for a report that doesn't appear on the list when this option is selected, you can clear it. Doing so for the previous dialog box produces a long list of reports.

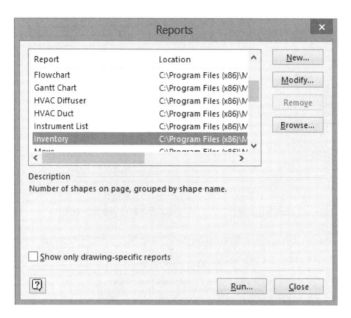

10 Click **Run**.

11 Double-click **Visio shape** in the **Run Report** dialog box to create a new Visio report shape showing a simple count of each shape type.

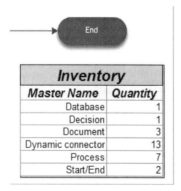

⊗ CLEAN UP Save your changes to the *HR Process Map Reports* drawing, but leave it open if you are continuing with the next exercise.

Creating a new report

Visio provides a Report Definition wizard so you can create new reports or modify existing reports. In this exercise, you will create a new report for the recruiting process.

➡ SET UP **You need the** *HR Process Map Reports* **drawing for this exercise. Either continue with the open copy from the previous exercise or open the** *HR Process MapE_start* **drawing located in the Chapter06 practice file folder and save it as** *HR Process Map Reports*. **Close the External Data window if it is open, and then follow the steps.**

1   On the **Review** tab, in the **Reports** group, click the **Shape Reports** button, and then click the **New** button to open the **Report Definition** wizard.

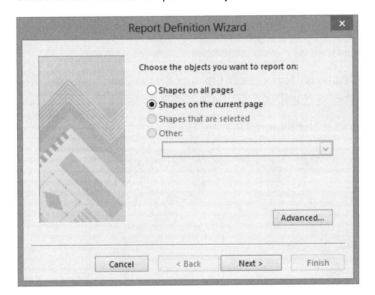

2   Click **Shapes on the current page** if it's not already selected, and then click **Next**.

This page of the Report Definition wizard shows the fields that you are most likely to want in your report. If the field you're looking for is not visible, select the Show All Properties check box.

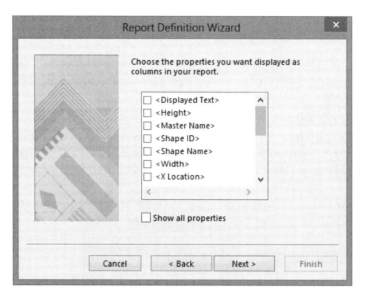

3   Select the **<Displayed Text>** check box, scroll down, and then select the check boxes for **Owner**, **Process Number**, **Start Date** and **Status**, and then click **Next**.

4   Type **HR Report** in the **Report Title** text box.

5   Click the **Sort** button so you can specify the order in which you want the data to appear in the report.

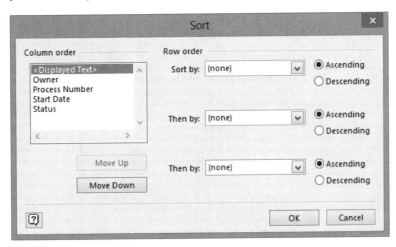

6   In the **Sort** dialog box, in the **Row Order** section, click the arrow next to **Sort by**, and then select **Process Number**.

TIP You can sort by as many as three fields in the Row Order section.

7   In the **Column Order** section, click once on **Process Number**, and then click the **Move Up** button twice to set the column sequence as shown in the following graphic.

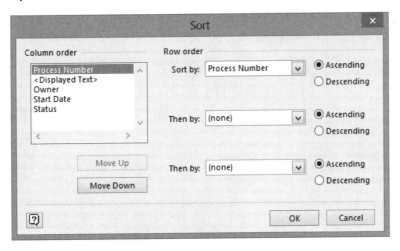

8   Click **OK** to close the **Sort** dialog box.

TIP The text under the Sort button identifies the sort field(s) you selected.

Be sure to note the Subtotals and Format buttons that allow you to customize the report output in additional ways beyond what you will use in this exercise.

9 Click **Next** to open the final page of the **Report Definition** wizard.

10 Type **Custom HR Report** in the **Name** text box.

11 Type **HR Process Report showing task number, task description, owner, start date and status** in the **Description** text box.

You can save the report definition in the current Visio drawing, which is the default, or you can save it to an external file.

TIP Save the report definition to an external file if you think you'll want to use it with multiple drawings. If you do, you can retrieve the report definition by clicking the Browse button in the Reports dialog box shown in the following graphic.

12   Click **Finish**. Your report appears in the list of available reports in the **Reports** dialog box and you can run it in the usual way.

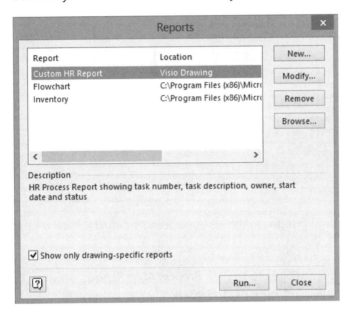

13   Click **Run** in the **Reports** dialog box.

14   Double-click **Visio shape** in the **Run Report** dialog box. Your custom report appears on the drawing page.

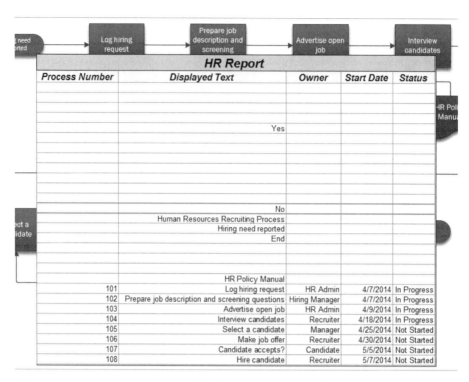

Process Number	Displayed Text	Owner	Start Date	Status
	Yes			
	No			
	Human Resources Recruiting Process			
	Hiring need reported			
	End			
	HR Policy Manual			
101	Log hiring request	HR Admin	4/7/2014	In Progress
102	Prepare job description and screening questions	Hiring Manager	4/7/2014	In Progress
103	Advertise open job	HR Admin	4/9/2014	In Progress
104	Interview candidates	Recruiter	4/18/2014	In Progress
105	Select a candidate	Manager	4/25/2014	Not Started
106	Make job offer	Recruiter	4/30/2014	Not Started
107	Candidate accepts?	Candidate	5/5/2014	Not Started
108	Hire candidate	Recruiter	5/7/2014	Not Started

When you save the changes to this file, your report definition will be saved with your drawing.

✖ CLEAN UP Save your changes to the *HR Process Map Reports* drawing but leave it open if you are continuing with the next exercise.

The report you've just created is interesting, but needs some fine tuning. For example, there are blank rows because some shapes on the page do not contain any data. To modify the report, continue reading in the next section.

Modifying an existing report

Whether you are using a predefined Visio report or one you've created, there are times when you may want to modify the output it produces.

In this exercise, you will modify the HR Report you created in the previous section to eliminate the blank rows.

 SET UP **You need the *HR Process Map Reports* drawing for this exercise. Either continue with the open copy from the previous exercise or open the *HR Process MapF_start* drawing located in the Chapter06 practice file folder and save it as *HR Process Map Reports*. If the HR Report is still on the drawing page, click it once to select it, and then press Delete. Next, follow the steps.**

1 Open the **Reports** dialog box, click **Custom HR Report** in the list of reports, and then click the **Modify** button to open the **Report Definition** wizard.

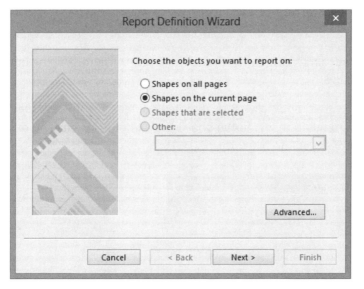

2 On the first page of the **Report Definition Wizard**, click the **Advanced** button.

   You can set selection criteria in the Advanced dialog box to control which shapes will appear in the report.

3 Under the **Property** heading, click the arrow, and then click **Process Number**.

4 Under the **Condition** heading, click the arrow, and then click **is greater than**.

5 Under the **Value** heading, type **0**.

6   Click the **Add** button to add your selections to the **Defined criteria** list.

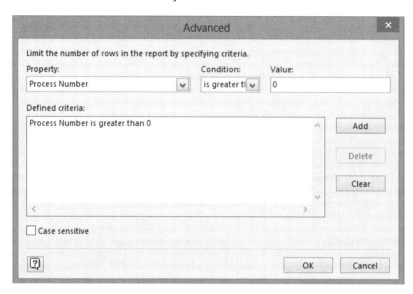

7   Click **OK**.

8   Click **Next** three times in the wizard, and then click **Finish** to save the updated report definition.

9   In the **Reports** dialog box, click **Run** and then double-click **Visio shape.** When you compare the resulting report to the one at the end of the preceding exercise you will discover that there are no blank rows.

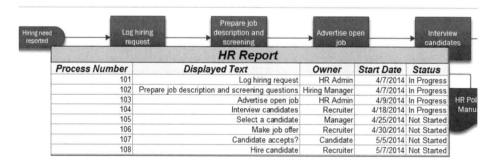

❌ CLEAN UP **Save and close the *HR Process Map Reports* drawing.**

TIP It would be a good idea to experiment with the other buttons and option settings in the Report Definition wizard while everything is fresh in your mind. There are many other ways that you can customize Visio reports.

Key points

- Shape data exists in, or can be added to, any shape on a Visio drawing page. A growing percentage of Visio drawings are valuable not just because they are attractive pictures, but because they are visual representations of real-world data.

- Visio diagrams do not need to exist in isolation. You can link your drawings to personal or organizational data repositories of almost any type, ranging from simple spreadsheets to SharePoint lists and almost any kind of database.

- The data in a linked Visio drawing can be updated manually or you can schedule updates to occur at a preset time interval.

- Many Visio templates include predefined reports that you can run to export summarized data to webpages, Excel files, and other formats. In addition, the Visio Report wizard steps you through editing existing reports or creating your own.

6

Chapter at a glance

Use

Use hyperlinks,
page 293

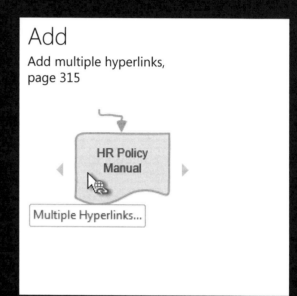

Add

Add multiple hyperlinks,
page 315

Link

Link to a specific location in a document,
page 299

Link

Link to another Visio page,
page 302

IN THIS CHAPTER, YOU WILL LEARN HOW TO

- Enhance diagrams by adding hyperlinks to a website and a document.

- Add even more value to diagrams by linking to a specific location in a document or to another Visio page.

- Use hyperlinks.

- Understand relative and absolute hyperlinks.

- Set the hyperlink base.

- Edit existing hyperlinks.

- Add multiple hyperlinks.

Aside from adding and using data in your drawings, one of the most significant ways to add value to a Microsoft Visio 2013 diagram is by adding hyperlinks. As you create or edit a drawing, try to anticipate what other resources your reader will require. With that in mind, create hyperlinks that lead the reader to documents, to webpages, to specific shapes elsewhere in the same or another Visio drawing—in short, to any location that will enhance the viewer's experience with your diagram.

A simple form of hyperlink might lead to another page in the same drawing, much like the off-page connector in the flowcharts you learned about in Chapter 4, "Creating flowcharts and organization charts." More sophisticated hyperlinks can lead the reader to a specific cell in a Microsoft Excel spreadsheet, or to a particular phrase in a Microsoft Word document.

In this chapter, you will learn how to create both simple and sophisticated hyperlinks. You will learn how to use both relative and absolute links and to set the hyperlink base. You will also find out how to edit links and attach more than one link to the same shape.

Enhancing diagrams by adding hyperlinks

Many business diagrams can be enhanced by adding hyperlinks. For example, if a step in your flowchart refers to a policy manual, add a link to the associated Word document or PDF. If your office layout is derived from a list of employees in Microsoft Access, link to the database. If the map of your new data center includes a move-in budget, link to the spreadsheet containing the budget.

One of the simplest ways to add a hyperlink to a Visio shape is to right-click the shape and click Hyperlink on the resulting shortcut menu, which opens the Hyperlinks dialog box.

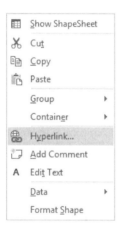

TIP You can also open the Hyperlinks dialog box from the ribbon after selecting a Visio shape. On the Insert tab, in the Links group, click the Hyperlink button.

KEYBOARD SHORTCUT After selecting a Visio shape, you can open the Hyperlinks dialog box by pressing Ctrl+K.

In the exercises that follow, you will use the Hyperlinks dialog box to create multiple types of hyperlinks.

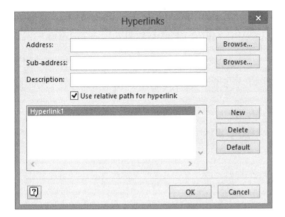

Using hyperlinks

After you've created any type of hyperlink in a Visio drawing, you will notice several things:

- Pointing to a hyperlinked object causes a hyperlink symbol to appear below the pointer (left graphic).

- Pausing on a hyperlinked object displays a tooltip containing a description of the hyperlink (center graphic).

- Right-clicking a hyperlinked object displays the shortcut menu, which includes a description of the hyperlink (right graphic).

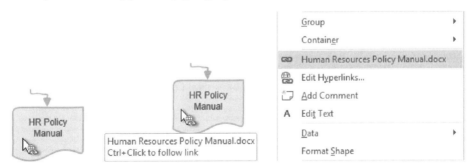

To follow a Visio hyperlink, simply right-click any hyperlinked shape, and then click the name of the hyperlink.

KEYBOARD SHORTCUT You can also follow a hyperlink on a Visio shape by holding down the Ctrl key and clicking the shape, as indicated in the tooltip text shown in the middle of the previous graphic.

If Visio warns that you are about to leave Visio and open another application, click Yes or OK as appropriate.

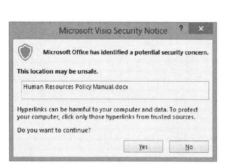

TIP The dialog box on the left appears if the drawing containing the hyperlink has not yet been saved; the dialog box on the right appears when the file has been saved.

Linking to a website

In this exercise, you will create a hyperlink to a current website. You can use the same technique to create links to any website on the public World Wide Web as well as to sites on your organization's intranet.

 SET UP **You need the** *HR Process Map_start* **drawing located in the Chapter07 practice file folder to complete this exercise. Open the drawing in Visio and save it as** *HR Process Map.*

TIP The HR Process Map you've just opened uses variant 4 of a theme called Pencil, which gives it a hand-drawn look. To learn more about hand-drawn themes—or any themes— refer to Chapter 5, "Adding style, color and themes."

1   Click **Advertise open job** shape and then open the **Hyperlinks** dialog box.

2   In the **Hyperlinks** dialog box, click **Browse** to the right of **Address**.

3   From the menu that appears, click **Internet Address.** Visio opens your web browser so you can provide the address of a website.

4   Navigate to **www.visiostepbystep.com**.

5   Click the Visio icon on the Windows taskbar to verify that Visio has inserted the correct URL into the **Address** box and that it has also copied the title of the webpage into the **Description** box.

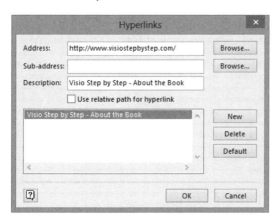

6   Click **OK**.

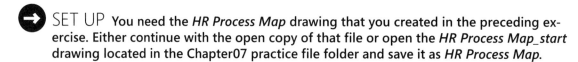 CLEAN UP **Save your changes to the** *HR Process Map* **drawing but leave it open if you are continuing with the next exercise.**

Now you can enjoy the result of the hyperlink by following the instructions in the "Using hyperlinks" section earlier in this chapter.

TIP If your target webpage contains HTML bookmarks, you can include a bookmark in the address for the page. Clicking this type of hyperlink will take the user directly to the part of the page containing the bookmark.

In addition to creating links to websites, you can also create hyperlinks to email addresses by prefixing the email address with *mailto:* when you type or paste it into the Address text box.

Linking to a document

In this exercise, you will create a link to a Word document.

SET UP **You need the** *HR Process Map* **drawing that you created in the preceding exercise. Either continue with the open copy of that file or open the** *HR Process Map_start* **drawing located in the Chapter07 practice file folder and save it as** *HR Process Map*.

1 Click the **HR Policy Manual** shape and then open the **Hyperlinks** dialog box.

2 Click **Browse** to the right of **Address**, and then click **Local File**.

TIP The use of the words Local File by Visio is a misnomer. Although you can select files on your local hard drive, you can also select files on a server, file share, Microsoft SkyDrive, or other nonlocal device.

3   Navigate to the **Chapter07** practice file folder.

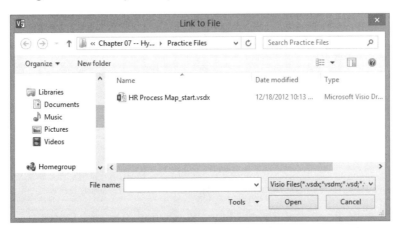

IMPORTANT Visio shows you only Visio files by default in the Link To File dialog box.

4   Click the box showing **Visio Files** to display a list of other file types.

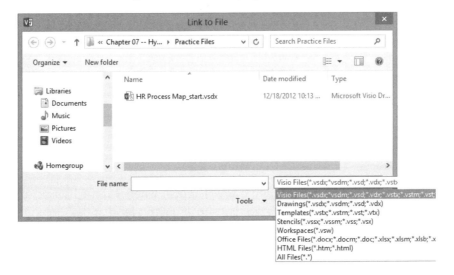

5   Click **Office Files** to display all types of Microsoft Office documents located in this folder.

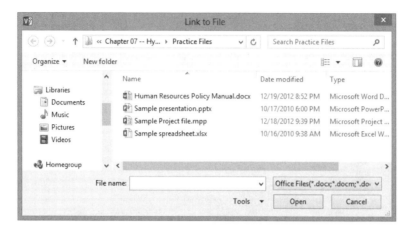

6   Click **Human Resources Policy Manual.docx**, and then click **Open**.

Visio shows the path to the target file in the Address box and places the target file name in the Description box.

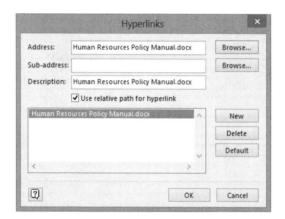

TIP The text in the Description box will appear whenever the user points to the hyperlinked object in your Visio drawing. If you prefer that the tooltip text display something other than the file name, you can type the text you want into the Description box.

7   Click **OK**.

8   Follow the hyperlink you've just created to verify that the Word document opens, and take note that it opens at the top of the document.

⊗ CLEAN UP **Save your changes to the *HR Process Map* drawing but leave it open if you are continuing with the next exercise. Close Word.**

Linking to a specific location in a document

One of the underused but incredibly valuable features in Visio is the ability to link not just to a document, but to a specific location inside a document. Imagine a process map that refers to a policy manual at 17 different steps in the process. If each of those 17 hyperlinks merely opens the document at the cover page, you will leave the reader wondering where the relevant material resides in the document.

Imagine instead that each of the 17 hyperlinks moves the reader to a specific page or even to a particular word or phrase on that page. Accomplishing this is quite easy from Visio when you are armed with key knowledge about Word, Excel, and Microsoft PowerPoint. Keep in mind the following guidelines:

- For Word, the key is knowing that you can create named bookmarks in two ways:

    - You can assign a name to the location of the insertion point.

    - You can assign a name to a range of text—anything from one character to multiple paragraphs.

    If you create a bookmark with the first method, your Visio hyperlink will jump to the part of the page containing the bookmark; if you create the second type of bookmark, your hyperlink will jump to and highlight the selected text.

- In Excel, you can assign names to individual cells or to cell ranges.

- In PowerPoint, you can't assign names to specific locations but you can refer to slides either by number or slide title.

In this exercise, you will create and follow a hyperlink to a bookmark in a Word document.

 SET UP **You need the *HR Process Map* drawing that you created in the preceding exercise. Either continue with the open copy of that drawing or open the *HR Process Map_start* drawing located in the Chapter07 practice file folder and save it as *HR Process Map*.**

1   Drag a **Document** shape from the **Basic Flowchart Shapes** stencil, drop it below the *Hire candidate* shape, and then open the **Hyperlinks** dialog box for the new shape.

7

2   Repeat steps 2–6 in the preceding section titled "Linking to a document."

> **IMPORTANT** Do not close the Hyperlinks dialog box.

3   In the **Sub-address** text box, type **Recruiting**.

> **TIP** *Recruiting* is the name of a bookmark that already exists in the *Human Resources Policy Manual* document. If you were creating a link to an Excel workbook, you would type a cell reference or the name of a cell or cell range to which you want to link.

4   Clear the **Use relative path for hyperlink** check box.

> **SEE ALSO** Refer to "Understanding relative and absolute hyperlinks" later in this chapter for more information about this important hyperlink qualifier.

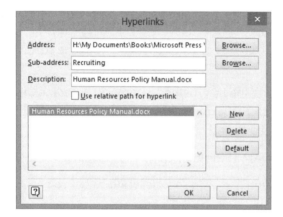

5   Click **OK**.

6   Follow the hyperlink you just created.

When you follow the hyperlink, the bookmarked text is highlighted automatically in the resulting document window. In this example, notice that the highlighted text is located on Page 3 of 5 (the page number is displayed in the status bar at the lower-left corner of the Word window), a clear indication that you can guide the user of your Visio drawing to any part of a document.

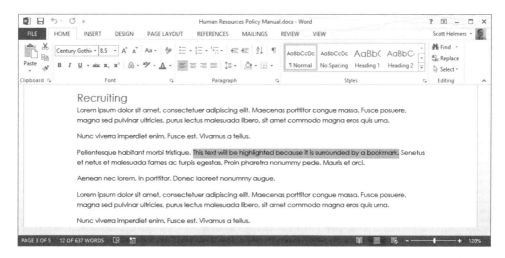

Recruiting

Lorem ipsum dolor sit amet, consectetuer adipiscing elit. Maecenas porttitor congue massa. Fusce posuere, magna sed pulvinar ultricies, purus lectus malesuada libero, sit amet commodo magna eros quis urna.

Nunc viverra imperdiet enim. Fusce est. Vivamus a tellus.

Pellentesque habitant morbi tristique. This text will be highlighted because it is surrounded by a bookmark. Senetus et netus et malesuada fames ac turpis egestas. Proin pharetra nonummy pede. Mauris et orci.

Aenean nec lorem. In porttitor. Donec laoreet nonummy augue.

Lorem ipsum dolor sit amet, consectetuer adipiscing elit. Maecenas porttitor congue massa. Fusce posuere, magna sed pulvinar ultricies, purus lectus malesuada libero, sit amet commodo magna eros quis urna.

Nunc viverra imperdiet enim. Fusce est. Vivamus a tellus.

✖ CLEAN UP Save your changes to the *HR Process Map* drawing but leave it open if you are continuing with the next exercise. Close Word.

By using targeted hyperlinks, you can bring users of your Visio drawings directly to the one place in the document that is relevant to them at this moment.

TIP To link to a location in a Word document, create one or more bookmarks in the document first, and then use the bookmark name in the Sub-address field. For information about creating bookmarks in Word documents, refer to *Microsoft Word 2013 Step by Step* by Joan Lambert and Joyce Cox (Microsoft Press, 2013).

To link to a location in an Excel workbook, create one or more named cells or named cell ranges first, and then use the cell or range name in the Sub-address field. You can also enter a standard cell reference such as "D5" or "Sheet3!H8" into the Sub-address field. For information about cell references or creating named cells or ranges in Excel documents, refer to *Microsoft Excel 2013 Step by Step* by Curtis Frye (Microsoft Press, 2013).

To link to a location in a PowerPoint presentation, type either the slide number or slide title in the Sub-address field.

Linking to another Visio page

It is often helpful to link from a Visio shape on one page to another Visio page, whether the target page is in the same drawing or in a different drawing. Sometimes your goal is to achieve *drilldown*, that is, to enable the reader to click a shape in a high-level view and be taken to the next lower level of detail. (You can continue to do this through as many levels of detail as you'd like.) Other times, your goal is just to take the reader to the next page or to related information on another page.

In this exercise, you will build Visio-to-Visio hyperlinks.

 SET UP **You need the *HR Process Map* drawing for this exercise. Either continue with the open copy of that drawing or open the *HR Process Map_start* drawing located in the Chapter07 practice file folder and save it as *HR Process Map*.**

1   Click the **Hire candidate** shape and then open the **Hyperlinks** dialog box.

2   Leave the **Address** field blank.

> **IMPORTANT** To link to another page in the Visio drawing you are currently editing, you *must* leave the Address field blank. If you do not leave this field blank and later decide to publish this map as a webpage, your hyperlink may not work.

> **TIP** If you want to link to a page in a different Visio diagram, complete steps 2–3 in the section titled "Linking to a document" earlier in this chapter, select the target Visio document, and then click OK.

3   Click **Browse** to the right of the **Sub-address** field. The **Sub-address** dialog box opens.

4   Click the arrow to the right of **Page**, and then click **Page-2** to select it as the name of the target page.

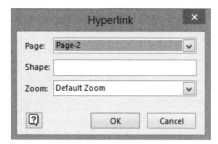

5   If you want to link to a specific shape on the target page, enter the shape name in the **Shape** text box.

SEE ALSO For information about finding and using Visio shape names, refer to the sidebar titled "What is a shape name? Where do I find it?" later in this chapter.

6   If you want to guide your reader to a specific page view, click the arrow to the right of **Zoom**, and then click a zoom level.

TIP The Zoom setting ensures that whenever someone follows your hyperlink, the target page will always appear with the same zoom setting. Select Page to show a full-page view, Width to show the full width of the page regardless of its height, and a percentage value to zoom in to that level of detail. If you don't select a zoom level, the target page will always be displayed at its most recent zoom level.

7   Click **OK** to return to the Hyperlinks dialog box.

TIP If you type text into the Description box, the description will appear whenever a user points to the hyperlinked object. If you leave the Description box blank, the popup will display the page name.

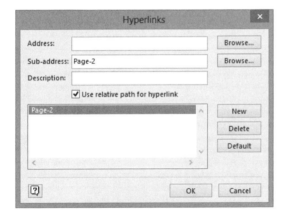

8   Click **OK**, and then follow the hyperlink.

✖ CLEAN UP **Save your changes to the *HR Process Map* drawing but leave it open if you are continuing with the next exercise.**

What is a shape name? Where do I find it?

Every shape in a Visio drawing is referred to internally as a **sheet**. Consequently, Visio shape names are often in the form *Sheet* or *Sheet.n*, where *n* is a number representing the ID of the shape, and is appended by Visio to ensure that every shape has a unique name/ID combination. Some shapes have names other than Sheet, so you will come across shapes with names like *Process* or *Process.12*.

The easiest way to determine a shape's name is to run Visio in **developer mode**, which adds the Developer tab to the ribbon. Follow these steps to determine a shape's name:

1   Turn on developer mode as described in the Appendix, and then select the target shape.

2   On the **Developer** tab, in the **Shape Design** group, click the **Shape Name** button to open the **Shape Name** dialog box.

3   Make note of, or copy, the text to the right of the **Name** text box, and then close the **Shape Name** dialog box.

> **TIP** Another way to determine the shape name is to open the Shape Data window, which is described in the section titled "Viewing shape data" in Chapter 6, "Entering, linking to, and reporting on data." As an example, look for the name Process.24 in the title bar of the Shape Data window shown in the following graphic.

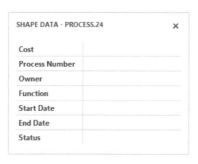

Understanding relative and absolute hyperlinks

You may have noticed a Use Relative Path For Hyperlink check box in the Hyperlinks dialog box. If you're *very* observant, you may also have noticed that this check box is unavailable if you haven't yet saved your drawing, but is available and selected by default if your current drawing has been saved. What's this all about?

With Visio, you can build two types of links:

- **A relative link** provides a path to a resource by assuming a known starting location.

  As an analogy in the physical world, let's say you need to attend a meeting in Room 216 at Lucerne Publishing. If you're standing at the reception desk in the lobby of the company's office and ask where the meeting is located, the receptionist might say, "Go up to the second floor and it's the second door on the right." Based on the known starting location you share with the receptionist—the lobby—that information is sufficient to get you to the intended location.

Relative links in a Visio drawing work in a similar way. The folder containing the Visio drawing serves as *the lobby*, and hyperlink targets on the same disk drive are found relative to that starting point.

For Visio drawings, relative links work very nicely when the relationship between the starting point and the hyperlink targets remains fixed. Problems can arise, however, if you need to move the Visio drawing file to another computer or even to another location on the same computer. In this case, you must preserve the relative relationships from the new location of the Visio file to the target folders and files. One way you can accomplish this is by copying the entire directory structure containing the Visio drawing and its hyperlink targets.

- **An absolute link** contains all of the information required to locate a linked resource, regardless of the starting point.

    Returning to our meeting analogy, if you're at home and need directions to the conference room at Lucerne Publishing, you need a lot more information to arrive at your destination. An absolute address for the meeting room would look more like the following:

    Lucerne Publishing, Room 216, 3456 Elm St., San Francisco, CA 94117 USA

    Armed with an absolute address, you can get to the meeting from your home, or for that matter, from any starting location in the world.

    For Visio hyperlinks, absolute links work regardless of where your Visio drawing is located. You can move the drawing to a different computer and the links will continue to function without requiring any other changes.

TIP Relative and absolute hyperlinks are not mutually exclusive in a single drawing. In fact, many Visio drawings contain a mix of the two link types.

What does all of this have to do with the check box in the Visio Hyperlinks dialog box?

For a saved drawing, Visio assumes that the path to the target of a hyperlink begins in the same folder that contains the Visio drawing. Thus, the default behavior in Visio is to create a relative hyperlink using the location of your Visio drawing as the starting point for the path. When someone clicks your hyperlink, Windows figures out where the target object is by navigating from the location of the Visio drawing.

Just knowing this much explains why the Use Relative Path For Hyperlink check box is unavailable if you haven't yet saved your drawing—Visio can't create a relative link yet because there is no known starting point for the Visio drawing. Consequently, the only option in this situation is to use an absolute path that contains all of the information Windows will need to track down the target object.

Although there are no firm guidelines on when to use relative links rather than absolute links, it's a good idea to think about your environment and the nature of your document collection before creating very many links in Visio. If all of your target documents are in their final resting place, on a network server, for example, then absolute links probably make the most sense. However, if your environment is more volatile, or you know in advance that you'll be moving your Visio drawing and its hyperlink targets to another computer or to a CD or DVD, then carefully constructed relative links are a good choice.

In addition to that advice, the following examples will help you to understand when Visio creates relative or absolute links.

> **IMPORTANT** When you use the Hyperlinks dialog box to browse to and select a target document, Visio fills in the Address box and selects the Use Relative Path For Hyperlink check box based on the locations of the Visio drawing and the target document.

For the examples that follow, assume that the *HR Process Maps* drawing is saved in C:\Human Resources\Process Maps\ and that the hyperlink target is one of the Word documents shown in the following directory listing.

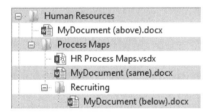

TIP The file name of each Word document includes a parenthetical note to indicate whether it is in a directory above or below the Visio document, or if in the same directory.

- When the target document is in the same folder as *HR Process Maps.vsd*, which obviously means that it is on the same disk drive as the Visio drawing, Visio creates a relative hyperlink and the **Address** box contains the following:

    MyDocument (same).docx

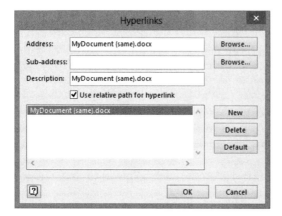

If you now clear the Use Relative Path For Hyperlink check box, the link becomes an absolute link that begins at the root of drive C. The Address box displays the full path to the document:

    C:\Human Resources\Process Maps\MyDocument (same).docx

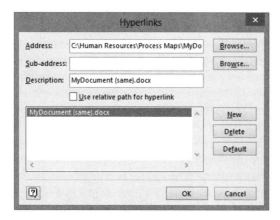

- When you link to a document in C:\Human Resources\Process Maps\Recruiting\, which is a subfolder of the one containing the Visio drawing, Visio creates a relative hyperlink and the **Address** box contains the following:

    Recruiting\MyDocument (below).docx

This indicates that the target document is in a folder called *Recruiting*.

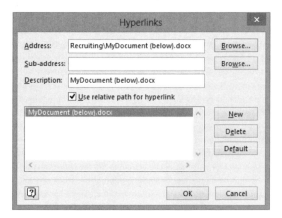

- When the target document is located in C:\Human Resources\, which is above the folder containing the Visio document, Visio creates a relative hyperlink and the Address box contains the following:

    ..\MyDocument (above).docx

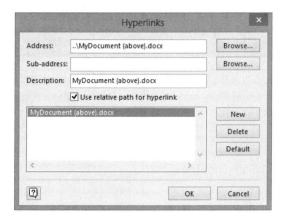

TIP "..\" is arcane syntax that predates Windows. It means "go up one directory level."

- When the target document is located on any drive other than the one containing the Visio document, for example, drive D, drive K, or a network share such as \\MyServer\Human Resources\FY2011\, Visio creates an absolute link and the Address box contains something like one of the following entries:

    D:\SomeFolder\MyDocument.docx

    \\MyServer\Human Resources\FY2011\MyDocument.docx

The following screen shot shows a target document on drive N.

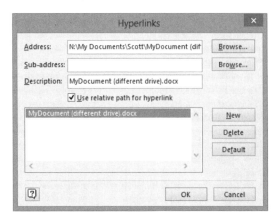

TIP Although the link shown in the previous graphic is an absolute link because the target object is located on a network drive, the Use Relative Path For Hyperlink check box still appears with a check mark. Just to confuse things further, if you try to clear the check box, you will find that you can't do so.

IMPORTANT You can only create relative links to files that are located on the same physical hard drive as the saved Visio drawing.

TIP Visio always creates an absolute link if you begin your address with a server name, drive letter, or web protocol. All of the following will create absolute links regardless of the location of the Visio drawing:

- *C:\SomeFolder\MyWorkbook.xlsx*

- *\\MyServer\Presentations\MySlideShow.pptx*

- *http://www.contoso.com/Somepage.html*

Setting the hyperlink base

One additional factor affects relative links in Visio: each Visio drawing has a property called the *hyperlink base* that is blank by default. Its purpose is to allow you to shift all relative links in a document from one location to another, perhaps because you want to move an entire collection of documents to a new server. If you enter a value for the hyperlink base, Visio will prepend all relative links in the document with the value in that field.

You set the hyperlink base using options in the Backstage view. For the sake of the next exercise, let's assume you want to change the hyperlink base to the following because your drawing contains relative links and you've moved all hyperlinked resources to that folder:

K:\HR Info

In this exercise, you will change the hyperlink base for a Visio drawing.

➡️ SET UP **You need the *HR Process Map* drawing for this exercise. Either continue with the open copy of that map or open the *HR Process Map_start* drawing located in the Chapter07 practice file folder and save it as *HR Process Map*.**

1　Click the **File** tab to display the **Backstage** view.

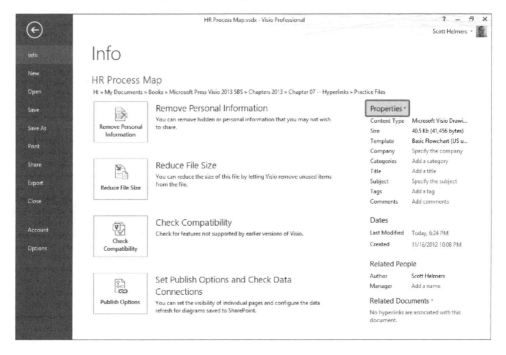

2　On the right side of the screen, click the **Properties** button. On the menu that appears, click **Advanced Properties**.

3 In the **Hyperlink base** text box, type **K:\HR Info**.

IMPORTANT Be sure to include a trailing backslash when you enter a hyperlink base.

4 Click **OK**.

TIP The physical location of your Visio diagram is no longer the starting point for relative hyperlinks. Instead, Visio will construct each hyperlink from the combination of K:\HR Info\ plus the address information from the Hyperlinks dialog box. Adding a hyperlink base has no effect on absolute hyperlinks.

✖ CLEAN UP **Save your changes to the *HR Process Map* drawing but leave it open if you are continuing with the next exercise.**

In this exercise, you created a hyperlink base for a location on a disk drive. The hyperlink base field can also be used to establish a base for web hyperlinks. For example, if you enter a hyperlink base such as the following:

http://OurIntranet/Finance/

and create a relative hyperlink of:

AuditInfo.html

Visio will combine the two to create a link of:

http://OurIntranet/Finance/AuditInfo.html

> **IMPORTANT** There is only one hyperlink base per Visio document. Consequently, if you create either a directory path hyperlink base or a web-based hyperlink base, Visio will use it for *all* relative links in your document. Consequently, you must be extremely careful when establishing a hyperlink base in a diagram.

Editing existing hyperlinks

You can both edit and delete existing hyperlinks.

In this exercise, you will change the description of an existing hyperlink.

 SET UP **You need the *HR Process Map* drawing for this exercise. Either continue with the open copy of that map or open the *HR Process Map_start* drawing located in the Chapter07 practice file folder and save it as *HR Process Map*.**

1   If the **HR Policy Manual** shape already contains a hyperlink, continue with step 2. Otherwise, follow steps 1–7 in the "Linking to a document" exercise earlier in this chapter.

2   Click the **HR Policy Manual** shape and then open the **Hyperlinks** dialog box.

> **TIP** If you use the right-click method to open the Hyperlinks dialog box, you might notice that the menu entry that formerly said Hyperlink now says Edit Hyperlink.

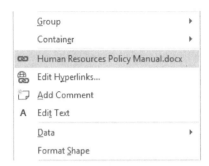

3   Select the hyperlink you want to change if it is not already selected. When it is selected, the hyperlink's details will appear in the appropriate boxes at the top of the **Hyperlinks** dialog box.

4   In the **Description** text box, type **HR Policy Manual**.

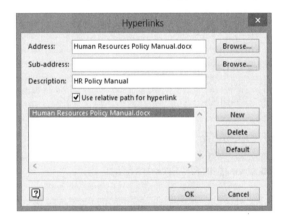

5   Click **OK**. The next time you point to or right-click the hyperlinked shape, the new description text will be displayed.

❌ CLEAN UP **Save your changes to the** *HR Process Map* **drawing but leave it open if you are continuing with the next exercise.**

TIP You can change the hyperlink destination for any existing link by clicking the Browse button to the right of the Address text box whenever you have the Hyperlinks dialog box open. You can also delete a hyperlink by selecting it in the Hyperlinks dialog box, and then clicking the Delete button.

Adding multiple hyperlinks

You can add more than one hyperlink to any object in Visio, offering your reader a choice of places to go or documents to view.

In this exercise, you will add a second hyperlink to a shape that already contains a hyperlink.

 SET UP **You need the** *HR Process Map* **drawing for this exercise. Either continue with the open copy of that map or open the** *HR Process Map_start* **drawing located in the Chapter07 practice file folder and save it as** *HR Process Map*.

1   If the **HR Policy Manual** shape already contains a hyperlink, continue with step 2. Otherwise, follow steps 1–7 in the "Linking to a document" exercise earlier in this chapter.

2   Click the **HR Policy Manual** shape and then open the **Hyperlinks** dialog box.

3   Click the **New** button. *Hyperlink2* appears below **HR Policy Manual** in the **Hyperlinks** dialog box.

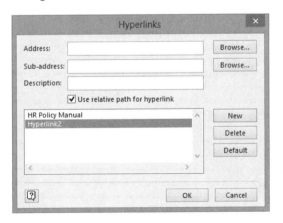

4   Create a hyperlink using any of the techniques described earlier in this chapter, and
    then click **OK**. When you point to the edited shape, Visio uses tooltip text to inform
    you that there are multiple hyperlinks.

Visio also displays the description of each hyperlink when you right-click a linked object. Notice that the previous link, HR Policy Manual, is now followed by the name of
an Excel workbook.

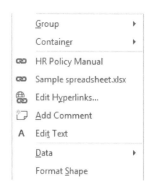

❌ CLEAN UP   **Save and close the *HR Process Map* drawing.**

Key points

- Visio contains an extremely flexible hyperlink mechanism that you can use to create links to webpages, Office documents, other Visio drawings, and more.

- You can enhance users' navigation experience within your Visio drawings by building links to other pages or even to specific shapes on other pages. This allows users to do things like drill down to a lower level of detail in a network diagram, or easily flip from page to page in a multipage drawing.

- Visio supports both relative and absolute hyperlinks, enabling you to create drawings that are connected to resources in a fixed location, or to create a portable Visio library that can be moved to another disk drive or be copied to a CD or DVD.

- Hyperlinks to Office documents can be very precise. You can easily build links that take users to particular phrases or sections of text in a Word document; to individual cells or cell ranges in an Excel workbook; and to specific slides in a PowerPoint presentation.

- Any Visio shape can include multiple hyperlinks, making it simple for you to build content-rich drawings that guide your readers to a variety of relevant resources.

7

Chapter at a glance

Preview

Preview diagrams before printing,
page 320

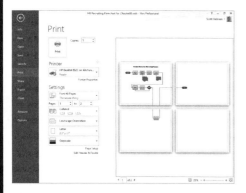

Create

Create graphics,
page 330

Create

Create custom templates,
page 338

Publish

Publish diagrams to the web,
page 344

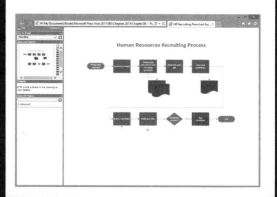

IN THIS CHAPTER, YOU WILL LEARN HOW TO

- Preview and print Visio diagrams.

- Remove personal information.

- Create graphics.

- Save drawings in other file formats.

- Create Visio templates.

- Share diagrams by using the Visio Viewer.

- Publish Visio diagrams to the web.

When you've worked hard to create a Microsoft Visio 2013 diagram, the chances are extremely good that you want to share it with other people. Sometimes you may simply want to share a printout, but in many cases, you want to share all or part of your diagram in electronic form. Visio has long provided an extensive list of alternative formats, and the list is even longer with Visio 2013.

In this chapter, you will learn how to use the diagram preview mode in Visio and then how to print Visio diagrams. You will learn about the private information that Visio stores and discover how to remove it from diagrams you want to share electronically. Then you'll create graphics from all or some of the shapes on a drawing page and will save drawings in various file formats, including creating a new Visio template. Finally, you'll learn how people without Visio can view your drawings by using the Visio Viewer and by using a web browser when you publish diagrams as webpages.

PRACTICE FILES To complete the exercises in this chapter, you need the practice files contained in the Chapter08 practice file folder. For more information, see "Downloading the practice files" in this book's Introduction.

Previewing and printing Visio diagrams

In this exercise, you will explore several options for previewing and printing your document.

 SET UP You need the *HR Process Map for Chapter08A_start* drawing located in the Chapter08 practice file folder to complete this exercise. Open the drawing in Visio and save it as *HR Process Map for Chapter08A*.

1 On the **File** tab, click **Print** to display the **Print** page of the Backstage view. The left side of the page displays print options and the right side is a print preview pane. If your drawing includes more than one page, the active page will appear in the preview pane, however, you can preview any page using the page controls that are highlighted at the bottom center of the following graphic. Note that you can also zoom in and out using the zoom slider and the buttons in the lower-right corner of the page.

TIP The print preview is displayed in grayscale by default. You can preview a pure black and white view by clicking the Grayscale button. There is not a color preview option.

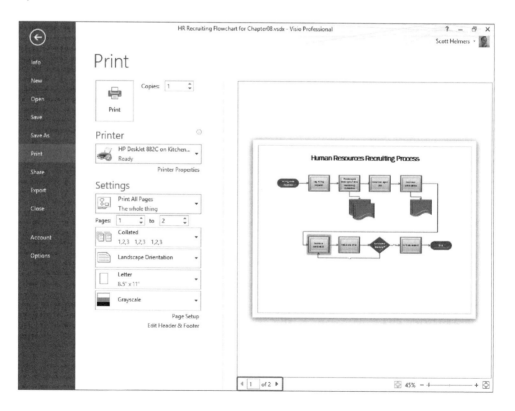

TIP When you move the cursor into the preview pane, the pointer changes to a hand. You can click anywhere on the preview image and drag to reposition the diagram.

2   Click the **Back** arrow in the upper-left corner of the window to return to the Visio diagram.

KEYBOARD SHORTCUT You can also close the print preview by pressing the Esc key.

3   Drag the **End** shape off the page to the right to add a new drawing page automatically, and then drag the **Hire candidate** shape down to create additional new pages.

SEE ALSO Refer to "Managing pages and page setup" in Chapter 3, "Adding sophistication to your drawings" for more information about the Auto Size feature in Visio 2013.

4   On the **File** tab, click **Print** to display the **Print** page of the **Backstage** view. Because the drawing page spans multiple print pages, the preview pane shows four separate printer pages; each page shows its print margins so you know exactly what will print.

KEYBOARD SHORTCUT You can open the print preview page using Alt+F, P, or to maintain compatibility with Visio 2007 and earlier, you can use Alt+F, V.

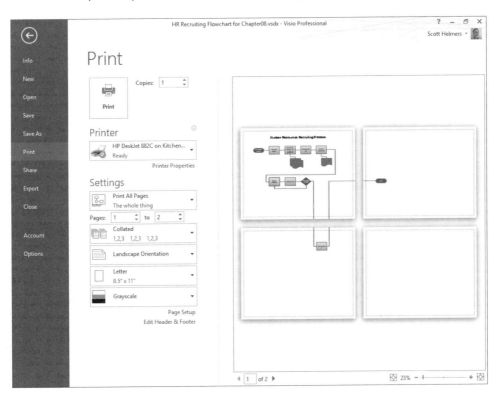

5   Close the print preview page and return to the Visio diagram.

6   Draw a bounding box to select the title at the top of the page and the first row of flowchart shapes, and then open the print preview page. The print preview looks the same as it did in the preceding image.

7   In the **Settings** section on the left side of the page, click the **Print All Pages** button, and then click **Print Selection**. The preview shows exactly what will print: just the selected shapes on one printer page.

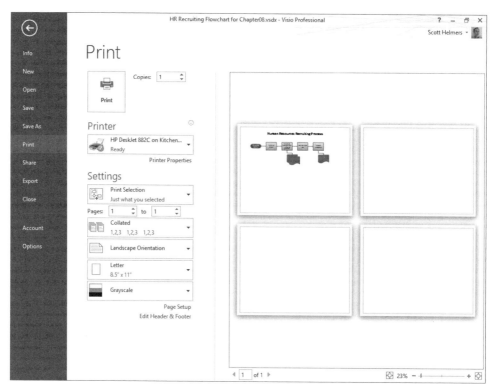

8   In the **Settings** section, click the button that is now labeled **Print Selection**, and then click **Print All Pages** to return to the previous view.

TIP The bottom of the menu on the print selection button that you used in the previous two steps includes two additional options:

■ **No Background** Toggles inclusion or exclusion of the page background from the print preview and printed output.

■ **High Quality** Toggles inclusion or exclusion of certain effects, such as reflections, from the print preview and printed output.

9   In the **Settings** section, click the **Landscape Orientation** button, and then click **Portrait Orientation**. The preview shows how your diagram will print in portrait mode.

10   Click the **Portrait Orientation** button and then click **Landscape Orientation** to return to the previous view.

11   In the **Settings** section, click the **Letter** button, and then click **Legal** to change the printer page size. The preview shows how your diagram will print using this new size.

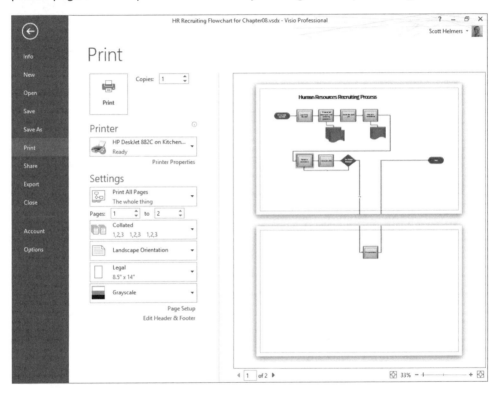

TIP If you create diagrams using metric templates, the page size buttons in the Settings section will be labeled with appropriate paper sizes, such as A4 or A3.

12   At the bottom of the **Settings** section, click **Page Setup**. The **Page Setup** dialog box opens to the **Print Setup** tab so you can make further adjustments, if desired.

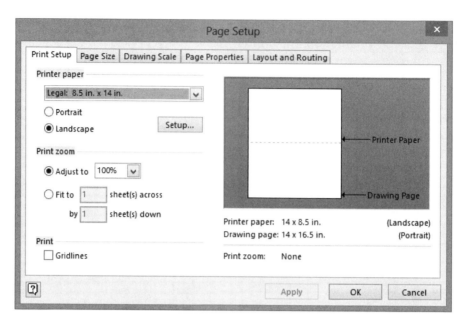

13   Close the print preview page and return to the Visio diagram.

14   At the bottom of the **Settings** section, click **Header & Footer** to open the **Header and Footer** dialog box, which allows you to set a three-part header or footer for this document. You can type text into any of the **Header** and **Footer** fields, or you can click the Right arrow next to each field to select a predefined value from the list. Note that you can also set page margins in this dialog box.

TIP Headers and footers print information on the top and bottom of each printer page and are independent of the drawing page. Consequently, headers and footers can be useful for Visio diagrams in which the drawing page is spread across multiple printer pages. They are used infrequently for the majority of Visio documents where each drawing page prints on a single printer page. In those cases, including header or footer information on background pages is a more common technique.

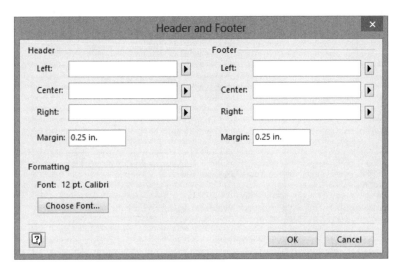

15   If you added header or footer information, click **OK**; otherwise click **Cancel**, and then close the print preview page.

❌ CLEAN UP Leave the *HR Process Map for Chapter08A* drawing open if you are continuing with the next exercise, otherwise close the file. It is not necessary to save changes.

8

Removing personal information

Every Visio document contains a collection of metadata about the document itself. Some of the data fields are supplied by Visio; some are prefilled based on the template from which you create a document; most are blank. You can view and change metadata fields either on the Info page in the Backstage view (on the left in the following graphic) or in the document's Properties dialog box, which is accessed by clicking the Properties button on the right side of the Info page. The Properties dialog box is shown on the right in the following graphic.

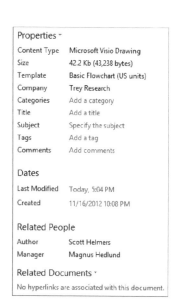

When you plan to share your Visio drawing in electronic form, you may want to remove personally identifiable information first.

In this exercise, you will remove personal information from a Visio diagram.

SET UP **You need the *HR Process Map for Chapter08A* drawing for this exercise. Either continue with the open copy from the previous exercise or open the *HR Process Map for Chapter08A_start* drawing located in the Chapter08 practice file folder and save it as *HR Process Map for Chapter08A*.**

1   Click the **File** tab. By default, Visio opens to the **Info** page when you click the **File** tab (as described in Chapter 1, "A visual orientation to a visual product.") The **Info** page shows the location of the current drawing on disk, the document properties, and several buttons.

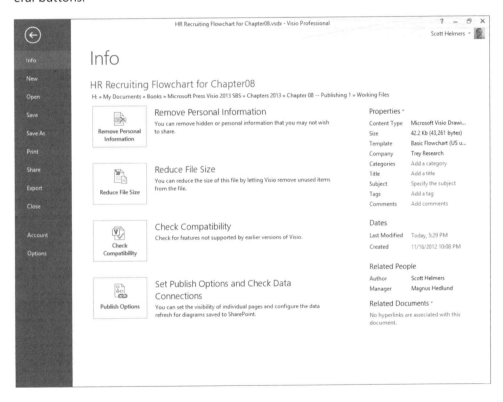

2   Click the **Remove Personal Information** button to open the **Remove Hidden Information** dialog box.

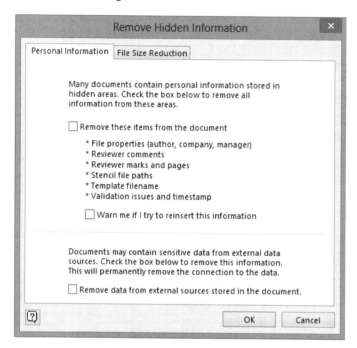

This dialog box offers three check boxes:

- **Remove these items from the document** Removes author, company, and other information shown in the Properties area of the Info page

- **Warn me if I try to reinsert this information** Protects you if you inadvertently add personal details back to the document after removing them

- **Remove data from external sources stored in the document** Removes private information from data sources to which this diagram has been linked using the techniques described in Chapter 6, "Entering, linking to, and reporting on data."

3   Select **Remove these items from the document**, click **OK**, and then compare the fol-
    lowing graphic with the graphic in the introduction to this exercise. Notice that the
    Company, Author, and Manager names have all been removed.

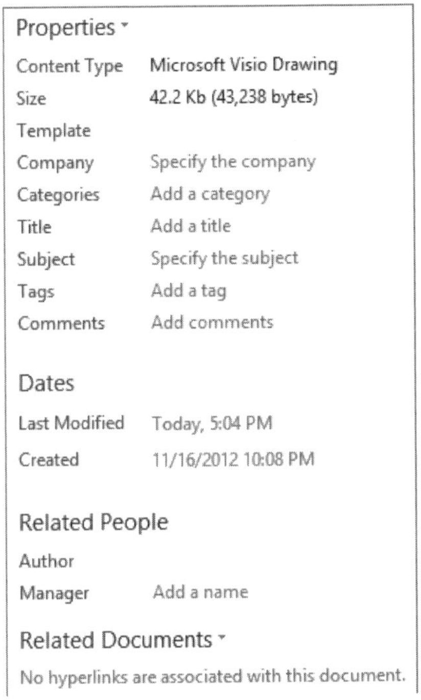

Properties ˅

Content Type	Microsoft Visio Drawing
Size	42.2 Kb (43,238 bytes)
Template	
Company	Specify the company
Categories	Add a category
Title	Add a title
Subject	Specify the subject
Tags	Add a tag
Comments	Add comments

Dates

Last Modified	Today, 5:04 PM
Created	11/16/2012 10:08 PM

Related People

Author	
Manager	Add a name

Related Documents ˅

No hyperlinks are associated with this document.

❌ CLEAN UP Leave the *HR Process Map for Chapter08A* drawing open if you are continuing with the next exercise, otherwise close the file. It is not necessary to save changes.

8

Creating graphics

The collection of "Save As" file types in Visio is extensive and includes options to create the following image types (listed in alphabetical order):

- **BMP or DIB** Windows Bitmap
- **EMF** Enhanced Metafile and
  EMZ Compressed Enhanced Metafile
- **GIF** Graphic Interchange Format
- **JPEG** Joint Photographic Experts Group
- **PNG** Portable Network Graphic
- **SVG** Scalable Vector Graphics and
  SVGZ Scalable Vector Graphics - Compressed
- **TIF** Tag Image File Format
- **WMF** Windows Metafile

TIP If you need a detailed description of any of these file formats, you can find plenty of information on the Internet. For example, the Wikipedia article at *www.wikipedia.org/wiki/ Image_file_formats* describes most of the formats in the previous list.

For all image formats except SVG/SVGZ, creating images in Visio is a shape-oriented, not a page-oriented, operation. To say that another way, with the exception of SVG, Visio does not provide a built-in method to create an image of an entire page. When you use Visio to create a graphic for all shapes on a page, Visio will create an image that is only as big as the rectangle surrounding the shapes. White space between that rectangle and the page boundaries will not be included. You will find an example of this behavior in the following exercise and will also learn an easy workaround.

In this exercise, you will create JPEG and PNG images from a Visio drawing.

 SET UP **You need the *HR Process Map for Chapter08A* drawing for this exercise. Either continue with the open copy from the previous exercise or open the *HR Process Map for Chapter08A_start* drawing located in the Chapter08 practice file folder and save it as *HR Process Map for Chapter08A*. Set the Recruiting page to whole page view.**

1   On the **File** tab, click **Export**, and then click **Change File Type**. Four of the most common image file types appear under the **Graphic File Types** heading. (At the end of this exercise, you will learn how to save to file types not listed here.)

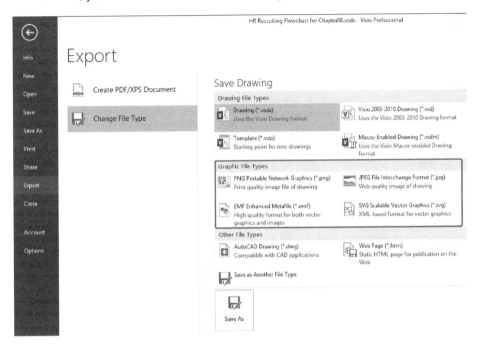

2   Double-click **JPEG File Interchange Format (*.jpg)** to open the **Save As** dialog box.

TIP The default save location for your image is the same folder that contains the Visio drawing. Because Visio uses the standard Windows Save As dialog box, you have the option to change the folder in which the image file will be saved. You can also click Save As Type to select a different file type.

3   In the **File name** field, type **Not quite full page**, and then click **Save**. The **JPG Output Options** dialog box lets you adjust how the image file will be created. In most situations, you can accept all default settings by clicking **OK**. However, if you require a specific JPEG file format that differs from the defaults shown in the following graphic, use the various drop-down lists, text boxes, and options to satisfy your needs.

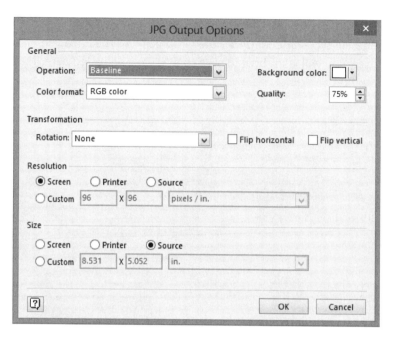

4   Click **OK**.

5   Open the **Not quite full page** image in any image viewing program. On most systems, you can do this by double-clicking the file name in Windows Explorer.

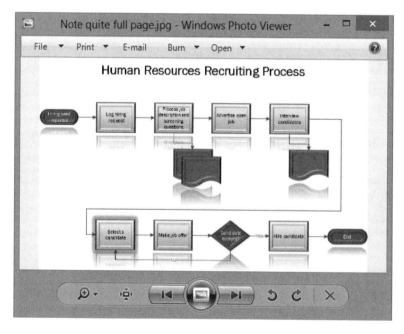

Notice that the image created by Visio does not include the full drawing page, but rather is just big enough to contain all of the shapes on the page. As noted in the introductory text for this exercise, this is normal Visio behavior when creating image files.

TIP If you want to create an image of an entire Visio drawing page, you must place one or more shapes at the page boundaries to force Visio to capture the entire page. The easiest techniques for accomplishing this are to: 1) draw a rectangle with no fill at the page margins, effectively creating a border around the page; or 2) place a pair of very small shapes in opposite corners of the page.

If you use the first technique, you can make the line nearly invisible by making it very thin and giving it a color that is almost the same as the page background. If you use the second method, you can make the small shapes nearly invisible by making them very, very tiny or by making their fill color nearly the same as the page background. In either case, do not use a color that is exactly the same as the page background. If your shapes and the background are the same color, Visio will not detect your shapes and will not include them in the exported image, so you will fail to capture the full page.

Next you will create a PNG image of a portion of the Visio recruiting diagram.

6   Use a bounding box to select the **Select a candidate**, **Make job offer**, and **Candidate accepts?** and **No** arrow shapes. Do not include the Yes arrow shape.

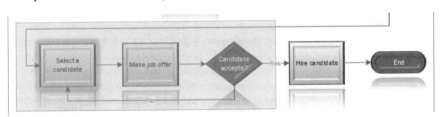

7   On the **File** tab, click **Export**, click **Change File Type**, and then double-click **PNG Portable Network Graphics (*.png)**.

8   In the **File name** field, type **Job offer shapes**, and then click **Save** to open the **PNG Output Options** dialog box. As with JPEG images, the default settings for PNG images are probably sufficient unless you have specific requirements that mandate other settings.

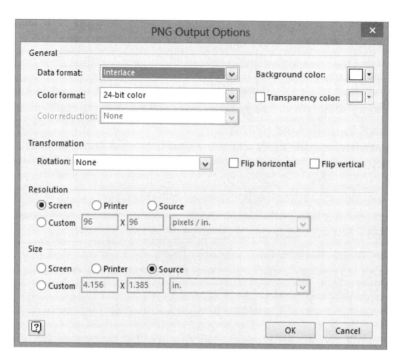

9   Click **OK**.

10   Open the **Job offer shapes** image in any image viewing program.

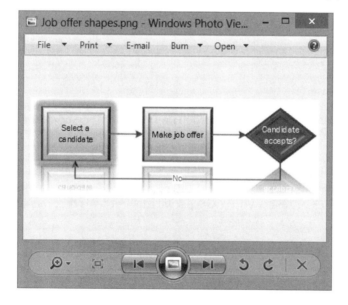

Notice that this image of a set of selected shapes exhibits the same behavior you saw when you created an image that contained all of the shapes on the page: the image is exactly as large as the set of shapes. If you require white space at the outside edges of your image, you will need to use one of the techniques described in the Tip after step 5.

Also notice that only fully selected shapes are included in the image: the Yes arrow and the arrow leading into the Select A Candidate shape are not included because they were only partially selected.

✖ CLEAN UP Close the *HR Process Map for Chapter08A* drawing. It isn't necessary to save your changes.

TIP The Graphic File Types section of the Export page shown in the graphic after step 1 in this exercise only includes the four most common image types. All image types are accessible in the Save As dialog box that you can open from the Save As page in the Backstage view. The list in the following graphic is from Visio Standard. The Professional edition includes one additional entry for backward compatibility: Visio 2010 Web Drawing.

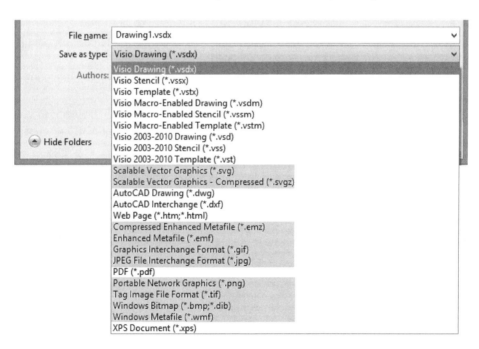

Saving drawings in other file formats

In addition to creating multiple types of graphics files for shapes located on a single page, Visio lets you save your entire drawing in more than a dozen formats. To access the file formats: on the File tab, click Save As, click Computer, click Browse, and then in the Save As Type list, select the desired file type.

TABLE 1 Visio file types

Save As format name	File extension	Description
Visio Drawing	.vsdx	Visio 2013 drawing (cannot contain macros)
Visio Stencil	.vssx	Visio 2013 stencil (cannot contain macros)
Visio Template	.vstx	Visio 2013 template (cannot contain macros)
Visio Macro-Enabled Drawing	.vsdm	Visio 2013 macro-enabled drawing
Visio Macro-Enabled Stencil	.vssm	Visio 2013 macro-enabled stencil
Visio Macro-Enabled Template	.vstm	Visio 2013 macro-enabled template
Visio 2003-2010 Drawing	.vsd	Visio drawing in file format used in Visio 2003 through Visio 2010
Visio 2003-2010 Stencil	.vss	Visio stencil in file format used in Visio 2003 through Visio 2010
Visio 2003-2010 Template	.vst	Visio template in file format used in Visio 2003 through Visio 2010
Visio 2010 Web Drawing	.vdw	Visio file format used to publish drawings to Visio Services on Microsoft SharePoint 2010 (Professional edition only)

Visio 2013 can create files that are compatible with Visio versions back to Visio 2003 but cannot create files that are compatible with Visio 2002 or earlier.

TABLE 2 Non-Visio (and non-image) file types

Save As format name	File extension	Description
AutoCAD Drawing	.dwg	AutoCAD drawing format; file can be opened directly by AutoCAD and other CAD systems that use this file format
AutoCAD Interchange	.dxf	AutoCAD drawing exchange format; intended to provide greater interoperability among systems that do not use DWG

Save As format name	File extension	Description
PDF	.pdf	Adobe Portable Document Format; accurate rendering of a Visio drawing, including most hyperlinks, that is intended to be read-only; requires free PDF viewer
XPS Document	.xps	XML Paper Specification; an alternative to PDF for creating high-quality, read-only renderings of a document; requires free XPS viewer
Web Page	.htm/.html	HTML rendering of a Visio drawing that is viewable with a web browser

All of the entries in Table 1 and the first two entries in Table 2 always save the entire Visio drawing in the new format. However, the last three entries in Table 2—PDF, XPS, and Web Page—give you the choice of saving a subset of your pages into the desired format. Each offers an options dialog box, similar to the one for PDF shown in the following graphic, in which you can select a range of pages along with other format-specific options.

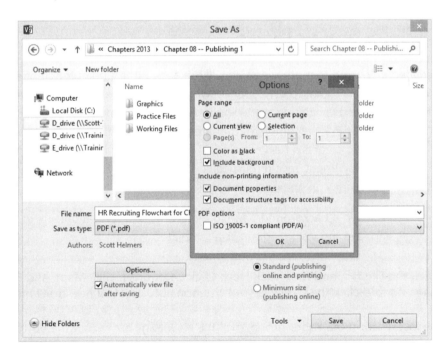

The inclusion of PDF as a built-in file format in Visio 2013 and Visio 2010 is a big advantage for many people. In previous versions of Visio, it was necessary to download PDF-creation software from Adobe, Microsoft, or another vendor in order to share Visio drawings in this popular file format.

XPS is an alternative to PDF that includes most of the same capabilities. Visio summarizes the benefits of PDF and XPS in the Backstage view: on the File tab, click Export, and then click Create PDF/XPS Document to display the text shown on the far right in the following graphic.

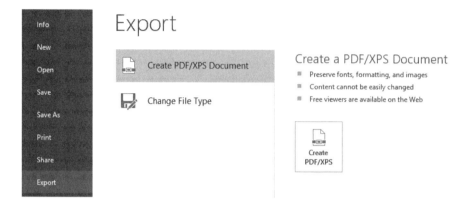

Creating Visio templates

If you have created a drawing that other people will use as a starting point for creating their own drawings, you may want to save your drawing as a Visio *template*. The advantage of sharing a template over sharing a drawing is that your document is not modified when someone uses it. Just like the templates that are packaged with Visio, whenever a user selects your template, Visio creates a new drawing. The new drawing inherits all of the attributes of your original document, including specific stencils, foreground and background pages, and even preset shapes on one or more pages.

In this exercise, you will add a background page to a drawing, add several objects to the background page, and save the Visio diagram as a template.

 SET UP **Click the File tab, and then click New. Click Categories, click Maps And Floor Plans, and then double-click the Office Layout thumbnail to create a new drawing.**

1   On the **Insert** tab, in the **Pages** group, click the **New Page** arrow (not the button) to display the submenu.

2   Click **Background Page**, and then in the **Page Setup** dialog box, click **OK**. Visio has created a new page called *Background-1*.

SEE ALSO For more information about background pages, refer to "Working with background pages and borders" in Chapter 3.

3 In the **Shapes** window, click **More Shapes**, point to **Visio Extras**, click **Title Blocks**, and then click anywhere on the drawing page to close the fly-out menus.

4 From the **Title Blocks** stencil, drag a **Drawn by** shape into the lower-right corner of the background page.

TIP The Drawn By shape automatically displays the contents of the Author field from the Visio document's properties.

5 Add a text box to the upper-left corner of the page, type **Trey Research**, and apply the following attributes to the text box: **30 pt.**, **Bold**, **Align left**.

You've created a background page and can now apply it to the foreground page in your document.

6 Right-click on the page name tab for **Page-1**, and then click **Page Setup**.

7 Click the **Background** drop-down list arrow, and then click **Background-1**.

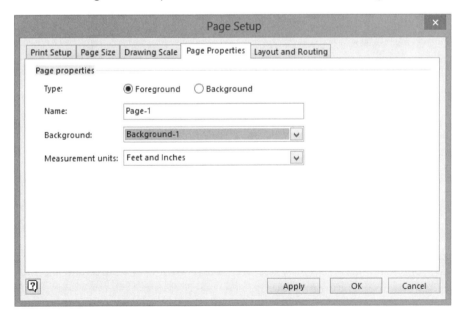

8   Click **OK**. Your drawing page now displays the company name and a *Drawn by* information block from the background page.

9   In the **Shapes** window, click the heading for **Walls, Doors and Windows** to activate that stencil so it will be the active stencil whenever a diagram is created from your template.

10 On the **File** tab, click **Save**, click **Computer**, and then click the **Browse** button.

11 In the **Save As** dialog box, navigate to the folder in which you'd like to save the template, and in the **File name** field, type **Trey Research Office Layout**.

12 In the **Save as type** drop-down list, click **Visio Template**.

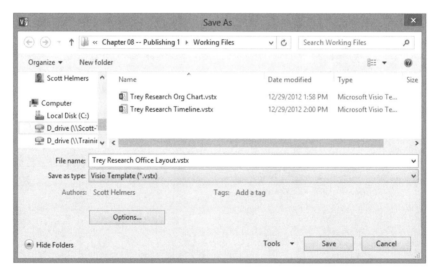

13 Click **Save**. You have created a template that can be used by other people to create office floor plans for Trey Research. Each drawing will automatically show the name of the author of the document.

❌ CLEAN UP   Close the template file.

Where do I store custom templates?

You can store custom templates in any location that you like. You might store them on your own system if you're the only person who will use them, or you might place them on a server so you can share them with others.

Regardless of their location, you need to tell Visio where you've put your templates in order for them to show up on the New page in the *Backstage view*. You will probably find it helpful to organize your templates by placing them in a folder. The following example uses a folder called *Trey Research Templates*.

To inform Visio of the location for your template folder:

1 On the **File** tab, click **Options**, and then click **Advanced**.

2 Scroll to the bottom of the **Advanced** settings, and click the **File Locations** button.

3 In the **Templates** field of the **File Locations** dialog box, enter the path to the folder that contains the *Trey Research Templates* folder.

> **IMPORTANT** Be sure to note the wording in the preceding sentence: "enter the path to the folder that contains the Trey Research Templates folder." In other words, do not include the name of the folder that contains the templates in the template path: stop one folder above your folder. This ensures that your folder name appears in the Template Categories panel along with the Visio-supplied template categories. For example, in the following graphic, the Trey Research Templates folder is located within the Chapter08 folder, so Trey Research Templates is not included in the path.

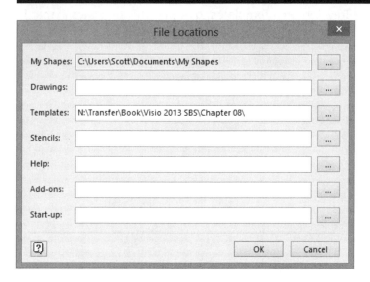

4   After entering the template path, click **OK** twice. The next time you start Visio, the **Template Categories** section of the **New** page on the **Home** tab should look something like the following graphic.

TROUBLESHOOTING If the *Trey Research Templates* folder doesn't appear as shown, refer to the Important note following step 3 in this sidebar.

5   Double-click **Trey Research Templates** to display the templates in that folder.

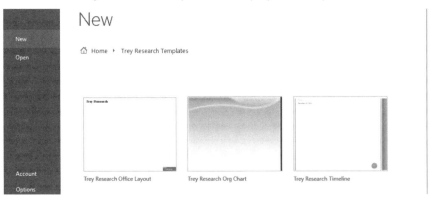

Sharing diagrams by using the Visio Viewer

Microsoft Office 2013 includes the Visio Viewer as a default installation option. Consequently, on a system that includes Office but not Visio, you can view any Visio diagram in Windows Internet Explorer (the Viewer runs as an Internet Explorer add-on). On a system that includes both Office and Visio, Visio drawings will always open in Visio and not in the Visio Viewer.

In this exercise, you will use the Visio Viewer to examine a Visio drawing.

 SET UP **You need the *HR Process Map for Chapter08A_start* drawing located in the Chapter08 practice file folder to complete this exercise.**

1   On a system that includes Office 2013 but not Visio, double-click the **HR Process Map for Chapter08A_start** drawing in Windows Explorer. If this is the first time you have used the Visio Viewer on this system, a warning like the one shown in the following graphic might appear.

This webpage wants to run the following add-on: 'Microsoft Visio Viewer' from 'Microsoft Corporation'.   What's the risk? | Allow | ×

2   Click **Allow**. A **Security Warning** dialog box appears.

3   Click **Run**. The Visio drawing appears in the Internet Explorer window, which includes a set of zoom controls in the upper left and familiar-looking page navigation controls in the lower left. There are also three buttons at the top of the window that give you control over display, layer, and markup information for the Viewer rendering of your drawing.

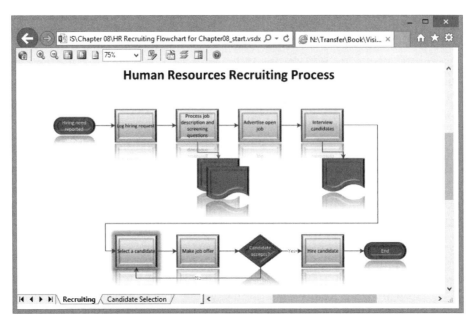

CLEAN UP Close Internet Explorer.

TIP After you have given Internet Explorer permission to run the Visio Viewer add-on, it will do so in the future without requiring any intervention.

Publishing Visio diagrams to the web

One of the most useful features for sharing Visio diagrams is the ability to create a website from a Visio document. The Visio-generated website includes all foreground pages, preserves both page-to-page and external hyperlinks, and includes the following bonus features:

- A table of contents that allows you to jump to any page

- A pan-and-zoom pane that lets you click and drag to zoom and navigate around any page

- A details window to present shape data for any shape

- Full-text search for all text in the entire drawing

If you haven't explored the Save As Web Page option in Visio, you owe it to yourself to do so. Whether you want to share drawings on your intranet site with colleagues who don't have Visio, or publish diagrams on the public World Wide Web, this Visio feature can make your diagrams more accessible.

In this exercise, you will create and explore a website generated with default Visio web publishing settings.

SET UP You need the *HR Process Map for Chapter08B_start* drawing located in the Chapter08 practice file folder to complete this exercise. Open the drawing in Visio and save it as *HR Process Map for Chapter08B*.

1   On the **File** tab, click **Export**, click **Change File Type**, and then double-click **Web Page (*.htm)**. A **Save As** dialog box appears with the **Save as type** drop-down list preset to **Web Page**. The dialog box also offers additional choices related to creating a website.

For this exercise, you will accept the default settings that lie behind the **Change Title** and **Publish** buttons. In Chapter 13, "Collaborating on and publishing diagrams," you will investigate the settings those buttons offer.

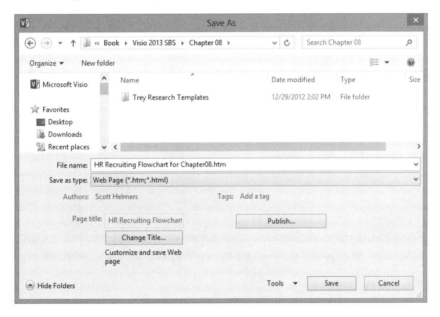

8

2   Click **Save**. One or more progress indicators appear, and then your Visio-generated website opens automatically in Internet Explorer. In addition to a viewing pane, notice the four-part navigation pane on the left side of the browser window.

IMPORTANT Internet Explorer requires you to install Microsoft Silverlight to view a Visio-generated website. If you have not previously installed Silverlight, a button will appear in Internet Explorer that you can click to install it. Information about Silverlight is available at *www.microsoft.com/silverlight/*.

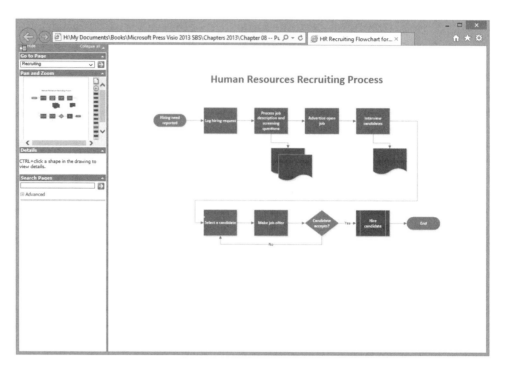

TIP Depending on where your Visio-created webpages are stored, a warning may appear when you attempt to view the pages. Simply click Allow Blocked Content to proceed.

Internet Explorer restricted this webpage from running scripts or ActiveX controls.   Allow blocked content   ×

3   Point to the **Hire candidate** *subprocess* shape. Because this shape contains a hyperlink, Internet Explorer displays a pop-up that contains up to three entries:

- The shape text, if any

- Instructions to hold down the **Ctrl** key and click to view shape details

- Instructions to click to follow the hyperlink

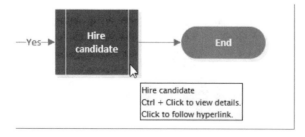

4   Click the **Hire candidate** shape. Internet Explorer follows the hyperlink to the subprocess page.

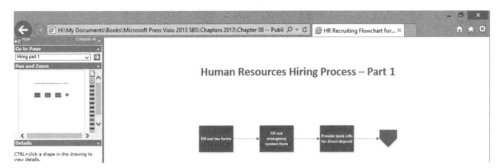

5   Click the browser's **Back** button to return to the first page.

6   Click the **Advertise open job** shape. This shape contains a hyperlink to *www.visiostepbystep.com*, so that webpage appears.

7   Click the browser's **Back** button to return to the first page.

8   In the **Go to Page** section of the navigation pane, click the down arrow, and then click **Hiring part 1**. Finally, click the green button containing the white arrow to go to the page you've selected. The viewing pane displays the selected page.

9   Click the browser's **Back** button to return to the first page.

10 In the **Pan And Zoom** section of the navigation pane, drag from the upper-left edge of the **Hiring need reported** shape to the right so you include the first four shapes in the top row. As you drag the pointer, a blue box appears; it will follow your pointer to the right and will also expand downward. When you release the mouse button, the border of the box you've drawn turns from blue to red and the viewing pane shows just that portion of the drawing page.

IMPORTANT You can't control the shape of the box you draw in the Pan And Zoom pane. It will maintain the same aspect ratio as the viewing pane to the right. With Internet Explorer opened to full screen on a system with resolution of 1024 × 768, the result looks like the following diagram.

Full page view

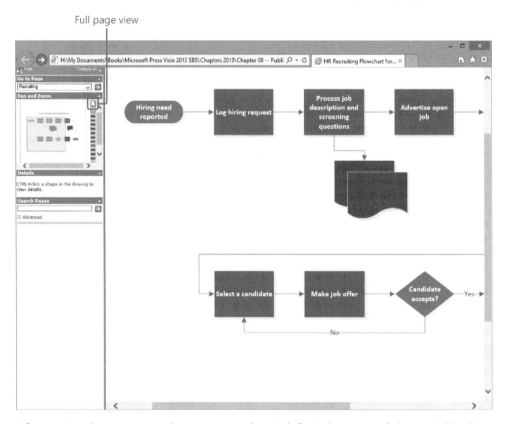

After you've drawn a zoom box, you can drag it left, right, up, and down within the Pan And Zoom pane to move the image in the viewing pane. You can also click the buttons and bars at the right edge of the Pan And Zoom pane to zoom in or out.

11   In the upper-right corner of the **Pan and Zoom** pane, click the **Zoom page to 100%** button to return the viewing pane to full page view. (The button looks like a piece of paper and is marked in the preceding graphic.)

TIP After returning to full page view, you'll find that the red-bordered box remains in the Pan And Zoom pane as shown in the following graphic.

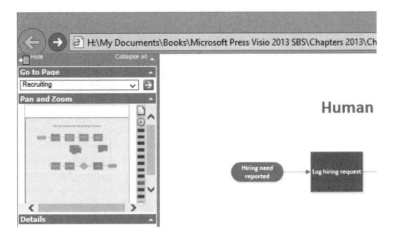

If you subsequently want to change the zoom level, you can either drag the edges of the zoom box or click the refresh button in Internet Explorer. The latter action reloads the drawing and removes the zoom box completely.

12 Hold down **Ctrl** and click the **Hire candidate** shape. The shape data for this shape appears in the **Details** pane, which is located just below the **Pan And Zoom** pane.

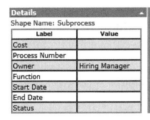

13 In the **Search Pages** pane, type **candidate**, and then click the arrow in the green square to execute the search. A list of all shapes that contain any form of the word *candidate* appears below the search box. What is particularly impressive about the full text search is that it presents more than just a list; it creates a hyperlinked list of search results, as you will discover in the next step.

14 Click the **Select a candidate** link in the **Search Pages** pane. Notice that an orange arrow appears over that shape for several seconds to show you exactly where on the page your search result is located. Try clicking the other entries in the search results list and you'll find that the arrow points to each of them.

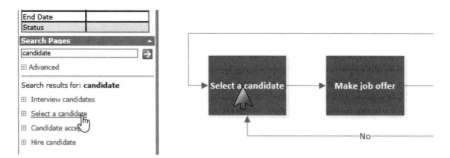

15   In the **Search Pages** pane, type **manager**, and then press **Enter** to execute the search.

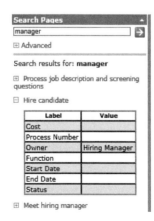

At first glance, the search results look incorrect because two of the three listed items don't contain the word *manager*. However, it's important to understand that the search function is looking at the shape data inside the shapes as well as the text on the shapes. Consequently, if you click the first or second entry and then hold down Ctrl and click the designated shape, you can confirm that the shape data in the Details pane does, indeed, include the word *manager*.

TIP Clicking the plus sign to the left of any search result also reveals the shape data associated with that result.

16   Click **Meet hiring manager** in the search results list. Even though the designated shape is located on another page, the target page will first appear in the viewing pane and then the orange arrow will appear.

❌ CLEAN UP **Close Internet Explorer and the *HR Process Map for Chapter08* drawing.**

Key points

- A significant part of the value of creating a Visio drawing comes from sharing it with others. Visio allows you to print diagrams as well as share them in many other formats.

- You can remove personal metadata from documents with a couple of clicks prior to sharing them electronically.

- You can create graphics from one or more shapes on a page in any of eight different file formats.

- You can save Visio diagrams, stencils, and templates in three different Visio formats: the new VSDX format that doesn't permit files to contain macros; the VSDM format that does allow macros; and the VSD format that is backward-compatible with Visio 2010, 2007, and 2003.

- You can create Visio templates that contain any document and page elements that you would like to have present every time you create a new diagram. Typical items to include in a template include company logos or other required graphics; legal notices or copyright statements; page numbering placeholders; customized background pages; and title blocks.

- The Visio Viewer that is included with every copy of Office 2013 lets anyone view Visio diagrams using nothing more than Internet Explorer.

- One of the most useful features in Visio is the ability to create an entire website from a Visio drawing. Graphic and text elements, all hyperlinks, and nearly every other Visio feature is preserved in the web rendering. In addition, a Visio-created website includes pan-and-zoom, shape data display, and full-text search capabilities.

8

Chapter at a glance

Build

Build network diagrams,
page 354

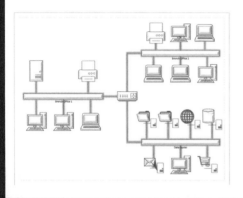

Organize

Organize network shapes,
page 363

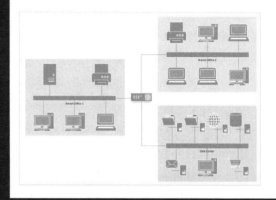

Add

Add equipment to rack diagrams,
page 370

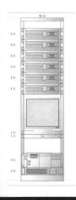

Run

Run network reports,
page 381

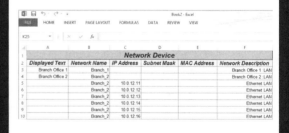

IN THIS CHAPTER, YOU WILL LEARN HOW TO

- Build basic and detailed network diagrams.

- Organize network shapes in a diagram.

- Create and add equipment to rack diagrams.

- Change the drawing scale.

- Run computer and network reports.

- Search and replace text.

- Map Active Directory and LDAP.

This chapter describes one of the most common uses for Microsoft Visio: creating network and data center diagrams. Whether your goal is to create simple, stylized representations of network connectivity or to create photo-realistic rack diagrams that show real-time equipment status, you can accomplish your goal with Visio.

Previous versions of Visio included several stencils containing computer and network shapes that had a three-dimensional (3D or 3-D) appearance. These stencils are still available in Visio 2013 and are packaged with two templates: *Basic Network Shapes - 3D* is included with both the Standard and Professional editions; *Detailed Network Shapes - 3D* is packaged with the Professional edition.

In addition, Visio 2013 includes new stencils containing two-dimensional (2-D) shapes that are fully compatible with Visio 2013 themes. These shapes are used in the templates called *Basic Network Shapes* and *Detailed Network Shapes* (Professional edition only).

In addition to the hundreds of computer and network shapes that are packaged with Visio, there are thousands of downloadable shapes, many of which were designed to look exactly like specific brands and models of equipment. You will find links to many sources of Visio shapes later in this chapter in the sidebar, "Where can I get shapes that look like my equipment?"

Early versions of Visio—Visio 2000 and earlier—included a network discovery and auto-mapping capability. In essence, you could point those early versions of Visio at a network and it would figure out what was out there and build a map for you. Although that capability no longer exists in Visio, several vendors provide Visio add-ins that have this capability. One place to look for Visio add-ins is the partner solutions page at *Visio.Microsoft.com*.

In this chapter, you will build basic and detailed network diagrams and learn one technique for organizing network shapes. You will create rack diagrams using equipment shapes designed to fit in the racks and will learn how to set the page properties so that all shapes on the page are drawn to scale. You will run computer and network reports from your diagrams and find out how to search and replace text in a drawing. Finally, you'll learn about two templates that help you create maps for an Active Directory and an LDAP Directory.

PRACTICE FILES To complete the exercises in this chapter, you need the practice files contained in the Chapter09 practice file folder. For more information, see "Downloading the practice files" in this book's Introduction.

Building basic network diagrams

Both editions of Visio 2013 include a network diagram template called *Basic Network Diagram*.

In this exercise, you will use that template to create a diagram of a simple corporate network.

 SET UP **Click the File tab, and then click New. Click Categories, click Network, and then double-click the Basic Network Diagram thumbnail. Save the drawing as *Network Diagram (Basic)*.**

1   Drag an **Ethernet** shape from the **Network and Peripherals** stencil onto the drawing page and position it in the vertical center of the page, a short distance from the left margin.

2   Drag the resize handle on the right end of the **Ethernet** shape until the network segment is approximately 100 mm (4 inches) long.

> **TIP** Remember that the Width button on the *status bar* displays the current length of any selected shape, so you can use it as a guide as you drag the resize handle.

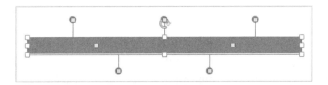

3   With the **Ethernet** shape still selected, type **Branch Office 1** to label the network segment, and then click anywhere on the background of the page.

4   Drag a **Server** shape onto the page and place it above and toward the left end of the **Ethernet** shape.

5   Click once on the **Ethernet** shape to select it, and then drag any yellow *control handle* toward the center of the server shape until a green square appears around the control handle (there's a *connection point* in the center of each of the computer and network shapes).

TIP If you drag a connector line before selecting the Ethernet shape, you will drag the entire shape and not just the connector. Be sure to select the Ethernet shape first.

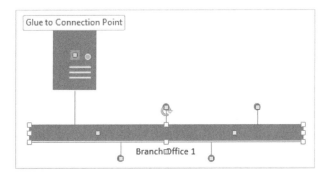

6   Drag a **Printer** shape above and toward the right end of the **Ethernet** shape, and then connect the printer to the network by dragging a yellow handle and gluing it to the printer.

TIP Notice that connector lines remain attached to the Ethernet as you drag control handles in any direction.

7   Drag two **PC** shapes and one **Laptop computer** shape from the **Computers and Monitors** stencil and drop them below the Ethernet shape.

     TIP Don't forget that you can use the *Dynamic Grid* to align the new shapes with each other and with the Ethernet segment.

8   Drag a yellow control handle to each of the **PC** shapes.

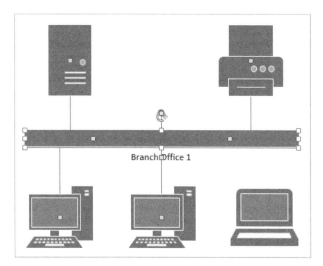

At this point, only one control handle remains below the Ethernet shape but its purpose is to move the text block. Consequently, you can't use it to link the laptop to the network.

9   Drag a control handle from the middle of the **Ethernet** shape and glue it to the **laptop** shape. The laptop is now connected to the Ethernet segment and there are still additional control handles available as shown in the following graphic.

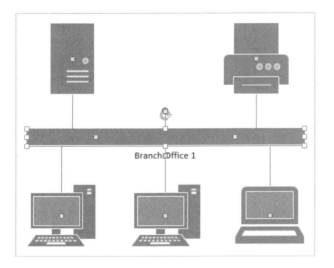

TIP In this graphic, there is an unused control handle/connector line just above the center of the Ethernet segment. If you don't want it there, don't try to delete it—you'll end up deleting the entire Ethernet segment. Instead, if you want to hide the unused connection, drag its control handle back into the interior of the Ethernet shape. Then it won't be visible unless the network segment is selected.

10   Drag another **Ethernet** shape into the upper-right corner of the page, leaving enough room to add shapes above it, and positioning it near the right margin.

11   Drag the left resize handle toward the left to lengthen the Ethernet segment. Continue dragging until a double-headed green arrow appears, indicating that the new network segment is the same length as the one that is already on the page.

9

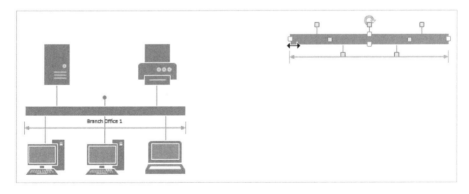

12 While the **Ethernet** shape is still selected, type **Branch Office 2**, and then click anywhere on the background of the page.

13 Drag a **Printer** shape, two **PC** shapes, and three **Laptop computer** shapes, and attach them to the new network segment so you have a network that looks something like the one on the right side of the graphic in step 16.

14 Drag a **Router** shape from the **Network and Peripherals** stencil into the center of the page.

15 Drag the remaining unused connector from the **Branch Office 1** *subnet* and glue it to the router. Notice that the connector repositions itself so the end attached to the **Ethernet** is closer to the **router**.

16 Drag a control handle from the **Branch Office 2** subnet and glue it to the **router**. The connector bends as you drag it toward the **router**—it behaves more like a *dynamic connector* than just a line. Your finished network diagram should look something like the following graphic.

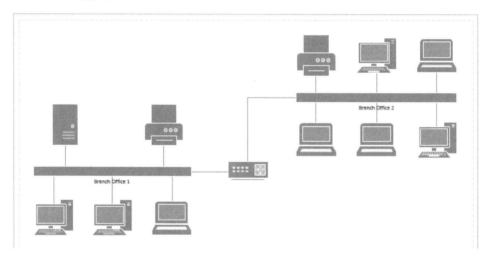

❌ CLEAN UP **Save your changes to the** *Network Diagram (Basic)* **drawing but leave it open if you are continuing with the next exercise.**

Don't forget that the new Visio computer and network shapes accept all of the new themes and effects you learned about in Chapter 5, "Adding style, color, and themes." The following example uses *Variant 4* of the *Zephyr* theme. In addition, the *Art Deco* bevel effect has been applied to the computer shapes and the *Dark Red, 8 pt, Accent color 6* glow effect has been added to the two network segments.

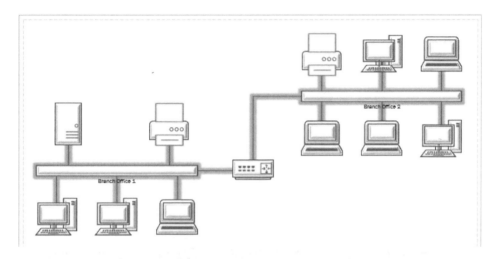

IMPORTANT The following section applies only to the Professional edition of Visio 2013.

Building detailed network diagrams

9

The Professional edition of Visio 2013 includes an advanced network diagram template that offers additional stencils you can use to create more sophisticated diagrams. The primary differences between the Basic and Detailed network templates are visible in the Shapes window. The Basic template (on the left in the following graphic) includes just two stencils: Computers And Monitors and Network And Peripherals. The Detailed template (on the right) includes those two, plus five additional stencils you can use to create more sophisticated diagrams.

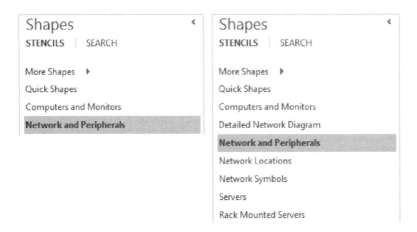

In this exercise, you will create a new drawing from the Detailed Network Diagram template. Then you will paste a copy of the network diagram you created in the previous section into the new drawing. Finally, you will add a network segment to the diagram by using shapes from the Detailed Network Diagram stencils.

SET UP You need the *Network Diagram (Basic)* drawing for this exercise. Either continue with the open copy from the previous exercise or open the *Network Diagram (Basic)_start* drawing located in the Chapter09 practice file folder. With the basic network diagram still open, click the File tab, and then click New. Click Categories, click Network, and then double-click the Detailed Network Diagram thumbnail. Save the drawing as *Network Diagram (Detailed)*.

> **IMPORTANT** If a scroll bar appears when you move the pointer into the upper part of the Shapes window, drag the separator between the title bar section and the shapes section down to reveal all of the stencil titles.

1   On the **View** tab, in the **Window** group, click the **Switch Windows** button and then click **Network Diagram (Basic)**.

    KEYBOARD SHORTCUT You can also press Ctrl+F6 to change windows within Visio.

2   Press **Ctrl+A** to select all shapes on the page, and then press **Ctrl+C** to copy them.

3   Switch Visio windows to return to the **Network Diagram (Detailed)** drawing and press **Ctrl+V** to paste the basic network diagram onto **Page-1**.

    TIP The enhanced copy-and-paste function in Visio 2013 remembers the exact location of the copied network shapes on the original page and places them in the same location on the new page.

4   Drag an **Ethernet** shape from the **Network and Peripherals** stencil onto the drawing page and position it in the lower-right corner of the page so the right end aligns with the right end of the network segment in the upper-right part of the page.

5   Drag the left resize handle until the Ethernet segment is approximately 100 mm (4 inches) long, and then type **Data Center** to label the network segment.

6   Drag and glue a yellow control handle from the **Data Center** network to the **router** shape in the center of the page.

7   Drag a **File server** from the **Servers** stencil onto the page and position it on the left end and above the **Data Center** network segment.

8   Drag one of each of the following server shapes from the **Servers** stencil: **File server**, **Web server**, **Database server**, **Mail server**, and **E-Commerce server**. Position the first three above the network segment and the last two below it.

9   Drag and glue a yellow control handle from the **Data Center** Ethernet to each server.

10 Drag a **PC** shape from the **Computers and Monitors** stencil; position it below and attach it to the **Data Center** network segment. One possible arrangement of your subnet is shown in the following graphic.

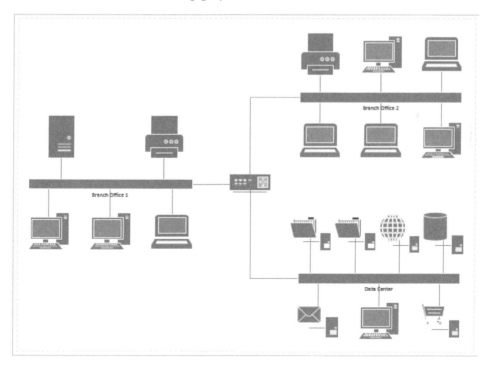

CLEAN UP Save your changes to the *Network Diagram (Detailed)* drawing but leave it open if you are continuing with the next exercise.

You have created a stylized view of the equipment attached to the Data Center network. In all likelihood, the actual equipment in the data center does not consist of stand-alone PCs, but consists of equipment mounted in racks. In two upcoming exercises, you will build a data center rack containing equipment that is equivalent to the previous graphic.

The stencils that are part of the Detailed Network Diagram template include many more shapes than the ones you used in this exercise. If you work with networks, it would be a good idea to spend a few minutes exploring the shapes in the other stencils before moving on to the next exercise.

The Servers stencil you used in this exercise contains 17 unique shapes that you can use to represent specific server types. The Rack Mounted Servers stencil, which is also opened with the Detailed Network Server template, contains a corresponding set of 17 rack-mounted server shapes.

SEE ALSO In Chapter 10, "Visualizing your data," you will learn additional methods for enhancing network and data center diagrams.

In the preceding exercises, you used the redesigned network and computer shapes in Visio 2013. Don't forget, however, that the traditional 3-D network and computer shapes are still available in two templates: *Basic Network Shapes - 3D* and *Detailed Network Shapes - 3D* (Professional edition only). Compare the diagram you created in this exercise with the graphic below that represents the same network but uses the 3-D shapes.

SEE ALSO Microsoft created a collection of server and network shapes for use in wall posters depicting product deployment scenarios. Though you may not need to create posters containing network shapes, the free, downloadable stencils offer an alternative to the traditional Visio shapes. To download these stencils, go to *www.microsoft.com/en-us/ download/details.aspx?id=21480*.

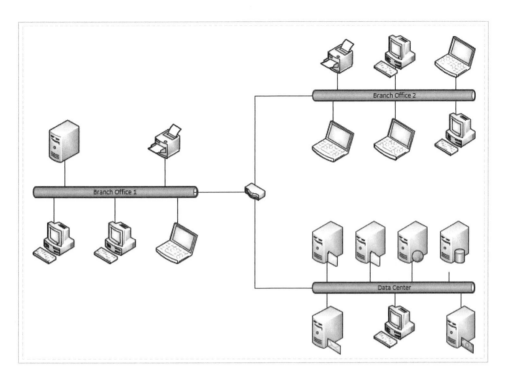

SEE ALSO If you would like to create your own customized server shapes, refer to the article on the Visio Guy website at *www.visguy.com/2009/09/11/visio-server-shape-icon-customization-tool*. Note, however, that this article applies to customizing the older, 3-D-style Visio server shapes.

Organizing network shapes in a diagram

It's quite common that once you've created a network drawing, you might want to organize subsets of the shapes. Sometimes the reason is aesthetic: you want to create visual groupings within your diagram. Sometimes the reason is practical: you want to rearrange the drawing and it's easier if certain shapes are grouped.

In this exercise, you will add a background shape to each section of your network diagram and then group the shapes in that part of the network.

SET UP You need the *Network Diagram (Detailed)* drawing for this exercise. Either continue with the open copy from the previous exercise or open the *Network Diagram (Detailed)_start* drawing located in the Chapter09 practice file folder and save it as *Network Diagram (Organized)*.

1   Right-click anywhere on the drawing page, click the arrow on the *Mini Toolbar* to open the **Drawing Tools** drop-down menu, and then click the **Rectangle** tool.

2   Draw a rectangle just large enough to surround everything in **Branch Office 1**.

3   Right-click the new rectangle, click the **Styles** button on the Mini Toolbar, and then click a light-colored background color in the **Theme Styles** section or using the **Fill** button.

4   Right-click the new rectangle, and then click **Send to Back** on the Mini Toolbar to place the rectangle behind the network shapes.

   SEE ALSO For information about the front-to-back positioning of Visio shapes, see the sidebar, "What's on top?" in Chapter 5, "Adding style, color, and themes."

5   Draw a bounding box around the new rectangle and the shapes within it.

6   On the **Home** tab, in the **Arrange** group, click the **Group** button, and then click **Group**.

   SEE ALSO Refer to Chapter 3, "Adding sophistication to your drawings," for more information about grouping and ungrouping shapes.

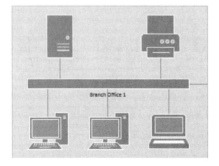

7   Repeat steps 1–6 for **Branch Office 2** but select a different fill color in step 3.

8   Repeat steps 1–6 for **Data Center** but select a different fill color in step 3.

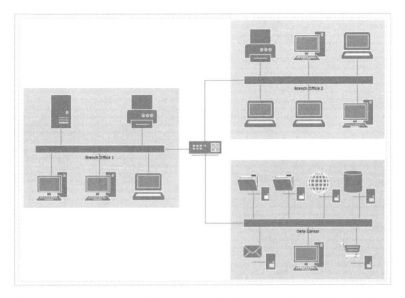

The approach you used in this exercise for grouping network shapes is very common. It offers the advantages, but also the disadvantages, of working with grouped shapes that were described in Chapter 3. In Chapter 11, "Adding structure to your diagrams," you will learn about a feature that was introduced in Visio 2010—containers—that offers most of the advantages of grouping shapes but few of the disadvantages.

✖ CLEAN UP **Save the changes to the *Network Diagram (Organized)* drawing but leave it open if you are continuing with the next exercise.**

IMPORTANT The following section applies only to the Professional edition of Visio 2013.

9

Creating rack diagrams

In the previous exercises in this chapter, you created a stylized representation of your network. To build a more complete network representation, you need to add a diagram of the network equipment rack in the data center. You will use some of the stencils from the Rack Diagram template to create that picture.

The Rack Diagram template includes four stencils, three of which contain equipment and rack shapes (the fourth contains annotation shapes). The three equipment stencils are shown side by side in the following graphic.

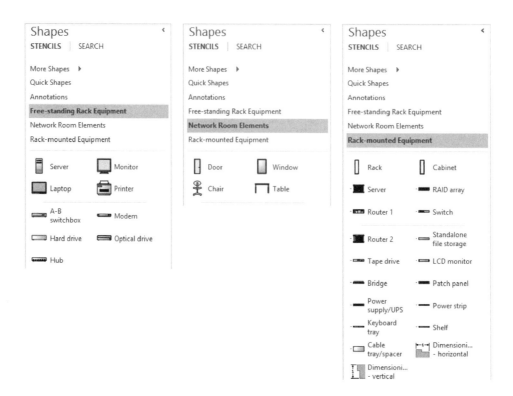

TIP You are not restricted to using just the stencils that are packaged with a Visio template. You can open any Visio stencil in any diagram.

In this exercise, you will create the foundation for building a rack diagram by adding two stencils from the Rack Diagram template to your current drawing. You will also add a new page and will set the page attributes so you can create a drawing whose shapes are drawn to scale. Finally, you will add a rack shape to the new page.

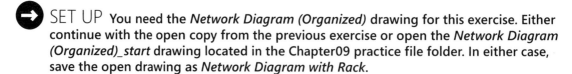 SET UP **You need the** *Network Diagram (Organized)* **drawing for this exercise. Either continue with the open copy from the previous exercise or open the** *Network Diagram (Organized)_start* **drawing located in the Chapter09 practice file folder. In either case, save the open drawing as** *Network Diagram with Rack*.

1 In the **Shapes** window, click **More Shapes**, point to **Network**, and then click **Free-standing Rack Equipment**. The fly-out menu remains open.

2   Click **Rack-mounted Equipment**, and then click anywhere on the drawing page to close the fly-out menus.

3   Double-click the **Page-1** name tab, type **Network Overview**, and then press **Enter**.

Next you will add a page that has the dimensions and drawing scale to hold an equipment rack.

4   Right-click the **Network Overview** name tab, and then click **Insert**.

5   Type **Data Center Detail**, click the **Measurement units** drop-down arrow, and then select **Meters**.

TIP Changing measurement units is not required. However, a standard equipment rack is just over 2 meters (6.5 feet) tall. By selecting Meters as the measurement unit, the rulers on the left and top of the drawing page will show dimensions in meters, which is likely to be more useful than showing thousands of millimeters.

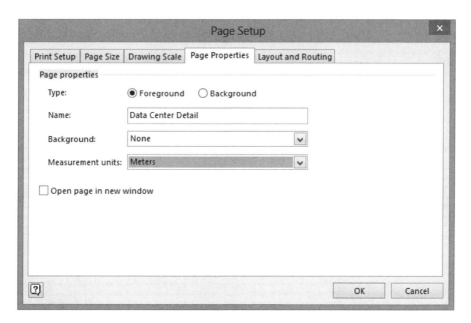

If you are working in US units, select either Feet And Inches or Feet (decimal) in the Measurement Units drop-down list on the Page Properties tab.

6 Click the **Drawing Scale** tab, click **Pre-defined scale**, and then select **Metric** in the first list and **1 : 10** in the second list.

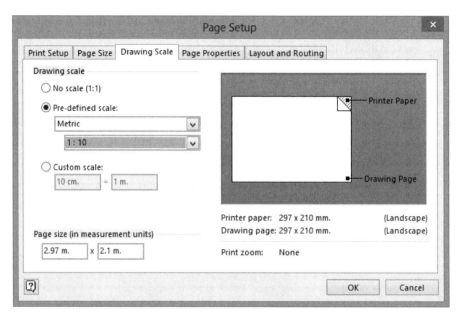

If you are working in US units, select Architectural in the first list and then select 1" = 1' 0" in the next list. Refer to the following graphic.

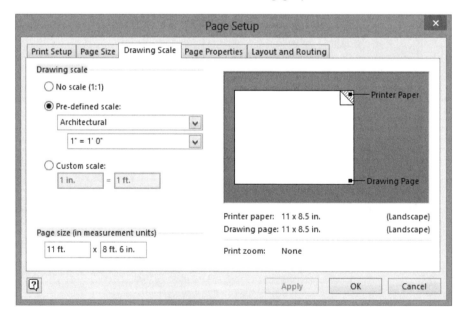

SEE ALSO For more information about drawing scale and its effects on shapes, refer to "Changing the drawing scale" later in this chapter.

7   Click **OK**.

8   Drag a **Rack** shape from the **Rack-mounted Equipment** stencil onto the center of the drawing page. Because of the measurement units and page scale you've set in the preceding steps, the rack will occupy the entire space between the top and bottom margins of the page. (If you are using US units, there will be some free space between the top and bottom margins.)

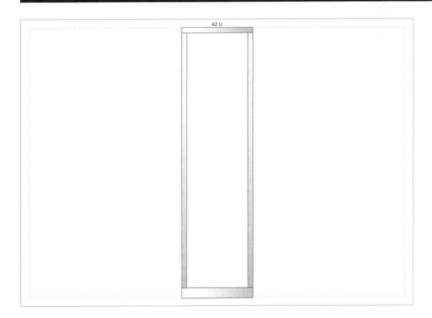

TIP The rack shape was designed to be included in a scaled drawing, as it is in this exercise. If you drop a rack shape onto a page that does not contain a drawing scale, the rack will be only 1U high.

✖ CLEAN UP Save your changes to the *Network Diagram with Rack* drawing but leave it open if you are continuing with the next exercise.

In the next exercise, you will add equipment shapes to your rack diagram.

IMPORTANT The following section applies only to the Professional edition of Visio 2013.

Adding equipment to rack diagrams

As you work with the equipment shapes that were designed to be used within a Visio rack, you will notice that they have a unique feature: the shapes look 2-D, yet they are actually one-dimensional (1-D) shapes. Because they are 1-D shapes, you will be able to glue both ends of each shape to the connection points on both sides of the rack.

SEE ALSO For more information about 1-D shapes and connection points, see Chapter 2, "Creating a new diagram."

In the previous exercise, you added a page with suitable dimensions and drawing scale to hold an equipment rack, and then you placed a rack onto the page.

In this exercise, you will add the following equipment to the rack: six servers, one PC, a router, and a power supply. In addition, you will build a drill-down hyperlink to the equipment rack from your stylized network drawing.

➡ SET UP 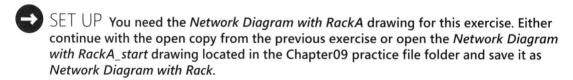 You need the *Network Diagram with RackA* drawing for this exercise. Either continue with the open copy from the previous exercise or open the *Network Diagram with RackA_start* drawing located in the Chapter09 practice file folder and save it as *Network Diagram with Rack*.

1   Drag a **Power supply/UPS** shape from the **Rack-mounted Equipment** stencil and drag it toward the bottom of the rack. The connection points on each side of the rack light up as the shape approaches, confirming that the **Power supply/UPS** shape can be glued to the rack. In addition, the U height of the rack appears to the left of the shape.

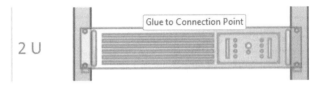

2   Glue the **Power supply/UPS** to the connectors at the bottom of the rack.

3   Drag a **Server** shape from the **Rack-mounted Equipment** stencil and drag it to the center of the rack.

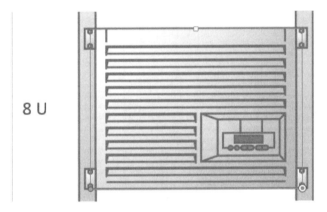

The default server shape is very tall—8U—but it's actually an interesting shape. Like many rack-mounted shapes, you can change its height, but this shape actually adjusts its appearance as you resize it; this will be illustrated in the next step.

4   Drag the resize handle at the top of the server shape downward until the label at the left says **3U**.

TIP As you drag the handle, notice that at 7U, 6U, and 5U, the bottom half of the shape remains unchanged as the upper half of the shape gets smaller. However, at 4U and below, the lower part of the shape begins to adjust as well. Even a seemingly simple Visio shape can have reasonably sophisticated behavior.

5   Press **Ctrl+D** five times to make duplicate copies of the 3U server shape. Drag each copy so it sits just above or below another server in the rack.

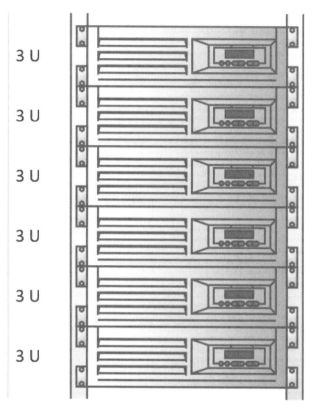

6   Drag a **Router 1** shape from the **Rack-mounted Equipment** stencil and position it at the bottom of the rack just above the power supply.

7   Drag a **Shelf** shape from the **Rack-mounted Equipment** stencil and attach it to the rack between the bottom server and the router.

8   Drag a **Keyboard tray** shape from the **Rack-mounted Equipment** stencil and attach it to the rack just below the shelf.

9   Drag a **Monitor** shape from the **Free-standing Rack Equipment** stencil and position it below the servers. If necessary, adjust the position of the shelf and the monitor so the monitor appears to be sitting on the shelf. Your finished rack should look like the one on the left in the following graphic.

     TIP If you prefer to display the rack without the U dimensions, right-click the rack or any rack-mounted shape and click Hide U Sizes. The result is shown in the graphic on the right. You can turn U sizes back on by right-clicking and selecting Show U Sizes.

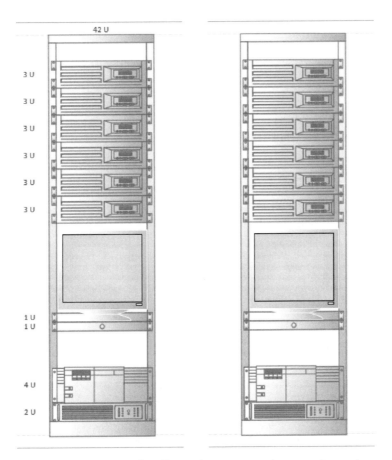

At this point, your rack reflects the same equipment shown in your stylized diagram on the Network Overview page. In the final steps for this exercise, you will create a drill-down hyperlink from the overview page to the rack.

10 Return to the **Network Overview** page and draw a bounding box around the **router** shape and the **Data Center** group in the lower-right corner of the page.

11 Press **Ctrl+K** to open the **Hyperlinks** dialog box.

SEE ALSO If you need a refresher on hyperlinks, see Chapter 7, "Adding and using hyperlinks."

12 In the **Hyperlinks** dialog box, click the **Browse** button to the right of **Sub-address**. The **Hyperlink** dialog box opens.

13   In the **Hyperlink** dialog box, select **Data Center Detail** from the **Page** list and select **Page** from the **Zoom** list.

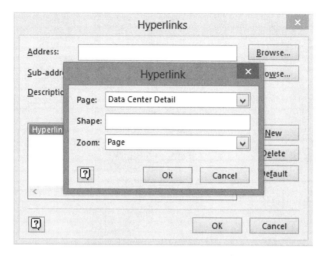

14   Click **OK**.

15   In the **Description** text box of the **Hyperlinks** dialog box, type **Drill down to Data Center**, and then click **OK**.

IMPORTANT It's very important to understand that you've just applied the identical hyperlink to all selected shapes in one step. The hyperlink is not attached to the part of the page you selected with the bounding box, but is attached to each selected shape. Visio makes it very easy to apply the same change to multiple shapes, which is great if that's what you want to do. However, you do need to be careful that you don't apply a change to multiple shapes by mistake.

16   Right-click any of the hyperlinked shapes, and then click **Drilldown to Data Center**. Visio switches to the **Data Center Detail** page and displays a full-page view of the rack diagram.

❌ CLEAN UP **Save your changes to the** *Network Diagram with Rack* **diagram but leave it open if you are continuing with the next exercise.**

Where can I get shapes that look like my equipment?

In the exercises in this and preceding sections, you built network and rack diagrams using stock shapes that are delivered with Visio. The shapes probably look something like your servers, routers, and other equipment, but they can't match exactly because they are generic shapes.

If you want to create more realistic diagrams, there are thousands of downloadable Visio stencils and shapes from various sources, such as the following:

- Network and computer equipment vendors often provide shapes for their equipment.

- Some companies design and sell both product-specific and generic Visio shapes.

- Individuals have created network and computer equipment shapes. Many provide them for free; some charge for their artwork.

For large collections of links to various stencil sources (most are free), go to the following sites:

- *visio.mvps.org/3rdParty/*

- *www.visiocafe.com*

You can also try the following commercial stencil vendors:

- *www.visiostencils.com*

- *www.shapesource.com*

Examples of shapes provided by equipment manufacturers are located at the following sites:

- **Cisco** *www.cisco.com/en/US/products/hw/prod_cat_visios.html*

- **Dell** *www.dell.com/us/en/esg/topics/segtopic_visio.htm*

9

The rack diagram you've created shows the key equipment in this simple data center. What might you do to enhance your rack drawing? Consider these ideas:

- Use *data linking* (refer to Chapter 6, "Entering, linking to, and reporting on data") to link the equipment in your rack to a spreadsheet or database containing asset IDs, serial numbers, and other inventory information.

- Link your rack equipment to a real-time or near-real-time data source so the equipment in your rack contains status information.

- Use data visualization techniques (refer to Chapter 10) to help the user of your diagram understand the data "behind the shapes."

- Add a patch panel and network cabling. Consider putting the cabling on a separate layer (refer to Chapter 3) so you can easily show or hide it.

- Add data to the rack shape so its location and other information is part of your network inventory reports.

- Add hyperlinks (refer to Chapter 7) to the rack and the equipment in the rack and link to photographs of the actual wiring closet or equipment.

- Change the hyperlinks on the **Network Overview** page so that instead of linking a group of servers to the **Data Center Detail** page, you link each server to a specific server shape in the rack. When you do this, try setting the hyperlink zoom level to **150%** or **200%**.

IMPORTANT The drawing scale concepts in the following section apply to all editions of Visio. However, the exercise uses rack shapes that are available only with the Professional edition of Visio 2013.

Changing the drawing scale

In "Creating rack diagrams" earlier in this chapter, you used options on the Drawing Scale tab in the Page Setup dialog box to change the ratio between the dimensions for the images on the page and their real-life counterparts. The ability to create scaled drawings is a very powerful feature in Visio.

Occasionally, after you have created a scaled drawing, you need to adjust the scale. As a simple example, you might have created a diagram containing a single rack. What happens when you want to add additional racks and there isn't enough room on the page?

In this exercise, you will add additional racks to a diagram and rescale the page as required.

 SET UP **You need the *Network Diagram with Rack* drawing for this exercise. Either continue with the open copy from the previous exercise or open the *Network Diagram with RackB_start* drawing located in the Chapter09 practice file folder and save it as *Network Diagram with Rack*.**

1 Drag a **Rack** shape from the **Rack-mounted Equipment** stencil and drop it to the right of the existing rack. Then drop another one on the left side.

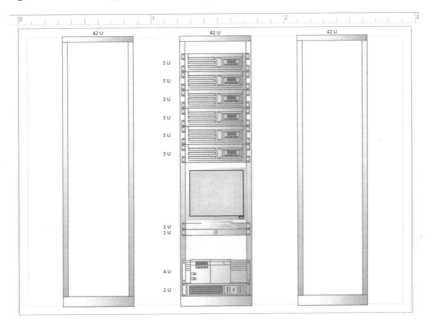

To represent a set of racks in a data center, you will need to abut the rack shapes on the page the way the racks are on the data center floor. If you do that on the previous page, you will only be able to add one or two more racks. In order to show additional racks, you could create another page and then add the racks there. However, if your goal is to represent a room full of racks on a single page, how can you accomplish that without overcrowding? The answer lies in adjusting the drawing scale.

2 Right-click the **Data Center Detail** page name tab, and then select **Page Setup**.

3   Click the **Drawing Scale** tab, and then select **1 : 20** in the list under **Metric**.

TIP If your drawing uses US units, select ½"=1'0" under Architectural.

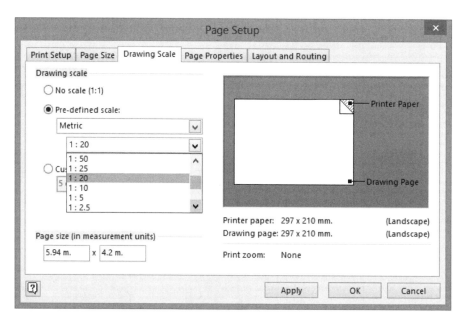

4   Click **OK**, and then press **Ctrl+Shift+W** to view the whole page.

IMPORTANT Look at the ruler at the top of the graphic in step 1 and you'll notice that the drawing represents approximately 3 meters of wall space in your data center. Now look at the ruler in the following graphic; your drawing page now represents 6 meters of wall space.

After cutting the page scale by half, you can certainly fit more racks onto the page, but the racks are very small. In addition, you may not need this much space. The good news is that Visio is very flexible, and you can specify your own scale factor to achieve the ideal balance.

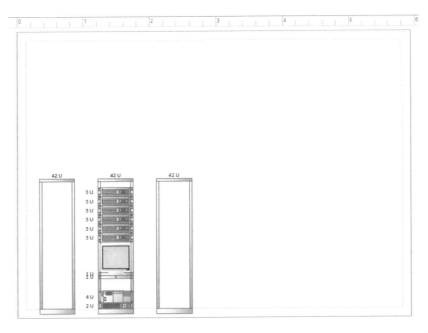

5 Right-click the **Data Center Detail** page name tab, select **Page Setup**, and then click **Drawing Scale**.

6 On the **Drawing Scale** tab, click **Custom scale**.

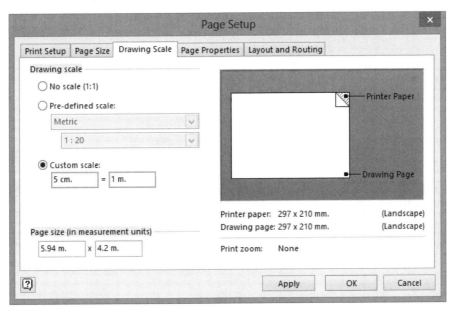

The current scale of 1:20 means that 5 cm. on the page equals 1 meter on the ground. If you had looked when the scale was 1:10, the settings would have been 10 cm = 1 m. You need to create a scaling ratio that is in between the two values you've already tried.

7   Type **7 cm.** in the first box under **Custom scale**, and then click **OK**. The resulting page size represents just over 4 meters of data center wall space and is appropriate for adding several additional racks. You can enter any other scale factors in the future to enlarge or reduce the working area of the page.

TIP If your drawing uses US units, try selecting ¾"=1'0" under Architectural.

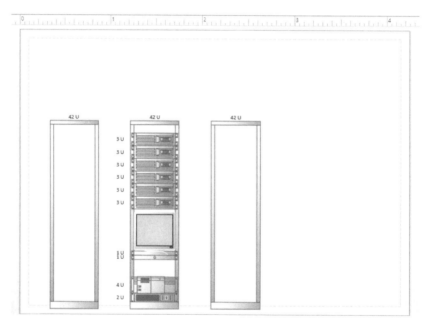

⊗ CLEAN UP **Save your changes to the** *Network Diagram with Rack* **drawing and close the file.**

IMPORTANT Not all shapes were designed to respond to changes in the drawing scale of the page. If you change the page scale and the shapes don't respond appropriately, either you're out of luck or you'll need to find replacement shapes.

Running computer and network reports

Many of the templates provided with Visio include predefined reports. Both the Basic and Detailed Network Diagram templates that were described earlier in this chapter include three reports that highlight different subsets of the *shape data* in the various computer and network shapes.

SEE ALSO Refer to Chapter 6 for a refresher on running Visio reports.

The following three graphics show part of the output available in the network and computer equipment reports. The sample reports were created by adding data to the basic network diagram you created earlier in the chapter. If you would like to run these reports yourself, you can open the *Network Diagram (Basic) with data_start* drawing located in the Chapter09 practice file folder.

TIP The Displayed Text column in the reports shows the text typed onto the shapes. In this network diagram, the only two shapes that contain text are the Ethernet segments.

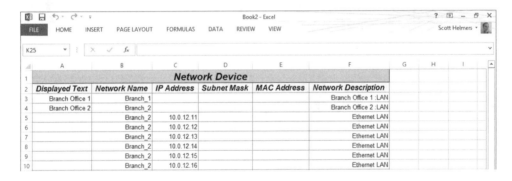

TIP Only part of the Network Equipment report is shown below; there are additional fields to the right of the Product Description column.

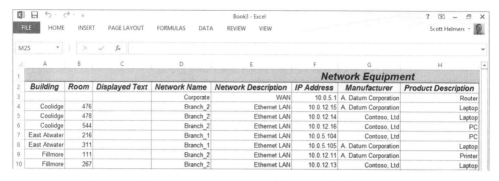

IMPORTANT The PC Report shown in the following graphic runs correctly with the network shapes in the Basic Network Diagram – 3D and Detailed Network Diagram – 3D templates. However, the new shapes in the Visio 2013 Basic Network Diagram and Detailed Network Diagram templates contain an error that prevents the PC Report from running. As a workaround, the author has posted a modified PC Report definition on his website at *www.visiostepbystep.com/downloads/2013/Visio_2013_Modified_PC_Report.zip*.

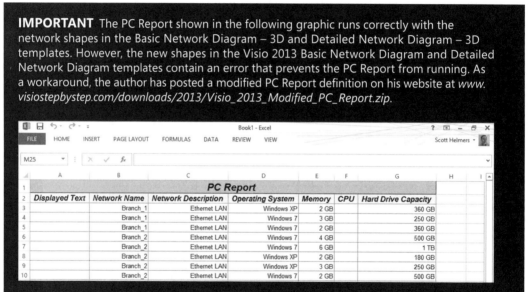

Searching and replacing text

Although the need to search and replace text isn't directly related to network diagrams, the subject is included in this chapter because network diagrams provide a useful example.

In this exercise, you will use the Visio find/replace features to locate and alter text.

 SET UP **You need the *Network Diagram (Basic) with data_start* drawing located in the Chapter09 practice file folder to complete this exercise. Open it in Visio and then close the External Data Window if it appears.**

1   On the **Home** tab, in the **Editing** group, click the **Find** button, and then click **Find**. The **Find** dialog box opens and allows you to type the search text as well as to define various search parameters.

KEYBOARD SHORTCUT You can also press Ctrl+F to open the Find dialog box.

In the next step, you will locate all computers that use Windows XP. According to the PC Report mentioned in the preceding section, "Running computer and network reports," there are three computers running Windows XP.

2   In the **Find what** text box of the **Find** dialog box, type **Windows XP**, and then click **Find Next**.

Even though you know there are three shapes containing *Windows XP*, it's clear from the preceding graphic that Visio did not find any of them. The problem lies in the default search parameters that are visible behind the search results message box: Visio only searched the ***shape text*** (the text displayed on a shape) and not the shape data.

3 Click **OK** to close the information dialog box, and then select **Shape data** in the **Find** dialog box.

4 Click **Find Next** again. This time the **Find** function identifies a PC with Windows XP in its shape data (look for the laptop that is selected in the Branch Office 2 network).

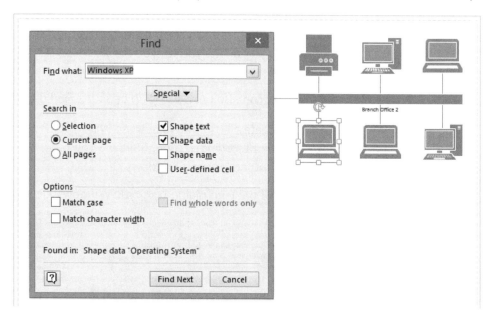

Continuing to click Find Next will identify other shapes that contain the search text (note that some shapes may be located under the Find dialog box). Eventually, clicking Find Next will display a dialog box indicating that Visio has finished searching the page.

TIP By using additional settings in the Find dialog box, you can limit a search to just those shapes that are currently selected or you can expand the search to all shapes on all pages. You can also search *shape names* and *user-defined cells*. The Options section of the Find dialog box lets you limit search results based on text case and other text attributes.

5 Click **Cancel** to close the **Find** dialog box.

6 On the **Home** tab, in the **Editing** group, click **Find**, and then click **Replace**.

TIP Both the Find and the Replace dialog boxes display the most recently used search string when you open them (see *Windows XP* in the following figure). In addition, both the Find What text box and the Replace With text box contain a drop-down arrow. Clicking the arrow displays recently used text strings.

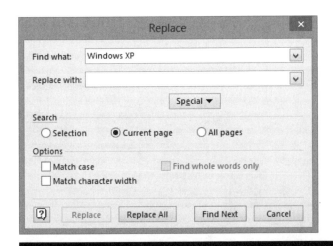

IMPORTANT Unlike the Find dialog box, the Replace dialog box does not include check boxes for Shape Data, Shape Name, or User-Defined Cell. Consequently, you can use the Replace function to change shape text but you cannot replace the text found in the other three locations.

7 In the **Replace** dialog box, type **Branch** in the **Find what** text box.

8 Type **Local** in the **Replace with** text box, and then click **Find Next**. Visio zooms in on the shape containing the search text and enters text-edit mode.

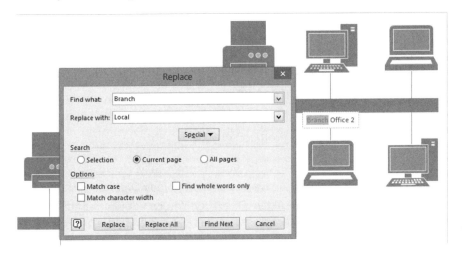

9   Click the **Replace** button. Visio makes the change, finds the next match, and enters
     edit mode.

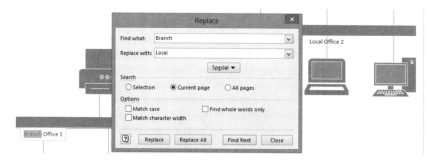

At any time, you can click Replace to make the next change, or Replace All to replace
all occurrences of the found text.

❌ CLEAN UP **Close your drawing file. It is not necessary to save changes.**

IMPORTANT The following section applies only to the Professional edition of Visio 2013.

Mapping Active Directory and LDAP

Visio Professional includes two templates in the Network category that help you create
logical maps of the directories that underlie many networks:

- The Active Directory template provides shapes that represent common Active
  Directory objects, sites, and services.

- The LDAP Directory template includes shapes that represent common LDAP (Light-
  weight Directory Access Protocol) objects.

Neither template creates a drawing for you automatically. However, Microsoft offers a free
download called the *Microsoft Active Directory Topology Diagrammer* that automatically
builds a Visio diagram from an Active Directory. You can download this add-in from *www.
microsoft.com/downloads/details.aspx?familyid=cb42fc06-50c7-47ed-a65c-862661742764.*

Key points

- Visio offers up to seven templates and nearly two dozen stencils for creating network, data center, and computer equipment diagrams.

- You can create both stylized network drawings and extremely realistic diagrams by using shapes supplied with Visio or that are available for download. Many equipment vendors provide stencils containing shapes for their products. In addition, other companies and individuals have created both generic and product-specific artwork.

- The Visio rack and equipment shapes were drawn to scale so that if you change the scale of the drawing page, the rack/equipment shapes will resize accordingly.

- One common way of organizing related sets of shapes in a network diagram is to group them together with a colored background shape. Although this technique creates a visually distinct group, it also inherits some of the disadvantages of grouping shapes (refer to Chapter 3). Visio 2013 offers another option for grouping shapes, called *containers*, that will be discussed in Chapter 11.

- The Visio text search feature is very flexible and allows significant control over how the search will be conducted. You can use it to locate text on and inside shapes. The text replace function is more limited and does not allow replacing anything other than the text that is displayed on a shape.

- Visio Professional includes templates for manually creating maps of Active Directory, Microsoft Exchange Server, and LDAP directories. In addition, Microsoft offers a free Active Directory Topology Diagrammer that automatically creates a Visio map from an Active Directory.

9

Chapter at a glance

Enhance

Enhance diagrams with data-driven graphics,
page 390

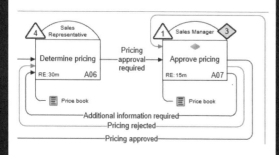

Edit

Edit data graphics,
page 399

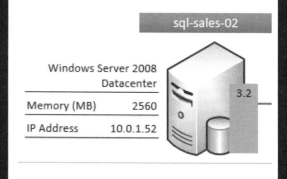

Create

Create data graphics,
page 406

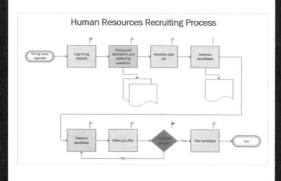

Add

Add data graphic legends,
page 412

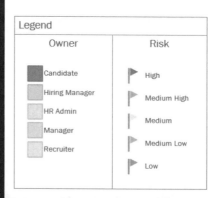

IN THIS CHAPTER, YOU WILL LEARN HOW TO

- Enhance diagrams with data-driven graphics.

- Use existing data graphics.

- Edit data graphics.

- Create new data graphics.

- Create data graphic legends.

- Refresh data and data graphics.

In Chapter 6, "Entering, linking to, and reporting on data," you learned how to enter data into Microsoft Visio shapes and how to integrate data from external sources into your diagrams. After you have data in your Visio diagram, you need techniques to make that data visible. With a Visio *data graphic*, you can do just that by displaying text or a graphic on a Visio shape based on the data inside the shape.

Data graphics are even more powerful when a diagram is connected to data that is dynamically refreshed from an external data source. In that situation, your Visio drawing becomes a dashboard showing near real–time status for your network, a business process, a restaurant seating chart, or a manufacturing assembly line; the possibilities are endless.

In this chapter, you will create, edit, and use Visio 2013 data graphics to present shape data in a variety of attractive and useful ways.

IMPORTANT The information in this chapter applies only to the Professional edition of Visio 2013.

PRACTICE FILES To complete the exercises in this chapter, you need the practice files contained in the Chapter10 practice file folder. For more information, see "Downloading the practice files" in this book's Introduction.

Enhancing diagrams with data-driven graphics

A person using a Visio diagram you create can learn a lot about the subject of the diagram based on your choice of shapes, their positions on the page, how they are connected, and many other visual cues. However, if your diagram is connected to an external data source, it can convey so much more information.

This section includes four examples of diagrams that employ data graphics to tell even more of the story behind the picture.

Network equipment diagram

The first example continues the network and rack diagram theme from Chapter 9, "Creating network and data center diagrams." The story behind this diagram is as follows:

- You are a data center manager and have created rack diagrams for each rack in your computer room.
- You've populated your drawing with data by using the techniques you learned in Chapter 6 to connect your diagram to a Microsoft Excel spreadsheet or to a database.
- Each rack-mounted server includes the data shown in the following graphic.

Height in U's	2	
Height	3.5 in.	
Asset Number		
Serial Number		
Location	Row 1 Rack 2	
Building		
Room		
Manufacturer	Contoso, Ltd.	
Product Number		
Part Number		
Product Description	database server	
Power Usage		
Network Name	sql-sales-01	
IP Address	10.0.1.51	
Subnet Mask		
Memory		
Operating System	Windows Server 2008 Datacenter	
Administrator	Anna Misiec	
CPU (MHz)	3	
Memory (MB)	2048	
Status	OK	

- The spreadsheet or database contains some static data about your equipment, but it also contains live status information that is updated periodically.

- You have configured your Visio diagram to automatically read the data source and refresh the drawing at a preset time interval.

The result is that you can use data graphics to turn your Visio drawing into a dashboard for viewing network and equipment status. In the following graphic, several data graphics have been applied to the equipment rack to highlight the following:

- Server name and type (left)

- Server status (center)

- CPU and memory (right)

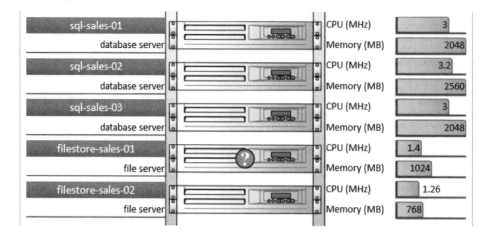

The following graphic shows the same equipment rack, at the same moment in time, but it uses different data graphics to highlight different information. In this version of the rack diagram, you find the following:

- Server name and IP address (left)

- Server status (center)

    TIP Instead of using an icon to represent the status of the server, the following diagram utilizes a color applied to the entire server shape.

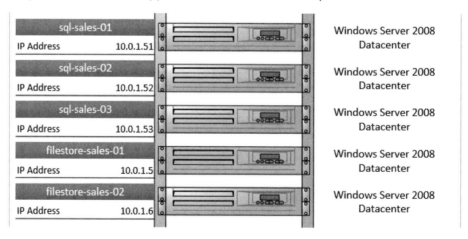

- Operating system name (right)

Part of the appeal of data graphics is represented by these two examples—you can apply different graphics at different times depending on what you need to know.

Process improvement workflow

In this example, data graphics have been applied to process steps in a swimlane diagram in order to show several process quality measurements. In the upper right of the diagram, you also find a *data graphic legend*. (You will learn more about legends in "Creating data graphic legends" later in this chapter.)

The metrics in this diagram:

- Show the duration of each step (look for a thermometer bar across the bottom of each task shape).

- Display a warning if the step is taking either 5–9 days or 10 or more days (lower-left corner of each step).

- Indicate whether each step is improving or being investigated (shape color).

The symbolism used for each of these metrics is explained in the legend that appears in the upper-right corner of the page.

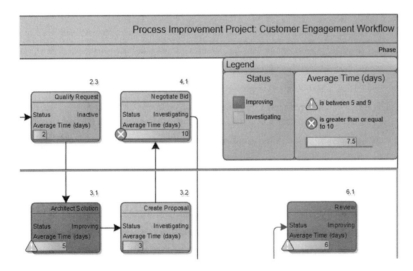

Casino operation

The third example illustrates the types of near real-time information that a casino manager might view in Visio with the goal of monitoring critical operations. In all likelihood, your job doesn't involve managing a casino, but you can probably think of important operations that you do need to monitor.

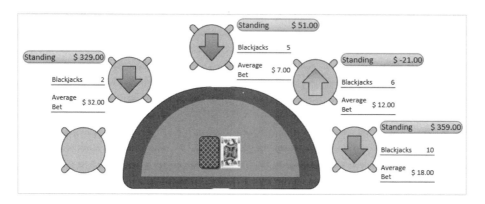

In the graphic, text callouts highlight each bettor's recent history, including current dollar standing, average bet, and number of blackjacks. In addition, there is a red or green arrow showing how each player is trending.

TIP If you would like to work with a very similar diagram to the preceding example, open the *Casino Floor* drawing in the Chapter10 practice file folder. Be sure to notice that the diagram has multiple pages showing different parts of the casino floor.

Risk management

In the final example, you are viewing part of a process map that was created using a Visio add-in called TaskMap (*www.taskmap.com*). The following graphic shows three tasks in the middle of a sales proposal process.

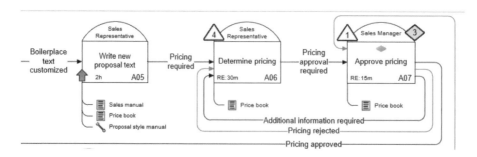

In this diagram, the data graphics depict two aspects of risk management:

- Yellow triangles identify risks; the number in each triangle relates to an entry in a master list of risks. Green diamonds show the corresponding controls that the organization has put in place to mitigate the risks. (An organization might maintain the master list of risks and controls in something as simple as a spreadsheet, or they might employ a formal risk management system.)

    In a task like the one in the center, the organization has identified a risk but not a control, so the risk is more significant.

- The red arrows identify tasks that exceed a defined time threshold—30 minutes in the case of this example.

There is a third data graphic in this example: the task on the right displays a red diamond to indicate that it is a decision point in the process.

TIP If you would like to look at the full page from which the excerpt above was taken, open the *Sales Proposal Process TaskMap* PDF in the Chapter10 practice file folder. In addition, a web-published version of this TaskMap that includes hyperlinks to Microsoft Word and Excel documents is available at *www.visiostepbystep.com/downloads/2013/RiskManagement.htm*.

The examples in this section highlight the importance of the data behind a diagram and suggest a variety of creative ways you can add value to your data-connected diagrams.

Using existing data graphics

Now that you've learned how varied and useful data graphics can be in real-world examples, it's time to work with them.

In this exercise, you will learn how to turn data graphics off, and then you will learn how to apply them to selected shapes. In contrast with the network shapes you used in Chapter 9, you will work with the legacy three-dimensional (3-D) network shapes that are still available in Visio 2013.

SET UP **You need the *Network Diagram_start* drawing located in the Chapter10 practice file folder to complete this exercise. Open the drawing in Visio, and then save it as *Network Diagram with Data Graphics*.**

1   Press **Ctrl+A** to select all shapes on the page.

2   On the **Data** tab, in the **Display Data** group, click the **Data Graphics** button. The **Data Graphics** gallery opens and displays available data graphics along with several menu entries. When you point to a data graphic, pop-up text displays its name and Live Preview shows how that graphic will be applied to the selected shapes on the page.

    TIP You must select one or more shapes *before* opening the Data Graphics gallery because you can only apply or remove data graphics on preselected shapes.

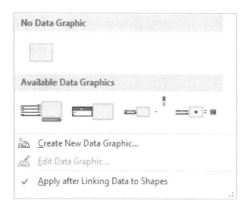

    TIP The selected Apply After Linking Data To Shapes check box at the bottom of the Data Graphics gallery causes the currently active data graphic to be applied each time you link data from the External Data window to one or more shapes on the drawing page. If you do not want a data graphic to be applied automatically, clear the check box to turn this option off. (Refer to Chapter 6 for more information about data linking.)

3   In the **Data Graphics** gallery, click the thumbnail below **No Data Graphic** to turn off data graphics on all shapes. The drawing page now shows the unadorned network diagram.

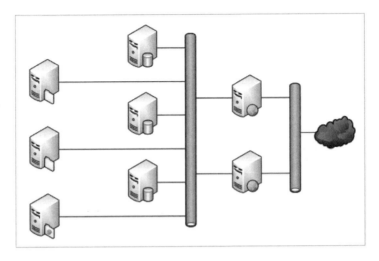

4   Select the six servers to the left of the longer network segment. (Do not include the network segment in your selection.)

5   On the **Data** tab, in the **Display Data** group, click the **Data Graphics** button to open the gallery, and then click the **Topology 1** thumbnail to apply that data graphic to the six servers.

6   Select the pair of web servers located between the two network segments.

7   On the **Data** tab, in the **Display Data** group, click the **Data Graphics** button to open the gallery, and then click the **Topology 2** thumbnail to apply that data graphic to the two servers.

8   Zoom in to view several servers in the center of the diagram.

10

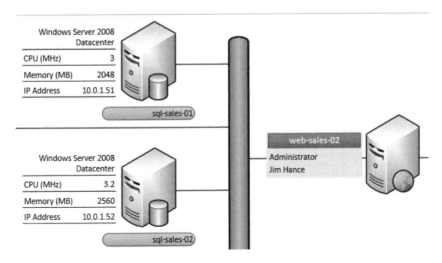

The servers on the left display a subset of the shapes' data using one style of presentation, whereas the servers on the right show different data in an alternate format:

- For the servers on the left, most of the data is displayed as underlined text to the left of the server icon, but the server name is displayed with a green background under the server.

- For the servers on the right, the name is displayed to the left of the PC shape with a blue background and the administrator name is displayed as plain text. In contrast with the servers on the left, there is also a border rectangle with light green fill surrounding the data graphic on this server.

You control all of these formatting options when you edit or create a data graphic as you will do in the exercises that follow.

TIP You can only apply one data graphic to any one shape at any one time. However, as the preceding figure shows, you can apply different data graphics to different shapes on the same page.

❌ CLEAN UP **Save your changes to the *Network Diagram with Data Graphics* drawing but leave it open if you are continuing with the next exercise.**

The data graphics used in this section all display text callouts in various formats. In upcoming exercises, you will discover several types of data graphic icons.

IMPORTANT Data graphics are applied to a single page at a time. If you want to apply the same data graphic to multiple pages, you must either apply it to each page separately, or write a Visio macro. As an alternative strategy, you can apply a data graphic to a shape and save the shape in a custom stencil. Then, whenever you drag the shape onto the drawing page, it will automatically display the data graphic. You will learn about macros and creating custom stencils in the Appendix.

TIP Visio data graphics are automatically assigned to a special layer in a diagram. (Refer to the "Understanding and using layers" section in Chapter 3, "Adding sophistication to your drawings.") If you want to hide data graphics without removing them, you can change the view properties for the data graphics layer.

Editing data graphics

The placement and appearance of data graphics are controlled by an editable set of parameters. Although you can't control every attribute of a data graphic without resorting to writing code, the Visio 2013 user interface provides tools to implement a surprising number of changes.

In this exercise, you will modify the data graphics that you applied in the preceding section. First, you will change the placement of one data graphic, and then you will alter the display attributes of several elements within a second data graphic.

 SET UP **You need the *Network Diagram with Data Graphics* drawing for this exercise. Either continue with the open copy from the previous exercise or open the *Network Diagram_start* drawing located in the Chapter10 practice file folder and save it as *Network Diagram with Data Graphics*.**

1   On the **Data** tab, in the **Display Data** group, click the **Data Graphics** button to open the gallery. (Refer to step 2 in the preceding exercise for an image of the Data Graphic gallery.)

2   Right-click the **Topology 2** thumbnail, and then click **Edit**. The **Edit Data Graphic** dialog box for **Topology 2** opens.

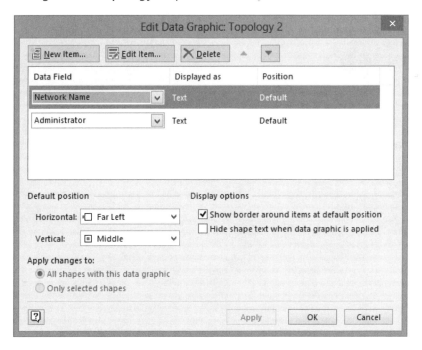

10

In the upper half of the Edit Data Graphic dialog box, you can add, edit, or delete individual items within the data graphic. In the lower half, you can modify the characteristics of the data graphic as a whole. You will use the lower half for this exercise.

> **IMPORTANT** You establish the default position for a data graphic in the lower-left corner of the Edit Data Graphic dialog box. (Both the horizontal and vertical positions are relative to the shape to which the graphic will be attached.) Data graphic items in the upper half of the dialog box whose Position is set to Default will appear at this location.

3   In the **Default position** section of the **Edit Data Graphic** dialog box, click the arrow next to **Horizontal**, and then click **Center**.

4   Click the arrow next to **Vertical**, and then click **Above Shape**.

   TIP You will need to scroll up to locate Above Shape in the list.

5   Click **OK**. You have relocated the data graphic so it appears above the center of the server shapes.

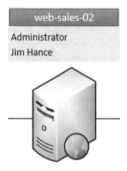

TIP The data graphic in the preceding graphic has a border rectangle around it. You can turn the border off by clearing the Show Border Around Items At Default Location check box in the Display Options section of the Edit Data Graphic dialog box shown in step 2.

In the remaining steps of this exercise, you will alter the *Topology 1* data graphic to make the display of the network name for the server consistent with the format used in the *Topology 2* data graphic. You will also change the display of CPU speed from text to a graphical presentation.

6   On the **Data** tab, in the **Display Data** group, click the **Data Graphics** button to open the gallery, right-click the **Topology 1** thumbnail, and then click **Edit**.

The upper half of the **Edit Data Graphic** dialog box shows the parameters for the items contained in this data graphic. The descriptions for the **Network Name** data field indicate that it is displayed as **Text** and is positioned in the **Center**, **Below** (the server) **Shape**. Similarly, the **CPU (MHz)** field is displayed as **Text** in the **Default Position** for the data graphic.

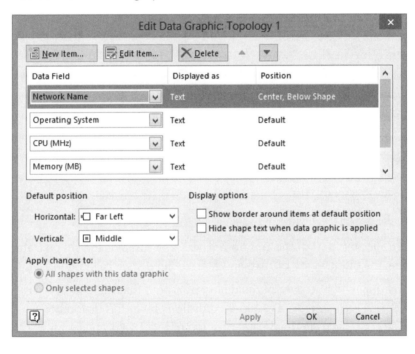

7   With **Network Name** already selected in the **Data Field** list (notice the highlight on that item), click the **Edit Item** button. The **Edit Item** dialog box opens.

TIP You can also double-click anywhere in an item row to open the dialog box.

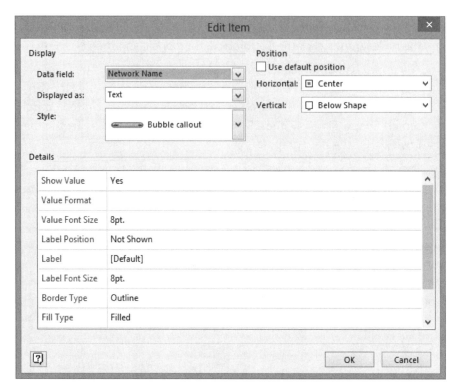

The upper-left part of the Edit Item dialog box contains the shape Data Field name, the display type of Text, and a predefined style called Bubble Callout.

In the upper-right corner of the dialog box, note that the Use Default Position check box is cleared. As a result, the positions set in this dialog box for Horizontal and Vertical override the default position of the data graphic as a whole.

The lower half of the dialog box displays customizable parameters for this data graphic item. Be sure to notice the scroll bar in the parameter list; there are additional parameters that are not currently visible.

8   In the **Display** section of the **Edit Item** dialog box, click the arrow next to **Style**. The list shows a set of predefined text callout styles. (Scroll to view all of them.)

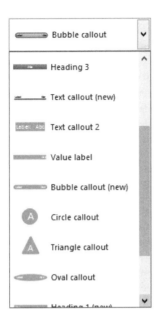

9   Click **Heading 3**.

10   In the **Position** section of the dialog box, display the **Vertical** list, click **Above shape**
       (you might need to scroll up to locate this selection), and then click **OK**. You have
       changed the location of the server name display; click the **Apply** button to make the
       change but keep the dialog box open. Next, you will change the way that CPU speed
       is presented.

11   In the **Edit Data Graphic** dialog box, double-click the row containing the **CPU**
       (MHz) item.

12   In the **Display** section of the **Edit Item** dialog box, click the arrow next to **Displayed**
       as. The list shows the four display options for data graphic items.

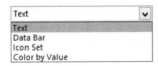

       TIP You will use Icon Set and Color By Value in the next exercise in this chapter.

13   Click **Data Bar**.

14   In the **Display** section of the **Edit Item** dialog box, click the arrow next to **Style**. The list shows the predefined data bar types. Data bars are designed for showing relative values in a variety of ways.

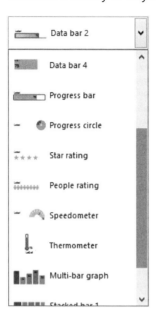

TIP The collection of data bars offers a variety of interesting ways to display numeric data. You will use one of them in this exercise, but you should take a few minutes to explore some of the other choices for potential future use.

15   Click **Data bar 3**.

16   In the **Details** section, of the **Edit Item** dialog box, type **5** in the **Maximum Value** field.

> **IMPORTANT** The Minimum Value and Maximum Value fields are critical for data bar graphic items. These two values set the boundaries for the values in the selected shape data field and enable Visio to scale the data bar graphic accordingly.

17   In the **Details** section, click in the **Label Position** field, and then click **Not Shown** from the list. This action turns off the display of the shape data field name.

18   In the **Position** section of the dialog box, clear the **Use default position** check box, click the arrow next to **Horizontal**, and then click **Right Edge**. The **Edit Item** dialog box should now look like the following graphic.

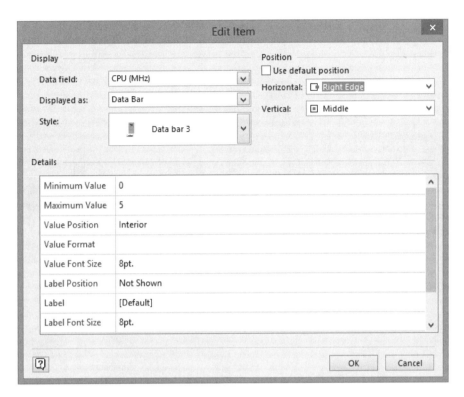

19   Click **OK** in both the **Edit Item** and **Edit Data Graphic** dialog boxes to view a presentation similar to the following graphic.

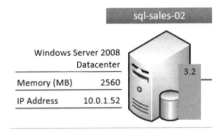

Overall, your revised diagram has several advantages over the initial version:

- It uses a consistent presentation style for the server names; they are displayed above the server in white text on a blue background.

- The display of CPU speed is much more effective as a proportionally sized icon than it was as text. It's easy to tell at a glance that several of the servers on the left of the diagram may be underpowered.

10

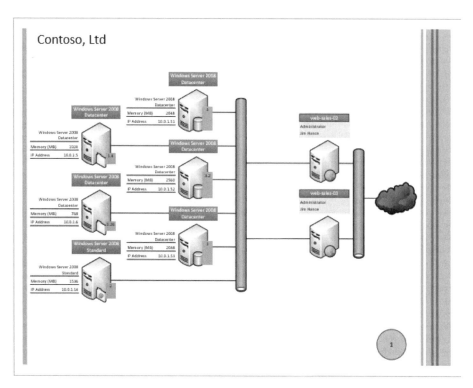

Contoso, Ltd

CLEAN UP Save your changes to the *Network with Data Graphics* drawing, and then close it.

Creating new data graphics

In the preceding exercise, you learned how flexible data graphics are and how easy it is to edit existing graphics.

In this exercise, you will create a new data graphic that contains two graphic elements and apply it to a flowchart that is similar to the one you created in Chapter 4, "Creating flowcharts and organization charts."

Your new data graphic will automatically apply color to process shapes based on who is responsible for them, making it very easy to understand who does what in the process. The graphic will also use icons to display the risk associated with each step in the process.

IMPORTANT Each process shape in this diagram contains several data fields, two of which you will use in your data graphic. One field is called *Owner* and identifies who is responsible for the process step. The other is called *Risk* and expresses the relative risk, on a scale of 1 (low) to 5 (high), of successfully completing that step in the process.

➡ SET UP You need the *HR Recruiting Flowchart_start* drawing located in the Chapter10 practice file folder to complete this exercise. Open the drawing in Visio and save it as *HR Recruiting Flowchart with data graphics*.

1   On the **Data** tab, in the **Display Data** group, click the **Data Graphics** button to open the **Data Graphics** gallery.

2   In the **Data Graphics** gallery, click **Create New Data Graphic**. An empty version of the dialog box you used in the preceding exercise appears and is titled **New Data Graphic**.

3   In the **New Data Graphic** dialog box, click **New Item**. The **New Item** dialog box appears.

4   In the **Display** section, of the **New Item** dialog box, display the **Data field** list, and then click **Owner**.

5   In the **Displayed as** list, click **Color by Value**. Visio creates a list of all of the values for **Owner** on this page and assigns a color to each one.

10

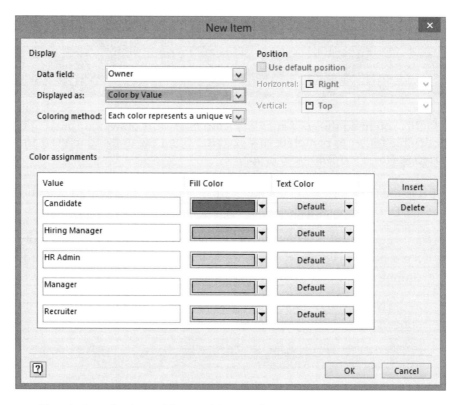

TIP The choice of colors Visio provides can be very suitable for some purposes but may be too bold for other purposes. In the latter case, you can display the Fill Color list for any field and change the color setting. You can also leave the Text Color of affected shapes at the default setting (as shown in the previous graphic) or you can manually change it. Finally, notice the Insert and Delete buttons to the right of the Color Assignments section. You can delete any field values or add new ones depending on what you want to highlight in the drawing.

6   Click **OK**.

7   In the **New Data Graphic** dialog box, click **New Item**.

8   In the **Display** section, in the **Data field** list, click **Risk**.

9   In the **Displayed as** list, click **Icon Set**.

10   Click the **Style** arrow to display a list of icon sets. (Scroll down to view all of them.)

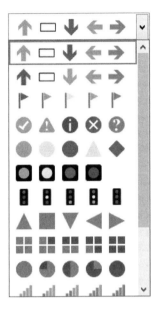

11   Click the set of colored pennants (flags) to select that icon set. The **New Item** dialog box should look like the following graphic.

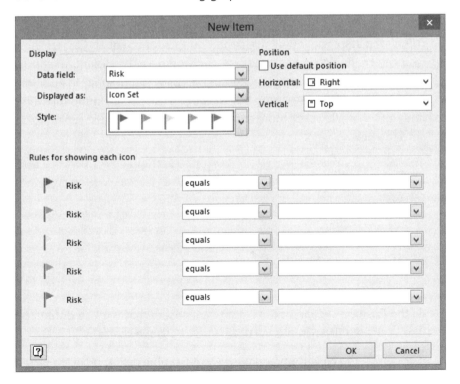

12   Type the following values in the empty text boxes to the right of the colored flags:

- Red flag: **5**

- Orange flag: **4**

- Yellow flag: **3**

- Green flag: **2**

- Blue flag: **1**

The center of the dialog box should look like the following graphic.

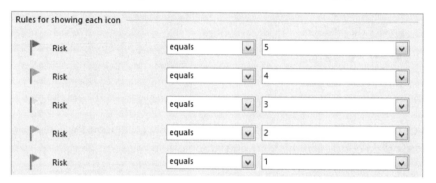

TIP In this step, you left all five condition lists set to Equals. Realize, however, that you can create nearly any condition you would like by clicking the arrow in that field to expose the list shown on the left in the following graphic. In addition, the text box on the right side of the dialog box includes a list, shown in the following graphic on the right that allows for more sophisticated values than just typing text or a number into the box.

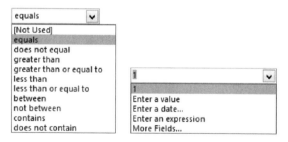

13   In the **Position** section of the dialog box, ensure that the **Use default position** check box is cleared. Then in the **Vertical** list, click **Above shape**.

14   Click **OK** in the **New Item** and **New Data Graphic** dialog boxes to close them.

15   Press **Ctrl+A** to select all shapes on the page.

16   On the **Data** tab, in the **Display Data** group, click the **Data Graphics** button, and
then click on your new data graphic.

TIP You'll notice when you point to the thumbnail for your data graphic that it has
been assigned the generic name *Data Graphic*. You can change the name by right-
clicking the thumbnail and selecting Rename.

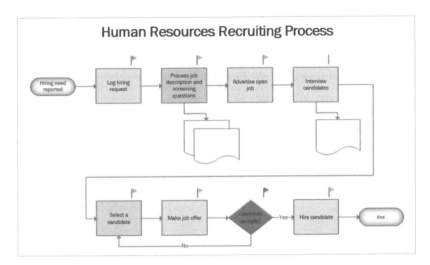

The process blocks in your diagram have been colored to reflect the owner of each
task. In addition, each step in the process shows a colored flag that indicates the relative risk associated with that step. At the moment, you don't know which owners or
risks are associated with which colors, but we'll solve that problem in the next section
of this chapter.

❌ CLEAN UP **Save your changes to the** *HR Recruiting Flowchart with data graphics* **but
leave it open if you are continuing with the next exercise.**

The display of data graphics is dynamic, which means that if the underlying data values
change, the data graphics will change. You can prove this to yourself by opening the shape
data window and changing the risk value for any shape. The pennant in the upper-right
corner of the shape will immediately change color.

TIP If you want to copy a data graphic from one Visio drawing to another, merely copy a
shape displaying the data graphic from the first drawing and paste it into the second one.
You can then delete the shape. The data graphic will remain behind.

Creating data graphic legends

In the preceding exercise, you created a diagram in which the color of the flowchart shapes and the color of an icon signify data values in the shapes. However, there's no way to tell what each color means.

In this exercise, you will add a *data graphic legend* to the page.

➡️ SET UP **You need the** *HR Recruiting Flowchart with data graphics* **drawing for this exercise. Either continue with the open copy from the previous exercise or open the** *HR Recruiting Flowchart with data graphics_start* **drawing located in the Chapter10 practice file folder and save it as** *HR Process Map with data graphics legend.*

1   On the **Data** tab, in the **Display Data** group, click the **Insert Legend** button, and then click **Vertical**. Visio always inserts the legend in the upper-right corner of the drawing page.

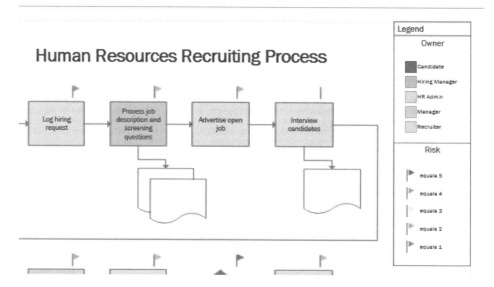

SEE ALSO Visio constructs the legend from a combination of containers and lists. Refer to Chapter 11, "Adding structure to your diagrams," for details about containers and lists.

After Visio has placed a legend on the page, you can edit it. In the next three steps, you will edit the legend to make it more descriptive.

2   Click once on the red pennant that displays **equals 5** and type **High**.

3   Click once on the orange pennant that displays **equals 4** and type **Medium High**.

Notice that Visio automatically expands the size of the legend shape because your replacement text is longer.

4   Continue typing descriptions for the remaining risk flags:

- Yellow: **Medium**

- Green: **Medium Low**

- Blue: **Low**

The Risk portion of the revised legend should look like the following graphic.

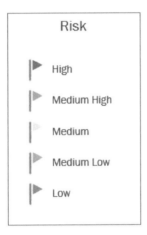

TIP To move the legend to another part of the page, click the header of the shape (where the word Legend is located) and drag the shape. You cannot select the legend by clicking anywhere in its interior; this behavior is characteristic of a list or container, as explained in Chapter 11.

CLEAN UP **Save your changes to the *HR Process Map with data graphics* drawing, and then close it.**

TIP After placing a data graphic legend on the page, Visio never updates it. Consequently, if you change the attributes of a data graphic in a way that affects the legend, you must delete the existing legend and insert a new one.

Refreshing data and data graphics

In Chapter 6, you learned how to link shapes in Visio diagrams to external data sources and then refresh the data in a diagram either manually or automatically.

In this chapter, you learned how to present data graphically.

Be sure to appreciate the power that exists when you combine these two operations: you can create a diagram whose data graphics change colors, appear or disappear, increase or decrease in size, or change icons merely because the data in a database or spreadsheet changed. If you would like to experiment with this idea, you can link the network diagram you worked with in the first two exercises in this chapter with the Contoso Network Data workbook that is located in the Chapter10 practice file folder.

Visio gives you the power to build compelling dashboards and business intelligence solutions. And you'll discover that the story gets even stronger when you explore publishing to Visio Services in Microsoft SharePoint in Chapter 13, "Collaborating on and publishing diagrams."

SEE ALSO For detailed descriptions of the reasons to use Visio as part of a business intelligence solution, including numerous examples, refer to Chapter 9, "Visio and Visio Services," in *Business Intelligence in Microsoft SharePoint 2013* by Norm Warren, Mariano Neto, Stacia Misner, Ivan Sanders, and Scott Helmers (Microsoft Press, 2013).

Key points

- Visio data graphics provide a powerful tool for visualizing the data behind the shapes on your page. Data graphics help you tell more of your story by:

    - Displaying text on or near a shape.

    - Highlighting data with data bars, star ratings, progress indicators, speedometers, thermometers, and other dynamic symbols.

    - Presenting an icon from an icon set, where each icon represents a specific data value or value range.

    - Changing the color of a shape based on a data value.

- If your diagram is linked to a live data feed or a near real-time data source, you can use data graphics to turn an otherwise ordinary Visio drawing into a dashboard for process monitoring, activity management, and status review.

- You can apply existing data graphics at any time by selecting one or more shapes and then choosing a graphic from the Data Graphics gallery.

- The appearance and location of data graphics are controlled by parameters that you can modify, making it easy to change any existing data graphic. It's also very easy to create a new data graphic by choosing the type and style from drop-down lists and then setting a handful of parameter values.

- It requires only two clicks to create a legend for the data graphics on your drawing page.

10

Chapter at a glance

Organize

Organize shapes with containers,
page 425

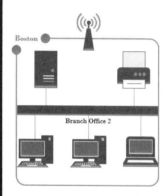

Add

Add shapes to lists,
page 431

Build

Build wireframes,
page 441

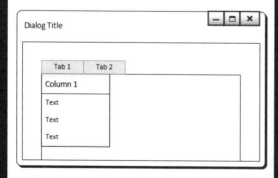

Annotate

Annotate shapes with callouts,
page 448

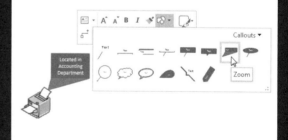

IN THIS CHAPTER, YOU WILL LEARN HOW TO

- Compare containers and groups.

- Work with containers and their contents.

- Format and size containers.

- Add shapes to lists.

- Format and size lists.

- Find containers and lists in Visio (swimlanes, wireframes, and legends).

- Annotate shapes with callouts.

In many types of Microsoft Visio diagrams, it is useful to create visual or logical relationships among a set of shapes. In previous versions of Visio, you could use background shapes and groups for this purpose. These capabilities are still available in Visio 2013 as you discovered when you created a network diagram in Chapter 9, "Creating network and data center diagrams." However, Visio 2013 offers three more effective ways to establish relationships and add structure to diagrams:

- **Containers** A *container* provides a visual boundary around a set of objects, but it also establishes a logical relationship between the container and the objects within it: shapes know when they are members of a container and containers know which shapes they contain.

    The key advantage of a container is that while you can move, copy, or delete it and its members as a unit, each contained shape maintains its independence. Selecting an object inside a container only requires one click, which makes it simple to access a container member's shape data and other properties.

    TIP A container can contain shapes, other containers, and lists.

- **Lists** A *list* is a special type of container that maintains an ordered relationship among its members. Each object in a list knows its ordinal position; new objects are not merely added to a list but are added to a specific position in a list.

  TIP A list can contain shapes and containers but cannot contain other lists.

- **Callouts** In previous versions of Visio, a callout was merely a shape that you glued to another shape to add a comment. A Visio 2013-style *callout* still provides a way to add annotation to a shape, but the callout knows the shape to which it is attached, and the shape can identify any attached callouts.

In this chapter, you will experiment with and learn the value of containers, lists, and callouts in Visio diagrams.

PRACTICE FILES To complete the exercises in this chapter, you need the practice files contained in the Chapter11 practice file folder. For more information, refer to "Downloading the practice files" in this book's Introduction.

Comparing containers and groups

You can use either groups or containers to visually connect a set of shapes. However, the two have key behavioral differences that are likely to lead you to use one or the other depending on your needs.

In this exercise, you will create both a group and a container, and then you will perform the same set of actions on each in order to examine the differences.

➡️ SET UP **You need the *Containers, Lists and Callouts_start* drawing located in the Chapter11 practice file folder to complete this exercise. Open the drawing in Visio and save it as *Groups vs. Containers*.**

1   Create a colored rectangle and group it with the network shapes on the left side of the page.

   SEE ALSO For a refresher on using a group with a background shape to organize a set of shapes, refer to "Organizing network shapes in a diagram" in Chapter 9.

2   Draw a bounding box around the **Branch Office 2** network shapes on the right side of the page.

3   On the **Insert** tab, in the **Diagram Parts** group, click the **Container** button. The **Container** gallery opens and as you point your mouse to the thumbnails in the gallery, *Live Preview* shows how each container style will look with your selected shapes. (Note that the **Belt** style is highlighted; you will use this style in the next step.)

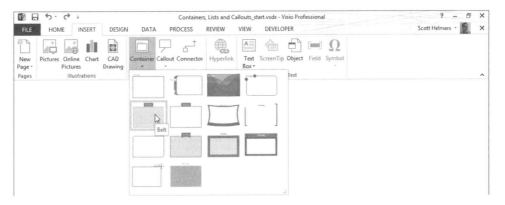

TIP The 14 container styles in the gallery range in appearance from subtle to bold so you have an option to match the style of the container to the style of your diagram. The following graphic offers five very different looks for a set of Network shapes.

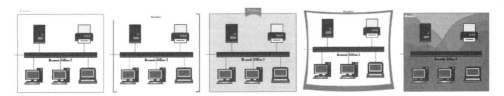

4   Click the **Belt** thumbnail in the **Container** gallery. Your diagram now shows a set of grouped shapes on the left and a container on the right.

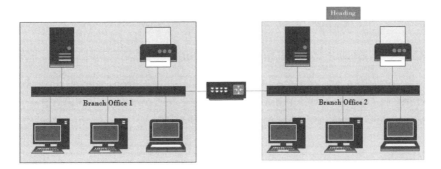

11

5   Click the **Branch Office 1** group once to select it, and then drag the bottom resize handle down to the bottom of the page.

6   Click the edge or heading of the **Branch Office 2** container once to select it, and then drag the bottom resize handle down to the bottom of the page.

> **IMPORTANT** One immediate difference to note is that you can select a group by clicking anywhere on its edge or interior, but you can only select a container by clicking its edge or its heading.

The following graphic illustrates that what you've previously learned about groups applies here: resizing the group resizes the shapes in the group. Look at the container on the right, however. The container is taller but its member shapes are unchanged.

TIP If you run Visio in developer mode, you can change the behavior of a group so the interior shapes do not resize. For more information about developer mode, refer to the Appendix.

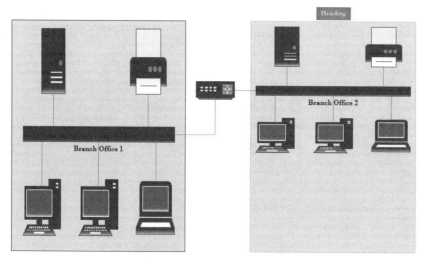

7   Press **Ctrl+Z** twice to undo both resize operations.

8   Drag two **PC** shapes from the **Computers and Monitors** stencil, dropping the first in the open area above the **Branch Office 1** network segment and the second in the open area of the container for **Branch Office 2**.

TIP Containers provide visual feedback when you drag shapes near or into them. (This is one way to distinguish a container from a group or an ordinary shape.) The border of the container on the right in the following graphic shows a green color that is very similar to the coloring used for Dynamic Grid lines (also visible in the graphic).

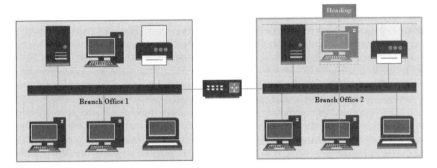

9 Hold down the **Shift** key while clicking both the group and the container to select them, and then drag the selection down to the bottom of the page. As the following graphic shows, dropping a shape on a group does not add it to the group—it remains behind when you move the group. In contrast, dropping a shape into a container adds it to the container, so it moves when you move the container.

TIP By default, shapes dropped on a group are not added to the group. However, if you run Visio in developer mode, you can change the behavior of a group so it will accept dropped shapes. For more information about developer mode, refer to the Appendix.

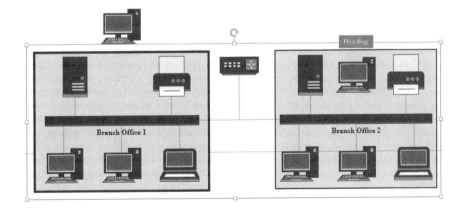

10   Press **Ctrl+Z** three times to undo the move operation and delete the two PCs you added.

11   Click once to select the **Branch Office 1** group, and then click the printer in the group. Drag it out of the top of the group rectangle.

TIP The default behavior for groups is that the first click selects the group; you must click a second time to select a shape in the group. If you run Visio in developer mode, you can alter the selection characteristics of a group. For more information about developer mode, refer to the Appendix.

12   Click once to select the printer in the **Branch Office 2** container, and then drag it out of the top of the container. The results of both this step and the previous step are shown in the following graphic.

TIP One click is sufficient to select any shape in a container because, by design, the fill of the container can't be selected with a mouse click.

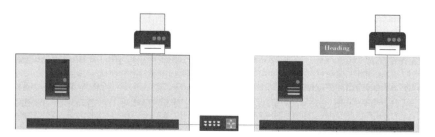

13   Hold down the **Shift** key while clicking both the group and the container to select them, and then drag the selection down to the bottom of the page. Although you have relocated the printer on the left outside the colored group rectangle, the shape is still part of the group. Consequently, the printer moves when you move the group. On the right, however, dragging a shape out of a container removes it from the container; therefore, it stays behind when you move the container.

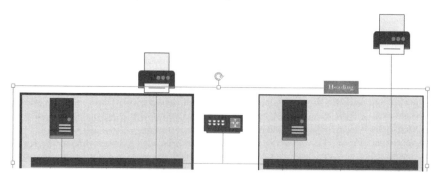

14   Press **Ctrl+Z** three times to undo the move operation and return the printers to their original locations.

15   Click and drag in the interior of the group and attempt to draw a bounding box around the two PCs below the network segment. The result will not be what you intended. You cannot select the two PCs with a bounding box because dragging within the group shape moves the group (refer to the left side of the graphic in the next step).

      TIP You can select shapes in a group with a bounding box—but only if you start the bounding box outside of the group.

16   Click once in the interior of the container and attempt to draw a bounding box around the two PCs below the network segment. A bounding box inside a container does select contained shapes for the same reason that you could select a contained shape with a single click in step 13: the container background is invisible to mouse clicks.

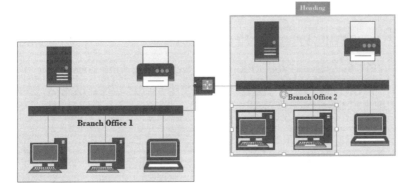

17   Click once to select the **Branch Office 1** group, type **San Francisco**, and press **Esc**. Then format the text to **16 pt.** and **Bold** to make it more visible. Because the new text falls directly on top of an Ethernet segment that is a similar color, the text is all but invisible.

18   Click once to select the container, type **Boston**, and press **Esc**. Then format the text to **16 pt.** and **Bold** to make it more visible. Notice that changing the font characteristics of the group makes the same changes to the text on all shapes within the group.

      In the following graphic, the text you added to the group on the left is positioned in the center of the group by default. Because the default position and color render

11

the text invisible, you may want to use the text manipulation skills you learned in Chapter 3, "Adding sophistication to your drawings," to move the text to a better position.

In contrast, a container has a built-in header. When you select a container and type text, the words automatically appear in the header. Changing the format of the header text does not affect the text on any shapes within the container.

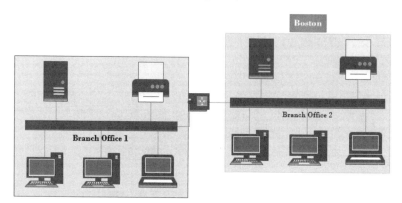

❌ CLEAN UP **Save your changes to the *Groups vs. Containers* drawing, and then close it.**

After completing this exercise, you should have a good working knowledge of the properties of groups compared to containers. For future reference, the following table contains a summary of the key differences.

Action	Groups	Containers
Resizing	Contents are resized with the group	Contents are not changed
Selecting an interior shape	Requires two clicks (unless default group behavior has been changed)	Requires one click
Selecting interior shape(s) with a bounding box	Cannot start a bounding box by clicking inside a group	Can start a bounding box by clicking anywhere
Dropping a new shape inside	Dropped shapes are not added to the group (unless default group behavior has been changed)	Dropped shapes are added to the container
Dragging a shape out	Shape is physically outside the group but remains part of the group	Shape is removed from the container
Typing text	Text is placed in the center of the group	Text is placed in the container's heading

SEE ALSO For more information about Visio 2013 containers, refer to the Visio development team blog at *blogs.office.com/b/visio/archive/2012/11/05/containers-and-callouts-in-visio.aspx*. Although the appearance of containers changed considerably between Visio 2013 and Visio 2010, the following Visio 2010 articles still contain useful information: *blogs.msdn.com/b/visio/archive/2009/08/25/organizing-diagrams-with-containers.aspx* and *blogs.msdn.com/b/visio/archive/2009/08/27/details-on-container-behaviors.aspx*. Finally, for the technically inclined, this post provides details about the inner workings of containers, lists and callouts: *blogs.office.com/b/visio/archive/2010/01/12/custom-containers-lists-and-callouts-in-visio-2010.aspx*.

Organizing shapes with containers

Group shapes are still valuable for many purposes, including holding collections of sub-shapes that will never change. However, Visio 2013 containers offer numerous advantages for dynamically grouping, moving, and managing a set of related shapes.

In this exercise, you will continue working with containers to learn more about their unique properties.

 SET UP **You need the *Containers, Lists and Callouts_start* drawing located in the Chapter11 practice file folder to complete this exercise. Open the drawing in Visio and save it as *Container Properties*.**

1   Draw a bounding box around the **Branch Office 1** network shapes.

2   On the **Insert** tab, in the **Diagram Parts** group, click the **Container** button, and then click **Wire**.

3   Right-click the edge or heading of the container to select it. Notice that whenever you select a container, the **Container Tools** *tool tab set* appears and includes the **Format** *tool tab*, as shown in the following graphic.

4   In the **Container Tools** tool tab set, click the **Format** tool tab to activate it.

5   On the **Format** tab, in the **Membership** group, click the **Select Contents** button. All contained shapes are selected.

> **TIP** You can also right-click the edge or heading of the container, click Container, and then click Select Contents to achieve the same result.

6   Draw a bounding box to select the **Branch Office 2** network segment and the PCs below it; do not select the server and printer above it.

7   On the **Insert** tab, in the **Diagram Parts** group, click the **Container** button, and then click **Wire**. You have created a container around part of the **Branch Office 2** network components.

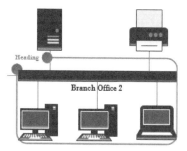

8   Click the edge or heading of the container you just created and drag the top resize handle up until the container surrounds the server and printer.

9   On the **Format** tab, in the **Membership** group, click the **Select Contents** button. Notice that the server and printer are not selected. Surrounding shapes with an existing container do not add them to the container.

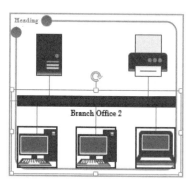

10   Click once on the server shape to select it.

11   Right-click the selected server, click **Container**, and then click **Add to Underlying Container**. The server shape is now a member of the container.

> **TIP** When you select any shape that is a member of a container, the green outline appears on the border of the container.

12   Click once on the edge or heading of the **Branch Office 2** container to select it, and then press the **Delete** key. The container and its contents are deleted.

If you want to remove a container but leave its contents, the simplest method is to disband the container.

13   Click once on the edge or heading of the **Branch Office 1** container to select it.

14   On the **Format** tab, in the **Membership** group, click the **Disband Container** button. The container is removed from the drawing but all of the previously contained shapes remain on the page.

> **TIP** You can also right-click the edge or heading of the container, click Container, and then click Disband Container to achieve the same result.

✖ CLEAN UP **Close the *Container Properties* drawing without saving changes.**

In this exercise and the preceding one, you selected a set of existing objects and created a container around them. You can also create an empty container and later add objects to it. To do so, ensure that nothing on the drawing page is selected. On the Insert tab, in the Diagram Parts group, click the Container button, and then click a container style in the gallery. The new container will be added to the center of the drawing window. You can then drop in new or existing shapes, lists, or other containers.

> **TIP** You can copy a container and paste it elsewhere in the same or a different drawing. A copy of the container and all its members will be pasted into the new location.

The Lock Container button in the Membership group of the Format tool tab prevents shapes from being added or removed; it also locks the container against deletion.

11

Formatting containers

When you drop a container onto the page, it includes a set of style attributes. You can change a container's formatting at any time by selecting it and then using the commands on the Format tab of the Container Tools tool tab set.

Container style drop down arrows   Heading style button

- You can use the **Style** gallery in the **Container Styles** group to select a different container style. (Be sure to notice the drop-down arrows at the right end of the **Container** gallery; use them to view additional container styles.) The container style options are also available by clicking the **Change Shape** button, either in the **Editing** group on the **Home** tab, or on the Mini Toolbar that appears when you right-click a container.

- You can choose alternate heading styles by clicking the **Heading Style** button in the **Container Styles** group. Visio offers either two or four heading styles, depending on the container.

There are two additional ways to alter the appearance of a container.

- Containers react to *Themes* and *Variants*. Consequently, the colors of the thumbnails in the **Containers** gallery and the containers on your drawing page can be very different from one diagram to the next.

- You can change the fill, line, and shadow attributes of a container by using the same techniques you use for any other Visio shape—on the **Home** tab, click any button in the **Shape Styles** group.

Sizing containers

The predesigned containers in Visio 2013 expand automatically when you add shapes near the edge of the container. You can change this default behavior by using the Format tool tab of the Container Tools tool tab set: in the Size group, click the Automatic Resize button to reveal three mutually exclusive options.

- **No Automatic Resize** The container will not expand when you drop shapes near the edge.

- **Expand as Needed** The container will expand when you drop shapes near the edge. The opposite is not true: however, the container will not shrink when you remove shapes.

- **Always Fit to Contents** The container will expand and contract automatically when you add or remove shapes.

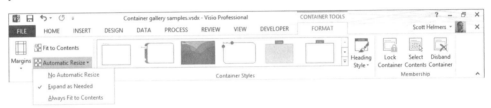

You can also affect container size with the two buttons located above and to the left of the Automatic Resize button shown in the preceding graphic:

- **Margins** Sets the spacing between the edges of the container and the contained shapes.

- **Fit to Contents** Sets the container size to the minimum required for the contained shapes plus the margin.

11

On the border

As you have already learned, when you drag a shape into a container, a green outline appears on the border of the container. This is true even when you drag most but not all of the shape into the container. In the following graphic, the wireless access point will be added to the container when the mouse button is released, even though it is not fully within the borders of the container. (Depending on the resize options described just before this sidebar, the container may expand to encompass the new shape.)

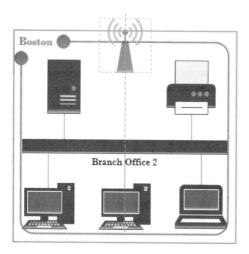

The following graphic on the left shows a different container behavior that you might use from time to time. In contrast to the previous graphic, the wireless access point has not been dragged quite as far into the container. The container signals the difference by displaying a green outline only on the top border and not all the way around. When the shape is dropped, the wireless access point will become a member of the container, but it will be attached to the edge of the container.

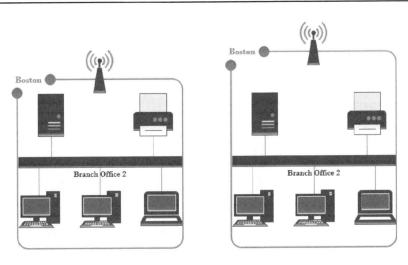

The key difference in behavior of a boundary shape is that when the container is re-sized, the boundary shape stays on the border. For example, when the resize handle on top of the container in the right-hand image in preceding graphic is dragged up-ward, the wireless access point remains on the container boundary.

You might use border shapes for a situation like the one shown in this network dia-gram because the wireless access point is attached to the branch office network but is also linked to other networks. Consequently, it makes sense to show it on the border rather than in the interior of the container. The "Wireframes" section of "Finding con-tainers and lists in Visio" later in this chapter, contains another use for border shapes.

Adding shapes to lists

A list is a special type of container that maintains its members in ordered sequence. When you drop an object into a list, it takes a specific place before, between, or after existing members. Each list member knows its relative position in the list.

Visio 2013 doesn't provide a list gallery on the Insert tab in the same way that it offers a container gallery. Consequently, creating a list either requires reusing an existing list shape or having enough technical knowledge to make changes to the *ShapeSheet*. (For more in-formation about modifying the ShapeSheet, refer to the Appendix.)

11

In this exercise, you will add shapes to a list, and then reorder the shapes within the list. For this hypothetical scenario, the list shape is called *My New PC*; you will add rectangular shapes that represent the software you will load onto your new PC. Your goal for this exercise is to create a list that shows the installation sequence for your new PC.

IMPORTANT The shapes you will drop into the list in this exercise have been prepared with two special attributes:

- Each shape displays the name of a software product. (The name of the product is stored in the shape as shape data.)

- Each shape displays its relative position in the list when it is in a list. When the shape is not in a list, it doesn't display any number.

- The first attribute uses a Visio field to display shape data; refer to Chapter 3 for more information about Visio fields. The second attribute was created specifically for this exercise and uses two ShapeSheet formulas to determine and present each shape's position in the list; refer to the Appendix for information about the ShapeSheet.

SET UP **You need the *Containers, Lists and Callouts_start* drawing located in the Chapter11 practice file folder to complete this exercise. Open the drawing in Visio and save it as *Lists*. Then go to the Lists page.**

1   Drag **Visio 2013** into the list.

TIP A list provides the same visual feedback—a green border—as a container when a shape approaches its interior.

The graphic on the left shows the list outlined as the Visio 2013 shape approaches, and the graphic on the right shows the shape inside the list. Notice that the shape now displays its ordinal position in the list in front of the product name.

2   Because you can't install Visio until after you've installed Windows, drag **Windows 8** into the list, above **Visio 2013**. As you approach the list with the **Windows 8** shape, notice that an orange *insertion bar* appears to tell you where you can add a new list member. In this example, you can insert the new shape after the existing shape (the following graphic on the left) or before the existing shape (graphic in the center).

When you drop Windows 8 above Visio 2013, notice that each rectangle displays its current position in the list. Visio 2013 is now #2.

TIP The blue triangle that appears at the end of the orange insertion bar in the previous left and center graphics and in several of the following graphics will be explained in the next section.

3   Insert **Office 2013** between **Windows 8** and **Visio 2013**.

4   Drop **Mozilla** at the end of the list.

5   Drag **Visio add-in** until the orange insertion bar appears below **Mozilla**, but stop when the pointer is on the edge of the list but most of the shape is still outside of it, as shown in the following graphic on the left.

6   With **Visio add-in** in the position shown on the left in the following graphic, release the mouse button. When you release the mouse button from this position, the shape jumps into the list producing the result shown on the right.

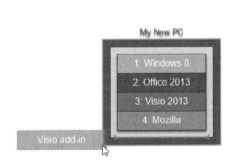

The behavior demonstrated by the *Visio add-in* shape highlights two differences between containers and lists:

- Container members can be located anywhere within a container; list members are always in fixed positions.

- Shapes that are dragged onto the border of a container can be attached to the border; shapes cannot be attached to the border of a list.

7   Drag **Mozilla** up so it is located between **Windows 8** and **Office 2013**.

The following graphic on the left shows the Mozilla shape as it is being dragged up the list; the graphic on the right shows the result. Notice that when you release the mouse button, each shape immediately reflects its new position in the list.

As this step illustrates, you cannot only add shapes to specific positions in a list, you can rearrange the shapes within a list.

Although you aren't likely to use a Visio list for the specific purpose suggested by this exercise, you can probably imagine your own applications for position-aware shapes. Refer to the subsections in "Finding containers and lists in Visio" later in this chapter for examples of several ways that lists are used in Visio 2013 templates.

The previous exercise used a vertical list with shapes automatically placed from top to bottom. A Visio list can be either vertical or horizontal and can order shapes in either direction within the list. Although these attributes are controlled by parameters and don't require writing code, you can't change them from the Visio ribbon; you must make changes to the ShapeSheet for the list.

SEE ALSO You will learn about the Visio ShapeSheet in the Appendix.

If you would like to experiment with a horizontal list, the Lists page in the *Containers, Lists and Callouts_start* drawing located in the Chapter11 practice file folder also includes a horizontal list called Store Shelf. Drag shapes from the Computers And Monitors or Network

And Peripherals stencils to create a list like the following example. The Store Shelf list is configured to add shapes from left to right so it expands to the right as you add shapes.

Store Shelf

SEE ALSO If you would like to know more about lists, go to *msdn.microsoft.com/en-us/library/ff959245.aspx*, which offers a comprehensive MSDN article on structured diagrams written by Mark Nelson of Microsoft.

❌ CLEAN UP **Save your changes to the *Lists* drawing, and then close it.**

Formatting and sizing lists

You can adjust most of the same format and size options for a list that you can for a container with one notable exception: you cannot change the size of a Visio list shape. Visio expands and contracts each list shape so it is the exact size of its member shapes plus the margin around the shapes.

The Format tool tab in the Container Tools tool tab set provides the functions described in the following list.

In the Size group:

- You can use the **Margins** button to adjust the spacing between the edges of the list and the contained shapes.

- Because Visio controls the size of a list shape, **Fit To Container** and **Automatic Resize** are disabled.

In the Container Styles group:

- If you open a diagram created in Visio 2010 that contains a list, you can select one of 10 alternate styles for the list. However, at present, Visio 2013 does not allow you to change the style of lists created in Visio 2013.

- The **Heading Style** gallery provides either two or four heading placement and style alternatives, depending on the list style.

11

In the Membership group:

- The **Lock Container**, **Select Contents**, and **Disband Container** buttons provide the same functions for lists that they do for containers.

Finding containers and lists in Visio

Several Visio 2013 templates take advantage of the properties of containers and lists to enhance ease of use and to add valuable features. In this section, you will discover three examples.

Swimlanes

One of the most prominent examples of list and container usage is for ***cross-functional flowcharts***, also known as ***swimlane*** diagrams. (Refer to Chapter 4, "Creating flowcharts and organization charts," for more information about this type of diagram.)

The swimlane add-in was completely redesigned for Visio 2010 in order to take advantage of both lists and containers, with the net effect that a cross-functional flowchart (CFF) is a list of containers! The Visio 2010 structure is also used for Visio 2013 swimlane diagrams:

- The framework that holds swimlanes is a list.

- Each swimlane is a container.

> **IMPORTANT** Because Visio 2010 swimlanes also use containers, if you open a 2010 swimlane diagram in Visio 2013, it will open directly. However, if you open a swimlane diagram created in an earlier version of Visio, it will be converted to the new swimlane structure and cannot subsequently be edited with the older software. To protect you, Visio presents the dialog box shown in the following graphic so you have the opportunity to save the older version of the diagram if you want to.

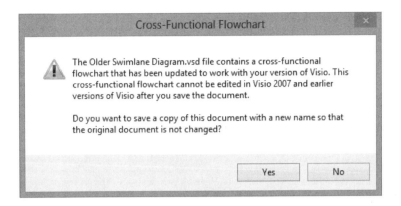

In this exercise, you will create part of a swimlane diagram to understand how lists and containers are used.

SET UP **Click the File tab, and then click New. Click Categories, click** *Flowchart*, **and then double-click the** *Cross-Functional Flowchart* **thumbnail to create a new drawing.**

1   Click the top edge of the CFF, and then type **Sample Swimlane Diagram**. Because the CFF structure is a list, the text you typed appears in the list heading.

2   Click the rectangle at the left end of the upper swimlane, and then type **Accounting**. Because the swimlane is a container, your text appears in the container heading.

3   Click the rectangle at the left end of the lower swimlane, type **Legal**, and then press the **Esc** key. The following graphic shows the results of steps 1, 2, and 3.

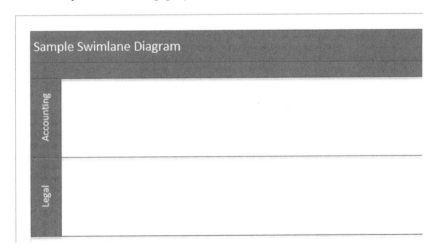

11

4   Drag a **Process** shape into the **Accounting** swimlane. Notice that the swimlane shows the green border that you previously learned was characteristic behavior for containers.

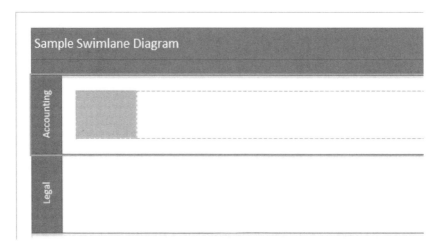

5   Drag a **Decision** shape into the **Legal** swimlane and position it to the right of the **Process** shape in the **Accounting** lane.

6   Drag the **AutoConnect** arrow on the right side of the **Process** shape to link that shape to the **Decision** shape.

SEE ALSO Refer to Chapter 2, "Creating a new diagram," for a refresher on using AutoConnect.

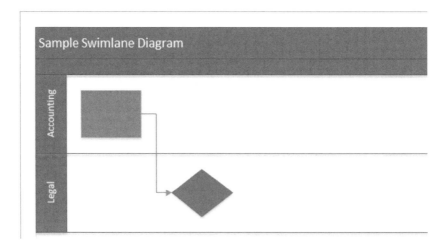

7   Position the cursor just outside the CFF frame at the junction between the
    Accounting and **Legal** swimlanes (the pointer is visible in the following graphic).

    TIP If the insertion bar isn't visible when you first position the cursor near the lane
    boundary, pause just a moment longer and it will appear.

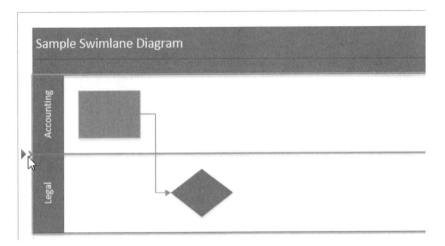

The presence of the list insertion bar on the boundary between the Accounting and
Legal lanes provides visible evidence that you are working with lists. Also, be sure to
note the blue insertion triangle that appears at the end of the insertion bar. Clicking
the blue insertion triangle automatically adds the default insertion object at the insertion bar location.

TIP Not all lists have a default insertion object. If you click the blue insertion triangle
on a list without a default, Visio will insert a copy of one of the adjacent list members.

8   Click the blue insertion triangle, shown in the previous graphic. Visio inserts a new
    swimlane between the other two and maintains all existing connections between
    shapes in the lanes.

11

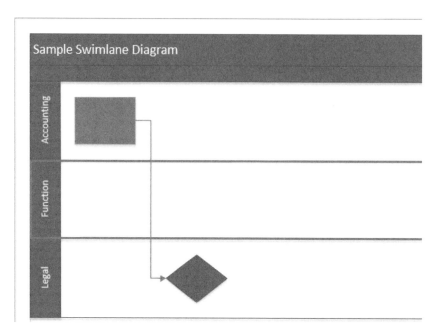

9   Click in the heading area of the **Accounting** swimlane and drag it down below the
     Legal lane. Visio moves the **Accounting** lane to the end of the list and maintains the
     connections between shapes within and across all swimlanes.

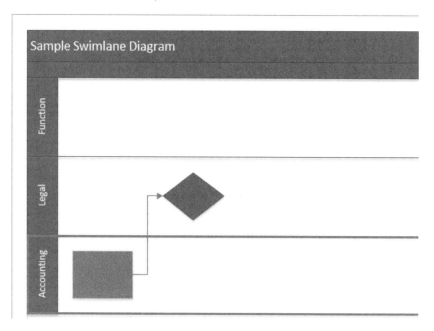

CLEAN UP **Save and close your diagram if you want to keep it; otherwise, just close it.**

Adding, deleting, and rearranging swimlanes is more predictable and logical in Visio 2013, because containers and lists provide the underlying structure.

Swimlane diagrams derive another benefit from being built as containers: shapes in the container know they are contained. To find evidence of this, examine the Function field in the shape data for any flowchart shape in a swimlane. As an example, the following graphics show the shape data for the process shape (on the left) and decision diamond shape (right) from the preceding graphic. The value in the Function field is derived dynamically from the swimlane heading; if you change the value of the swimlane title, the Function field will be updated for all contained shapes.

SEE ALSO For more about swimlane containers, go to the Visio development team blog at *blogs.msdn.com/b/visio/archive/2009/09/01/cross-functional-flowcharts-in-visio-2010.aspx.*

IMPORTANT The following section applies only to the Professional edition of Visio 2013.

Wireframes

Visio 2013 includes a revamped set of user interface (UI) design shapes that were initially introduced in Visio 2010. For this chapter, the key point of interest about the redesigned shapes is that many of them are either containers or lists.

Software designers use wireframe shapes to create mockups of dialog boxes and other visual elements that will be displayed by their applications. When you use Visio 2013 to create a mockup of a dialog box, you will find that the Dialog Form shape is a container. Consequently, as you add buttons and controls to your dialog form, they become container

11

members. If you move, copy, or delete your dialog box, all of the contained shapes are included. If you have ever created a UI mockup using Visio 2007 or earlier, it won't take more than a moment or two of experimentation to realize how significant an improvement this is.

Some Visio 2013 UI shapes are lists, including, not surprisingly, the List Box control. When you drop one into a dialog form container, the list is prepopulated with three list members. You can add, delete, and resequence list members by dragging them, as you learned in "Adding shapes to lists" earlier in this chapter.

In this exercise, you will use the Wireframe template to build a prototype of a simple dialog box that looks like the one in the following graphic. Even if you aren't a UI designer, you should find this exercise useful in learning more about the behavior of containers and lists.

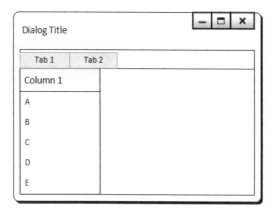

➡ SET UP Click the File tab, and then click New. Click Categories, click *Software and Database*, and then double-click the *Wireframe Diagram* thumbnail to create a new drawing.

1   Drag a **Dialog form** shape from the **Dialogs** stencil, drop it on the page, and then zoom in so you can work with the shape.

2   Drag a **Dialog button** shape from the **Dialogs** stencil and glue it to a connection point in the upper-right corner of the dialog form.

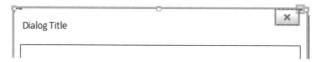

TIP As soon as you drag the Dialog Button shape into the Dialog Form shape, notice that the edges of the Dialog Form shape are marked with the green outline that characterizes a container.

When you drop a Dialog Button shape onto the page, it automatically opens the Shape Data dialog box.

3 In the **Shape Data** dialog box, click **OK** to accept the default value for **Type**.

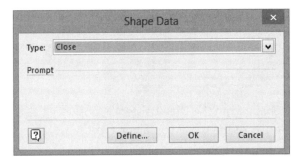

4 Drag another **Dialog button** shape into the dialog form container and glue it to the left end of the previous one; when the **Shape Data** dialog box opens, click **Maximize** in the **Type** list, and then click **OK**. Repeat a third time and select **Minimize** in the **Type** list.

TIP The Dialog Button shape is a *multi-shape*; the data value you select in the Shape Data dialog box determines the appearance of the shape.

The top of your dialog form container now looks like the following graphic.

5 Drag a **Panel** shape from the **Dialogs** stencil and drop it onto the page below (not inside) the dialog form. You need to drop it outside the dialog form, because it is too large to fit inside, and you want it to become a member of the **Dialog** container. (If a shape doesn't fit inside a container, it will not become a container member.)

6 Use the **Size & Position** window or the resize handles to change the width of the **Panel** shape to approximately 3 inches (75 mm) and its height to about 1.25 inches (30 mm).

7 Drag the **Panel** shape into the dialog form and position it in the bottom center.

TIP The Panel shape is a container, so you can only select and drag it by its edges.

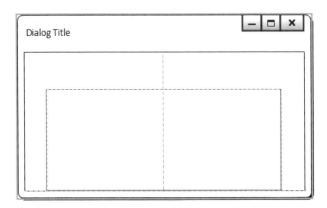

8   Drag an **Upper tab item** shape from the **Dialogs** stencil, position it as a **Boundary** shape at the upper-left corner of the panel container, type **Tab 1**, and press **Esc**.

TIP You want the Upper tab item shape to be on the boundary of the Panel shape and not inside it. Consequently, when you position the Upper tab item shape, make sure that only the top border of the panel container shows the green highlight, as shown in the following graphic. Refer to the sidebar "On the border" earlier in this chapter for more information about border shapes.

By attaching the Upper tab item shape to the boundary of the panel container, you have "welded" them together. If you reposition the panel container, the tab follows along.

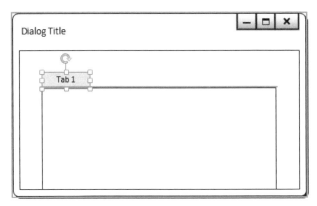

TIP Notice that the top border of the panel container is not the only thing with a green outline in this graphic. There is also a green outline surrounding the dialog form container. This is because you are adding the Tab shape to a container that is nested inside another container; both containers reflect your action.

9　Drag another **Upper tab item** shape from the **Dialogs** stencil, position it as a **Boundary** shape to the right of the previous tab, type **Tab 2**, and press **Esc**.

10　Drag a **List box** from the **Controls** stencil and position it in the upper-left corner of the panel container as shown in the following graphic.

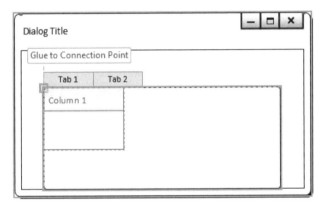

TIP The List Box shape exhibits behavior you haven't learned about yet in this chapter. When you release the mouse button to drop the new list, it automatically adds several list items, as shown in the following graphic. A List shape that automatically adds list entries can be very useful, but creating one that behaves this way is beyond the scope of this book.

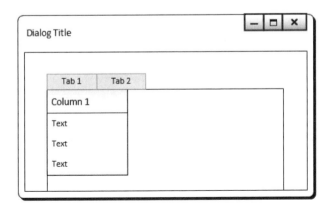

11

11   Select the uppermost **Text** item and type **A**, select the middle **Text** item and type **D**, and then select the bottom **Text** item and type **E**.

12   Position the cursor just to the left of the **Column 1** list shape, between the **A** and **D** labels.

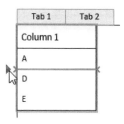

13   Click the blue insertion triangle twice to add two entries to the **List Box** shape, and then type **B** into the upper item and **C** into the lower one.

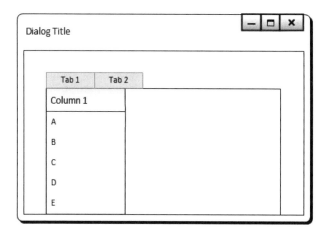

TIP The Dialog Form shape in this graphic is taller than the ones in step 10. That's because the list box, panel container, and dialog form container are all configured for automatic expansion. When you added new list items, the list expanded, which, in turn, caused both of the surrounding containers to expand.

14   Click once on the outer edge of the **Dialog form** shape to select it.

15   On the **Format** tab of the **Container Tools** tool tab set, in the **Size** group, click **Fit to Contents**. The **Dialog form** container shrinks to fit the size of the **Panel** container located within it.

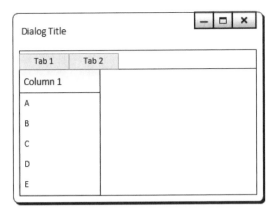

![Clean Up icon] **CLEAN UP** **Save and close your diagram if you want to keep it; otherwise just close it.**

The dialog box mockup you've created in this exercise isn't going to win any design awards. If you wanted to create a real mockup, you would add additional controls, text, colors, and themes. However, by completing this exercise, you have created a practical application for nested containers and lists, and have an example of a container with a border shape.

SEE ALSO For more information about wireframe design, refer to the Visio development team blog at *blogs.msdn.com/b/visio/archive/2009/12/22/wireframe-shapes-in-visio-2010.aspx*.

> **IMPORTANT** The following section applies only to the Professional edition of Visio 2013.

Legends

In Chapter 10, "Visualizing your data," you learned about *data graphics* and created a legend for your data graphics. A data graphics legend is actually a structure consisting of an outer list, one or more containers as list members, and lists within those containers. For example, the same legend is shown in both of the following graphics. The structure is loosely visible on the left. However, after drawing a bounding box around the entire legend, the structure is very apparent on the right: the legend consists of three containers (Legend, Owner, Risk) and two lists, all of which are outlined in green.

11

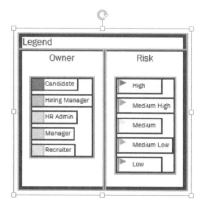

If you return to the data graphics diagram you created in Chapter 10 (or open the *Data graphics legends_start* file in the Chapter11 practice files folder), you will find that you can add, delete, rename, and move legend components. Throughout your changes, however, the legend maintains its overall structure because of the nested containers and lists.

Annotating shapes with callouts

In previous versions of Visio, you could drag a callout from the Callouts stencil onto the drawing page. The Callouts stencil still exists: in the Shapes window, click More Shapes, click Visio Extras, and then click Callouts to reveal more than three dozen callout types. The following graphic shows four examples.

Old-style callouts are useful for their intended purpose: you can type text into the text box and glue the tail onto another shape. Some even have attractive or clever designs.

The underlying problem with the older callouts, however, is that most of them are just shapes. Although you can attach them to other shapes, they aren't associated with those shapes in any useful way. For example, start with the printer and callout on the left in the following graphic.

- Moving the printer to the right (center image), doesn't change the location of the callout.

- Deleting the printer shape (rightmost graphic) doesn't affect the callout.

It's also easy to accidentally detach the callout from the printer by dragging the text box portion of the callout while trying to relocate it.

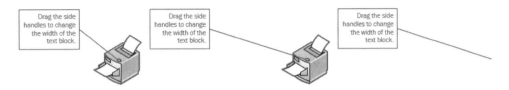

In this exercise, you will discover that Visio 2013 callouts are associated with the shapes to which they are attached in ways that make sense; the callout and its attached shape act in tandem.

SET UP **You need the *Containers, Lists and Callouts_start* drawing located in the Chapter11 practice file folder to complete this exercise. Open the drawing in Visio and save it as *Callouts*. Then go to the Callouts page.**

1   Click once on the **Printer** shape to select it.

2   On the **Insert** tab, in the **Diagram Parts** group, click the **Callout** button. The **Callout** gallery opens.

3   Point to various callout images in the gallery and notice that Live Preview shows what each callout will look like when attached to the printer shape.

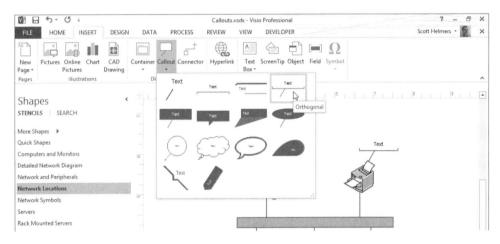

4   Click **Orthogonal** (as shown in the previous graphic). The callout is added to the page and attached to the printer.

5   With the callout still selected, type **Located in Accounting Department**, and then press **Esc** to exit text edit mode.

TIP Notice that when the callout is selected, there is a green border around the printer to signal the association between the two shapes. The reverse is not true: if you select the printer, the callout does not have any kind of border.

6   Select and drag the printer to the right (shown on the left in the following graphic), and then release the mouse button (graphic on right). The callout moves with the printer.

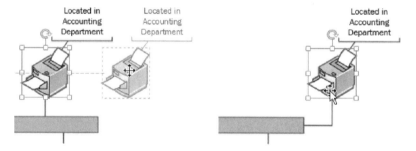

7   Select and drag the callout to the left side of the printer.

As you drag the callout, it looks like it's been detached from the printer (left graphic). However, as soon as you release the mouse button, it is still attached to the printer (right graphic).

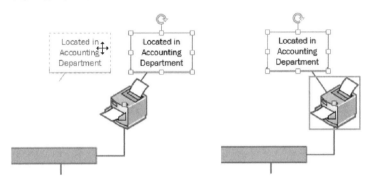

⊗ CLEAN UP Save and close your diagram if you want to keep the changes; otherwise just close it.

Unlike containers and lists, callouts do not have a context tab on the Visio ribbon. However, you can take advantage of the new change shape feature in Visio 2013 to switch any callout to a different style. Click the Change Shape button, either in the Editing group on the Home tab, or on the Mini Toolbar that appears when you right-click a callout. The following graphic takes advantage of Live Preview and the Mini Toolbar to illustrate changing the callout from the preceding graphics to the Zoom style.

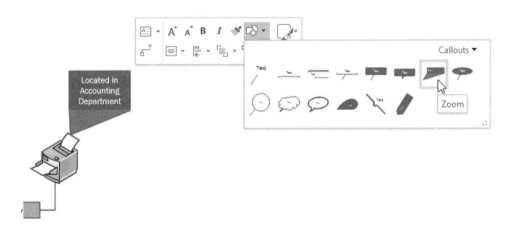

11

There are a few other useful things to know about callouts:

- If you delete a callout, it doesn't affect the shape to which it was attached. However, if you delete the shape, the callout is also deleted.

- If you copy a shape that has a callout attached, both the shape and the callout are copied.

- You can attach more than one callout to a shape.

- If you do not have any shapes selected when you insert a callout, Visio inserts the callout in the center of the drawing window.

- If you select more than one shape before inserting a callout, Visio will attach a callout to each selected shape.

- Callouts respond to Themes and Variants so their appearance on the page will remain consistent with the rest of your diagram.

SEE ALSO For more information about callouts, refer to the Visio development team blog at *blogs.office.com/b/visio/archive/2012/11/05/containers-and-callouts-in-visio.aspx*.

Key points

- You can use containers and lists to achieve many of the same results that you can by creating a background shape and grouping it with a set of shapes. However, containers offer considerable advantages over grouped shapes:

  - When you move, copy, or delete a container or a list, the member shapes in the container or list are also moved, copied, or deleted.

  - Even though the previous statement is true, each shape in a container or list maintains its independence. It's easy to select a container member with a single click and to access its shape data and other properties.

  - Shapes in containers and lists know they are contained and can derive data from the parent container. (Refer to the example at the end of the Swimlanes topic in "Finding containers and lists in Visio," earlier in this chapter.)

- Visio 2013 lists are a special type of container in which shapes are maintained in a specific sequence. Each shape knows its ordinal position in the list even when shapes are added, deleted, or rearranged.

- Visio 2013 uses containers and lists for cross-functional flowcharts, wireframe diagrams, data graphic legends, and other purposes. Visio also provides generic containers that you can use for any purpose you would like.

- Visio 2013 callouts are much more intelligent than the callouts provided with previous versions of Visio. In Visio 2013, each callout is associated with a specific target shape and is copied, moved, or deleted with that shape.

11

Chapter at a glance

Validate

Validate flowcharts,
page 457

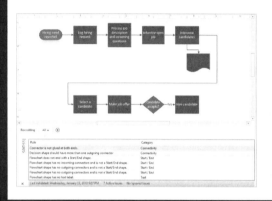

Create

Create and validate BPMN diagrams,
page 464

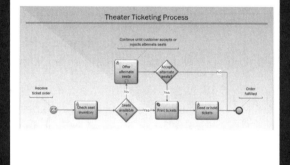

Create

Create SharePoint workflow diagrams,
page 472

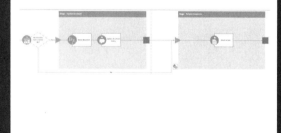

Reuse

Reuse validation rules,
page 479

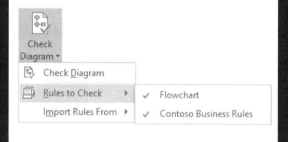

IN THIS CHAPTER, YOU WILL LEARN HOW TO

- Understand Visio rules.

- Validate flowcharts.

- Create and validate BPMN diagrams.

- Create subprocesses.

- Create SharePoint Workflow diagrams.

- Reuse existing validation rules.

- Create new validation rules.

A *business process*, also known as a *work process*, or just a *process*, is a collection of *tasks* or *activities* that leads to a desired result. A diagram of a work process is often referred to as a *process map*. In Chapter 4, "Creating flowcharts and organization charts," you worked with the *flowcharts* and *swimlane diagram* templates, both of which can be used to create process maps.

Microsoft Visio 2010 introduced a significant set of enhancements for creating process diagrams and ensuring that those diagrams are correct. Visio Professional 2013 builds on the work begun in the 2010 edition and includes a Process tab on the Visio ribbon.

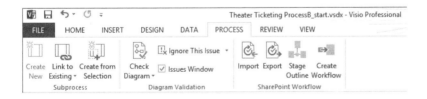

In this chapter, you will use a facility in Visio Professional 2013 to validate a Visio diagram against a set of rules. You will also learn about new process-oriented templates that are included with Visio Premium: *Business Process Model and Notation* (*BPMN*) and SharePoint Workflow.

> **IMPORTANT** The information in this chapter applies only to the Professional edition of Visio 2013.

TIP The default font size for shapes in the drawings you will create in this chapter is 8 pt. To improve the readability of the figures in this chapter, the shapes in most screen shots use a larger font size. Consequently, the text in the shapes on your Drawing page may appear smaller than in the graphics in this chapter.

PRACTICE FILES To complete the exercises in this chapter, you need the practice files contained in the Chapter12 practice file folder. For more information, refer to "Downloading the practice files" in this book's Introduction.

Understanding Visio rules

The diagram validation capabilities of Visio 2013 are built around collections of rules. A Visio *rule* can check a diagram for a very simple or a very complex condition. For example, a rule developer might create a rule to answer any of the following questions:

- Are there any shapes on the page that have one connection but not two?
- Are there any unconnected shapes on the page?
- Does every *two-dimensional (2-D) shape* contain text?
- Are there more than three blue shapes on any one page or more than five red shapes in the entire diagram?
- Are there any containers with fewer than three or more than seven shapes?
- Are there any shapes of type X, containing a field named Y, with a value of Z?

These are just representative questions. Visio rules are sufficiently flexible that the real question becomes: "What problem do you need to solve?"

Validation rules are packaged into *rule sets*. Five Visio templates include predefined business rules:

- Basic Flowchart
- Cross-Functional Flowchart
- BPMN
- SharePoint 2010 Workflow
- SharePoint 2013 Workflow

It's also possible to create your own custom rule sets for validating process diagrams, or, for that matter, for validating any kind of Visio diagram. Although the specific techniques for editing or creating custom rule sets are beyond the scope of this book, you will find links to appropriate resources in the sections titled "Reusing existing validation rules" and "Creating new validation rules," later in this chapter.

Validating flowcharts

One of the easiest ways to understand and begin using Visio validation is to work with something familiar—a flowchart you created in Chapter 4. The difference between the flowchart you'll work with in this exercise and the one in Chapter 4 is that this version contains deliberate errors.

In this exercise, you will use flowchart validation rules to discover and correct errors in a flowchart.

 SET UP **You need the *HR Recruiting Flowchart Validation_start* drawing located in the Chapter12 practice file folder to complete this exercise. Open the drawing in Visio and save it as *HR Recruiting Flowchart Validation*.**

1   On the **Process** tab, in the **Diagram Validation** group, click the **Check Diagram** button to run the default set of flowchart validation rules. Visio opens an **Issues** window to display the problems it found in the diagram. In addition to displaying the rule and rule category for each validation error, the bottom of the **Issues** window shows the date and time of the most recent validation.

12

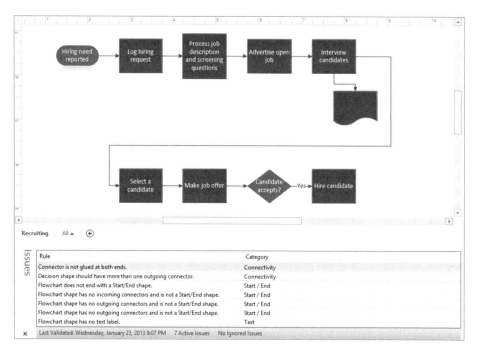

TIP You can re-sort the list of issues by clicking the Rule or Category column headings. You can also right-click anywhere in the Issues window, click Arrange By, and select Rule, Category, or Original Order.

2   In the **Issues** window, click once on **Connector is not glued at both ends.** The unlinked connector is highlighted.

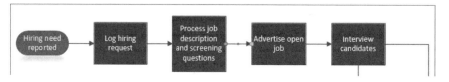

This error is an excellent example of the value of diagram validation. When you look at the flowchart image in step 1, it's not at all obvious that there is an unlinked connector, and yet successful process execution may depend on valid connections between shapes.

3   In the **Issues** window, click once on **Decision shape should have more than one outgoing connector.** Visio selects the **Candidate accepts?** shape, demonstrating yet another valuable reason to use validation: as you're creating a flowchart, it's easy to forget a path. This rule ensures that decisions always have at least two outcomes.

4   In the **Issues** window, click once on **Flowchart does not end with a Start/End shape.** Because this rule is about a missing shape, there is nothing highlighted in the drawing, but it is correct—there is no **End** shape.

5   In the **Issues** window, click once on **Flowchart shape has no incoming connectors and is not a Start/End shape.** Visio highlights the **Advertise open job** shape because of the unlinked connector described in step 2.

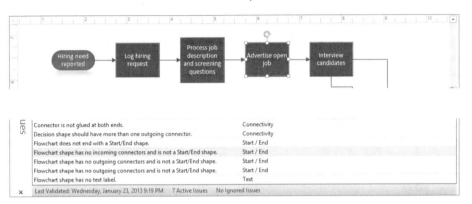

6   In the **Issues** window, click once on the first instance of **Flowchart shape has no outgoing connectors and is not a Start/End shape.** The **Hire candidate** shape is highlighted because there is no End shape.

7   In the **Issues** window, click once on the second instance of **Flowchart shape has no outgoing connectors and is not a Start/End shape.** The **Document** shape is highlighted.

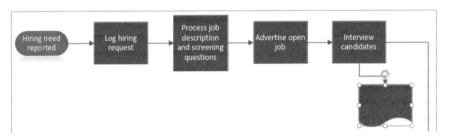

The error message is correct. The document shape does not have any outgoing connectors. For this shape, however, that is acceptable because a document isn't a process step but is a representation of a process artifact. Consequently, you will tell Visio to ignore this rule for this shape.

12

8   Right-click the already-selected issue description, and then click **Ignore This Issue**.

> **IMPORTANT** When you right-click, be careful of the distinction between Ignore This Issue and Ignore Rule. The former ignores a single issue; the latter ignores all issues created by a rule. Use Ignore Rule very carefully or you may inadvertently hide important problems.

Notice that the second occurrence of the *Flowchart shape has no outgoing connectors and is not a Start/End shape* issue has disappeared from the Issues window. Also, the status bar at the bottom of the window now indicates that there is one ignored issue.

Rule	Category
Connector is not glued at both ends.	Connectivity
Decision shape should have more than one outgoing connector.	Connectivity
Flowchart does not end with a Start/End shape.	Start / End
Flowchart shape has no incoming connectors and is not a Start/End shape.	Start / End
Flowchart shape has no outgoing connectors and is not a Start/End shape.	Start / End
Flowchart shape has no text label.	Text

Last Validated: Wednesday, January 23, 2013 9:19 PM   6 Active Issues   1 Ignored Issues

9   In the **Issues** window, click once on **Flowchart shape has no text label.** This issue also applies to the **Document** shape. If you don't want to put text on this shape, you can ignore the issue as you did in the preceding step. However, for this exercise, you will add text to the shape.

10 Double-click the **Document** shape, type **HR Policy Manual**, and then press **Esc**.

In the remaining steps of this exercise, you will resolve more of the diagram issues you reviewed in the previous steps.

11 Click once on the connector between the **Prepare job description and screening questions** shape and the **Advertise open job** shape, and then glue its ends to the adjacent shapes.

TIP You can click the Check Diagram button at any time to refresh the Issues window.

12 Draw a connector from the **Candidate accepts?** shape to the **Select a candidate** shape. While the connector is still selected, type **No**, and then press **Esc**.

13 Add a **Start/End** shape after the **Hire Candidate** shape, and then draw a connector from the **Hire Candidate** shape to the **Start/End** shape.

14 On the **Process** tab, in the **Diagram Validation** group, click the **Check Diagram** button. There is one remaining issue, which you can choose to resolve by adding text to the **End** shape or you can ignore it.

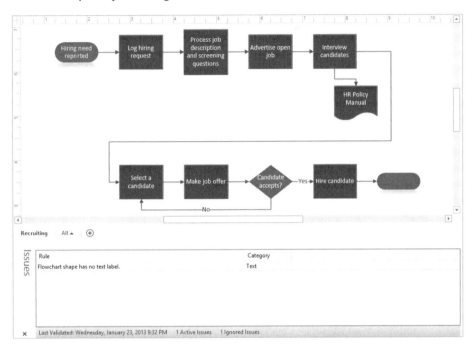

CLEAN UP **Save your changes to the *HR Recruiting Flowchart Validation* drawing, and then close it.**

TIP You can close the Issues window at any time by clicking the *X* in the lower-left corner or by clearing the Issues Window check box in the Diagram Validation group on the Process tab.

Understanding BPMN

Business Process Model and Notation (BPMN) was created to represent work processes in diagrams that are readily understandable by business people, yet are rich enough in detail to allow IT departments to translate process maps into technical specifications. The goal for BPMN is to enhance communication about processes across an organization. For automated processes, BPMN diagrams can serve as a bridge between process participants and the IT staff that build systems to support their work.

12

At one level, a BPMN diagram is like a flowchart or swimlane diagram. However, the symbol set is significantly larger than the one used for a conventional flowchart or swimlane diagram. This one fact leads both to strong advocacy for and strong resistance to BPMN.

Advocates assert that it is the combination of visual richness and underlying data attributes that allows BPMN diagrams to convey complex system and human interactions. Critics complain that the sheer number of symbols and symbol variants is off-putting to many people; they feel it makes diagrams more complex and less understandable to the business people who are half of the intended audience for BPMN.

Visio 2010 introduced a template for BPMN version 1.2 and it included stencils with dozens of shapes. Since the 1.2 version of the standard, the creators of BPMN have worked hard to make BPMN usable by a larger number of people. One result is that BPMN 2.0 defines a smaller working set of shapes and symbols that should be familiar to anyone who has created traditional flowcharts, and it is this version of BPMN on which the Visio 2013 template is based.

SEE ALSO For more information on the specific BPMN 2.0 features that are included with or excluded from the Visio 2013 BPMN template, refer to *blogs.office.com/b/visio/ archive/2012/11/19/introducing-bpmn-2-0-in-visio.aspx*.

The first thing to know about creating BPMN diagrams from the Visio Professional 2013 template is that there are four core shape types: *Events*, *Activities*, *Gateways*, and *Connecting Objects*, with multiple variations of each.

The BPMN 2.0 symbol set includes the following:

- Three types of Events, classified as **Start**, **Intermediate**, and **End**, and represented by different kinds of circles as shown on the left in the following graphic.

  Each of the BPMN shapes in Visio can display a modified appearance in order to represent a variation on the basic shape type. For example, each Event shape can show a trigger or result through the addition of an icon to one of the basic circles. The trio of images on the right in the preceding graphic represent a timer start event, a message intermediate event, and an error end event.

- Two Activity types, **Tasks** and **Sub-Processes**, each of which has multiple variations as you will discover in the exercise that follows.

- Six Gateway types, all of which are variations of the Diamond shape.

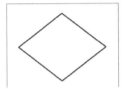

- Three Connector types, representing **Sequence Flows**, **Message Flows**, and **Associations** between shapes (left to right in the following graphic), with optional condition attributes for Sequence Flows and direction attributes for Associations.

If you create process documentation in any form today, or expect to in the future, it is worth learning more about BPMN. The next two exercises in this chapter will guide you through creating and validating a BPMN diagram, but they barely scratch the surface of what BPMN is about. The website and books in the following list provide further details and a web search will reveal many additional sources.

- Object Management Group/Business Process Management Initiative: *www.bpmn.org*.

- Silver, Bruce. 2011. *BPMN Method and Style, Second Edition, with BPMN Implementer's Guide*. Cody-Cassidy Press.

- White, Stephen A., and Derek Miers. 2008. *BPMN Modeling and Reference Guide*. Future Strategies Inc.

12

Creating and validating BPMN diagrams

Microsoft provides 16 shapes in the BPMN Basic Shapes template as shown in the following graphic. This may not seem like a sufficient number considering the BPMN shape variations described in the previous section. However, as you will discover in this exercise, most shapes offer one or more right-click menu options that produce a total of several hundred variations of these basic shapes.

In this exercise, you will start with a partially completed BPMN diagram of a theater box office ticketing process. You will set a trigger for the start event that launches the process, add a task and a gateway to offer the purchaser alternatives if the requested seats are unavailable, and set BPMN task types for various shapes.

 SET UP **You need the** *Theater Ticketing ProcessA_start* **drawing located in the Chapter12 practice file folder to complete this exercise. Open the drawing in Visio and save it as** *Theater Ticketing Process*.

> **TIP** The appearance of the document you just opened is based on Variant 4 of the Ion theme. In addition, the author applied the Whisp effect and Bevel shape style, and also increased the font size to 12 pt. Refer to Chapter 5, "Adding style, color, and themes," for information about *themes*, *variants*, *effects*, and *shape styles*.

1 Right-click the **Start** shape. The shortcut menu includes two BPMN entries at the top that enable you to alter the appearance of the shape to convey the proper BPMN information. The **Event Type** entry lets you change the current shape to any other event type. The **Trigger/Result** entry lets you select a subtype for the **Start** event.

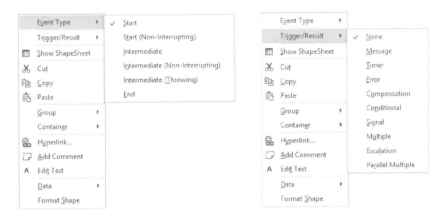

Each type of BPMN shape has its own set of shortcut menus.

2 With the shortcut menu open, point to **Trigger/Result**, and then click **Message**. The **Start** shape displays a white envelope, indicating that a message triggers the launch of this process.

3 Drag a **Task** shape from the **BPMN Basic Shapes** stencil, position it above the **Seats available?** shape, and drop it on the connector labeled **No**. The Visio 2013 AutoAdd feature splits the connector and inserts the new shape.

SEE ALSO For information about *AutoAdd* and *AutoDelete*, refer to Chapter 2, "Creating a new diagram."

4 With the new task still selected, type **Offer alternate seats**, and then press **Esc**.

5 Drag a **Gateway** shape from the **BPMN Basic Shapes** stencil, position it above the **Print tickets** shape, and drop it on the unlabeled connector.

6 With the new gateway still selected, type **Accept alternate seats?** and then press **Esc**.

7 Use the **AutoConnect** arrow under the **Accept alternate seats?** shape to draw a connector to the top of the **Print tickets** shape.

SEE ALSO For information about AutoConnect, refer to Chapter 2.

8 Click the new connector to select it, and then type **Yes**.

12

9   Click once on the connector from the **Accept alternate seats?** shape to the **End** shape, type **No**, and then press **Esc**.

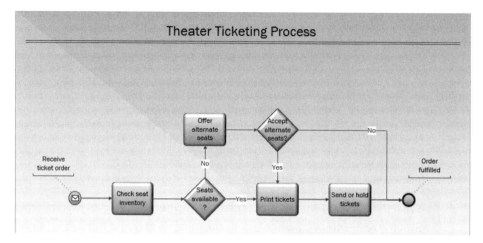

To finish this exercise, you will mark each task with a BPMN symbol to designate the task type.

10 Right-click the **Check seat inventory** shape, point to **Task Type**, and click **User**. A person icon appears in the upper-left corner of the shape.

11 Right-click **Offer alternate seats**, move to **Task Type**, and click **User**.

12 Right-click **Offer alternate seats** again, point to **Loop**, and click **Standard**. A loop symbol appears in the **Task** shape, indicating that this task will be repeated until certain conditions are met. You will describe those conditions with a text callout in the next step.

13 Drag a **Text Annotation** shape from the **BPMN Basic Shapes** stencil, attach the tail to the **Offer alternate seats** shape, type **Continue until customer accepts or rejects alternate seats**, and then press **Esc**.

TIP You can resize and reposition the Text Annotation shape. Note that the Text Annotation shape is a Visio 2013 callout, so it exhibits the callout behaviors described in Chapter 11, "Adding structure to your diagrams."

14　Right-click the **Print tickets** shape, point to **Task Type**, and click **Service** to indicate that this activity is performed by a system.

15　Right-click the **Send or hold tickets** shape, point to **Task Type**, and click **User**.

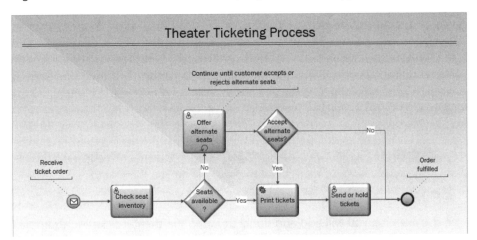

Earlier in this chapter, you validated a flowchart using built-in rules supplied by Visio Professional 2013. Visio also provides rules—a total of 76—for validating BPMN diagrams. The BPMN rule set shares some of the connectivity rules used for flowcharts, but it also includes many BPMN 2.0–specific rules.

In the final step of this exercise, you will validate your BPMN drawing.

16　On the **Process** tab, in the **Diagram Validation** group, click the **Check Diagram** button. Visio displays a dialog box reporting "Diagram validation is complete. No issues were found in the current document."

❎ CLEAN UP **Save your changes to the** *Theater Ticketing Process* **drawing but leave it open if you are continuing with the next exercise.**

The ticketing process used in this exercise is deliberately very simplistic. You could easily argue that more of the steps are automated in most theater box offices and that there should be other tasks involved. All of that is true, but the purpose of this exercise is to learn a bit about BPMN and not to create the ultimate theater ticketing process.

12

Creating subprocesses

As you document, define, and refine a business process, you will typically add more detail and additional steps to your process map. At some point, your map is likely to become unwieldy and difficult to read and maintain.

One common solution for a cluttered process map is to select a group of related process steps and replace them with a single *subprocess* symbol. You then move the selected steps to another page where you have room to spread them out and continue to work on that section of the overall process. Visio Professional 2013 includes several subprocess buttons that automate much of the work of creating subprocesses.

IMPORTANT You will use the subprocess functions in this exercise with a BPMN diagram, however, you can also create subprocesses in conventional flowcharts and swimlane diagrams.

In this exercise, you will add additional detail to the theater ticketing example by defining a subprocess for two of the existing tasks.

 SET UP **You need the *Theater Ticketing Process* drawing for this exercise. Either continue with the open copy from the previous exercise or open the *Theater Ticketing with SubprocessB_start* drawing located in the Chapter12 practice file folder and save it as *Theater Ticketing Process*.**

1   Draw a bounding box to select both the **Print tickets** and **Send or hold tickets** shapes.

2   On the **Process** tab, in the **Subprocess** group, click the **Create from Selection** button. Visio does four things for you: it replaces your selected shapes with a subprocess shape; adds a new page to the drawing; places your selected shapes on the new page; and builds a hyperlink from the new subprocess shape to the subprocess page.

    TIP The plus sign at the bottom of the new shape is the BPMN notation for a subprocess.

3   With the **Subprocess** shape still selected, type **Fulfill ticket order**.

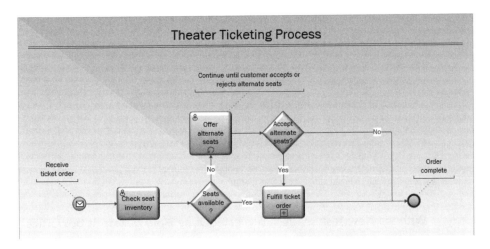

Theater Ticketing Process

4 Hold down the **Ctrl** key and click the **Print and fulfill ticket order** shape to move to the subprocess page where you will discover your two original activities on the new page.

In the remaining steps of this exercise, you will define a more complete subprocess.

5 Drag a **Gateway** shape from the **BPMN Basic Shapes** stencil, and drop it on the connector between the **Print tickets** and **Send or hold tickets** shapes. Visio inserts the new shape and moves the **Send or Hold Tickets** shape to the right to make room.

6 With the gateway still selected, type **More than 7 days 'til show?** and then press **Esc**.

7 Draw a bounding box around the **Print tickets** and **More than 7 days 'til show?** shapes, and drag them down until their top edges are approximately aligned with the bottom edge of the **Send or Hold tickets** shape.

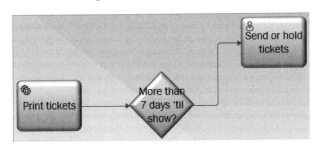

12

8   Click the arrow leading to **Send or Hold tickets**, type **Yes**, click the **Send or Hold tickets** shape, and then type **Send tickets**.

9   Point to the **AutoConnect** arrow on the right side of the gateway, and from the **Quick Shapes** menu, add a **Task**. Depending on the precise location of the **Gateway** shape, the new task may appear directly to the right of the gateway or it may be below it. If necessary, hold down the **Shift** key and drag the new task down so its top edge is just below the bottom edge of the gateway.

TIP Holding down the Shift key while dragging a shape constrains shape movement to a single direction.

10   With the **New Task** shape still selected, type **Hold tickets at box office**, and then press **Esc**.

11   Right-click the **Hold tickets at box office** shape, point to **Task Type**, and click **User**.

12   Click the arrow leading to **Hold tickets at box office**, type **No**, and then press **Esc**.

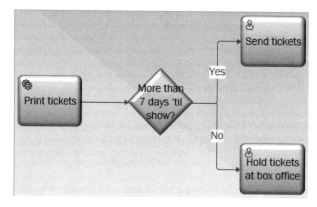

13   Drag an **End Event** shape from the **BPMN Basic Shapes** stencil and drop it to the right of the two new tasks.

14   Drag the **AutoConnect** arrow on the right of the **Ship tickets** task and connect it to the **End** shape; then do the same thing for the **Hold tickets at box office** task.

15   Drag a **Text Annotation** shape from the **BPMN Basic Shapes** stencil, attach it to the **End** shape, and type **Tickets processed**.

16   Double-click the **Page-2** page name tab and type **Print and Fulfill**.

17   On the **Process** tab, in the **Diagram Validation** group, click the **Check Diagram** button to open the **Issues** window. The messages that appear in the **Issues** window result from a deliberate omission in this exercise: there is no Start event. A BPMN subprocess that includes an End event should also include a Start. You can resolve the error by adding a Start event.

TIP Because of the potential complexity of BPMN diagrams, the text of many BPMN issue descriptions is longer than the width of the Issues window. However, if you position the pointer over any item in the Issues window, Visio displays the full text in a pop-up message.

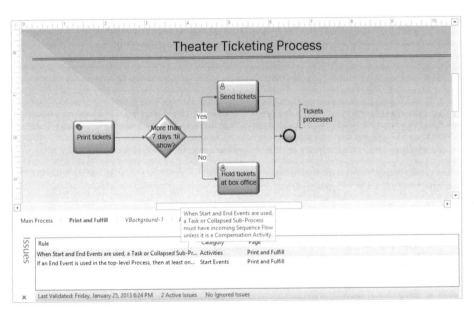

CLEAN UP Save your changes to the *Theater Ticketing Process* drawing, and then close it.

12

Your completed BPMN diagram now shows the main process flow on Main Process and the detailed subprocess on Print and Fulfill.

TIP In this exercise, you created a subprocess from existing tasks. The Subprocess group on the Process tab includes two additional subprocess functions:

- **Create New** To create a new, blank subprocess page, select any existing Task. When you click the **Create New** button, Visio inserts a new page and names it using the text from the selected task. Visio also creates a hyperlink from the selected shape to the new page.

- **Link to Existing** You can create a hyperlink to any existing subprocess page, whether it's located in the current drawing or another one. To do so, select any task, and then click the **Link To Existing** button. Visio presents a list of the pages in the current diagram as well as two options: **Browse To Other Document** and **Edit Link**. The former lets you link to any existing document; the latter opens the **Hyperlinks** dialog box so you can edit an existing link. The end result of selecting any of the **Link To Existing** menu items is a hyperlink to a page or document.

Creating SharePoint workflow diagrams

A *workflow* is a set of process steps, some or all of which have been automated. For the automated parts of a workflow, documents and files are stored and moved electronically, according to a set of predefined rules, so that they are available to participants as required.

To define a workflow, you need to identify three things:

- The participants (both people and systems)
- The sequence of activities
- The documents, databases, and other required work items

Common workflow examples in many organizations include the following:

- Approving employee expense reports
- Getting approval and then registering for a seminar
- Writing, editing, getting approval for, and publishing a new policy manual

Microsoft SharePoint 2013 includes a variety of predefined workflows, and you can both customize the existing workflows and define new workflows using SharePoint Designer. More relevant for this chapter, Visio Professional 2013 includes a SharePoint Workflow template so you can create and edit workflows in Visio and then open them in SharePoint Designer.

Whereas Visio 2010 offered a semblance of this capability but required you to export workflows in a special file format, SharePoint Designer 2013 reads and writes the new Visio 2013 .vsdx files directly. (Refer to the Appendix for a description of the Visio 2013 file formats.)

SEE ALSO The Microsoft Developer Network (MSDN) includes a series of very useful articles about the workflow capabilities in SharePoint. Two that provide helpful details about Visio are:

- "Workflow development in SharePoint Designer 2013 and Visio 2013" *msdn.microsoft.com/en-us/library/sharepoint/jj163272*

- "Shapes in the SharePoint Server 2013 workflow template in Visio 2013" *msdn.microsoft.com/en-us/library/sharepoint/jj164055*

In addition, the following blog posts, from the Visio and SharePoint Designer teams, respectively, will round out your knowledge on the subject.

- "SharePoint 2013 workflows in Visio" includes an excellent example that shows workflow creation steps in both Visio and the Visio ActiveX control in SharePoint Designer: *blogs.office.com/b/visio/archive/2012/11/12/sharepoint-2013-workflows-in-visio.aspx*

- "Introducing the new Visual Designer" demonstrates the advantages of SharePoint Designer 2013 and Visio 2013 over the text-based workflow designer: *blogs.msdn.com/b/sharepointdesigner/archive/2012/10/22/introducing-the-new-visual-designer.aspx*

When you create a new SharePoint Workflow diagram, Visio opens three stencils—Actions, Conditions, and Components—and places several shapes on Page-1 for you.

12

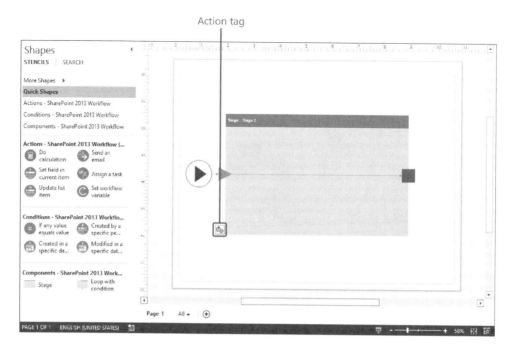
Action tag

The large shape in the center of the page is a container for the first stage in the workflow. Visio 2013 now supports the SharePoint notion of using stages to organize logically related, separable sets of workflow steps. A simple workflow might consist of a single stage, while a more complex workflow might include many stages.

Outside the stage container to the left is a workflow Start shape. On the left border of the stage is a green, triangular Entry shape; on the right border is a red, square Exit shape. In the lower left corner of the stage shape is a Visio **Action Tag**. In Visio, the action tag menu will contain one or more grayed out entries, however, when you open this diagram for visual editing in SharePoint Designer, you will use Action Tag entries to refine and complete the workflow definition.

Visio 2013 and SharePoint Designer 2013 also support SharePoint Workflow loops and steps, however, you will not use either of them in this exercise.

In this exercise, you will create a simple workflow to check a document out of a SharePoint repository, verify the creation date of the document, and revise the document if it is more than six months old. You will create the workflow using the SharePoint 2013 Workflow template and will validate it against the SharePoint Workflow rule set in Visio.

Of the several dozen rules in the SharePoint workflow rule set, the primary rules that apply to this exercise are as follows:

- Every workflow must have one **Start** shape. (A terminate shape is not required.)

- Every workflow must contain at least one **Stage**.

- Every **Stage** must have exactly one **Entry** and one **Exit** shape.

- All connections to a **Stage** must go in or out through the **Entry** and **Exit** shapes.

- The only shapes allowed outside a **Stage** are **Start**, **Terminate** and **Conditional** shapes.

- A **Conditional** shape must have at least one Yes and one No outcome.

➡ SET UP **Click the File tab, and then click New. Click Categories, click Flowchart, and then double-click the Microsoft SharePoint 2013Workflow thumbnail. Save the drawing as *Document Revision Workflow*.**

1 Click the **Stage 1** shape, type **Get Document**, and then press **Esc**.

2 From the **Actions – SharePoint 2013 Workflow** stencil, drag a **Check out item** shape into the **Get Document** stage, and then drop it on the connector near the center of the stage.

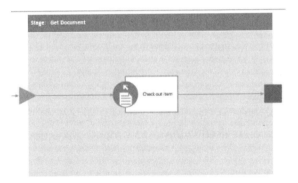

3 From the **Components – SharePoint 2013 Workflow** stencil, drag a **Stage** shape, and then drag and drop it off the right end of the Drawing page so Visio adds a new page. (Be sure to use the Dynamic Grid to align the new stage with the previous stage.)

4 With the new stage still selected, type **Update Document**, and then press **Esc**.

5 Right-click the **Drawing** page, click the **Connector Tool** on the Mini Toolbar, and then draw a connector from the **Exit** shape of the **Get Document** stage to the **Entry** shape of the **Update Document** stage.

12

6   Repeat steps 3-5 to create a third stage on a new page, and then type **Return Document** on the new stage.

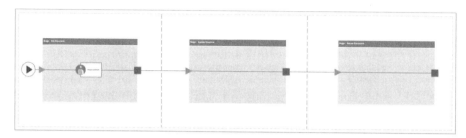

7   From the **Actions – SharePoint 2013 Workflow** stencil, drag a **Start a task process** shape into the **Update Document** stage, drop it on the connector, and then type **Revise document**.

8   Drag an **Add a comment** shape into the **Update Document** stage, drop it on the connector, and then type **Update document history**.

9   Drag a **Check in item** shape into the **Return Document** stage and drop it on the connector.

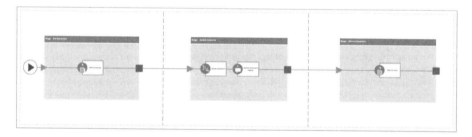

At this point, your workflow is nearly complete. However, you need to add a condition: if the document has been revised in the last six months, you don't need to update it again.

10   From the **Conditions – SharePoint 2013 Workflow** stencil, drag a **Modified in a specific date span** shape onto the connector between the **Get Document** and **Update Document** stages, and then drag the **Condition** and **Stage** shapes so they are both fully on **Page-2**.

11   Click the **New Condition** shape, type **Modified less than 6 months ago?** and then press **Esc**.

12   Right-click the **Drawing** page, click the **Connector Tool** on the Mini Toolbar, and then draw a connector from the connection point on the bottom of the **Modified less than 6 months ago?** shape to the green entry triangle on the **Return Document** stage.

> **IMPORTANT** When you glue the connector to the Modified Less Than 6 Months Ago? shape, be sure to glue it to the *connection point* on the bottom of the shape in order to create *static glue*. Do not create *dynamic glue*. Although this distinction does not affect the workflow for SharePoint, it creates a better layout for the connector.

SEE ALSO For information about static and dynamic glue, refer to Chapter 2.

13   With the connector still selected, drag the Move Midpoint handle downward so the line is below the **Update Document** stage.

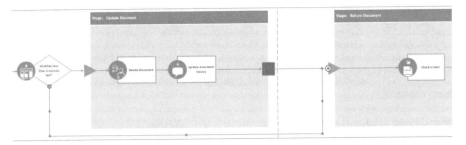

14   On the **Process** tab, in the **Diagram Validation** group, click the **Check Diagram** button. The **Issues** window appears and notifies you of two problems. Both are related to the connectors leading from the **Condition** shape.

You need to add Yes or No labels to the condition's outgoing connectors. Unlike the flowchart shapes, the connectors in the SharePoint Workflow stencil have been given shortcut menu options for exactly this purpose.

12

15 Right-click the connector to the right of the **Modified less than 6 months ago?** shape and click **Yes** on the context menu.

> **TIP** You can also use the Shape Data window to set the Yes/No/Blank option for a connector because the value is stored in a shape data field.

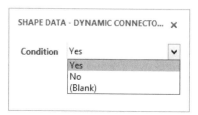

16 Right-click the connector that leads from the **Modified less than 6 months ago?** shape to the **Entry** shape for the **Return Document** stage, and then click **No**. You can rerun diagram validation if you'd like, in order to ensure that the diagram is now correct.

✖ CLEAN UP **Save your changes to the** *Document Revision Workflow* **drawing, and then close it.**

The workflow you created in this exercise is not very complex and doesn't really require three stages. However, creating it that way gave you an opportunity to work with stages and inter-stage conditions.

> **IMPORTANT** Creating a workflow in Visio Professional 2013 does not eliminate the need to use SharePoint Designer. Although you can use Visio to define and illustrate the flow of the work in a process, you must still use SharePoint Designer to provide the rest of the information that is required to execute the workflow.

> **TIP** Previous versions of SharePoint Designer were text editing tools. However, SharePoint Designer 2013 now hosts Visio 2013 as an ActiveX control. As a result, you can create and edit visual workflows directly in SharePoint Designer 2013 on any computer that also contains Visio Professional 2013.

Reusing existing validation rules

As you've already learned in this chapter, five Visio 2013 templates include predefined validation rule sets. Their existence raises a number of questions, such as the following:

- Is it possible to use those rule sets with other documents?
- Is it possible for a diagram to have more than one rule set?
- How do you find out what rules comprise an existing rule set?
- Is it possible to modify an existing rule set?
- Is it possible to create new rules?

In this exercise, you will learn the answer to the first question by importing a rule set into a flowchart created with Visio 2007. You will learn the answers to the second and third questions in the text at the end of this section, and you'll learn about modifying and creating rule sets in the next section.

 SET UP **You need the** *Visio 2007 Flowchart_start* **drawing located in the Chapter12 practice file folder to complete this exercise. Open the drawing in Visio and save it as** *Visio 2013 Flowchart*, **but change the file type to Visio Drawing (*.vsdx).**

1   On the **Process** tab, in the **Diagram Validation** group, click the **Check Diagram** button.

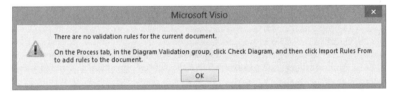

Visio tells you that the document does not contain any rule sets and also tells you what to do about it. Because you've opened a flowchart created in an older version of Visio, you will import the flowchart rule set.

2   Click **OK**.

12

3   On the **Process** tab, in the **Diagram Validation** group, click the **Check Diagram** arrow (not the button), and then point to **Rules to Check**. The submenu confirms that there are no rules in this document.

4   Point to **Import Rules From**, and click **Flowchart Rule Set**. Visio displays a dialog box confirming that one rule set was copied to the current document.

TIP The flowchart rule set is available to import into any diagram. In addition, if you have other diagrams open that contain rule sets, you will find them listed and can import their rules.

5   On the **Process** tab, in the **Diagram Validation** group, click the **Check Diagram** button. Visio runs the imported rule set against your diagram and reports the results in the **Issues** window.

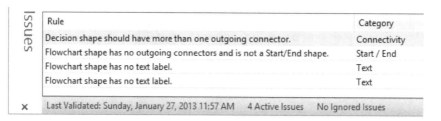

✖ CLEAN UP **Save your changes to the *Visio 2013 Flowchart* drawing but leave it open if you are continuing with the next exercise.**

Now that you know you can import a rule set into a diagram, you have probably guessed the answer to the second question in the list at the beginning of this section: you can have more than one rule set attached to a Visio diagram.

The following graphic indicates that the current diagram uses two rule sets. The check marks in front of both Contoso Business Rules and Flowchart indicate that both rule sets are active. Consequently, when you click the Check Diagram button, the diagram will be validated against both of them.

TIP You can clear the check box for any rule set to remove it from the active list.

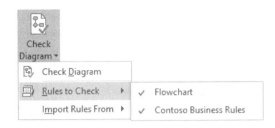

The answer to the third question posed at the beginning of this section is a bit trickier, because the Visio 2013 user interface does not provide a way to list the rules in a rule set. However, an experienced Microsoft **Visual Basic for Applications (VBA)** programmer can write a short program to list the rules contained in a rule set. Even better, Visio MVP David Parker has already done the work for you by including code samples for this and other diagram validation purposes in an article he wrote for MSDN. Although he wrote the article about the 2010 release of Visio, it applies equally to Visio 2013.

SEE ALSO David Parker's article, "Introduction to Validation Rules in Visio Premium 2010," is located at *msdn.microsoft.com/en-us/library/ff847470.aspx*.

You will find listings of all of the rules in each of the five Visio 2013 rule sets in the Chapter12 practice file folder. Look for the five .html files whose names start with the word *RuleSets*. The listings were produced using David Parker's Rules Tools, which are described in the next section.

Creating new validation rules

Now that you've experienced the value of the predefined rule sets in Visio 2013, you're probably beginning to think of other diagram types and ways that you would like to validate aspects of those drawings. Perhaps you want to do one of the following:

- Verify network shape connections.

- Ensure that the number of connections per network device doesn't exceed the maximum allowable for that brand and model of equipment.

- Confirm that each piece of furniture in an office floor plan was selected from an approved list and meets budget guidelines.

- Verify that all parts of an electrical schematic meet minimum and maximum power thresholds.

- Ensure that a building plan conforms to local building codes.

12

Regardless of the type of validation you want to perform, the good news is that you can both edit existing rules and create new rules. The bad news is that Visio does not provide an easy means to accomplish either task. In addition, doing so requires technical skills that are beyond the scope of this book.

The best resource for learning more about editing and designing validation rules is a book written by David Parker, who is mentioned at the end of the previous section. His book, *Microsoft Visio 2010: Business Process Diagramming and Validation* (Packt Publishing, 2010) provides extensive, technical coverage of many of the topics in this chapter, as well as details about many parts of Visio that touch, or are touched by, diagram validation. The validation features of Visio 2013 are largely unchanged from Visio 2010, so David's book is still relevant.

David also filled a significant gap left by Microsoft: he wrote software called *Rules Tools* that provides a user interface for exploring and working with validation rules. If you install David's Rules Tools and run Visio in **developer mode**, you'll find an additional group of buttons on the right end of the Process tab.

SEE ALSO You will learn about running Visio in developer mode in the Appendix.

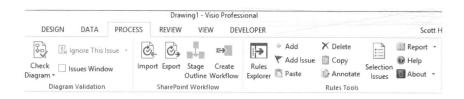

SEE ALSO For information about David Parker's book and about Rules Tools, go to *www.visiorules.com*.

In addition to David's book and MSDN article referred to in the previous section, the Visio development team wrote a brief article on custom rule development. Though it was written for Visio 2010, the article still applies to Visio 2013 and can be found at *blogs.msdn.com/b/visio/archive/2009/09/10/creating-custom-validation-rules-for-visio-2010.aspx*.

Key points

- The Process tab on the Visio Professional 2013 ribbon contains a collection of features that provide business process functions.

- Five Visio Professional 2013 templates include predefined rule sets that you can use to validate your Visio drawings. In addition, you can import those rule sets into existing drawings, including drawings created with previous versions of Visio, in order to enhance the validity of older diagrams.

- You can use the Visio 2013 BPMN template to create business process maps that comply with version 2.0 of the BPMN standard and can check the validity of your diagrams using built-in validation rules. Visio 2013 can also open and edit Visio 2010 BPMN 1.2 diagrams.

- With the subprocess feature in Visio Professional 2013, you can select one or more tasks in a drawing and automatically create a subprocess definition on a new page. You can also create blank subprocess pages with the click of a button.

- You can create graphical workflow maps in Visio and open them in SharePoint Designer in order to have them executed by the SharePoint workflow engine. In addition, because SharePoint Designer 2013 includes a Visio ActiveX control for visual editing, you no longer need to edit text-based workflow files in Designer.

12

Chapter at a glance

Save

Save Visio drawings to SharePoint 2013,
page 495

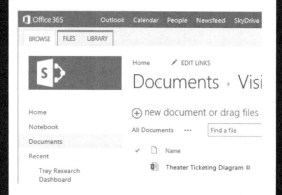

Refresh

Refresh diagram views in SharePoint,
page 503

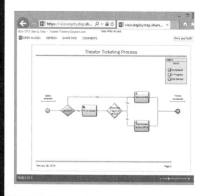

Comment

Comment on diagrams,
page 511

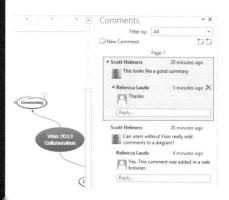

Coauthor

Coauthor Visio diagrams,
page 517

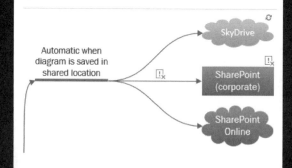

IN THIS CHAPTER, YOU WILL LEARN HOW TO

- Customize websites created by Visio.

- Understand Visio Services in SharePoint 2013.

- Save Visio drawings to SharePoint 2013.

- Refresh diagrams published to Visio Services.

- Collaborate on Visio diagrams (commenting and coauthoring).

In Chapter 8, "Printing, reusing, and sharing diagrams," you learned how to save Microsoft Visio 2013 drawings in a variety of formats, including as collections of webpages.

In this chapter, you will learn advanced techniques for customizing the websites you can create with Visio. You will learn about the structure of the resulting website, enabling you to move it to an intranet or other location when you want to share your drawing with people who don't have Visio.

You will also learn about *Visio Services*, which is part of Microsoft SharePoint 2013. Visio Services provides another technique for sharing diagrams with people who don't have Visio, and it offers several advantages over conventional web-published diagrams. Unlike websites created using *Save As Web Page*, drawings published with Visio Services can be updated dynamically as the underlying data changes. In addition, multiple people can view and comment on a diagram—even if some of them don't have Visio.

Finally, you will explore new collaboration capabilities that allow multiple people to create and edit Visio diagrams simultaneously.

PRACTICE FILES To complete the exercises in this chapter, you need the practice files contained in the Chapter13 practice file folder. For more information, refer to "Downloading the practice files" in this book's Introduction.

Customizing websites created by Visio

Web-published Visio drawings already include full support for embedded hyperlinks along with rich navigation and search capabilities, as you learned in Chapter 8. However, you don't necessarily need all of those capabilities in every Visio-generated website, so it is convenient to be able to change the publishing options.

In addition, you might want to change the format in which Visio creates your website. By default, Visio 2013 creates webpages using the *Extensible Application Markup Language (XAML)*, which is a different format from Visio 2007 and earlier versions. XAML requires that you install Microsoft Silverlight on your computer to view Visio-created websites. If you prefer a different webpage format that doesn't require Silverlight, you can select one of the five alternatives described later in this section.

In this exercise, you will use the Publish button in the *Save As* dialog box to customize Visio webpage output.

 SET UP **You need the *Timeline diagram_start* drawing located in the Chapter13 practice file folder to complete this exercise. Open the drawing in Visio and save it as *Timeline diagram*.**

1 On the **File** tab, click **Export**, and then click the **Change File Type** button.

2 In the **Other File Types** section, click **Web Page (*.htm)**, and then click the **Save As** button. The lower portion of the **Save As** dialog box includes two buttons for customizing webpage output.

   TIP Visio defaults to saving webpages in the folder that contains your Visio drawing file.

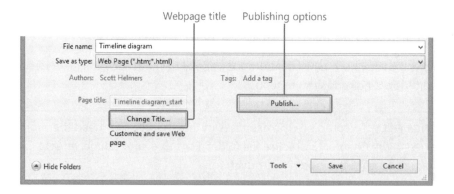

You can click the Change Title button to modify the text that will be displayed in the title bar of the web browser. The default page title is the file name of the Visio drawing.

The Publish button offers multiple options that you will explore in subsequent steps.

3 In the **Save As** dialog box, click the **Publish** button. The **Save as Web Page** dialog box opens.

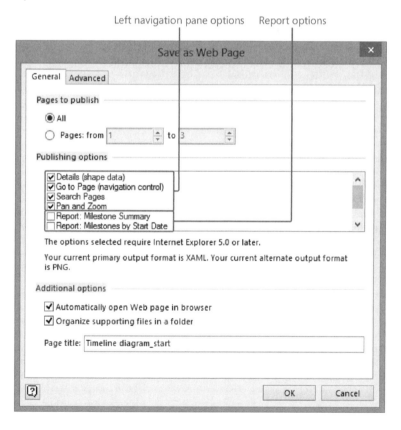

The Save as Web Page dialog box provides various ways to customize your website:

- In the **Pages to publish** section, you can select a subset of the diagram's pages to include in the web-published output.

- In the **Publishing options** section, you can select which navigation pane options, and which reports, if any, should be included in your website.

> **IMPORTANT** The only way to view reports in your web-published drawing is via the Go To Page navigation panel. Consequently, if you include reports as part of your website, you must leave the Go To Page check box selected.

- When Visio creates a website from your drawing, it automatically opens it in your browser. You can clear the **Automatically Open Web Page In Browser** check box in the **Additional Options** section to prevent this from occurring.

- By default, Visio creates a folder to store the majority of website files. You can clear the **Organize Supporting Files In A Folder** check box in the **Additional Options** section to have Visio store all website files in a single folder.

  SEE ALSO Refer to the sidebar, "What's in a Visio-created website and where is it stored?" later in this section for additional information about the files created by the Save As Web Page function.

- In the **Additional Options** section, you can type a different title in the **Page Title** text box. (This is an alternate method to using the Change Title button mentioned in step 2.)

4   In the **Publishing Options** section of the **Save as Web Page** dialog box, clear the **Details (shape data)** and **Search Pages** check boxes.

  TIP Visio remembers the settings for these options; the same settings will appear the next time you save a drawing as a webpage.

5   In the **Publishing Options** section of the **Save as Web Page** dialog box, select the **Report: Milestones by Start Date** check box. If your Visio drawing includes more than two reports, use the scroll bar in the **Publishing Options** section to view the full list of reports.

TIP Visio *does not* remember the settings for the reports you choose; none of the report check boxes will be selected the next time you save a drawing as a webpage.

6   Click **OK**. One or more progress indicators will appear before your browser displays your new website.

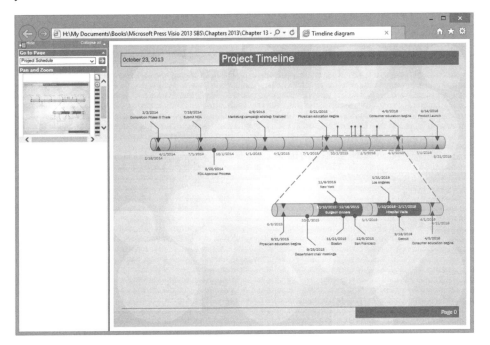

The result of the navigation pane choices you made in step 4 appear on the left side of the browser window. Only the Go to Page and Pan and Zoom panels are visible.

SEE ALSO If you need to review the full set of navigation pane options in web-published Visio drawings, refer to "Publishing Visio diagrams to the web" in Chapter 8.

13

7   In the **Go to Page** section, click the arrow next to **Project Schedule**. The Go to Page
     list includes entries for each page in the diagram and for each report you selected.

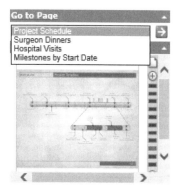

8   To view the milestone report, click **Milestones by Start Date** in the drop-down list,
     and then click the green button containing the white arrow.

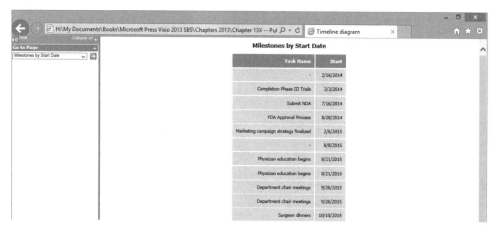

TIP To view other reports or to return to viewing the drawing pages, use the Go to Page
list. You can also click the browser's back button to return to the previous page.

✖ CLEAN UP **Save your changes to the *Timeline diagram* drawing, and then close it.**

You may have noticed in step 3 that the Save as Web Page dialog box includes a second tab labeled Advanced.

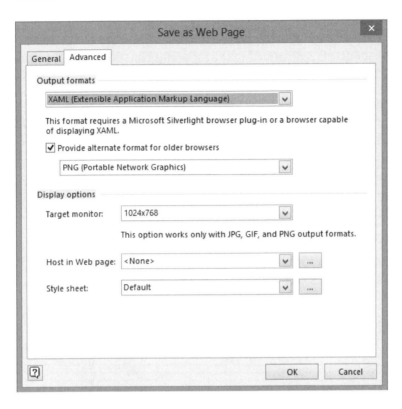

The Advanced tab provides additional customization options, such as the following:

- In the **Output formats** section, you can use the drop-down list to select one of the alternate webpage formats.

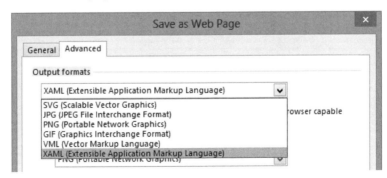

- *VML* is the webpage format created by versions of Visio prior to Visio 2010. The features of VML websites are very similar to websites created with XAML but only provide all features when viewed with Internet Explorer.

- *SVG* is a specialized format that is supported by some but not all browsers. Like the three image formats described in the following bullet point, SVG websites display fixed-size pages with no Pan and Zoom panel.

- *GIF*, *JPG*, and *PNG* provide fewer capabilities than either VML or XAML. For example, the viewing window for these formats is a fixed size and does not include the Pan and Zoom panel in the left navigation pane. However, websites produced in these formats retain all hyperlinks and are likely to be compatible with a wider range of web browsers. (Note that you can have the best of both worlds—full navigation functions in Windows Internet Explorer and support for older browsers; refer to the following bullet point.)

- If you select XAML, VML, or SVG as the output format, Visio defaults to selecting the **Provide alternate format for older browsers** check box. You can use the drop-down list under this heading to select GIF, JPG, or PNG output as a backup to your primary choice.

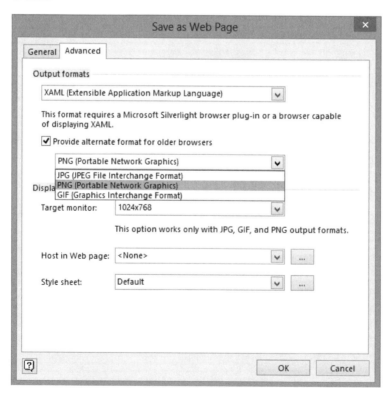

- In the **Display Options** section, you can use the **Target Monitor, Host In Web Page,** and **Style Sheet** settings to further customize your webpages. The second and third settings, in particular, are intended to help you integrate a Visio-created website with another existing website.

What's in a Visio-created website and where is it stored?

When you use the Save as Web Page function, Visio generates a webpage that is loaded into your browser and that provides access to the rest of your website. It also creates a supporting files folder that contains various graphics and webpages for each page in the drawing, as well as *JavaScript*, *Extensible Markup Language (XML)*, and other files that comprise the website.

By default, the Visio-generated files are stored in the same Windows folder that contains your Visio drawing. Visio gives the webpage file the same name as the drawing plus an *.htm* file extension. For English versions of Visio, the name of the supporting files folder is the same as the drawing name appended with *_files*.

If you completed the preceding exercise using an English language version of Visio, for example, the folder that contains *Timeline diagram.vsd* also contains the following:

- A file called *Timeline diagram.htm*

- A folder called *Timeline diagram_files*

If you want to copy or move your new website, it's important to copy/move both the .htm file and the supporting files folder to the new location. You can copy your website to a shared drive, to your organization's intranet, or to any web server in order to provide access to your Visio diagram.

> **IMPORTANT** The default name for the companion subfolder varies based on the language version of Microsoft Office that is installed on your computer. For a complete list of default names for various language versions, go to *office.microsoft.com/en-us/excel-help/language-specific-names-for-web-page-supporting-folders-HP001049381.aspx*. Even though the article applies to Microsoft Office Excel 2003, the list is also correct for the Visio 2013 website folder.

13

Understanding Visio Services in SharePoint 2013

Visio Services is a Microsoft SharePoint Server 2013 feature you can use to share diagrams with people who don't have Visio. There are three key advantages to sharing diagrams via Visio Services instead of publishing static webpages as described in the preceding section and in Chapter 8:

- The Visio Web Access browser view is dynamic and reflects nearly all diagram changes. (Diagrams published to SharePoint with Visio 2010 only displayed a subset of diagram changes.) The web view can be updated either automatically by a program or timer, or manually by the user.

- Visio Services supports interactive commenting on diagrams by any combination of people using the Visio client or viewing the diagram with a web browser.

- You can incorporate Visio diagrams into SharePoint applications:

    - You can embed a Visio web drawing in a SharePoint Web Part.

    - You can create dynamic connections between Web Parts that contain Visio web drawings as well as between them and other types of Web Parts.

    - You can use the Visio Services Mash-up API to program dynamic changes in the browser as the user navigates around a drawing or takes other actions in a SharePoint page.

In addition to the advantages just listed, the user experience in the web browser is enhanced in Visio web drawings when compared to Visio websites:

- Pan and zoom are provided by click-and-drag and rolling the mouse wheel, respectively. (Other techniques are also available.)

- Shape data is easier to view via a floating properties window.

- The properties window that displays shape data also lists the hyperlinks, if any, that are attached to the selected shape.

TIP One key feature is missing from Visio web drawings: full-text search. It is an important part of Visio-created webpages but is not part of web drawings saved to Visio Services.

Saving to Visio Services from Visio 2010 required a special intermediate file format, however, that is no longer true with Visio 2013 and SharePoint 2013. The same Visio file—in the new .vsdx file format—works in the Visio client and on the SharePoint server. In addition, Visio 2010 diagrams saved to SharePoint required Silverlight for optimal browser viewing; that requirement no longer exists for Visio 2013. Refer to the Appendix for more information about the new file format.

Data-connected Visio diagrams that use data graphics provide particularly impressive results when published to SharePoint, because whenever a user or a program changes the source data, the data graphics on the webpage change dynamically.

Data connections in a diagram published to SharePoint are refreshable if you link your diagram to one of the following data sources:

- Excel workbooks that were previously stored on the SharePoint site

- SharePoint lists

- SQL Server tables and views

- Databases accessed via OLEDB or ODBC drivers

TIP Linking to SQL Server and OLEDB/ODBC databases is supported for SharePoint but is not supported for SharePoint Online in Office 365.

Visio has always been good for building data-driven, visual representations of processes, networks, organizations, or other entities. When you add the capability to create dynamically updateable webpages via SharePoint, Visio becomes a key contender for building business intelligence solutions in almost any work domain.

SEE ALSO For detailed descriptions of the reasons to use Visio as part of a business intelligence solution, including numerous examples, refer to Chapter 9, "Visio and Visio Services," in *Business Intelligence in Microsoft SharePoint 2013* by Norm Warren, Mariano Neto, Stacia Misner, Ivan Sanders, and Scott Helmers (Microsoft Press, 2013).

Saving Visio drawings to SharePoint 2013

In the previous section, you learned that Visio Services on SharePoint reads Visio 2013 files directly. As a result, *publishing* a diagram to Visio Services can be accomplished by simply uploading the file to SharePoint. From there, anyone with a web browser can click to view the diagram.

13

However, in this exercise, you will use a different technique: you will save a diagram to SharePoint from within Visio and will then view the diagram in your web browser. The diagram you will work with was created using the Business Process Model and Notation (BPMN) 2.0 template that is packaged with Visio Professional 2013. (For more information about BPMN, refer to Chapter 12, "Creating and validating process diagrams.")

IMPORTANT You need access to Visio Services on a SharePoint 2013 server to complete this exercise. Visio Services are available with a SharePoint Server 2013 Enterprise Client Access License (ECAL) or by using SharePoint Online in Office 365. The screen shots in this section were created using SharePoint Online.

→ SET UP You need the *Theater Ticketing ProcessA_start* drawing located in the Chapter13 practice file folder to complete this exercise. Open the drawing in Visio and save it as *Theater Ticketing Diagram*.

1   On the **File** tab, click **Save As**.

If you have previously configured a SharePoint server on your Save As list, it will appear similar to Visio Step By Step in the preceding graphic, and will display a list of recently used folders on the server. You can select one of the recently used folders or you can click the **Browse** button to navigate to any folder on the server.

If you have not already configured a SharePoint server, you have two options.

■ For SharePoint Online, click **Add a Place** and then click **Office 365 SharePoint**.

■ For either SharePoint Online or an in-house server, click **Computer**, and then click the **Browse** button. When the Save As dialog box appears, navigate to and select your SharePoint server.

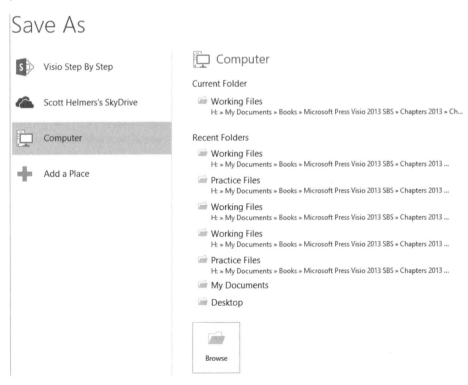

2   Either click the button for your SharePoint Server or use the Browse button to navigate to it.

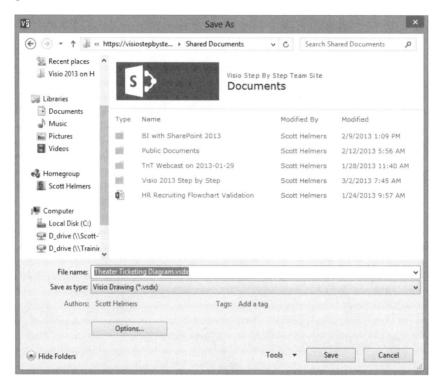

Clicking the Options button in the Save As dialog box displays the Publish Settings dialog box.

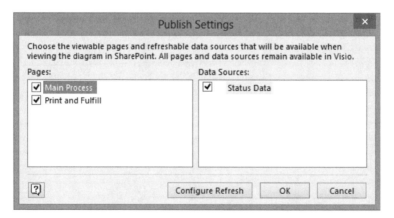

In the Pages section on the left, you can select a subset of the diagram's pages if you don't want to include all of them in your web-published drawing.

If your diagram is linked to one or more data sources, you can use the Data Sources section on the right to select which ones will refresh their data to the browser.

TIP Be sure to notice the comment at the top of the Publish Settings dialog box: unchecking pages or data sources in this dialog box eliminates them from the browser view of the drawing. However, the unchecked pages and sources are still available to anyone who opens the diagram in Visio.

3   In the **Save As** dialog box, navigate to the folder in which you would like to save your diagram, and then click **Save**.

TIP Often the easiest way to select the desired folder on the correct SharePoint site is to navigate to it first in your web browser. After locating the correct folder, copy and paste its URL into the address bar at the top of the Save As dialog box.

4   Start your web browser and navigate to the SharePoint folder in which you saved the Visio diagram.

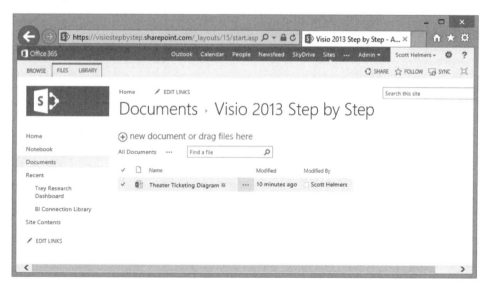

13

5   Click **Theater Ticketing Diagram** to open the drawing in the browser.

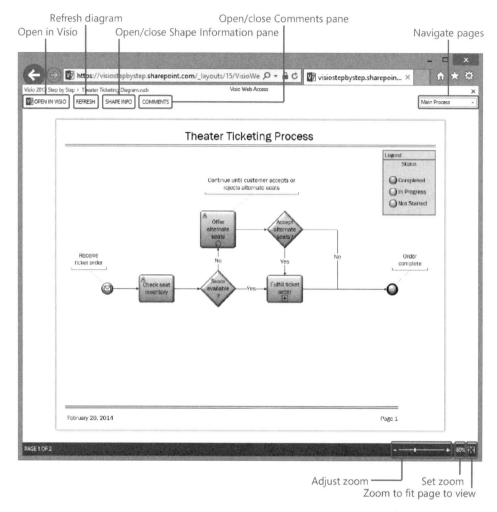

In the web drawing view, you can drag the diagram in any direction to change which portion of the page is visible.

Use the buttons in the upper-left browser window to adjust the view of your diagram.

- Click **Open in Visio** to view and edit the diagram using the Visio desktop application instead of the web browser.

- Click **Refresh** to update the diagram from any connected data sources.

- Click **Shape Info** to toggle the appearance of the **Shape Information** pane.

- Click **Comments** to toggle the appearance of the **Comments** pane.

You can roll your mouse wheel to zoom in or out, or you can use the controls in the lower-right corner of the browser window to change zoom settings:

- Click the plus or minus signs to increase or decrease the zoom level.

- Use the zoom slider to change the zoom level.

- Click the displayed percentage and type a new percentage.

- Click the **Zoom To Fit Page To View** button to view the entire Visio page in the browser window.

Use the page list in the upper-right corner to view a different page.

In the upcoming steps, you will apply data graphics and make other changes in Visio and then will view those changes in the published drawing.

6   Return to Visio (do not close the web browser).

> **IMPORTANT** You are no longer editing the Visio diagram you started with, but you are editing the Visio drawing that is stored in SharePoint.

7   Press **Ctrl+A** to select all shapes on the **Main Process** page. Then on the **Data** tab, in the **Display Data** group, click **Data Graphics**. In the **Available Data Graphics** section of the gallery, click **Color by Status**. Visio applies the color-by-value data graphic to the shapes on this page.

> **SEE ALSO** To learn about data graphics, refer to Chapter 10, "Visualizing your data."

8   Click the **Print and Fulfill** page name tab, select all shapes on that page, and then apply the same data graphic.

9   On the *Quick Access Toolbar*, click the **Save** button.

10 Return to your open web browser and click the SharePoint **Refresh** button (do not click the browser refresh button). The browser view now reflects the current state of the Visio diagram.

13

11   In the upper-left corner of the Visio diagram, click **Shape Info** to open the shape information pane, and then click the **Fulfill ticket order** sub-process shape.

The results of both steps 10 and 11 appear in the following graphic. The color of the shapes reflects their current status and the **Shape Data** section of the information pane displays the shape data for the sub-process shape. Note also that the **Hyperlinks** section of the information pane reveals one hyperlink that connects the sub-process shape to the **Print and Fulfill** page.

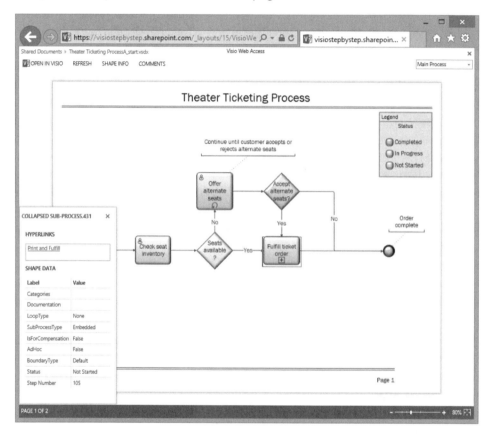

❌ CLEAN UP Save your changes to the *Theater Ticketing Diagram* file, but leave it open if you are continuing with the next exercise.

Refreshing diagrams published to Visio Services

In the preceding section, you saved a diagram to Visio Services, applied a data graphic, saved the changes, and then refreshed the web view of the drawing.

In this exercise, you will make more extensive changes to the diagram, including linking it to an Excel workbook, changing the data in the workbook, and then observing how those changes ripple through the diagram and the web rendering.

 SET UP **You need the *Theater Ticketing Diagram* drawing for this exercise. If the drawing is still open from the previous exercise, proceed to step 1. Otherwise, open the *Theater Ticketing DiagramB_start* drawing located in the Chapter13 practice file folder, and then save it to SharePoint 2013 as *Theater Ticketing Diagram*.**

You also need the *Theater Ticketing Process Status Data_start* workbook located in the Chapter13 practice file folder. Open the workbook in Excel and save it to the same SharePoint folder that contains your Visio diagram using the name, *Theater Ticketing Process Status Data*. Leave the workbook open in Excel.

> **IMPORTANT** In order for Visio Services to have access to data in an Excel workbook, the workbook must be stored in SharePoint prior to linking to it from your Visio drawing.

1   On the **Data** tab, in the **External Data** group, click **Link Data to Shapes**.

   SEE ALSO Only a subset of the pages from the Data Selector wizard are shown in this exercise. For assistance with data linking, and to view all of the wizard pages, refer to Chapter 6, "Entering, linking to, and reporting on data."

2   On the first page of the **Data Selector Wizard**, click **Microsoft Excel workbook**, click **Next**, click the **Browse** button, and then navigate to, and open, the copy of the Excel workbook that you saved to SharePoint.

   TIP When you click the Browse button in the wizard and the Open dialog box appears, it may be easier to navigate to your Excel workbook first in your web browser. After locating the correct document, simply copy and paste its URL into the address bar in the Open dialog box.

13

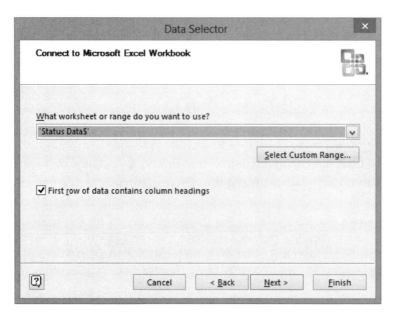

3   On the third page of the **Data Selector Wizard**, select the worksheet named **Status Data$**, and then click **Next**.

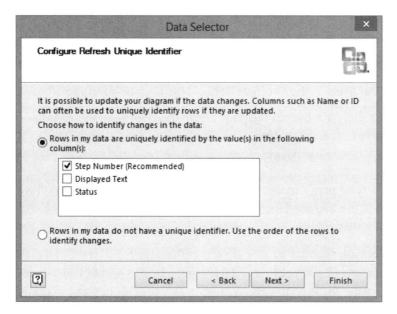

4   Accept the recommendation to use **Step Number** as the unique identifier in the status data, click **Next**, and then click **Finish**. The **External Data** window opens.

5 On the **Data** tab, in the **External Data** group, click **Automatically Link**, and then click **Next** on the first page of the **Automatic Link Wizard**.

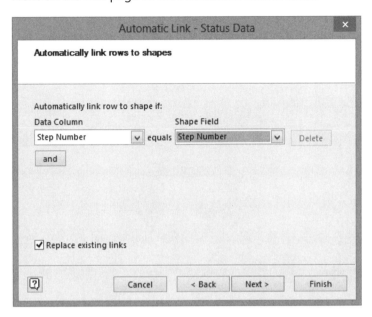

6 Select **Step Number** from the drop-down list under both **Data Column** and **Shape Field**, click **Next**, and then click **Finish**. You have linked data from your Excel workbook to the shapes on the **Main Process** page of your diagram. Notice that the fill colors of some shapes have changed because the status values in the linked data are different.

> **IMPORTANT** The automatic linking function in Visio works on one page at a time. You can confirm this by viewing the left end of the External Data window: a link symbol appears for steps 101–105 but not for the steps in the 200 range that are on the other page. You will link the 200-series steps to shapes on the Print and Fulfill page later in this exercise.

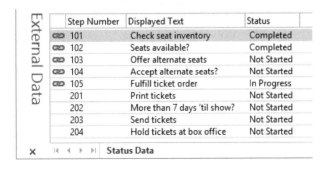

13

7   On the **Quick Access Toolbar**, click **Save**, then switch to your web browser and click the **Refresh** button in the upper-left corner of the Visio diagram (do not click the browser's refresh button). The color changes now appear in the web rendering.

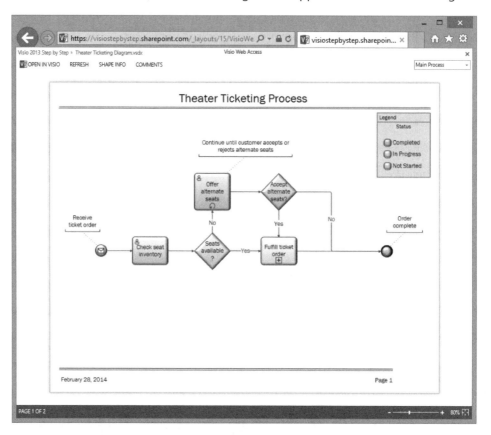

8   In the upper-right corner of the Visio diagram, click **Main Process**, and then click **Print and Fulfill** to view that page.

TIP Because the Fulfill Ticket Order shape contains a hyperlink to page 2, you can also point to that shape and then press Ctrl+click to move to the second page.

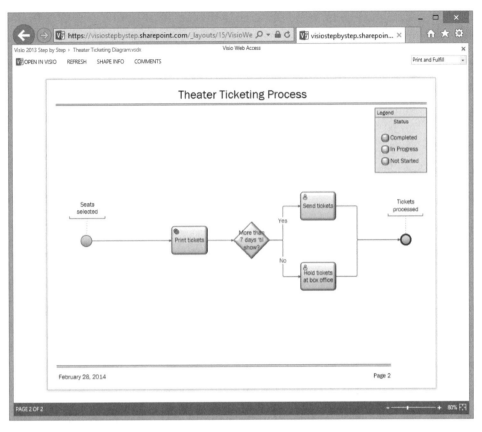

9   Switch to Visio, click the page name tab for **Print and Fulfill**, and then apply the **Color by Status** data graphic to all shapes on this page.

10   On the **Data** tab, in the **External Data** group, click **Automatically Link**, and complete the **Automatic Link Wizard** for this page just as you did in steps 5 and 6 earlier in this exercise. The shapes on this page are now linked to Excel data on SharePoint as you will demonstrate in the remaining steps of this exercise.

11   Switch to Excel. Use the drop-down list in the **Status** column to change the status for **Step Number 201** to **Completed**, change the **Status** for **Step Number 202** to **In Progress**, and then on the **Quick Access Toolbar**, click **Save**. At this point, you have changed the data in the copy of the workbook that resides on SharePoint.

13

12   Switch to Visio. On the **Data** tab, in the **External Data** group, click **Refresh All**, and then click **Close**.

13   On the **Quick Access Toolbar**, click **Save**. The changes from Excel that are now visible in Visio have been saved in SharePoint.

14   Return to your open web browser. If the web view of the diagram has not already updated, click the **Refresh** button.

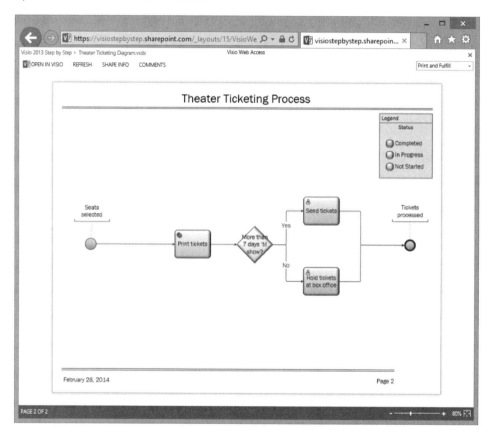

The web view of your Visio diagram reflects much more than changes in data graphics. In the final steps of this exercise, you will add several shapes to the Visio diagram and observe those changes in the browser.

15   Switch to Visio. Drag a **Gateway** shape from the **BPMN Basic Shapes** stencil and drop it on the connector between the **Start Event** shape and the **Print tickets** shape, and then add a new connector from the top of the gateway to the **Send Tickets** shape.

16 Type text on three shapes:

  ▪ On the new gateway, type **etickets?**

  ▪ On the connector from **etickets?** to **Print tickets**, type **No**.

  ▪ On the connector from **etickets?** to **Send tickets**, type **Yes**.

17 On the **Quick Access Toolbar**, click **Save**.

18 Switch to your browser and click the **Refresh** button. The browser view of your diagram shows the new shapes.

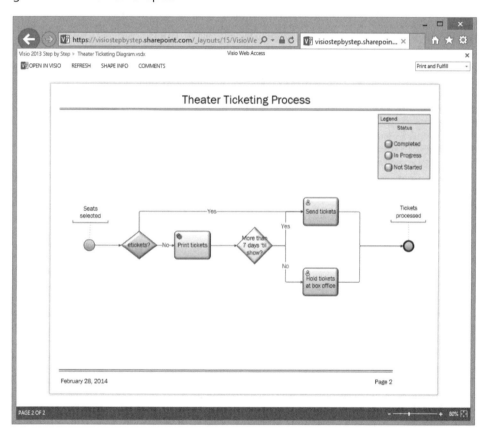

❌ CLEAN UP **Save your changes to the *Theater Ticketing Diagram* file and close it. Close your web browser.**

This exercise involved a lot of switching between applications in order to demonstrate the interactions among those applications. In the real world, you are unlikely to be moving back and forth as much. For example, in a typical scenario, you would have linked your diagram to data and selected a data graphic once, prior to saving to SharePoint. From then on, you might periodically update a database or Excel workbook and occasionally view the changes in your browser. In another common scenario, you might be responsible for maintaining and updating the data, while many other people use their web browsers to view the dashboard you created.

Collaborating on Visio diagrams

The enhanced collaboration capabilities in Visio 2013 take two principal forms: commenting and coauthoring. Both capabilities recognize the growing importance of collaboration among geographically dispersed workers by providing extra features when used with Visio Services, either via SharePoint within an enterprise or SharePoint Online. In the following section, you will learn how a group of people can write and read comments in a Visio drawing, even when some of them do not have Visio. In the section after that, you will explore the coauthoring capabilities of Visio 2013. Both exercises utilize the following Visio Brainstorming Diagram that summarizes the collaboration capabilities in Visio 2013.

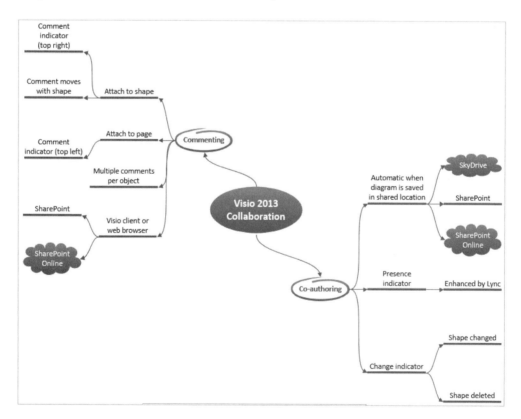

Commenting

Commenting in Visio 2013 is much more flexible than in previous versions of the product and includes several important enhancements.

- You can attach comments to shapes as well as to the drawing page.

  TIP If one shape is selected when you add a comment, the comment will be attached to that shape. If more than one shape is selected when you add a comment, the comment will be attached to the *anchor shape* (refer to Chapter 5, "Adding style, color, and themes" for information about anchor shapes). If no shapes are selected, the comment will be attached to the drawing page.

- When you move or copy/paste a shape containing a comment, the comment travels with the shape.

- A comment indicator appears on the top right of a shape or top left of a page that contains a comment.

- You can view all comments at once by opening the **Comments** pane.

- In addition to writing and reading comments in Visio, you can take the same actions in a web browser when the Visio diagram is located on a SharePoint server or in SharePoint Online.

SEE ALSO The fundamentals of commenting are described in Chapter 3, "Adding sophistication to your drawings."

In this exercise, you will add comments to a Visio diagram. If you have access to either SharePoint or SharePoint Online, you will also read and write comments using a web browser.

> **IMPORTANT** You need access to Visio Services on a SharePoint 2013 server to complete all of the steps in this exercise. Visio Services are available with a SharePoint Server 2013 Enterprise Client Access License (ECAL) or by using SharePoint Online in Office 365.

 SET UP You need the *Collaboration Brainstorm DiagramA_start* drawing located in the Chapter13 practice file folder to complete this exercise. Open the drawing in Visio. If you have access to SharePoint or SharePoint Online, save the diagram there as *Collaboration Brainstorm Diagram*. Otherwise, save the diagram locally as *Collaboration Brainstorm Diagram*.

13

1   Right-click the **Commenting** topic shape in the diagram, and then click **Add Comment**. Visio drops a comment indicator and an edit box for the comment body onto the page. The indicator is located in the upper-right corner of the shape and looks like a cartoon dialog balloon; the edit box appears above or near it.

2   Type **Can users without Visio really add comments to a diagram?**

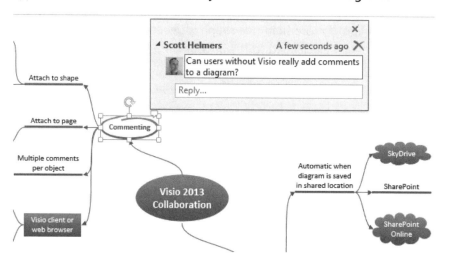

3   Right-click anywhere on the page background, click **Add Comment** to page, type **This looks like a good summary**, and then press **Esc**. A comment balloon appears in the upper-left corner of the page.

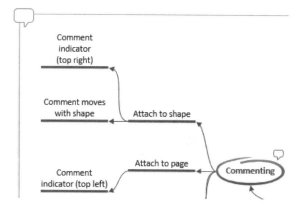

4   On the **Review** tab, in the **Comments** group, click **Comments Pane**. The **Comments** pane opens and displays all comments that exist on this or any other pages in the diagram as shown on the left.

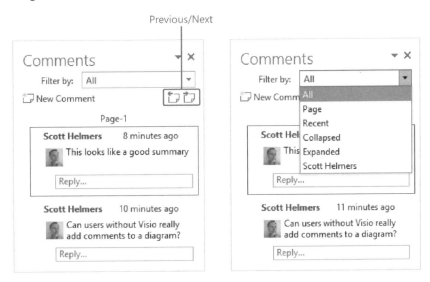

Be sure to notice the navigation controls at the top of the Comments pane:

- The previous and next buttons allow you to move through the comments sequentially (left graphic).

- The **Filter by** drop-down list lets you select categories of comments that you want to review or edit (right graphic).

5   Save changes to the diagram and then close it, but leave Visio running.

6   Switch to your web browser, navigate to the SharePoint folder in which you saved your diagram, and then click **Collaboration Brainstorm Diagram**. When the diagram opens, you'll notice that there aren't any visible comment indicators.

TIP The default view for Visio Web Access is to hide the comment balloons unless the Comments pane is open, which is why no balloons are visible in your web view. However, the default presentation for comments in Visio is to show the comment balloons whether or not the Comments pane is open; the graphic that accompanies step 3 shows this behavior.

13

7   In the upper left of the browser window, click **Comments**. The **Comments** pane opens on the right side of the window, and comment balloons appear on both the page and the shape in the same locations where they appeared in Visio.

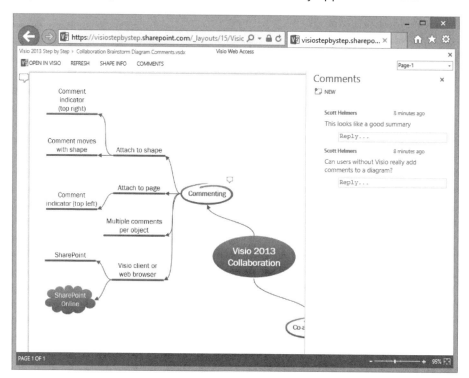

8   In the **Reply** box beneath **This looks like a good summary,** type **Thanks**, and then click anywhere outside the **Reply** box. Visio Services writes your comment to the Visio diagram.

> **TIP** If you or someone else has the diagram open in the Visio client when you attempt to add comments via your web browser, you will receive an error message like the one shown in the following graphic.

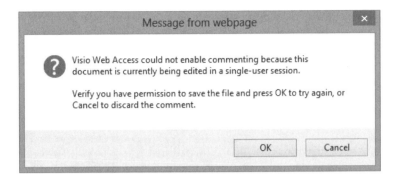

9   In the **Reply** box beneath **Can users without Visio really add comments to a diagram?** type **Yes. This comment was added in a web browser.**, and then click anywhere outside the **Reply** box. Visio Services updates the Visio diagram.

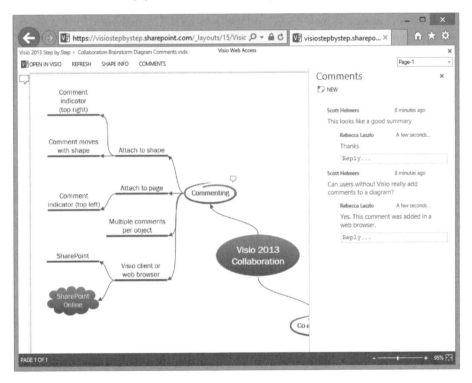

10   Switch to Visio and open **Collaboration Brainstorm Diagram**.

13

11   On the **Review** tab, in the **Comments** group, click **Comments Pane**, which opens the
pane and reveals the new comments that were entered in your browser.

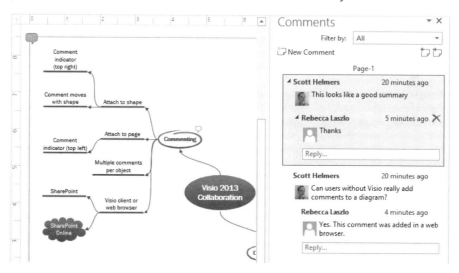

⊗ CLEAN UP **Save your changes to the *Collaboration Brainstorm Diagram* drawing, but
leave it open if you are continuing with the next exercise.**

The Visio commenting feature makes it easy to connect with another person who has
entered comments. If you point to the commenter's name or photograph, a pop-up box
displays his/her photo and up to four ways to connect with that person, including live chat
if both parties are online at the same time. In the following graphic, only the email icon is
active, because the other three require Microsoft Lync.

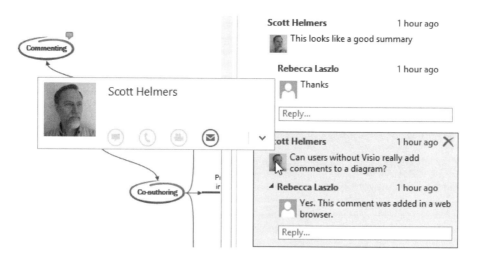

Clicking the arrow in the lower-right corner of the pop-up box opens a contact card for this person. The information that appears on the contact card will vary depending on what the user has made public in his/her profile. An example of the full contact card appears in the following graphic.

IMPORTANT The following section applies only to the Professional edition of Visio 2013.

Coauthoring

Coauthoring in Visio 2013 means that multiple people can edit the same diagram simultaneously when the diagram is stored on SkyDrive, SharePoint, or SharePoint Online. Nothing else is required other than opening the drawing—coauthoring is automatic.

In the Visio 2013 implementation, shapes and pages are not locked during a coauthoring session. The assumption is that there are so many possible things to change in a Visio diagram that it's unlikely two people will be changing exactly the same thing at the same time. On the rare occasions when that does occur, the last change wins.

13

To prevent possible conflicts and to help everyone working on a diagram to understand what is happening, Visio provides several markers on the upper-right corner of a shape during coauthoring sessions. The markers indicate when another user is editing some aspect of a shape (refer to the following graphic on the left), has altered a shape (center), or has deleted a shape (right).

IMPORTANT Normally, if one coauthor deletes a shape and then saves changes, the shape will disappear from other authors' diagrams when they apply updates. There is an important exception: the shape will be retained and marked as shown in the preceding graphic on the right if one of the coauthors has made what Visio determines to be significant changes to the shape. If that author then saves the diagram, Visio reinstates the shape for all authors and adds a special marker icon. The exercise that follows includes an example of this sequence and the special icon.

The status line at the bottom of the Visio window shows important coauthoring information.

- Toward the left, an icon indicates that other users are editing the diagram and displays how many are doing so. Each time a new coauthor opens the diagram, he or she is announced in a text box (following graphic on the left). At any time after the announcement box has disappeared, clicking the icon produces a list of coauthors (right).

Pointing to one of the coauthor's names produces a short form contact card that indicates how the person can be contacted via a series of icons. Additional icons are illuminated if both authors are using Lync.

Clicking the arrow in the lower-right corner yields a full contact card that displays as much information about the coauthor as that person has chosen to make available.

- Toward the right end of the status bar, the words *Updates Available* notify you that other users have saved changes. Clicking Updates Available applies any pending changes to your diagram and saves your changes to the server.

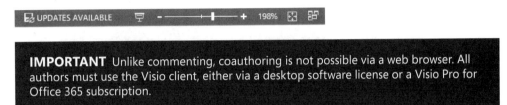

> **IMPORTANT** Unlike commenting, coauthoring is not possible via a web browser. All authors must use the Visio client, either via a desktop software license or a Visio Pro for Office 365 subscription.

In this exercise, you will make changes to a diagram that you have opened with two copies of Visio. You can start both copies of Visio on a single PC or on two different PCs. Although you can perform all of the steps in this exercise by yourself, it will be more interesting if you and another person work together.

The portion of the diagram you will be using in this exercise is shown in the following graphic.

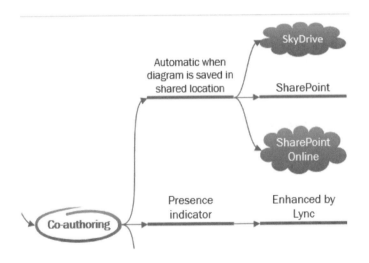

→ SET UP You need the *Collaboration Brainstorm Diagram* drawing for this exercise. Either continue with the open copy from the previous exercise or open the *Collaboration Brainstorm DiagramB_start* drawing located in the Chapter13 practice file folder.

To complete this coauthoring exercise, you must save the diagram as *Collaboration Brainstorm Diagram* on SkyDrive, SharePoint, or SharePoint Online. In addition, you or another person must open the saved diagram in a second copy of Visio.

13

1 PC2: Right-click the **SkyDrive** shape, click **Styles** on the Mini Toolbar, click any color other than blue in the **Theme Styles** section, and then click **Save**. Your updates are sent to the server. After a brief delay, the symbol indicating that another user is editing the **SkyDrive** shape will appear on PC1.

2 PC1: Click **Updates Available**. The color change is applied to the **SkyDrive** shape and the icon indicating that changes have been made by another user appears.

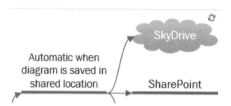

3 PC1: Select the **SkyDrive**, **SharePoint**, and **SharePoint Online** shapes, drag them far enough to the right so that Visio creates a new page, and then click **Save**.

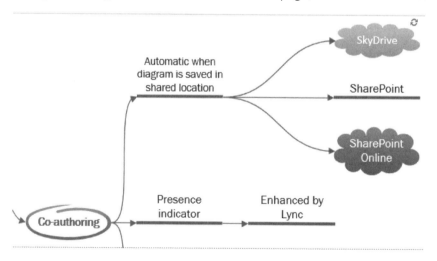

4   PC2: Click **Updates Available.** The relocated shapes appear in their new positions.

You have now made and saved changes on each PC and have verified that the results appear on the other computer. In the remaining steps of this exercise, you will make changes to a shape on PC1 while the user on PC2 deletes the same shape.

5   PC1: Right-click the **SharePoint** shape and click **Change Topic Shape.**

6   PC1: In the **Change Shape** dialog box, click **Rectangle**, and then click **OK.**

7   PC1: Double-click the **SharePoint** shape and change the text from **SharePoint** to **SharePoint (corporate)**. Do not save your changes.

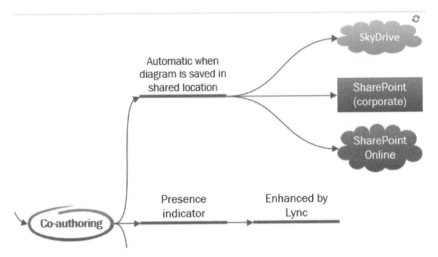

8   PC2: Delete the **SharePoint** shape and then click **Save**. The Visio AutoDelete function also deletes the connector leading to the SharePoint shape.

IMPORTANT At this point, you have unsaved changes pending for the SharePoint shape on PC1 and have just deleted that shape on PC2. After a brief pause, deleted shape warning icons will appear on PC1 for the SharePoint (corporate) shape and the connector leading to it.

13

9   PC1: Wait for deleted shape icons to appear.

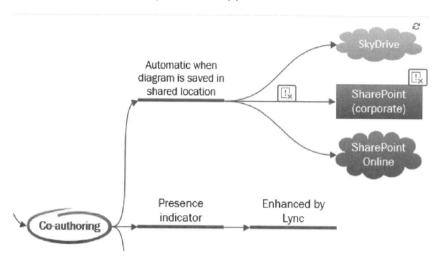

10   PC1: Click **Updates Available.** Because you made multiple changes to the **SharePoint (corporate)** shape before the user on PC2 deleted it, Visio retained the shape and added a marker icon above the upper-right corner.

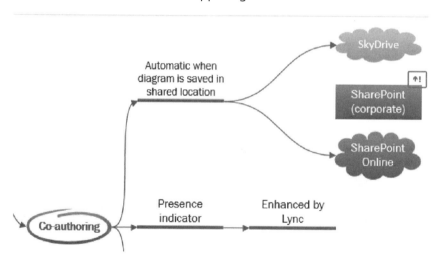

TIP The connector leading to the SharePoint (corporate) shape, which was deleted automatically when the primary shape was deleted on PC2, has not been preserved—there were no changes to the connector on PC1 that caused Visio to retain it.

11   PC2: Click **Updates Available.** The formerly deleted **SharePoint (corporate)** shape reappears in the diagram.

❌ CLEAN UP **Save your changes to the *Collaboration Brainstorm Diagram* drawing and close it on both PCs.**

Key points

- When you use the Save as Web Page function, you can customize the website that Visio creates. You can include or exclude navigation features, include reports, and even change the format and style of the website.

- Saving Visio diagrams to Visio Services on SharePoint provides high fidelity rendering of Visio drawings and simple user navigation controls. In addition, the Visio Services rendering of a diagram can be refreshed manually or automatically whenever there are changes in either the underlying Visio diagram or in data sources linked to the diagram.

- Multiple authors can enter and read comments in a Visio diagram using the Visio client software. In addition, if the diagram has been saved to SharePoint, users can write and read comments via a web browser.

- Simultaneous coauthoring is an automatic feature whenever more than one person opens a Visio 2013 diagram that is stored on SkyDrive or SharePoint.

13

Looking under the hood

Microsoft Visio 2013 serves two distinct communities that sometimes overlap. On one hand, there are people who create diagrams using just the tools on the standard user interface. The diagrams they create may be very simple or very sophisticated, but this group of people completes their diagrams without needing to look "under the hood." The second group of people loves to push Visio beyond its off-the-shelf capabilities by exploring and modifying the *ShapeSheet* or by writing code to drive the behavior of Visio.

The purpose of this appendix is not to turn members of the first group into coders and ShapeSheet developers. However, there is so much more you can accomplish with Visio if you have just a little bit of extra knowledge. Consequently, the goal for this appendix is to equip you with a few extra tips, techniques, and tools so you can customize Visio and create even more interesting, attractive, and functional diagrams.

Customizing the Visio user interface

Because Visio 2013 employs the second generation *fluent user interface*, you can customize both the ribbon and the *Quick Access Toolbar* very easily.

The ribbon

On the ribbon, you can alter the built-in tabs by adding or removing buttons. You can also create your own tabs so that all of your most frequently used buttons are arranged as you would like them.

To customize the ribbon, on the File tab, click Options. Then on the left side of the Visio Options dialog box, click Customize Ribbon. Use the main part of the dialog box to add, remove, or rearrange buttons on any existing tab.

To create your own tab, on the lower-right side of the dialog box, click the New Tab button, and then add and arrange buttons from the built-in tabs. You can create groups by clicking the New Group button, and can rename tabs or groups by clicking the Rename button. Finally, you can change the position of your new tab relative to the other tabs on the ribbon by using the Move Up and Move Down arrows located on the right side of the Main Tabs dialog box.

The following graphic defines a tab called *My Tab* to which several buttons have been added in a group called My Favorite Buttons.

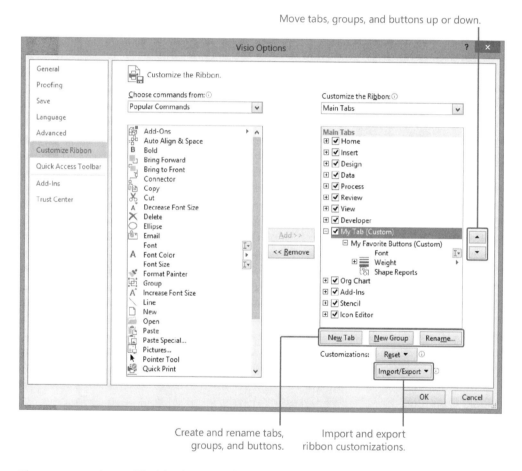

Move tabs, groups, and buttons up or down.

Create and rename tabs, groups, and buttons.   Import and export ribbon customizations.

The custom tab specified in the preceding graphic, with font selection, line weight, and shape reports buttons, is shown in the following graphic.

If you create a combination of tabs and buttons that you like and want to use them on another computer or share them with colleagues, it's easy to do. Simply use the Import and Export buttons in the lower-right corner of the dialog box.

SEE ALSO For more information on customizing ribbon tabs, go to *office.microsoft.com/en-ca/visio-help/customize-the-ribbon-HA010355697.aspx.*

The Quick Access Toolbar

The purpose of the Quick Access Toolbar, which resides in the upper-left corner of the Visio 2013 window, is exactly as its name suggests: to provide easy access to commonly used buttons. One of its best features is that you can easily add whatever additional buttons you would like. It's as simple as right-clicking any button on the ribbon (on the left in the following graphic) and selecting Add to Quick Access Toolbar to produce the result shown on the right.

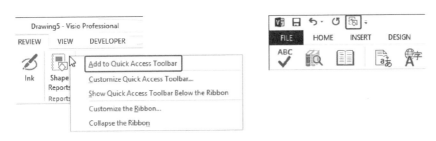

To add or remove commonly used functions, click the down arrow on the right end of the toolbar as shown in the following graphic, and then select or deselect any entry.

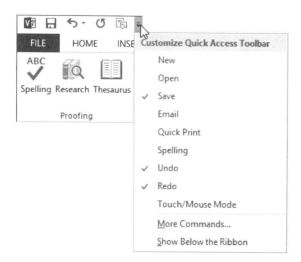

You can also add buttons for functions that are not shown on the list in the preceding graphic. On the File tab, click Options. Then on the left side of the Visio Options dialog box, click Quick Access Toolbar. Use the main part of the dialog box to add, remove, or rearrange the buttons on the toolbar.

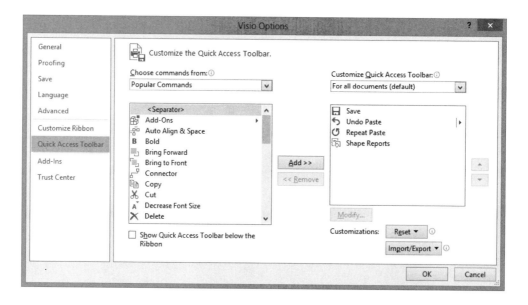

One convenient combination of file and window management functions includes Save, Save As, Open, Undo, Redo, and Switch Windows.

Although the Quick Access Toolbar usually shows file and window management functions, don't restrict your thinking to those categories. Do you use a certain fill color regularly? Do you frequently open and close the Shape Data window? Do you use the Check Diagram button (Visio Professional only) multiple times per day? You can add those and almost any other buttons to the Quick Access Toolbar.

Creating custom shapes and stencils

In this book, you've learned many ways to create and alter Visio shapes. Regardless of the techniques you use to build or modify shapes, there may come a time when you would like to save a customized shape so you can reuse it. Doing so is as easy as dragging a shape into an open *stencil* in order to create a new *master*. For this example, you'll drag a freeform shape similar to one you created in Chapter 2 into a new stencil.

1   Open the **Basic Shapes_start** diagram located in the **Appendix** practice files folder.

2   In the **Shapes** window, click **More Shapes**, and then click either **New Stencil (US Units)** or **New Stencil (Metric)**. A new stencil header appears in the **Shapes** window and it displays a red asterisk on its right end to indicate that the stencil is open.

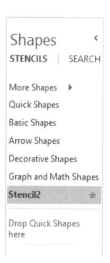

Also notice that like all Visio 2013 stencils, the new stencil is divided into two parts by a horizontal gray line. If you drop a shape above the line, it will appear on the *Quick Shapes* menu; if you drop it below the line, it will be in the stencil but will not be a Quick Shape.

3 Drag the freeform shape from the upper-right corner of the drawing page into the **Quick Shapes** area of the open stencil. A preview icon appears next to the name of the new master, in the form of *Master.n*, where *n* is an integer. The red asterisk changes to a diskette icon, indicating that the stencil contains unsaved changes. At this point, your new master behaves like any other: you can drag it onto the drawing page to create a new shape. To make the master more useful in the future, however, you will give it a more meaningful name.

4 Right-click the new master, click **Rename Master**, and then type **Freeform**.

5   Right-click the header of the new stencil, and then click **Save**. By default, the **Save As** dialog box opens to a special folder called **My Stencils** that is located in your Windows **Documents** folder.

6   Type **Custom Shapes**, and then click **Save**. Your new stencil name appears on the stencil header.

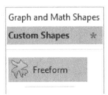

The new stencil is available for use in any Visio diagram. To open it, point to More Shapes, and then point to My Shapes. A menu containing a list of any stencils you've saved in the My Shapes folder appears; click a stencil name to open it in the shapes window.

SEE ALSO To learn more about the interactions among stencils, masters, and shapes, refer to "Visio Stencils, Masters and Shapes: How are they related?" written by Scott A. Helmers and published by Experts Exchange at *rdsrc.us/ybma5n*.

Running in developer mode

When you decide to step beyond the ranks of ordinary Visio users, one of the first things you should do is run Visio in *developer mode*. Don't let the name frighten you; there are no programming or hardcore technical requirements for running Visio in this mode.

The primary advantage of developer mode is easy access to a number of very useful features. In developer mode, you can perform the following functions:

- Create and run macros to automate Visio functions.

- Manage add-in programs.

- Add custom controls to Visio shapes.

- Design new shapes and alter the appearance and behavior of existing shapes.

- Create new stencils.

- View "behind the scenes" parts of Visio documents, most notably, the ShapeSheet. (Refer to the following section, "Viewing and modifying the ShapeSheet," for more information about the Visio ShapeSheet.)

To activate developer mode, on the File tab, click Options. Then on the left side of the Visio Options dialog box, click Customize Ribbon. On the right side of the dialog box, select the Developer check box.

After you activate developer mode, the most obvious difference is the addition of a Developer tab to the ribbon.

You will also find that the shortcut menu for any Visio object includes an option to open the ShapeSheet.

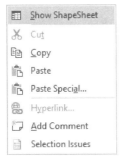

TIP There is no downside to running Visio in developer mode, even if you don't regularly use the features it provides.

SEE ALSO The Visio blog contains an article that provides details on Developer tab functions: *blogs.msdn.com/b/visio/archive/2009/09/02/the-developer-tab-in-visio-2010.aspx*. The article was written for Visio 2010, and though some of the button icons have changed for Visio 2013, the functions of the Developer tab are the same in both versions.

Viewing and modifying the ShapeSheet

There are three elements that combine to give Visio its power and versatility:

- **Visio engine** The *Visio engine* is the preprogrammed heart of Visio.

- **Add-in programs** *Add-ins* typically extend Visio by providing features that the Visio engine does not. They are created by Microsoft, other software companies, or individuals.

- **ShapeSheet** The *ShapeSheet* is a spreadsheet-like data store that exists behind every object in Visio. Every two-dimensional shape, every line, every container, every page, and even the document itself, has a ShapeSheet. The values and formulas in the ShapeSheet, in conjunction with the Visio engine and add-in code, control every aspect of the appearance and behavior of Visio objects.

    TIP For the technically inclined, you might prefer to think of the ShapeSheet as a window into parts of the Visio object model.

IMPORTANT You must be running in developer mode to access the ShapeSheet.

The remarkable thing about the ShapeSheet when you first start to explore it—or, for that matter, after you've been working with it for 10 years—is that changing one value or formula can have a profound effect on what appears on the page.

To view the ShapeSheet for any shape on the drawing page, select the shape, and then on the Developer tab, in the Shape Design group, click the Show ShapeSheet button. To view the ShapeSheet for the page or the document, click the lower half of the same button (do not click the icon) and choose an entry from the menu.

TIP There is a quick alternative method for opening the ShapeSheet for the three primary types of Visio objects:

- **Shape** Right-click the shape and click Show ShapeSheet.

- **Page** Right-click the page background and click Show ShapeSheet.

- **Document** Right-click the page background, hold down the Shift key, and click Show ShapeSheet.

The cells in the ShapeSheet are organized into sections and each section has a specific format. In the following graphic, some sections are open and visible, such as Shape Transform, and some are closed, such as Protection. You can open or close any section by clicking the blue section header.

TIP Notice the tool tab set at the top of the Visio window. The Design tool tab in the ShapeSheet Tools tool tab set provides ShapeSheet-specific functions.

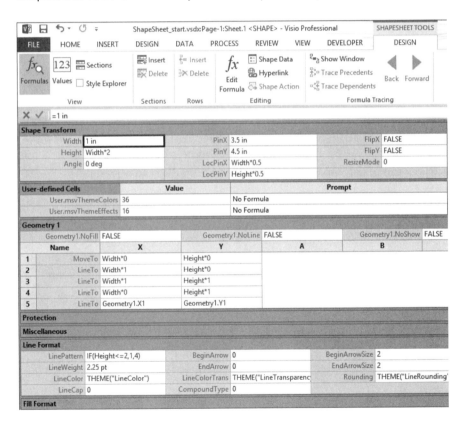

You can use ShapeSheet cells for two purposes: to observe the current attributes of a Visio object or to change the object's appearance or behavior. To do the latter, you can type either a constant or a formula into a ShapeSheet cell. Examples of both appear in the preceding graphic, which is part of the ShapeSheet for a rectangular shape.

The Width cell in the Shape Transform section for the rectangle has a value of one inch, so the shape on the page is exactly one inch wide. If you drag either the left or right *resize handle* on the shape, the value in the Width cell will change to reflect the new width. Conversely, if you type a different value into the Width cell, the shape on the page will react accordingly.

In contrast to that cell, you will find a formula of "Width*2" in the Height cell, ensuring that the height of the rectangle will always be two times its width. If you change the width of the shape by dragging a resize handle or by typing a new number into the Width cell, the height of the shape will adjust automatically. (In contrast, if you change the height of the shape by dragging the top or bottom resize handle, the height formula will be overwritten by the new height value. It is possible to prevent a formula from being overwritten by actions in the user interface, but the techniques for doing so are outside the scope of this appendix.)

"Width*2" is obviously a very simple formula. Many Visio shapes employ much more complex formulas. In addition, there are dozens of ShapeSheet functions that can take actions, such as reading data from other cells in this ShapeSheet; reading data from the ShapeSheets of other objects in the document; performing sophisticated calculations; setting a value based on an "if" condition; triggering actions in the drawing; and responding to events.

The formula in the LineColor cell in the Line Format section provides an example. The THEME() function retrieves the default line color used in the current theme and applies it to the line on this shape. If a user applies a different theme to the diagram, the line color for this shape will automatically change to the line color used in the new theme.

SEE ALSO For information about Visio 2013 themes, refer to Chapter 5, "Adding style, color, and themes."

As a second example, look at the formula for LinePattern in the Line Format section. The IF() function is interpreted this way: if the height of the shape is less than or equal to 2 inches, set the line around the shape to pattern number 1; if the height is greater than 2 inches, set the line pattern to 4. The results of this formula are apparent in the two shapes shown in the following graphic:

- In the ShapeSheet cells for the rectangle on the left, the Width is 1 inch, which means the height is 2 inches. Because the height equals 2 inches, the line pattern is set to pattern 1 (a solid line).

- For the rectangle on the right, the Width is 1.25 inches and the shape displays the cascading effects of the formulas and functions: the height now exceeds 2 inches, so the line pattern has changed.

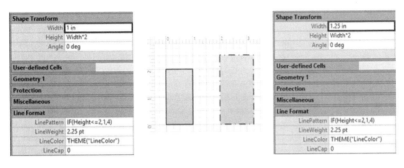

TIP If you would like to experiment with a rectangle configured like the one just described, open the *ShapeSheet_start* drawing located in the Appendix practice files folder.

The preceding example is a very simple one, but it should help you to understand the central role played by the ShapeSheet. It should also help you realize that one section in the appendix to a book like this can barely scratch the surface of the uses and functions of the ShapeSheet. Use the following references to continue your exploration of the Visio ShapeSheet:

- United Kingdom–based Visio Most Valuable Professional (MVP) John Goldsmith started his Visio blog in 2007 with a concise, nicely organized tutorial on the ShapeSheet: *visualsignals.typepad.co.uk/vislog/2007/10/just-for-starte.html*. Be sure to check out other posts on John's blog for additional ShapeSheet-related examples.

- Two other Visio MVPs blog regularly about a broad array of topics and frequently describe very clever manipulations of the ShapeSheet:

  - **Chris Roth**, aka The Visio Guy *www.visguy.com*

  - **David Parker** *blog.bvisual.net*

- The aforementioned David Parker wrote a book on business process validation that is cited in Chapter 12, "Creating and validating process diagrams." Chapter 3 of David's book is available at *msdn.microsoft.com/en-us/library/gg144579.aspx*. The first third of the chapter is an excellent ShapeSheet overview.

- The ultimate reference for the ShapeSheet is contained in the Visio 2013 Software Development Kit (SDK), online at *msdn.microsoft.com/en-us/library/ff768297.aspx* and in downloadable form at *www.microsoft.com/en-us/download/details.aspx?id=36825*.

Inserting fields: advanced topics

In Chapter 3, "Adding sophistication to your drawings," you learned how to display the value of a *shape data* field on a shape. Although that simple action is very helpful, you can do so much more than that with the Field dialog box.

To open the Field dialog box, select a shape, and then on the Insert tab, in the Text group, click the Field button. The first thing to notice about the Field dialog box is that the Category section includes seven entries underneath Shape Data. Each of these categories contains multiple data fields. The Date/Time category, for example, shows four types of dates.

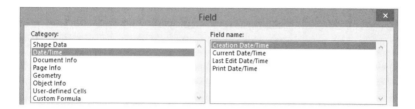

Other categories display data about the document (shown in the following graphic), the page, or various attributes of the selected object.

Finally, you can insert just about anything you'd like by selecting the Custom Formula category. A custom formula can include math and text functions, references to any of the data elements in the other seven field categories, and almost any ShapeSheet cell or function.

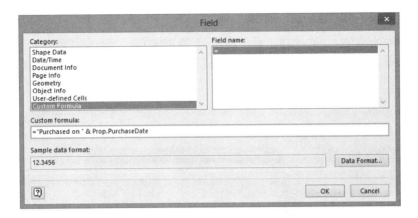

As one example, the custom formula shown in the preceding graphic consists of two parts: a text label, "Purchased on", concatenated with a value stored in the PurchaseDate shape data field. The result, inserted on a conference table shape from the Office Layout template, is shown in the following graphic.

The Field dialog box offers a rich set of options for making the data in your document visible to users of your drawings.

Recording and running macros

As with most of the programs in the Microsoft Office suite, you can record and run macros in Visio 2013. A *macro* is a stored set of instructions, and macros are a great way to perform repetitive actions: you record a set of actions once and can replay it as many times as you'd like. To start recording a macro, click the Macro button to the right of the Language section of the Visio status bar (refer to the following graphic on the left).

In the Record Macro dialog box that appears, click OK to begin recording. Note that the appearance of the button changes to a square stop button, as shown in the following graphic on the right.

Macro button
(recording not started)

Macro button
(recording started)

When you have completed the steps you want to capture, click the Macro button again.

IMPORTANT The macro recorder does not record mouse movements or specific keystrokes. Instead, it records the instructions that produce the result of your actions.

To run a macro that you've recorded, on the View tab, in the Macros group, click the Macro button. Select the appropriate macro in the Macros dialog box, and then click Run.

Although you are not required to be in developer mode to record and run macros, you can do both things very easily using buttons in the Code group on the Developer tab.

SEE ALSO Refer to the section titled, "Running in developer mode" earlier in this appendix.

Macro security in Visio

The default security setting for macro code is Disable All Macros With Notification, which means that Visio opens any diagram containing macros in protected mode and displays a security warning bar above the drawing page.

If you ignore the warning, you will be able to edit the drawing but not run macros. If you click Enable Content, the drawing will close and reopen with macros enabled.

To change macro security settings, on the File tab, click Options. Then on the left side of the Visio Options dialog box, click Trust Center, and then click the Trust Center Settings button on the far right. When the Trust Center dialog box opens, click Macro Settings if it's not already selected.

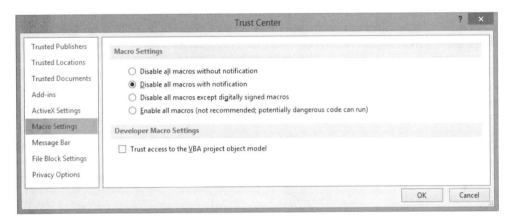

Click whichever of the other three settings meets your needs, and then click OK.

TIP If you are running Visio in developer mode, you can view the Macro settings with a single click: on the Developer tab, in the Code group, click Macro Security.

Programming Visio by using Visual Basic for Applications

Microsoft *Visual Basic for Applications* (*VBA*) is the built-in programming language that accompanies most Microsoft Office applications. With VBA, you can extend or change the way that an Office application functions. In Visio, for example, you can automate tasks, add new features, or integrate Visio with other members of the Office suite.

Using VBA to integrate one Office application with another can yield very interesting results. For example, you can write Visio VBA code that creates a Microsoft Excel workbook and writes diagram data to it, or saves all drawing pages as images and creates a Microsoft PowerPoint presentation from them. These are just two examples among many other possibilities.

SEE ALSO To read an article and view sample code for creating a PowerPoint presentation from a Visio diagram, refer to "How to Create PowerPoint Slides from a Visio Drawing" by Scott Helmers, published by Experts Exchange at *rdsrc.us/RQKWeK*.

To write a VBA program, you need to open the **Visual Basic Editor** (**VBE**): on the Developer tab, in the Code group, click Visual Basic. The VBE window opens, allowing you to create and debug your program.

KEYBOARD SHORTCUT Press Alt+F11 to open the VBE window.

You will not learn how to write VBA programs in this book, but you can find many books and online tutorials about VBA. The following links will get you started:

- An overview of VBA in Office is at *msdn.microsoft.com/en-us/library/ee814735.aspx*. Note that Visio is not included in the "Applies to" list of products on the page, but the material is relevant nevertheless.

- The Visio 2013 page on the Microsoft Developer Network (MSDN) website at *msdn. microsoft.com/en-us/library/fp161226.aspx* includes links to a number of helpful pages including those listed below.

  - Welcome to the Visio 2013 Automation reference: *msdn.microsoft.com/en-us/ library/ee861526.aspx*.

  - What's new for Visio 2013 developers: *msdn.microsoft.com/en-us/library/ ff767103.aspx*.

- The Visio SDK contains dozens of code samples that are excellent starting points for writing programs: *www.microsoft.com/en-us/download/details.aspx?id=36825*.

If you've never created a macro or written a VBA program, you might be wondering about the difference between the two because they sound similar. The answer is that a Visio macro is nothing more than a VBA program created for you by Visio. To discover this for yourself, record a macro by using the instructions in the preceding section, and then open the Visual Basic Editor window. The module called NewMacros contains the code.

Because VBA and macros are closely related, recording macros is one of the best ways to learn how to write VBA programs. Let Visio generate the code for a task that you want to perform, examine the code, and then incorporate it into your VBA program. Although this is an excellent strategy, you should be aware that automatically generated macro code tends to be very verbose. Over time, you will learn which parts of the macro code you need, which parts you don't need, and which parts you need to modify.

Creating containers and lists

In Chapter 11, "Adding structure to your diagrams," you learned about containers, lists, and callouts. You learned how to insert preformatted containers from the container gallery, and how to add callouts from the callout gallery. You also learned that there isn't a corresponding list gallery, which means that you can't create a list by using the Visio user interface.

So how do you create a list? Or a custom container? The answer is surprisingly simple: you add one entry to the ShapeSheet for any shape and it becomes a structured diagram component.

SEE ALSO If you're not familiar with modifying the ShapeSheet, refer to the section titled "Viewing and modifying the ShapeSheet" earlier in this appendix.

> **IMPORTANT** You must be running in developer mode to access the ShapeSheet.

To create a list, follow these steps:

1. On the **Home** tab, in the **Tools** group, click the **Rectangle** Tool and draw a rectangle.
2. Right-click the rectangle, and then select **Show ShapeSheet**.
3. Right-click anywhere in the **ShapeSheet** window, and then click **Insert Section**.
4. In the **Insert Section** dialog box, select **User-defined cells**, and then click **OK**.

User-defined Cells	Value	Prompt
User.Row_1	0	""

5. Click **User.Row_1**, type **msvStructureType**, and then press **Enter**.
6. Click the **Value** cell, type **"List"** (include the quotation marks), and then press **Enter**.

User-defined Cells	Value	Prompt
User.msvStructureType	"List"	""

You've just created a list! It isn't fancy and doesn't have any of the niceties like margins, a header, color, or style, but it is a list.

To test your new list, close the ShapeSheet window and drag a shape into the list. Drag several more shapes into the list. As you add each shape, you'll find that your rectangle behaves exactly like the lists you worked with in Chapter 11.

Creating a container is as easy as creating a list: simply type "Container" in the Value cell for msvStructureType. Creating a callout requires a few extra steps but can also be done fairly easily.

SEE ALSO If you would like to enhance the appearance and behavior of your list, container, or callout, you will need to add additional rows to the User-defined Cells section of the ShapeSheet. For an excellent summary of the user-defined rows and values required for structured diagram components, go to *blogs.msdn.com/b/visio/archive/2010/01/12/ custom-containers-lists-and-callouts-in-visio-2010.aspx*. For additional technical details, including sample code for working with structured diagram components in VBA, go to *msdn.microsoft.com/en-us/library/ff959245.aspx*.

The Visio 2013 file formats

All versions of Visio before the 2013 release utilized a proprietary file format. With the 2013 release, Visio joins most other members of the Office product family in using the Extensible Markup Language (XML)-based Open Packaging Convention file format. The change won't be particularly noticeable to most Visio users, with the exception of encountering new file extensions, however, the new file format offers multiple advantages.

- Most diagram files are significantly smaller than they were in the previous file format.

- Diagrams can be saved to, and then opened and read by, Visio Services on Share-Point. Neither a file conversion nor a special file format is required.

- Diagrams can be opened directly in SharePoint Designer for editing and preparation for SharePoint Workflow. An intermediate file format is not required.

- Files are readily accessible to software developers because they are in XML rather than a proprietary format.

The Visio files for drawings, templates, and stencils each have two variations in the new file format: one that prohibits macros and one that allows macros.

Macro-free file types and extensions:

- Drawing: .vsdx

- Template: .vstx

- Stencil: .vssx

Macro-enabled file types and extensions:

- Drawing: .vsdm
- Template: .vstm
- Stencil: .vssm

Several comments related to opening files from previous versions of Visio:

- Visio 2013 can open all files created in Visio 2010 through Visio 2003 and can save files in most 2010-2003 formats. Refer to Chapter 8, "Printing, reusing, and sharing diagrams," for details about saving Visio diagrams in other formats.

- Visio 2013 can open .vsd and .vdx files from Visio 2002 but cannot save in either of those formats.

- When you open a file from an earlier version of Visio, the words *Compatibility Mode* appear after the file name in the Windows title bar. The compatibility marker indicates that some newer features, including themes, variants, styles, and coauthoring, have been disabled.

- Opening and then saving a file created in an older version of Visio into the Visio 2013 file format is not sufficient to enable Visio 2013 features. To upgrade a file that you have opened in compatibility mode, you must click File, and then click the Convert button on the Info page.

Developers interested in learning how to work with the new XML file formats have several resources available.

- "Welcome to the Visio 2013 file format reference" includes links to multiple articles: *msdn.microsoft.com/en-us/library/office/jj684209.aspx*

- Visio MVP, Al Edlund, created a set of utilities for investigating and manipulating Visio 2013 files: *pkgvisio.codeplex.com/documentation*

Glossary

1-D shape A Visio shape that has two endpoints and behaves like a line, sometimes in spite of its physical appearance. 1-D is an abbreviation for one-dimensional.

2-D shape A Visio shape that has a border and an interior and behaves like a polygon. 2-D is an abbreviation for two-dimensional.

absolute link A type of hyperlink that contains all of the information required to locate the linked object. Examples: D:\MyFolder1\MyFolder2\MyDocument.docx or *http://www.taskmap.com/Downloads.html*. See *relative link*.

action tag Visio shapes can be designed to display a special icon when you point to the shape. Clicking an action tag displays a menu that contains one or more items. Prior to Visio 2010, action tags were called smart tags.

active page The drawing page that has the focus within the drawing window.

active window Of the windows inside the Visio window, this is the one that has the focus; most often the active window is the drawing window.

Activity (BPMN) One of a set of rectangle shapes that represents a step in a BPMN diagram. See *Business Process Model and Notation*.

Activity (General) A task or step in a *work process*.

add-in Software written by Microsoft, other companies, or individuals that adds features and capabilities to Visio.

add-in tab A tab on the Visio ribbon that is present only when a Visio add-in is running. Example: the Org Chart tab for the Organization Chart add-in.

anchor shape The primary shape when multiple shapes are selected. If you select multiple shapes at one time using a bounding box, the anchor shape is the one farthest to the back (see *Z-order*). If you select multiple shapes one at a time, the anchor shape is the first one you select. The anchor shape affects the results of alignment, spacing, and numbering operations.

area select A Visio technique for selecting multiple shapes within a rectangular area. See *bounding box*; compare with *lasso select*.

Auto Size A Visio option that automatically expands or contracts the drawing page as you move shapes across page boundaries. Introduced in Visio 2010.

AutoAdd Occurs when you drop a shape onto an existing dynamic connector that is glued to two shapes. Visio disconnects the dynamic connector from shape #2, glues it to the shape you dropped, and automatically adds a new dynamic connector, which it then glues to the new shape and to shape #2. See *AutoDelete*.

AutoConnect A Visio feature that glues a dynamic connector from one shape to another with a single click; AutoConnect arrows are small blue triangles that appear when you point to a shape.

AutoDelete Occurs when you delete a shape that is connected to two other shapes with dynamic connectors. Visio removes the deleted shape, deletes the dynamic connector glued to shape #2, and then glues the remaining dynamic connector to shape #2. See *AutoAdd*.

background An area of the drawing page that does not contain any shapes.

background page A Visio page that can be attached both to foreground pages and to other background pages. Shapes on a background page appear on other pages to which the background page is attached; however, the shapes can only be selected or altered when the background page is the active page.

Backstage view A central location for managing files and setting options that control how Visio 2013 operates; you access the Backstage view by clicking the File tab.

bounding box A temporary rectangular shape created by clicking the background of a page and dragging the mouse to select one or more shapes. By default, Visio selects all shapes that are fully contained within the area of the bounding box. Also referred to as *area select*.

BPMN See *Business Process Model and Notation*.

business process A collection of tasks and activities that leads to a desired result; also known as a *work process*, or just a *process*.

Business Process Model and Notation (BPMN) A standard for graphically representing business processes. Visio 2013 conforms to the 2.0 version of the standard.

callout A shape you use to annotate other shapes in a drawing. Visio 2013 callouts exhibit more intelligent behavior, because they maintain a logical association with the shapes to which they are connected.

canvas See *drawing canvas*.

collaboration Visio 2013 features that enable multiple authors to edit a diagram simultaneously, and enter comments in a diagram by using either Visio or a web browser.

color by value A type of data graphic that applies color to shapes based on data values within the shapes.

comment A Visio annotation object that can be attached to a shape or the drawing page. Compare with *ScreenTip*.

Connecting Object One of a set of arrow shapes that links other shapes in a BPMN diagram. See *Business Process Model and Notation*.

connection point A location on a Visio shape to which other shapes can be glued; represented by a small, dark square that appears when you point to a shape.

Connector Tool A Visio tool that lets you add dynamic connectors to a drawing by dragging from one shape to another or from one connection point to another.

container A Visio 2013/2010 structured diagram shape that can contain other shapes. Containers know which shapes are members; member shapes know the identity of their containing shape.

control handle A yellow square that you use to alter the appearance or function of a shape. Most shapes do not have control handles; when they do exist, they appear when you select a shape.

cross-functional flowchart A type of flowchart in which each process step is placed into a horizontal or vertical lane based on which person, department, or function is responsible for that step. Commonly referred to as a *swimlane diagram*.

custom properties Data values that are stored inside a Visio shape. Starting with Visio 2007, custom properties are known as *shape data*.

data graphic A Visio feature that lets you annotate a shape with icons, text callouts, and color based on data in the shape.

data graphic legend A key to the data graphics used on a Visio drawing page.

data linking The act of building a dynamic connection between a Visio diagram and an external data source; the data in the diagram can be refreshed manually or automatically whenever the linked data changes.

developer mode A special Visio operating mode that provides additional features and tools beyond the normal user interface. When you turn on developer mode, Visio activates a Developer tab on the ribbon.

diagram See *drawing*.

drawing A Visio document that contains a drawing window and may contain other open windows. Also referred to as a diagram. Visio drawings use the .vsdx file extension.

drawing canvas The space in the drawing window that is outside the Visio drawing page. If the Auto Size option is turned on, when you place an object on the drawing canvas, Visio automatically expands the page size to include the shape. If the Auto Size option is turned off, you can store shapes on the canvas; they are saved with the drawing but do not print.

drawing page The printable drawing surface within the drawing window. In some templates, the drawing page displays a grid to aid in positioning and aligning shapes. Compare with *drawing canvas*.

drawing scale A ratio that expresses the size of an object in a drawing compared to its counterpart in the real world. In a metric drawing, 1:10 means that 1 cm on the page represents 10 cm in the real world. In a US units drawing, 1":1' means that 1 inch in the drawing represents 1 foot in the real world.

Drawing Tools A set of six tools—rectangle, ellipse, line, freeform, arc, and pencil—that enables the creation or alteration of shapes.

drawing window The Visio window that contains the drawing page.

dynamic connector A special type of line that adds and removes bends as the shapes to which it is glued are moved or resized. Each end of a dynamic connector can be glued to another shape.

dynamic glue The result of attaching a dynamic connector to the body of a shape. When you move dynamically glued shapes, the point of attachment of the connector can change. See *static glue*.

Dynamic Grid A Visio feature that provides visual alignment and positioning feedback when you move shapes near other shapes or near the page margins. Visio 2013 also provides dynamic feedback as you resize shapes.

effect A coordinated set of fonts, fill patterns, gradients, shadows, and line styles. See *themes*.

embellishment An extension of the *theme* concept that helps set the overall tone of a diagram by altering the geometry of selected shapes. Each theme has a default embellishment level, but you can choose a different level.

Event One of a set of circle shapes that mark start, intermediate, and end events in a BPMN diagram. See *Business Process Model and Notation*.

Extensible Application Markup Language See *XAML*.

Extensible Markup Language See *XML*.

flowchart A diagram that illustrates the activities, decisions, and events that occur in a work process or the logic of a program.

fluent user interface The official name of the user interface style introduced in selected Microsoft Office 2007 products. Commonly referred to as the *ribbon*, it was added to the 2010 release of Visio.

foreground page A Visio drawing page. Can be attached to a background page.

functional band A vertical or horizontal rectangle in a cross-functional flowchart that contains process steps. Also known as a *swimlane*.

Gateway One of a set of diamond shapes that identify divergence and convergence in a BPMN diagram; gateways often represent decisions. See *Business Process Model and Notation*.

GIF Graphic Interchange Format; a common format for storing graphics and images on computers.

glue A property of a Visio shape that lets it remain attached to another shape. See *dynamic glue* and *static glue*.

gravity In Visio, a mathematical function that gives the appearance of gravity; rotating a shape or text that contains the gravity function will keep the shape/text upright.

grid The background pattern of intersecting, perpendicular lines on a drawing page. By default, shapes on a Visio drawing page snap to the grid lines as you move the shapes across the page.

guide A Visio shape you create by dragging either the horizontal or vertical ruler onto the drawing page; used to align other shapes.

handle See *selection handle*.

htm/html File extension for webpages; short for *Hypertext Markup Language*.

hyperlink base The starting point for determining the path to a hyperlink target; Visio documents include a hyperlink base field, which is blank by default.

Hypertext Markup Language (HTML) A markup language used to define and render webpages.

insertion bar An orange horizontal or vertical line that appears when you drag a shape near the edge of a shape that is already in a Visio list; the insertion bar indicates where the shape you are dragging will be inserted. See *list*.

JavaScript An object-oriented scripting language used by Visio to implement some navigation functions for websites created using Save As Web Page.

JPG/JPEG Joint Photographic Experts Group; a common format for storing graphics and images on computers.

lasso select A Visio technique for selecting multiple shapes within a freeform area drawn by the user; compare with *area select*.

layer A means for organizing sets of shapes in a drawing; layers have properties that affect all shapes in the layer at once. For example, with one or two clicks, you can show or hide all shapes on a layer, prevent shapes on a certain layer from printing, and recolor all shapes on a layer.

list A Visio 2013/2010 structured diagram shape that can contain other shapes. A list maintains its member shapes in ordered sequence; member shapes know their ordinal position within the list.

Live Preview An Office feature that shows the results of many operations before you implement the change. Used in Visio for many font, size, color, alignment, theme, and data graphic operations.

macro A stored set of instructions; in Visio, you can record a macro and play it back to repeat a set of actions.

master An object in a Visio stencil. Dragging a master from a stencil onto the drawing page creates a shape.

metric A system of measurement used in Visio drawings and templates in most countries outside North America. See *US Units*.

Mini Toolbar A floating toolbar accessed by right-clicking either a shape or the drawing page. It contains the Drawing and Connector Tools; alignment and send to front/back buttons; font and text enhancement buttons; the Format Painter; and access to shape styles.

multi-shape A Visio shape whose appearance changes as data or attributes of the shape change.

org chart See *organization chart*.

organization chart A diagram that represents the structure of an organization.

page controls A collection of buttons and tabs at the bottom of the Visio drawing window that you can use to navigate from one page to another within the drawing.

page name tab A tab at the bottom of the Visio drawing window that displays the name of a page. Right-clicking the tab provides access to page management functions.

pan To change which part of a drawing is visible by moving the page horizontally, vertically, or both.

pin The center of rotation for a shape.

PNG Portable Network Graphics; a common format for storing graphics and images on computers.

Pointer Tool A Visio tool that you can use to select shapes on the drawing page.

print tile The portion of the drawing page that is the size of a physical printer page; tiles are marked by dashed lines in print preview mode and on the drawing page if the Page Breaks check box is selected in the Show group on the View tab.

process See *business process*.

process map A diagram that shows the tasks and activities that comprise a *business process*.

Quick Access Toolbar A collection of buttons for frequently used functions that appears in the title bar of the Visio window and is always visible; can be customized.

Quick Shape One of up to four masters that appear on a Mini Toolbar when you point to the *AutoConnect* arrow for a shape on the drawing page; click a Quick Shape to add it to the drawing page.

Quick Styles A set of predefined colors and styles that can be applied to one or more shapes. Each theme has its own set of Quick Styles, ensuring that you can apply styles while maintaining the overall look of the theme.

rack unit A unit of measure for the space occupied by equipment mounted in a network or data center equipment rack. Each rack unit or U equals 1.75 inches (44.45 mm); equipment height is described as a multiple of U's, for example, 3U or 5U.

relative link A type of hyperlink that contains only part of the information required to locate the linked object. The remainder of the required information is derived from the location of the document containing the hyperlink. Example: MyFolder2\MyDocument.docx or Downloads.html. See *absolute link*.

report A Visio feature that you can use to generate a summary of the data on one or more pages in a drawing. A report can be exported in HTML, Excel, or XML format or can be dropped on the drawing page as a Visio shape.

resize handle One of up to eight squares that appear when you select a shape; two handles adjust the width; two adjust the height; the four corner handles adjust both dimensions proportionally.

ribbon Common name for the fluent user interface. The ribbon consists of a collection of tabs, each of which contains a set of buttons that provide related functions. See *fluent user interface*.

ribbon UI Ribbon user interface; see *ribbon*.

rotation handle A circle that appears when you select a shape using the Pointer Tool, or select text with the Text Tool; dragging the handle rotates the shape or text.

rule A condition to be validated in a Visio drawing. For example, a Visio validation rule might specify that all 1-D shapes must be connected on both ends.

rule set A collection of Visio validation rules, for example, the flowchart rule set or the BPMN rule set.

ScreenTip Text annotation that can be added to a shape; the ScreenTip appears when you point to the shape on the drawing page. Compare with *comment*.

selection handle Small circles, diamonds, or squares that appear when you select a shape; used to resize or adjust the appearance of a shape. See *control handle*, *resize handle*, and *rotation handle*.

shape An object on a Visio drawing page. You create shapes in three ways: 1) using tools from the Tools group on the Home tab to draw them; 2) dragging masters from stencils; or 3) pasting objects from the Clipboard. Alternatively, a program can create shapes for you.

shape data Data values stored inside a Visio shape; known as custom properties prior to Visio 2007. See *custom properties*.

Shape Data window A window that displays shape data names and values for a selected shape. See *shape data*.

shape name Internal name of a Visio shape.

shape text Text that is part of a shape and appears on or near the shape.

Shapes window A Visio window that contains one or more stencils.

ShapeSheet A spreadsheet-like data store that exists behind every object in Visio: every 1-D or 2-D shape, every container, every page, even the document itself. The values and formulas in the ShapeSheet in conjunction with the Visio engine and add-in code, control every aspect of the appearance and behavior of Visio objects. See *Visio engine* and *add-in*.

sheet Internal Visio term for a shape.

static glue The result of attaching a dynamic connector to a connection point on a shape. When you move statically glued shapes, the point of attachment for the connector remains fixed. Compare with *dynamic glue*.

status bar A region at the bottom of the Visio window that displays information about the drawing page and selected shapes; also contains buttons and controls to adjust the page and selected shapes.

stencil A Visio document that contains a collection of masters. Stencils use a .vssx file extension.

subnet A section of a network.

subprocess A subset of a process. In Visio, a subprocess shape on one page represents a collection of process steps that are typically located on another page; the subprocess shape is usually hyperlinked to the other page.

SVG Scalable Vector Graphics; an XML-based format for describing and rendering vector graphics.

swimlane A vertical or horizontal rectangle in a swimlane diagram that contains process steps.

swimlane diagram A type of flowchart in which each process step is placed into a horizontal or vertical lane based on which person, department, or function is responsible for that step. Sometimes known as a *cross-functional flowchart*.

tab On the Visio 2013 ribbon, a set of buttons that provide related functions.

task A step or activity in a process map.

task pane A small, special-purpose window within the main Visio window.

template A Visio document that includes one or more drawing pages with preset dimensions and measurement units. A template may also include one or more stencils; it may include background pages and designs; its pages may contain shapes or text. A template may also include special software that only operates in that template. Templates use a .vstx file extension.

text block The part of a shape that contains text.

Text Tool A Visio tool that you can use to manipulate shape text when you use the tool to select a shape; also lets you create a text-only shape by clicking and dragging across the background of the drawing page.

theme A coordinated set of colors and *effects* designed to enhance the presentation of a Visio diagram.

tile See *print tile*.

tool tab A tab on the Visio ribbon that appears only when you select an object for which it is relevant. Tool tabs are organized into tool tab sets.

tool tab set A collection of one or more tool tabs that appears only when you select an object for which it is relevant. Example: the Container Tools tool tab set appears when you select a container or a list.

U See *rack unit*.

URL Uniform Resource Locator; used to identify the location of a document or other electronic object.

US Units A system of measurement used in Visio drawings and templates in the United States and parts of Canada and Mexico. See *metric*.

user-defined cells Data names and values that can be stored in the User section of the *ShapeSheet* for a Visio shape.

validation A Visio Professional feature that you can use to verify that a drawing meets certain predefined requirements; see *rule* and *rule set*.

variant One of four variations on a theme that includes alternate colors and shape designs so you can add your own flair to a drawing while retaining the overall look of the theme.

VBA See *Visual Basic for Applications*.

.vdw File extension for a Visio 2010 web drawing; see *Visio web drawing*.

Visio engine The core software that provides Visio features and functions. See *add-in*.

Visio Services A service provided by SharePoint; you can use it to publish dynamically updateable Visio drawings that can be viewed by people without Visio.

Visio web drawing A Visio 2010 file format that you can use to publish Visio drawings to SharePoint sites using Visio Services; Visio web drawings can be viewed by anyone with Internet Explorer; web drawings can be dynamically updated when the data in the Visio drawing changes. Uses .vdw file extension. No longer used in Visio 2013.

Visio Workflow Interchange A Visio 2010 file format used to exchange Visio SharePoint Workflow drawings with SharePoint Designer. Uses .vwi file extension. No longer used in Visio 2013.

Visual Basic for Applications (VBA) A programming language built into many Microsoft Office products including Visio.

VML Vector Markup Language; a markup language used to define and render webpages created using Save As Web Page. VML was the primary Save As Web Page output format in versions of Visio before Visio 2010; it is still available in Visio 2013 and Visio 2010 as an alternate output format.

.vsdx New file extension introduced with Visio 2013. Utilizes Open Packaging Conventions to store Visio diagrams in a standards-based XML format.

.vwi See *Visio Workflow Interchange*.

work process See *business process*.

workflow A set of process steps, some or all of which have been automated. For the automated parts of a workflow, documents and files are stored and moved electronically according to a set of predefined rules, so that they are available to participants as required.

workspace A collection of Visio windows and window settings. At minimum, the workspace consists of the drawing window and the zoom settings for the pages in the drawing; frequently, it also includes a Shapes window containing one or more stencils.

X The X coordinate; defines the horizontal position of a shape on the drawing page.

XAML Extensible Application Markup Language; a markup language based on XML that was created by Microsoft. Used by many Microsoft products. Visio creates XAML documents when you use the Save As Web Page function.

XML Extensible Markup Language; a text-based markup language for defining objects and their values.

Y The Y coordinate; defines the vertical position of a shape on the drawing page.

zoom To magnify (zoom in) or shrink (zoom out) the display of a drawing.

Z-order Defines the relative front-to-back position of a shape on the drawing page. The first shape you add to a page is at the back, and each subsequent shape is in front of all previous shapes. You can change the Z-order by using the Send Forward/Send Backward or Send To Front/Send To Back buttons.

Index

Symbols

A

B

About the author

Scott A. Helmers is a Microsoft Most Valuable Professional (MVP) for Microsoft Visio and is the primary Visio expert at Experts-Exchange.com. He has helped companies create custom Visio add-ins to enhance organizational efficiency and employee productivity, and has taught thousands of people how to use technology more effectively.

He is Vice President of Product Planning and Support at the Harvard Computing Group, a software and consulting firm that helps clients understand and implement business process solutions. Scott is a co-inventor of TaskMap (*www.taskmap.com*), a Visio add-in that allows anyone to document all of the important aspects of any business process.

Scott has worked with clients in Afghanistan, Egypt, India, Ireland, Jordan, Malaysia, Saudi Arabia, Singapore, Canada, and the United States on projects involving knowledge management, specification of new IT systems, process mapping and redesign, and technology training. In addition, he has been an Adjunct Professor at both Northeastern University and Boston University.

Scott is the author of two previous books: *Microsoft Visio 2010 Step by Step* (Microsoft Press, 2011) and *Data Communications: A Beginner's Guide to Concepts and Technology* (Prentice-Hall, 1989). He also contributed Chapter 9, "Visio and Visio Services," to *Business Intelligence in Microsoft SharePoint 2013* by Norm Warren, Mariano Neto, Stacia Misner, Ivan Sanders, and Scott Helmers (Microsoft Press, 2013). Information about Scott's books is available at *www.VisioStepByStep.com*.

When not working or spending time with his family in Andover, Massachusetts, Scott can usually be found on his bicycle or working with a local community theater company.

How To Download Your eBook

Thank you for purchasing this Microsoft Press® title. Your companion PDF eBook is ready to download from O'Reilly Media, official distributor of Microsoft Press titles.

To download your eBook, go to
http://aka.ms/PressEbook
and follow the instructions.

Please note: You will be asked to create a free online account and enter the access code below.

Your access code:

> # MLWJPNM

Microsoft Visio 2013 Step by Step

Your PDF eBook allows you to:

- Search the full text
- Print
- Copy and paste

Best yet, you will be notified about free updates to your eBook.

If you ever lose your eBook file, you can download it again just by logging in to your account.

Need help? Please contact:
mspbooksupport@oreilly.com
or call 800-889-8969.

Now that you've read the book...

Tell us what you think!

Was it useful?
Did it teach you what you wanted to learn?
Was there room for improvement?

Let us know at http://aka.ms/tellpress

Your feedback goes directly to the staff at Microsoft Press,
and we read every one of your responses. Thanks in advance!

 Microsoft